CBS's DON HOLLENBECK

Radio and television newscaster Don Hollenbeck sits before a CBS microphone in New York City on September 5, 1950.

LOREN GHIGLIONE

CBS's DON HOLLENBECK

AN HONEST REPORTER
IN THE AGE
OF McCARTHYISM

 COLUMBIA UNIVERSITY PRESS   NEW YORK

Columbia University Press
Publishers Since 1893
New York   Chichester, West Sussex
Copyright © 2008 Loren Ghiglione
All rights reserved

A Caravan book. For more information, visit www.caravanbooks.org

Library of Congress Cataloging-in-Publication Data
    Ghiglione, Loren.
        CBS's Don Hollenbeck: an honest reporter in the age of McCarthyism / Loren Ghiglione
            p. cm.
        Includes bibliographical references and index.
        ISBN 978-0-231-14496-4 (cloth : alk. paper) — ISBN 978-0-231-51689-1 (e-book)
        1. Hollenbeck, Don. 2. Television journalists—United States—Biography.
    3. Journalist—United States—Biography. I. Title.

PN4874.H62G45   2008
070.92—dc22   200801686
[B]

Columbia University Press books are printed on permanent and durable acid-free paper.
This book is printed on paper with recycled content.
Printed in the United States of America
c 10 9 8 7 6 5 4 3 2 1

To Ted Geiger

Contents

Introduction

Don Hollenbeck . . . was always a non-conformist, a dissenter, an individual ualist, a free and independent man who in the Shakespearean sense spoke truth and shamed the devil. . . . He . . . may be considered a martyr . . . in the unending war for freedom of the press in America.

—George Seldes, *Witness to a Century*

When I started this book thirty-five years ago, I planned to write the definitive history of U.S. press criticism. But then I discovered a press critic whose career so intrigued me that I revised my plan. I chose instead to write the story of Don Hollenbeck, a story of firings and failed marriages, McCarthyism and suicide, conscience and courage.

In researching Hollenbeck's story I felt at times like a forensic psychologist. Why did the gifted journalist—described by a Columbia Broadcasting System president as "one of the few great writers that broadcasting has produced"—take his own life?[1] Who or what was to blame for his death?

Hollenbeck's story also intrigued me because his life of personal misfortune and professional success tantalizingly married American tragedy to the American dream.

Hollenbeck succeeded in virtually every aspect of twentieth-century American journalism, both print and broadcast. Early in his career Hollenbeck wrote for heartland newspapers—the *Journal,* the most important paper in Lincoln, Nebraska, the state capital, and the *Omaha Bee-News* of William Randolph Hearst's chain, the classic media conglomerate with an ideological agenda. Hollenbeck edited photos for the preeminent news service, the Associated Press, in an era when pictures were dramatically altering forever the appearance and content of newspapers.

He helped create *PM,* the innovative, ad-free New York City paper that attracted some of America's most gifted writers, artists, and photographers. He wrote thought-provoking articles about the press for important magazines like the *Atlantic Monthly.* At great personal risk he reported the Allied invasion of Italy during World War II for NBC radio. And, as a member of Edward R. Murrow's legendary news team at CBS, he broadcast groundbreaking television news programs during the 1950s, the decade that gave birth to television news.

Hollenbeck also fascinated me because of his press criticism. *CBS Views the Press,* his radio program on WCBS, exhibited extraordinary skill, insight, and independence. From 1947 to 1950, a time of crisis about Communism, Hollenbeck's candid, fifteen-minute program dared each week to make enemies in the powerful New York media. The program was feisty, said Mike Wallace, the *60 Minutes* correspondent who worked in broadcasting for two-thirds of a century: "It named names and kicked ass."[2]

In more than 130 broadcasts Hollenbeck examined almost every element of the New York press, from the Communist Party's *Daily Worker* on the left to Hearst's *Journal-American* and *Mirror* on the right. Hollenbeck criticized Henry Luce and the *Time* machine when Luce's magazine insisted on censoring the outside writing of its employees.

Hollenbeck pricked the ponderous prose of New York's dailies, including the elite *Times* and *Herald Tribune.* He challenged the *Sun,* the *Journal-American,* and other papers that saw Communists everywhere, even where they were not.

Finally, I was drawn to Hollenbeck because he represented the timeless tale of good versus evil, as relevant in today's age of anxiety about terrorism as in the age of McCarthyism. In times of peril and panic—when, in Murrow's words, "the tide runs toward a shore of conformity, when dissent is often confused with subversion, when a man's belief may be subject to investigation as well as his action"—the individual of integrity plays a special role as defender of the people's rights.[3]

Hollenbeck never denied Soviet-sponsored U.S. spies existed and that they warranted the nation's serious concern and action. But he worried, even before Senator Joe McCarthy's famous 1950 speech about Communists in the State Department, that innocent Americans were losing their freedoms and jobs to a witch-hunt. Nat Brandt, a CBS newswriter who worked with Hollenbeck, said he was "early on, when it wasn't fashionable,"[4] against

McCarthyism—indeed, prior to the word's invention. In confrontations that seem surprisingly contemporary, Hollenbeck defended due process and other principles of the Constitution and the Bill of Rights. For that, he "was rapped as a pinko," Brandt said.[5] Wallace said that early in his career he viewed Hollenbeck as "dead honest and brave. And I hoped as I got older I would be like him." Wallace proposed in recent years that Hollenbeck's *CBS Views the Press* be revived. Then Wallace turned realistic. "I shall not hold my breath," he said, as if recalling the cost to Hollenbeck of broadcasting an independent assessment of New York's newspapers.[6]

CBS, arguably the best of the networks for news in the early days of radio and television, featured a team of celebrated newscasters. Hollenbeck—more than Murrow, Eric Sevareid, Charles Collingwood, Howard K. Smith, and the others—was the uncompromising knight, fighting anonymously, by comparison, for journalistic first principles, said Jack Walters, a CBS newswriter.

"Of them all," Walters added, "Hollenbeck bore the truest lance. The fact is that he succeeded in one giant step for journalism, where the more favored, the more self-controlled were afraid to tread." Robert Lewis Shayon, a CBS producer in the 1940s and early 1950s, said Hollenbeck "was one of the heroes of the time."[7]

I was not surprised when the movie director George Clooney sought to explain the extraordinary relevance of the age of McCarthyism to this age by portraying in *Good Night, and Good Luck* (2005) not only the celebrated confrontation between McCarthy and Murrow but also the equally dramatic, if uncelebrated, final days and death by suicide of Hollenbeck.

Hollenbeck's death is a tale of two men. Primarily, it is the story of Hollenbeck, his depression and despair as well as his prize winning, enemy-producing journalism. But it is also the story of Jack O'Brian, radio and television critic for Hearst's flagship *New York Journal-American*. The evening after Hollenbeck killed himself, Murrow asked in a radio tribute what caused the "considerable steel" in his friend to snap.[8]

Part of the answer was the badgering by O'Brian, the journalistic personification of McCarthyism. In column after column in the early 1950s O'Brian smeared Hollenbeck as a soft-on-Communism traitor.[9]

John Horn, a CBS field producer in the 1950s, said that to read O'Brian's columns is to "discover the true climate of McCarthyism—how jackals such as O'Brian hounded men such as Don with continual abuse, hatred, and vicious demagoguery."[10]

To understand Hollenbeck's end it is necessary to understand how

O'Brian's columns helped snap Hollenbeck's steel. For this reason I have included four short biographical chapters about O'Brian among the chapters that focus on Hollenbeck's broadcast career at CBS, beginning with his controversial *CBS Views the Press*.

O'Brian represents what the historian Richard Hofstadter calls the American "paranoid style" of mind. Paranoid, said Hofstadter, because the word "evokes the qualities of heated exaggeration, suspiciousness and conspiratorial fantasy" evident in the fanaticism of those obsessed with what they perceive as a powerful, un-American cabal. The practitioners of the paranoid style have taken various forms—the anti-Chinese Supreme Order of the Caucasians, the antiblack–anti-Catholic–anti-immigrant–anti-Semitic Ku Klux Klan, and the anti-Communist McCarthy and his followers. With O'Brian the paranoid style may have been as much tactical as ideological. He intended his polarizing, pulverizing rhetoric to destroy his targets.[11]

O'Brian regularly laced his radio and television criticism with venomous personal attacks. *Time* magazine introduced a profile of O'Brian with quotes from anonymous sources. A "TV star" described O'Brian as "the only TV critic in the nation who is rude, inaccurate, un-Christian and vengeful." A television network executive said, "He's a murderer. Anyone who gives him the time of day has lost his mind."[12]

O'Brian's targets feared that if they responded he would resort to even more vitriolic character assassination. Lawrence K. Grossman, a six-year CBS employee who became president of PBS and then NBC News, called O'Brian "really over the edge." The historian Neal Gabler said O'Brian "didn't care one whit for the sophisticates or the intellectuals or the liberals; he cursed them all." Nat Hentoff, writing in the *Village Voice,* focused on O'Brian's pro-McCarthy, anti-CBS orientation: "I don't know whether he thinks Edward R. Murrow is a paid agent of the Kremlin or is only doing it for kicks." In a 2005 interview Hentoff added that O'Brian, "for a guy who made his living as a critic, compartmentalized. He wanted the First Amendment for himself," not for those who failed to share his anti-Communist beliefs.[13]

Hentoff said O'Brian saw himself and the *Journal-American* columnist George E. Sokolsky as holy warriors, defending the flag, patriotism, and congressional investigators like McCarthy, whose exaggerations, inaccuracies, and irresponsible methods were being questioned by Murrow, Hollenbeck, and others. The CBS correspondent Bob Schieffer said O'Brian declared war on Hollenbeck: "The attacks were relentless."[14]

Sally Bedell Smith, biographer of CBS chairman William S. Paley, said O'Brian repeatedly harassed Hollenbeck, suggesting he was a Communist: "CBS News shamefully kept a discreet distance. Finally, in the summer of 1954, Hollenbeck cracked under the strain and committed suicide."[15] O'Brian, the holy warrior, continued to use his *Journal-American* column to revile Hollenbeck, even after he killed himself.

The year that Hollenbeck died, 1954, was the year of the televised Murrow-McCarthy showdown and Army-McCarthy hearings—events that contributed to the eventual demise of McCarthyism and of the blacklisting associated with McCarthyism. In the more than half-century that has followed, those events have been mythologized in historians' accounts, biographies, memoirs, Hollywood films, and such made-for-television movies as *Murrow* and *Fear on Trial*.[16] Hollenbeck, a complicated person, has become almost a cardboard character. He has become merely a victim of O'Brian, symbol of McCarthy and McCarthyism.

To the Murrow biographer Bob Edwards, Hollenbeck was one of the "victims of the anti-Communist hysteria."[17] In Clooney's black-and-white *Good Night, and Good Luck,* the actor Ray Wise also portrayed Hollenbeck as victim. The film captured Hollenbeck's dark days and death.[18] But it elected to show neither the complexity nor the controversial career of the working-stiff newsman, as Hollenbeck called himself.[19]

This biography attempts to fill that void. Whatever Hollenbeck's failings and failures, his life indicates he was, in the words of Yeats, "bred to a harder thing than Triumph."[20]

Milton Stern, a friend who was among the last to see him alive, said, "One of the reasons why Don Hollenbeck's life and death made such an impression on me—I've known other people who've killed themselves— was a special, mythic quality about the nature of his death, what he was being subjected to externally and internally."[21]

Hollenbeck's death represented evil's triumph over good. The CBS newscaster Ned Calmer compared Hollenbeck to "a kind of classic Greek protagonist destroyed by forces fated to defeat his purpose."[22]

In a time of crisis and widespread fear Hollenbeck pursued the truth, risking his career, even his life, to do so.

CBS's DON HOLLENBECK

CHAPTER 1

The Boy *from* Lincoln

I am the boy from Lincoln.
—Don Hollenbeck

Don Hollenbeck looked back on Lincoln, Nebraska, as a hellish hometown of despair and defeat. His years at the University of Nebraska–Lincoln ended without a degree. His marriage quickly collapsed. His mother killed herself.

But boosters of Lincoln in the mid-1920s portrayed their growing city (1920 population: 54,948) as a cosmopolitan center of commerce and culture, government and godliness.[1] More than one hundred passenger trains a day of the Chicago, Burlington and Quincy and four other railroads helped make Lincoln the "Retail Capital of the Midlands," the boosters said. Dozens of homeowners' insurance companies promoted a vision of Lincoln as "the Hartford of the West."[2]

As Nebraska's capital, Lincoln amassed many state "businesses"—it was home to the state university, state penitentiary, state insane asylum, state reform school, a state agricultural college, and the state government. As a capital of culture, Lincoln bragged about the *Prairie Schooner*, a literary quarterly with a national reputation; the Circlet Theater, a community drama group that occasionally performed in the city bathhouse; and the Nebraska Art Association. The novelist Mari Sandoz depicted the association as comprised of the city's better folk, who sponsored annual exhibits of sentimental "flower pictures and still-lifes."[3]

Lincoln also billed itself as the "Athens of the West."[4] About 13,500 students attended three church-related schools—Cotner College, Nebraska Wesleyan University, and Union College—and the main campus of the

University of Nebraska and its College of Agriculture. John D. Hicks, history professor and later dean at the University of Nebraska, said it "carried the brightest torch for learning to be found anywhere between the Missouri River and the Pacific Coast."[5]

But John Andrew Rice, a Rhodes scholar who taught Greek and Latin at the university, saw it as an "imitation university," turning students away from academic pursuits and toward "fraternity life, for there was no other." The line between fraternity and nonfraternity students, Rice said, was forever.

"The Lincoln *Journal* kept a file of student names, and the society editor might scout birth and breeding, but the Greek letters had better be there," Rice said.[6] He described Lincoln as the ultimate stronghold of bourgeois respectability, smug in its ninety-eight churches, expurgated movies, Sunday blue laws, Emily Post manners, and near beer.

Clyde Edward Hollenbeck and Clara Genevieve Hollenbeck, parents of Don Edward, an only child born March 30, 1905, embraced that cult of respectability. Of Scottish, Irish, Dutch, and German descent, they pursued a version of the American dream—a life of hard work, home ownership, church gatherings, potluck dinners at friends' homes, and a university education and a career as a doctor or other professional for their son.

Clara had grown up in Malcolm, Nebraska, a frontier village of fifty people that was visited regularly by Native Americans and Roma, or Gypsies, as Malcolm residents called them. Her father, James Ezekial Davey, owned a two-hundred-acre homestead as well as three lots in Malcolm. The village consisted of a dozen or so small dwellings, a blacksmith shop, railroad depot, grade school, Methodist church, and two stores, Malcolm Showers's and Ira Bishop's. Bishop's contained the post office. The 1890s brought a creamery, barber shop, implements business, stockyards, and even a weekly newspaper, the *Malcolm Messenger*, but Malcolm remained a village.[7]

Clara's move to Lincoln after her marriage on June 8, 1904, to Clyde Hollenbeck of Lincoln represented a passage to a new world. Gilbert M. Savery, who as a boy delivered the *Lincoln Journal* on horseback in the village of Shelby, recalled what moving to Lincoln from a frontier village was like: "I was awestruck—the state capital, with a university, and stores you would never dream of, lights at night, such a big place."[8]

Clara herself saw Lincoln as passage to a new way of life. She was wife to Clyde, an office worker, and soon-to-be mother to Don. In 1902, two years before Clyde and Clara married, Clyde worked as a clerk at the B & M freight depot. Then he became an assistant cashier for the Chicago, Burlington and Quincy railroad. During the next dozen years the railroad pro-

Don Edward Hollenbeck, an only child born in 1905, with his parents, Clyde and Clara Hollenbeck.

Courtesy Harold L. Davey.

moted him to cashier and then chief clerk.[9] He joined Union Central Life Insurance Co. in 1923 as cashier. Eventually, as financial correspondent for Union Central's investment department, he managed the company's farm loan program in several midwestern states.[10]

Clara Hollenbeck went to work soon after Don entered grammar school. In an era when few middle-class women worked, she earned $300 a month writing insurance policies and processing new applications at Bankers Life Insurance Co. She wanted a better life for her son. "He was just the apple of her eyes," said Kathleen Weller, a family friend. "She put a lot of money into him." She hoped he would study medicine at the five-hundred-year-old University of Heidelberg in Germany and become a doctor.[11]

Clara Hollenbeck's dream for her son was never fulfilled. As close as Don Hollenbeck got to a career in medicine was his Lincoln High School chemistry club. But he was bookish and "had 'smarts,'" said a classmate, Monte Kiffin.[12] Without real effort Hollenbeck maintained an A-minus average in English, Latin, French, algebra, geometry, botany, chemistry, physics, and history.[13]

At sixteen, when other boys were memorizing batting averages, Hollenbeck was reading H. G. Wells's *Tono-Bungay*, a study of late nineteenth-century English society in dissolution. Hollenbeck was not interested in sports. He received his lowest grade in physical education. He later described himself as a "case of arrested development" in high school. He did not wear long pants until his freshman year and had neither "a sweetheart nor a date" throughout his four years.[14]

His main extracurricular activities were theater and music. In his senior year he earned a lead role—Eliphalet Hopper, villainous Northern hypocrite—in an adaptation of the American novelist Winston Churchill's *The Crisis*, a drama about the slave South. Hollenbeck played two instruments—clarinet in the band for two years and violin in the orchestra for four years. In his senior year, 1920–21, he was elected vice president of the forty-nine-student orchestra.[15]

Hollenbeck bowing his violin looked a bit like a whooping crane flapping one of its wings. Carl Sandburg, poet and author of a six-volume life of Abraham Lincoln, later would say that the 150-pound, almost six-foot Hollenbeck resembled Lincoln as a young man, before he grew a beard—dark-haired, heavy browed, lean, almost frail, with long, delicate fingers.[16]

The girls of Lincoln High School saw Hollenbeck as a handsome, if shy, heartthrob—"the 'White Knight' of my freshman year," said Marion Easterday Kingdom, a classmate who played violin with him in the school orchestra. "A delightful young boy, tall and handsome, brilliant, sophisticated, friendly, and sensitive."[17]

Other female classmates called Hollenbeck intelligent, well groomed, and well mannered. Amorette Pardee Page said he was also "a quiet person, never pushy, always cheerful and pleasant, a leader without trying to be."[18]

Hollenbeck said his one significant sexual encounter involved his seduction at age thirteen by a Russian maid who worked for his parents. "The only thing I can really recall acutely about the business was that she didn't smell very good," he wrote to his third wife, Anne, two decades later. "It was a terrifying and uncomfortable experience, that introduction to Life."[19]

Otherwise, his high school years were marked by their ordinariness. No

HOLLENBECK, DON
"I never do commonplace things."
Band, 7, 8; orchestra, 4-8; vice-
president of orchestra, 8; *The
Crisis;* Chemistry Club.

Don Hollenbeck's entry in the 1921 edition of *The Links*, the Lincoln (Nebraska)
High School yearbook. The quote accompanying his photograph is prescient.

Courtesy William Bogar.

academic honors. No athletic achievements. No student government posts.
Yet the 1921 edition of *The Links*, in the overblown prose typical of many a
high school yearbook, published next to his photo a portentous sentence: "I
never do commonplace things."[20]

Hollenbeck was only sixteen when he, like a third of his classmates,
enrolled at the University of Nebraska ("Not too many of those actually finished," said Roy F. Randolph, a fellow student[21]). Hollenbeck majored in
English and continued his violin studies. Although he had been an excellent

student in high school, he quickly lost interest in his university courses. Encouraged during his freshman year to become a member of Phi Kappa Psi, one of the university's most prestigious fraternities, Hollenbeck did so and proceeded to flunk "almost all courses in the last semester except orchestra, where I finally achieved first section. I would now and then have a terrific bout of studying, but it was seldom," he said.[22]

Hollenbeck also failed to focus on his favorite extracurricular activities, even on his music. "I could have done a lot, but when the going got tough and called for five or six hours of finger-breaking work a day, I said the hell with it. . . . Everything always came too easily for me," he said. "I mean in a superficial way, and I was always able to charm and palaver my way around."[23]

Hollenbeck directed his charm and palaver at his female classmates. "At first Don was withdrawn," said Philip Aitken, a university classmate, "probably because of immaturity coupled with some degree of shyness. After a year at the university, he seemed to have acquired more confidence."[24] W. E. Bradley, a fraternity brother, remembered that Hollenbeck, who had not dated in high school, "carried on during his early college days."[25]

One of the women he dated was Jessie Snively Seacrest, daughter of J. C. Seacrest, publisher and majority owner of Lincoln's leading daily newspaper, the *Journal*. Jessie had attended Whitton-Carlisle, a local private school, and, after three years at Lincoln High School, had traveled to Staunton, Virginia, for two years of finishing at Mary Baldwin Seminary and Mary Baldwin College.[26] Then she had returned to Lincoln in June 1924 to take two summer courses—public speaking and dramatics—at the University of Nebraska. She enrolled at the university full time as a fine arts major in September 1924.[27]

She was a beauty—dark hair, a coquettish smile—and "fun to be around," said Carol Reeve Burchette, a Lincoln prep school classmate of Jessie's. Burchette and Seacrest were "more like sisters" than close friends, "just brought up together," Burchette said.

"All the men were crazy about Jessie, and she was crazy about them," Burchette said. Jessie had the reputation, justified or not, of being sexually liberated. "Jessie's girl 'crowd' was considered a 'fast' sisterhood in sporty cars," said Arthur H. Hudson, who became a *Lincoln Journal* reporter. Jessie refused to sit still for a foursome of bridge, a favorite pastime of young Lincoln ladies. She would choose, instead, dances, parties, and shopping sprees that might end with the whimsical purchase of a $1,000 diamond wrist watch, Burchette said. "She knew her father would foot the bill."[28]

Jessie Seacrest, daughter of the publisher of the major newspaper in Lincoln, Nebraska, married Don Hollenbeck in 1926. They were divorced in 1928.

Courtesy Joe W. Seacrest.

"She didn't like school," Burchette added. "She didn't care about reading. [She liked] society butterfly stuff—it was just come easy, go easy." Jessie was the kind of Nebraska woman who worried Willa Cather, the Pulitzer Prize– winning novelist who had attended the University of Nebraska and written part time for the *Journal*. "Too much prosperity, too many moving-picture shows, too much gaudy fiction," Cather wrote in 1923, describing "girls who try to look like heroines of the cinema screen."[29]

Jessie's main reason for attending the university was "to have as good a time as possible," said her brother Joe Seacrest.[30] She flunked first-semester English, German, chorus, a design course, and even physical education. Finally, on February 11, 1925, the university suspended her.

Jessie's fairytale life fascinated Hollenbeck, if only because it was so different from his. She lived with her parents, siblings, and their servants at Wayside, the three-story, white-pillared mansion on the edge of Lincoln. She regularly participated in garden parties of one hundred to two hundred people on the twenty-three-acre grounds, complete with gentleman's farm.

While her brothers, Joe and Fred, were inventing Latin names for Wayside barn pigeons, entering them in the state fair, and winning "best of breed" from stumped judges, Jessie was roller skating, swimming, and motor boating with friends. "She was well known for spunk and her love of a good time," said Jettie, her daughter. James C. Seacrest, Jessie's nephew, recalled her impishly signing a family guest book as "Jessie Seek Rest." He added, "She brightened everybody's day."[31]

Jessie bought a horse—"She thought it was swanky to ride horseback," said Burchette—but her interest waned. Jessie continued, even so, to pay $100 a month for the horse's board and keep. She borrowed money from loan sharks at 10 percent, which so angered her father that he set up a trust for her to ensure "he wouldn't lose his temper and cut her off or do something he shouldn't," explained her brother Joe. "She was a lovely person," he added, smiling. "Full of piss and vinegar. Going all the time. She had no concept of the value of money. . . . I used to have to bail her out."[32]

Jessie found Hollenbeck fascinating, too. He was Hollywood handsome, a beautiful dancer, and a charming conversationalist, not with small talk but with insights derived in part from the books he devoured. Hudson recalled that while his own reading rarely went beyond the journalists Lincoln Steffens and Richard Harding Davis, "the titles more common in Don's reading were Gibbon, Ibsen, Colette, Andre Gide, Oscar Wilde, Dostoevsky, Tolstoy." [33]

Hollenbeck, in addition, had a quick mind and quick reflexes. Horace Noland, a fraternity brother, remembered a double date with Don and Jessie. They were returning from a party and Hollenbeck stopped the car near the railroad tracks for an unobstructed view of the New Year's Eve moonlight. "Suddenly [the view] was completely eradicated from our car by the beams of the headlight from an oncoming Rock Island passenger train," Noland said. "Don, fortunately, reacted quickly, typical of him, and we raced across safely."[34]

Don and Jessie grew close, but Jessie's family questioned a Seacrest-Hollenbeck marriage. Don appeared unconcerned about whether he ever graduated from the university. During his junior year he took a full-time job at the county courthouse. His father by then handled the investments of Union Central Life Insurance in farm mortgage loans.[35] Through his contacts he was able to get his son a position as a clerk in the county treasurer's office. Then Don, in the middle of his senior year, left the university to become a deputy county treasurer, not a position that impressed the Seacrests.

Jessie's parents discouraged their daughter from continuing to date Hollenbeck. Burchette said, "So I remember Jess and I had lunch at Miller and Paine, that's the big department store, and they had a tearoom. She was crying.

"She said, 'Mother and Dad are going to send me to Europe to get over Don and I'll never get over him.'

"And I said, 'You'll have fun in Europe. You may meet someone else.'

" 'No, it's Don.'

"And it was Don."[36]

On April 15, 1926, Don and Jessie were married at Wayside, the Seacrests' mansion. On consecutive Sundays the front page of the *Journal's* society section featured the wedding as "outstanding" among Lincoln nuptials. The wedding gifts included silver, crystal, an oriental rug, and, from the Seacrests, a baby grand piano, a maid, and a two-bedroom cottage at 2811 Cedar Avenue, not far from the Country Club of Lincoln and the Sheridan Elementary School, an excellent grammar school attended by many members of the Seacrest family. Burchette explained, "Jess was only used to the finest of everything."[37]

Don loved Jessie, but he may have also seen his marriage as a ticket out of a world that seemed increasingly claustrophobic and oppressive. He, like many University of Nebraska students, dreamed of escaping Lincoln. Professor John Andrew Rice wrote: "Some rebelled and, as soon as they could, hurried away, to be buried in time in the cities of the East; others, a few of these, remained and were defeated."[38]

Lincoln prided itself on being a city of respectability, religion, and rules. It enforced stringent Prohibition-era regulations against student drinking. When an undergraduate group called for a campus referendum on ending Prohibition, Chancellor Samuel Avery acknowledged similar surveys at eastern colleges but announced, "Such a proposal, however, in the University of Nebraska is preposterous."[39]

Lincoln, because of its churches' war on drinking and other forms of sin, became known as "The Holy City."[40] Many a Lincoln newspaper report exposed those not sufficiently devoted to Prohibition: an attorney convicted of moral turpitude and disbarred for three years for manufacturing seven hundred quarts of beer at his home; a detective chided for being caught with an uncolored moonshine whiskey called "white mule" ("Cop Is Hooch Sniffer—'Suspicious' Suitcase Yields Three and a Half Pints of Alleged Booze").[41]

Hollenbeck's parents—particularly his father—symbolized the Lincoln he wanted to escape. In a letter twenty years later Hollenbeck would describe his father as a Roosevelt-hating Republican, a backbone-of-America businessman—a man of conventional tastes, catchwords, and ambitions: "He hums, he drums. I can see him eating what is good for him, buying conservative worsted suits (but a loud sports outfit because that is the proper costume for relaxing), stolidly playing golf or tennis or squash to 'keep fit,' putting sex on a time clock basis, reading *Gone With the Wind*, playing contract [bridge] un-erratically, attending concerts, lectures, plays for their conversation value, scared of his life or a new thought, or a departure from the climate of his kind."[42]

Throughout his time at the University of Nebraska, Don Hollenbeck exhibited independence. "He had his own ideas about things," said Harold Stebbens, a fraternity brother. "He didn't care whether you agreed with him or not." Noland, another Phi Psi, said Hollenbeck "seemed to enjoy standing alone and being different."[43]

In 1926, about the time Hollenbeck married Jessie, he became a reporter at the Seacrest paper, which was not the career path his parents had hoped he would take. When he walked the worn pine stairs to the *Journal*'s second-floor newsroom at P and Ninth streets, he found a calling that would be one of the few constants in his life for the next three decades. He also developed an understanding of American journalism at the grass roots that would inform his pioneering press criticism two decades later.

The *Journal* of the late 1920s—*Nebraska State Journal* in the morning, *Lincoln State Journal* in the afternoon—symbolized the nationwide shift of most dailies away from personal, partisan journalism toward more detached, heavily local coverage. The more neutral reporting offended fewer advertisers and permitted the newspapers' owners to guarantee their not insubstantial incomes. The local coverage played to the strength of the *Journal*'s reporting staff—educated by many years of familiarity with Lincoln organizations and government agencies.

J. C. Seacrest, the majority owner of the *Journal* beginning in 1924, had entered journalism at the age of fourteen as a printer's devil on the *Greencastle (Pa.) Press*. Eventually, he had risen to editor-owner. He had come to the *Journal* in 1887 looking for a reporting job. His success at the *Journal*, however, was related to more than his skill as a $15-a-week reporter. He quit three times to start his own newspaper. Each paper failed. But Seacrest learned the business of news.[44]

When he returned to the *Journal* the third time, he proved he could sell advertisements and subscriptions. He jumped circulation to ten thousand and sold a $1,200 contract to publish a merchant's half-page ad every Sunday for a year.[45] Seacrest became business manager of the State Journal Company and, later, a director of the First National Bank and other financial organizations. He was businessperson first, journalist second.[46]

Will Owen Jones, the *Journal*'s editor, cited Seacrest's "early discovery of the business trend that was to revolutionize the newspaper business in a very few years. . . . The newspaper is now a completely 'commercialized' institution. It is operated for a profit, like a store, a bank or a railroad." The *Journal* of Hollenbeck's era—twelve to twenty pages for two cents—exemplified the kind of conventional paper that H. L. Mencken loved to disparage. "The *average* American newspaper," Mencken wrote, overstating his case, "*especially* of the so-called better sort, has the intelligence of a Baptist evangelist, the courage of a rat, the fairness of a Prohibitionist boob-bumper, [and] the information of a high-school janitor."[47]

In truth, the *Journal* provided a thorough, if dry, report of local news. Dry in two senses. First, Seacrest, to satisfy his wife, had ended his "goodfellow tendencies toward saloons, cigars and a night out with the boys."[48] His *Journal* supported adoption of Prohibition. Second, the dryly written *Journal* looked and read—with reason—a bit like a paper ready for retirement or a rest home.

Hugh G. McVicker, the night editor, who had telegraphed news of the Wounded Knee Massacre in 1890, and Editor Will Owen Jones had worked at the *Journal* for forty years. John M. Thompson, statehouse reporter who covered seventeen governors, had lasted thirty-six years. Ammi Leander ("Doc") Bixby, poet, philosopher, and columnist, had trumpeted the GOP for thirty-five years. Harry T. Dobbins, who had begun working at the *Journal* in 1888 as a Linotype operator and would retire sixty-four years later as its associate editor, had just started his thirty-eighth year at the *Journal*.

Those senior staffers served as journalism professors, even if most lacked college degrees, to Hollenbeck and other newsroom cubs, full and part time. The *Journal* relied heavily on student part-timers, taking advantage of the inexpensive labor market provided by the University of Nebraska. A majority of the university's students worked. The smartest journalists-to-be attended classes during the day and ran Linotypes at night, making union salaries several times that of cub reporters' and escaping the reporters' frenetic schedules.

Hollenbeck's father-in-law insisted he start at the bottom of the *Journal*'s newsroom ladder. As a $20-a-week cub reporter, Hollenbeck was expected to read the police station's blotter at 8 a.m. for the night's booze-and-bordello arrests and return immediately to the paper to write up the blotter stories, call hospital emergency rooms and mortuaries for overnight deaths, and accept other assignments.

The assignments ranged widely: human-interest features, major fires and crimes, interviews of visiting celebrities, occasional federal-building and statehouse specials, and frequent city-hall stories (pinch-hitting for the city hall reporter, who drank heavily). After finishing articles in the morning to make the state edition of the evening *Journal*, he rushed to Lamson Brothers, a brokerage firm, at noon for the grain and produce quotations and, later, for two hundred to three hundred stock prices.

Hollenbeck then hurried back to the paper to write and edit stories and make up pages in an antiquated design style that one journalism historian described as "drab *New York Times* tombstone."[49] Though Hollenbeck's workday was officially over at 4:30 p.m., he was regularly asked to "volunteer" for a night assignment. His workweek was often seventy-two hours, at less than 30 cents an hour.

Frank L. Williams, the tight-fisted managing editor who began as a journeyman printer, served on the Republican State Committee and died at his desk of a heart attack in 1943 at age seventy-seven. He had enjoyed telling the story about a *Journal* reporter who discovered an extra ten dollars in his paycheck. The reporter assumed it was a raise. Later that day he was called to the office of the cashier. A mistake had been made. The reporter had been given the janitor's check. The reporter quit. "I can make more money preaching than reporting," he said, "and I'll be damned if I won't try."[50]

Reporters were not given bylines, because, Joe Seacrest said, "It was the newspaper that counted, not the writers." But the reporters knew better. "Bylines encouraged egos, illusions, and requests for salary increases," Arthur H. Hudson said. "It was preferable [from management's perspective] for the staff to function unimpeded by glory and hanging tenaciously to their respective jobs." When a reporter proudly informed J. C. Seacrest that four of his exclusives had been published in the previous four days, Seacrest harrumphed, "We do not praise a man for doing his duty. . . . We merely call attention to his shortcomings."[51]

The *Journal*'s management was devoted not only to profitability but also to the Republican Party. In pre-Seacrest days Charles H. Gere, editor-in-chief and majority owner as well as state senator, drafted state Republican

Party platforms, negotiated disputed planks, and wrote pro-Republican editorials. His editorials summarily dismissed Populist leaders as hayseed "hogs in the parlour." The Populists retaliated for years by routing their parades past the *Journal* office for a chorus of high-decibel hog calling.[52]

Jones, J. C. Seacrest's cautious editor, was more discreet in his Republicanism. One reporter described Jones's editorial policy as "particularly unenthusiastic about being enthusiastic about anything."[53] Francis S. Drath, the assistant to the editor who wrote *Journal* editorials, instructed fledglings on the paper's style of noneditorial editorial writing: Introduce your subject, marshal the facts, link them together, and, in the last paragraph, draw your conclusion. Then take a pair of scissors and cut off the last paragraph.[54]

However milquetoast the editorials and Republican the paper's views, the *Journal's* reporters and editors helped Hollenbeck learn how to dig up news and catch the reader's eye. The *Journal's* experienced hands, said Gilbert M. Savery, later the paper's managing editor, "knew more about certain facets of government than any of the officeholders, whom they had seen come and go."[55] The editors crammed the front page with as many as twenty-six news articles (today's *Lincoln Journal Star* often runs only three).

Not all front-page articles dealt with government news. A *Journal* editorial explained that the news editor was "guided somewhat by flapper philosophy by which we mean that he puts the most attractive things he has right out where they cannot be missed by the naked eye." Sometimes the "most attractive thing" for Page One was a gory death by suicide, a fiery Ku Klux Klan rally, or Mlle. Neryda, who "narrowly escaped death in her hotel room last night in the coils of the seven-foot python which she uses in her dancing act."[56]

The *Journal's* "good wholesome reading" standard usually encouraged abundant coverage of other kinds of activities. Savery recalled that the *Journal* "covered the dickens out of local news," from "Society with a capital S," to secret meetings of the city council, which Phil Wadhams, the city hall reporter, disparaged as "star chamber sessions." Reports on the Bruner Bird Club, the Knights of Pythias, and other local organizations, news of record (births, deaths, real estate transfers), "What's Doing Tonight," and church notes filled inside pages. The *Journal* billed itself as "the first Nebraska newspaper to have a church and religion page."[57]

The paper devoted special attention to downtown business people, known as the O Street Gang. When Don and Harry Ludwig joined the sales staff at Speir's, an O Street clothing store, their hiring merited top-of-the-page photos and stories. The *Journal* reported meetings of the Lincoln

Rotary Club in detail. A typical account applauded meeting attendance—91.9 percent of the membership on December 7, 1926—and recounted verses of a ditty, sung to "Reuben, Reuben, I've Been Thinking." Club members dedicated the song to the new governor of the Rotary district ("We're a bunch of right good fellows / And we're ready at your call"). Seacrest, the *Journal's* publisher, happened to be a member of Rotary.[58]

Occasionally, the local news coverage engaged in moralizing. A Page One story reported that Douglas Orr had warned World Forum students "not to be shocked when the international student council comes to Lincoln." Orr had attended a council meeting in Ann Arbor and said he was surprised and embarrassed when a Vassar girl offered him a cigarette.[59]

The *Journal* also contained large quantities of wire service news—Associated Press in the morning, United Press in the afternoon—and syndicated material: "Mutt and Jeff," "Little Nap," and other cartoons; serialized soap operas ("Revelations of a Wife"); "Tomorrow's Horoscope" by Genevieve Kemble; and a battery of advice columnists, including Dr. Royal S. Copeland ("Pains that Wander Over the Body").[60]

Amid the syndicated material, soap operas, front-page sermons, and Rotary reports, Hollenbeck's writing stood out. "His writing wasn't florid like the exciting sentences, even razzle-dazzle, that had made Floyd Gibbons and Richard Halliburton," celebrity journalists of the 1920s, said Hudson, who followed Hollenbeck as the *Journal's* utility reporter. "It was a simple recitation of facts, arranged for brevity and written 'cleanly.'"

The clarity of Hollenbeck's writing began with the way he took notes on twice-folded sheets of newsprint, Hudson said. "Don's hastily jotted notes were neat and readable, like his orderly mind. . . . I was unprepared for the clearness of the writing. . . . Not a stroke of 'knows God' *Time*-style and tangential asides beginning then to tycoonize city room typewriters."[61]

Hollenbeck, at twenty-two, "was young and inexperienced," said Nell Greer, a reporter at the *Lincoln Star*, the evening competitor of the morning-evening *Journal*. But already he was a professional. "His intelligence, personality, and talent spilled out," Hudson said. Despite his status as the boss's son-in-law, Hollenbeck commanded the respect of his supervisor, Maurice Clifford, the thirty-five-year-old city editor–cum–managing editor. "They were on good terms," Hudson added.[62]

But Hollenbeck was not on good terms with Jessie, his wife. The battle line between their self-images had been drawn. She was the society beauty, an active member of the Junior League of Lincoln and the Lincoln Garden Club. He was the urbane intellectual who was not above twitting Jessie for her disinterest in the cerebral. At a dinner party Jessie's friend Carol Reeve Burchette asked whether she had read a new best seller. "No, no," Jessie said. "No, I haven't." Hollenbeck looked at Burchette, pretending sternness. "Carol, Jessie's already read a book."[63]

Hollenbeck's and Jessie's separate, sometimes antagonistic, lifestyles led to acrimony. The friction surprised few of their friends. "Jessie was inclined to do what Jessie wanted to do," including seeing other men, Greer said. At the time of the Hollenbeck-Seacrest marriage the local gossip, recalled Noland, Hollenbeck's fraternity brother, was "that Jessie would settle down, which she didn't, and Don had made an excellent association for his future, which he did, in spite of the devastating situations during their marriage."[64]

On April 13, 1927, Jessie gave birth at Lincoln General Hospital to a girl, Jessie, nicknamed Jettie. Even that happy event was tinged with unpleasantness. Rumors circulated that Don was not the father. Robert Y. Ross, a fraternity brother of Hollenbeck's, said, "Don's wife bore a daughter . . . (not Don's)." Anne, Don's third wife, said he told her that during a heated argument, Jessie revealed that she had been seeing another man while Don was at work and that man was Jettie's father. Anne said, "That pretty much worked on Don as much as anything." Burchette agreed, saying, "I don't think he really ever got over that."[65]

Charles E. Oldfather, a lawyer representing Joe Seacrest, Jessie's brother, said Joe checked with his two children and the two children of his deceased brother, Fred: None had ever heard a question about Jettie's father. Oldfather also noted that Joe and Jessie were close; she never said anything to her brother that led him to doubt Jettie was Don's daughter.[66]

The Seacrests' prominence in small-city Lincoln meant, Oldfather said, that at least one of the family members would have heard something. This led Seacrest and Oldfather to insist that Don was Jettie's father. If Jessie did tell Don that Jettie was not his daughter, Jessie said it to hurt Don, not because it was true, Oldfather concluded. (When success came to Hollenbeck—when he was first included in *Who's Who in America* and *Current Biography* in the early 1950s—he listed Jettie as his daughter.)[67]

Just weeks after Jettie's birth, Don and Jessie separated, divorcing in March 1928. "After the baby was born, Don moved in with his parents," Anne said. Jessie returned to Wayside, her family's home. She tried to persuade Hollenbeck to rejoin her, but her efforts failed. Two years later she married Alan McIntosh, a *Lincoln Star* advertising salesman and then *Journal* reporter-photographer, who adopted Jettie. Jessie filed a petition for divorce from Alan in 1940. Later that year Jessie visited Honolulu with friends, underwent emergency surgery for an "intestinal obstruction," and died. She was thirty-five.[68]

Hollenbeck's 1928 divorce from Jessie crushed him. But he said nothing about it to people at the *Journal*. Mildred Raleigh, Hollenbeck's second wife, to whom he was married from 1934 to 1941, declined to discuss what Hollenbeck told her about his first marriage and divorce. Anne, Hollenbeck's third and final wife, whom he married in 1941, recalled almost forty years after his first marriage and divorce that this devastating period for him "was something that I avoided dragging out. I was hoping that our life together would be enough to cover, to disguise, 'cosmeticize' the agony." The writer Margaret Halsey, a friend of Don's, said, "He lived in such pain that I wouldn't have wanted to touch on anything that he had built up defenses against."[69]

Clara Hollenbeck also was devastated by the rumors about the paternity of her granddaughter and the disintegration of her son's marriage, Anne recalled. "Don did say that at the time, too, she [Clara] was going through menopause, which unbalances some people." When Don told his parents that Jessie had said the baby was not his, "Clara really decided this was all a reflection on her," Anne said. "She [Clara] had failed, she couldn't hold her head up in public."[70]

Clara also thought it important to maintain the reputation of her family—of her father, James Davey, and her mother, Rosaltha Emma Hornung Davey. They had raised Clara and her four siblings to be upright Christians. Clara had taught Sunday school for years at Malcolm's Methodist church.[71]

Clara's father, who had begun his life in Nebraska as a farmer-carpenter, had become Malcolm's "well-connected and popular grain buyer."[72] He had moved his family from the farm into one of the village's largest houses, formerly the Methodist parsonage, at Lincoln and Second streets, the village's main intersection. As the oldest daughter of Malcolm's "leading citizen," Clara felt shame and fury about the paternity rumors and the dissolution of her son's marriage, Don said later. That shame and fury, he believed, led his mother to try to kill herself.[73]

A few days after her daughter-in-law filed for divorce, Clara Hollenbeck went on a lake outing and swam away from everyone. Clyde, her husband, rescued her. Then, early on the morning of August 1, 1927, she walked from her bedroom to the bathroom, took out her husband's razor, and slit her jugular vein.[74]

She felt such anger and frustration, Halsey said, that "she stomped out of life in a sheer temper." Harold Davey—Clara's grandnephew and the histo-

Clara Hollenbeck, Don Hollenbeck's mother, in an undated photo. In 1927 she used her husband's razor to kill herself.

Courtesy Harold L. Davey.

rian of her family—believed "Clara committed suicide from her abrupt loss of the high social position she had achieved through Don's marriage into the prestigious Seacrest family."[75]

Hollenbeck tried to get the Seacrests to keep the news of his mother's death by suicide out of the *Journal*. Joe Seacrest remembered that the Seacrests advised, "For your own selfish good, put it on the front page and you'll be through with the damned thing. Otherwise it will live forever."[76]

The story ran on Page One. The *Journal's* straightforward headline read: "LINCOLN WOMAN IS FOUND DEAD—Mrs. Clara Hollenbeck Discovered Monday Morning in Bath Room With Jugular Vein of Throat Cut." The *Lincoln Star* reported that she had been "suffering from one of the terrific headaches to which she was subject. Mrs. Hollenbeck had been in poor health for some time."[77]

Whatever the effect of the Seacrests' advice to report the death by suicide straightforwardly, Hollenbeck was never "through" with his mother's death. His psychic scars refused to heal.

"Mothers are people that exert unreasonable and too-emotional influence on us," Hollenbeck wrote later, "although the fact that I have lost my own, under such tragic circumstances, perhaps makes me overestimate their importance: I envy anyone who can say, 'My mother thinks,' etc. . . . I am honest, I admit that probably there would be nothing but battles between us, because she was as much of an individual as I am; and she did her best to make me fit into the mold she thought I belonged in. That kind of an individualist I am not; I am satisfied with my own mold, and others can have theirs, or go in the common button caster's pot, like Peer Gynt."[78]

Anne Hollenbeck believed that her husband's mother—her physical and emotional absence and rejection of Don while he was a boy—doomed him. Clara Hollenbeck, the busy businesswoman, "just wasn't sensitive enough to meet the needs of a little boy," said Anne. "So he started this thing which was tight inside him—gnawing resentment about the fact that she was never there when he came home and it was grandma or the housemaid."[79]

Despite Hollenbeck's divorce, and his dislike for the way the *Journal* reported his mother's suicide, he stayed at the paper. He tried to improve his writing. During the summer of 1928 he took two journalism courses—news editing and community news—at the University of Nebraska.

But haunting images of his mother's death by suicide—the razor blade, the bloodied bathroom, the lifeless body—remained with him. So he hoped to leave them and his failed marriage by escaping the city. He insisted that he would never return: "I am the boy *from* Lincoln."[80]

CHAPTER 2

Working for William Randolph Hearst in Omaha

*The young man or woman had to go east instead of west; in search of
freedom . . . , a "style" . . . , culture and sophistication.*
—Frederick J. Hoffman, *The Twenties*

Omaha was as close to naughty New York City in spirit as Hollenbeck could
get and still be in Nebraska. It was a blood, guts, and sperm city: packing-
houses and twenty six hundred prostitutes; the heritage of five-term mayor
James C. Dahlman, who bragged that he grew up with a branding iron
glued to one hand and a six-shooter stuck to the other; and a $20-million-
a-year liquor-vice-crime-graft-gambling industry nurtured by the political boss Tom Dennison. Omaha during Prohibition, recalled the reporter
Sam Mindell, "was a wide-open town—nightclubs, gentle women, a little
Las Vegas."[1]

With three years of experience Hollenbeck landed a $35-a-week report-
ing job in May 1929 at William Randolph Hearst's *Omaha Bee-News*. Archie
Jacobs, an editor, remembered Hollenbeck's coverage of the legislature for
the *Nebraska State Journal*. "He was a very good reporter," Jacobs said. "He
was a pro when he came from Lincoln." Fred Hunter, managing editor of
the *Bee-News*, agreed. "We'd keep an eye on papers around us. Hollenbeck
attracted attention early in the game. Politically, he leaned to the liberal
side. But he was objective at all times—he didn't let it affect his writing."[2]

Hearst's Omaha paper acted right at home in Sodom amid the corn-
fields. The *Lincoln Journal*'s Gilbert M. Savery called the *Bee-News* "a rowdy
paper, quite sensational in makeup and content." Bought by Hearst in 1928,
it published crime-and-sex stories topped by reverse banners (white type

on a black background) or gaudy, black headlines ("Girl Bandits in Daring Raid") that often ended in exclamation points. In a letter to his publishers Hearst argued for entertaining news with a touch of humor or pathos: "The romance and tragedy of life figure largely in the news and always will just as they figure in literature and in the drama."[3]

Joseph Willicombe, Hearst's secretary, sent daily to the *Bee-News* and the other Hearst papers Olympian wire dispatches that began "The Chief says" or "The Chief wants." That summer the Democrats nominated Al Smith for president. Smith, the de facto head of the Democratic Party in New York State during the early 1920s, had kept Hearst from becoming a U.S. senator in 1922 by refusing to run for governor of New York on the same ticket with Hearst. So some of Willicombe's "The Chief wants" dispatches in 1928 made clear Hearst's preference "hook, line and sinker" for the corn-belt Republican ticket, Herbert Hoover of Iowa for president and Charles Curtis of Kansas for vice president, over Smith's Democratic ticket.[4]

Political gossips whispered that Hearst had bought the *Bee-News* and installed as its publisher the former governor Henry J. Allen of Kansas, who also served as director of publicity for the Hoover-Curtis campaign, so that the Omaha paper could help defeat Smith by electing Hoover. The *Bee-News* predicted Smith's defeat and dutifully cheered Hoover as "a steam shovel with a soul and a vision."[5]

Other Willicombe memos dealt with Hearst's demand that news articles be tossed out to make room for his rambling front-page editorials or for a complimentary review of a movie that featured Marion Davies, his mistress. "We were Hearst's employees, and everything he said to do we did," Mindell said. "We followed his instructions to the letter."[6]

Hearst's advice wasn't all bad. He commanded that articles be written simply; even a person with a fifth-grade education should be able to understand them. Hearst wanted punchy stories and headlines—like "Kills His Bride for Smoking!"—that would make readers rise out of their rocking chairs and shout, "Great God!" Irving Baker, a *Bee-News* reporter, said Hollenbeck was capable of "doing things the way Hearst liked things done. Hearst took a thing with flair, milked a thing for all it was worth. Don fit the job like a glove."[7]

During his first year at the *Bee-News* Hollenbeck transformed a mundane, disturbing-the-peace incident into a Twain-type tale. It began irresistibly: "This story has to do with the drama, with the artistic temperament of actors, with bridge clubs, with bachelors, with husbands, with the Y.M.C.A., and finally, with the city jail."

The article prompted Hunter, the managing editor, to write a note to the editor who supervised Hollenbeck: "My compliments to the author of the story on the drama. Those are the kinds of stories that make readers."[8]

When Omaha mayor Dan B. Butler refused Irving Becker's request for a permit to put on his traveling stage version of *Tobacco Road*, Hollenbeck reported the confrontation as if it were a boxing match. The mayor had a weight advantage and "a horseshoe in his glove." Ringside seats for *Tobacco Road* were selling well and the odds were even, although Sam House of the Diamond Cigar Store, Omaha's preeminent bookie joint, was betting 50 to 1 that "the show would never go on if Mayor Butler said it would not."[9]

Hollenbeck became the *Bee-News*'s zany affairs specialist. He tackled everything—from a firsthand account of a get-rich-quick stag party business to a humorous piece about three and one-half-inch grasshoppers (chests unexpanded) to a rhyming report on Mrs. Joe Somalzek's charge that Joe Zinsky had stolen her pig. The news department shipped its kook correspondence to Hollenbeck. He prized a letter from Peter Johnson, a farmer in Alvo, Nebraska: "I have on my farm here a hog weighing about 90 lbs., is in good health and . . . doing well and said hog have [sic] no rectum. This seems unbelievable but I have the hog here to prove it."[10]

Hollenbeck also reported crimes and other bread-and-butter news. He had a reputation for accurate, ethical journalism. "In those days, a lot of funny things happened with reporters," said Hunter, the managing editor. "If you were a police reporter, you made forty bucks a week and what you could steal." Hunter recalled Hollenbeck's erring only once. High school boys had been staging impromptu wrestling matches in a barn. Hollenbeck's story placed the barn one block from its actual location. The man whose property had been mistakenly fingered sued the paper for libel. He claimed he had been disgraced by Hollenbeck's article. A judge threw out the suit.[11]

Hollenbeck covered the odyssey of A. Paul Wupper, president of the Beemer, Nebraska, bank for more than twenty years and mayor of Beemer for sixteen years. The police sought Wupper for embezzling one million dollars from the bank. Wupper was found in 1931 in Philadelphia, where he was facing charges of nonsupport by his Philadelphia wife, who knew nothing about his wife in Beemer. Wupper said he was willing to return to Nebraska for trial.[12]

Hollenbeck rushed to Philadelphia and rode the train back to Nebraska with Wupper. Hollenbeck described how Wupper had remained free. "I looked everyone in the eye," Wupper said. "And they got out of my way. . . . Anyone will look away from a person who looks him straight in the eye."[13]

Eventually, the *Bee-News* billed Hollenbeck as its "ace feature writer." He produced a series titled "Back to School at 35," reprinted and distributed under the headline "What Parents Should Know about Our Schools." Filled with humor, the series offered a reformer's critique of Omaha's under-funded schools. Hollenbeck reported that Miss Emma Fullaway, a kinder-garten teacher at Druid Hill School, "out of her pocket, has bought dolls, a little wash tub, electric iron and washboard, a set of dishes."[14]

He wrote "Omaha's Neighbors," visiting small towns like Weeping Water (population 1,029) with the photographer John Savage to interview the bar-ber, banker, and bandleader. The newspaper used Hollenbeck's series as a pro-motional tool. Boxed, boldface paragraphs within each story called attention to regular *Bee-News* features—the radio columnist "Judge Puffle," and the syndicated columnists Walter Winchell, Damon Runyon, O. O. McIntyre, and "Bugs" Baer. Advertisements bordering Hollenbeck's feature articles plugged *Bee-News* accident insurance ("protection up to $13,000 for only 5 cents per week") and the thirteen-thousand-member *Bee-News* Homemakers Club.[15]

The paper promoted Hollenbeck to night editor in 1930. Byron Reed, who worked at the *Bee-News* for ten years as police reporter and then as bureau chief in Council Bluffs, Iowa, said, "We listened to him. He was the guy in the slot who read everybody's copy, and he was tough." The reporter J. Wilson "Red" Gaddis said, "He was never nasty but he could be rather crisp. I didn't take this amiss. I looked up to him." Volta Torrey, night editor on the competing *Omaha World-Herald*, summarized the feelings of Hol-lenbeck's newsroom colleagues when he said, "He ran a good paper."[16]

The *Bee-News* newsroom was well managed, but the after-work con-versations of its reporters and editors often failed to rise much above the off-color joke of Jim O'Hanlon on rewrite about a short Eskimo in heat—a frigid midget with a rigid digit. "In those days," Hollenbeck wrote later, "I was rather ashamed that I did have some tastes a little more refined than those of the people I was running with, and I didn't indulge them much. If ever I did say anything, I got nothing but that kind of silence which tells you more plainly than words, 'For Christ's sake, quit showing off, and have another drink, and forget it.' "[17]

Victor Haas, a cub reporter with the *Bee-News* in 1936, said, "Don Hol-lenbeck was a kind of maverick. He didn't take kindly to criticism, frankly, because he was three steps ahead of them [other staff members] and he knew it. He belonged in New York City. All of Nebraska was just a stopping-off place for Don. He was always reading books that most of the journalists couldn't understand anyway. He didn't fit the *Bee-News* at all."[18]

Don Hollenbeck, camera in hand, talks to Officer Joseph Libershal during a 1936 visit to Plattsmouth, Nebraska, for an "Omaha's Neighbors" feature article in William Randolph Hearst's *Omaha Bee-News*.

Courtesy John S. Savage.

Hollenbeck tried to disguise the difference and become one of the boys. The sixty- to seventy-two-hour workweek left him little time to build friendships outside the *Bee-News*. He spent many of his free hours with the reporter, then telegraph editor, Mindell; Reed, the police reporter, and O'Hanlon, the rewrite person. They worked until early morning, six days a week, sometimes seven. After work they would go drinking at one of the speakeasies—the City Club, 60 Club, or Stork Club.

Occasionally, they would visit one of Omaha's houses of prostitution. Hollenbeck contracted gonorrhea. "From then on," recalled Anne Hollenbeck, his third wife, "whenever they did a [fertility] test, he was sterile." Reflecting on the impact of Hollenbeck's divorce from Jessie Seacrest, his mother's death by suicide, and his whorehouse visits, Anne said Don became in Omaha "a young man in search of a way to die." He would continue to "embrace the black angel," she said.[19]

In addition to Hollenbeck's duties as reporter, rewrite person, and occasional local-news columnist, he served as the paper's book editor. "Don was quite an erudite fellow," Fred Stouten, an editor, said, "and no one else wanted the job." A 1937 review by Hollenbeck, not so ironically, applauded a book by the U.S. surgeon general on the prevention of venereal disease. Hollenbeck argued that if ever it might be beneficial to have a dictator of literature, that person should order everyone who was ostrich-like about venereal disease to read the surgeon general's book.[20]

Sometimes as the sun came up, Hollenbeck, Mindell, O'Hanlon, and Reed would head for an intoxicated round of golf—no one kept score. Other times they would rent bicycles for a ride around the city. They would get to bed at noon, wake up in the late afternoon, and go to work.

As a tippler, Hollenbeck was a close second to O'Hanlon, who eventually drank himself to death. "I can't think of much else I did at that time that I enjoyed so much," Hollenbeck wrote later.[21]

Hollenbeck gained the reputation of being a connoisseur of cocktails. Bess Furman, a *Bee-News* reporter from "a strict Prohibition family," consulted him when she wanted to write about a make-believe cocktail that would have the kick of an Omaha campaign speech by Al Smith. "Now, what would you put into a drink that would symbolize satire?" Furman asked Hollenbeck. "Vermouth," he replied. "Unquestionably vermouth." Furman's article said Smith's "campaign concoction" was flavored by "that mint called humor" and topped by a "big maraschino cherry of his own personality."[22] The article won her a Washington correspondent's position with the Associated Press.

Mindell characterized Hollenbeck as a Dr. Jekyll–and–Mr. Hyde drinker: "Happy-go-lucky when he was sober, he would say the wildest things when he was drunk." Hollenbeck reminisced about "getting pie-eyed every night after work in a favorite speakeasy run by a sinister brotherhood of Syrians in the worst neighborhood of Omaha." Hollenbeck wrote, "I was unbearably cocky at 29." His indifference to a woman's play for drinks led her to snap that he looked like a pimp. "That's right, and you'll get every third call," Hollenbeck answered. "Wow! She swung right from the bar, and I stung for a week," Hollenbeck recalled. "Such a surprise it was, although I suppose I had it coming."[23]

Hollenbeck tore around town in a maroon roadster, until one morning he piled it into a tow truck. "I spent five awful hours in the bullpen in the company of a lot of flea-bitten canned-heat victims," Hollenbeck said, "and for all I was an Editor, the lieutenants (I knew them, too) just went on smiling. It seems the man whose truck I had scarcely dented was affronted because I profanely accused him of being in the way. I had crossed to the left side of the street to hit him. He filed charges against me. So I waited bail, and had to eat crow to get the thing canceled. That scared me to death, and I sold the roadster as soon as it was soldered together."[24]

The party was coming to an end, for Hollenbeck and for the *Bee-News*. Despite his hijinks Hollenbeck also had a second, quieter life with a close female friend and his father. Clyde Hollenbeck had wanted to escape Lincoln after his wife's death by suicide. He moved to Omaha and shared an apartment with his son.

Don dated Mildred Raleigh, a secretary-stenographer from Iowa who worked for the *Bee-News* and then for Nebraska Power. "If I describe her as being nondescript, perhaps of worthy rural parentage, simple, plain, unassuming yet trying to overcome it, I may be unjust because she is really little more than a blank in my mind," said Hudson. "But my vagueness may describe her best."[25]

After his failed marriage to Jessie Seacrest, Hollenbeck had thought he wanted an old-fashioned woman for a wife. He had been like the man at the bar in an old cartoon, toasting the assembled barflies, "To women, as we once knew them." Any woman, as Hollenbeck once knew women, seemed acceptable, regardless of intellect or sophistication. He had nurtured, he wrote later, "the opinion that all women were alike; in five minutes you know them all; throw a sack over their heads and what's the difference?"[26]

Anne, Hollenbeck's third wife, said Mildred and Don "had the usual lay-in affair. Lay in and laissez faire, you know. They went together for . . . years. One snowy night his father said, 'Well, why don't you marry the girl?'" Don was almost thirty, Mildred twenty-seven. So Don told his father, "All right," and, Anne said, "he pulled on his boots . . . and he went over and he knocked on the girl's door and he said, 'Will you marry me?' And they were married. And there was no more about it than that."[27]

The wedding on December 20, 1934, was described by the *Bee-News* as "a quiet ceremony at the First Central Congregational church." Pastor Frank G. Smith officiated. Only family members and two female friends of the bride attended. After the wedding Mildred and Don moved to an apartment at the Logan, a downtown residential hotel.[28]

As the Depression deepened, the financial condition of the *Bee-News* worsened. Hearst's corporate executioners made regular visits, replacing

Bee-News employees at dinner in the mid-1930s. From left, John S. Savage, *Bee-News* photographer, and his wife; Mrs. Bill Wiseman, wife of a *Bee-News* reporter, and the Hollenbecks. Mildred Raleigh, an Omaha secretary-stenographer from Iowa, and Hollenbeck (leaning out of the photo) married in 1934. They divorced in 1941.

Courtesy John S. Savage.

Bee-News advertising executives and editors and changing the paper's content and design. Some changes were only cosmetic, and few took hold. "Hearst would send his boys from the West to perk up the paper," said Stouten. "They would change sliding heads to inverted heads. Then he would send his boys from the East to perk up the paper. They would change the inverted heads to sliding heads. Fred Hunter [the managing editor] would do whatever anyone wanted him to do. After they had left, he would go back to doing things his way."[29]

The *Bee-News*'s problems were more deeply rooted than headline styles. The Depression, the *Bee-News*'s emphasis on syndicated material instead of local news, the paper's editorial attacks on Franklin D. Roosevelt, Hearst's financial demands on the paper, and competition from the *World-Herald* took their toll. "Omaha is in the heart of the Midwest, the heart of the Bible belt," said Hunter. "Senator [Gilbert M.] Hitchcock and his family [owners of the *World-Herald*] knew the ways of the people, and the Hearst kind of paper didn't have appeal. It lost readers and advertisers."[30]

The *Bee-News* published a sensational series on sin in Omaha—gambling, drinking, and soliciting. The series infuriated readers. The *World-Herald* responded with an upbeat series—"This, too, goes on in Omaha"— that included articles and photographs about a prominent banker who played with toy trains.[31] The *World-Herald* made more friends.

The *World-Herald* focused on local news. It ran charity drives that netted $10,000 to $15,000 a year for the local poor, including $3,000 for a children's camp. It set up a $4,000 contest for promoting the progress of city and state. It undertook a campaign to collect scrap metal, a campaign that later served as a national model and won the paper a Pulitzer Prize for meritorious public service.[32]

The *Bee-News* appeared by comparison to concentrate on the nonlocal. The paper regularly published atop its editorial page a five-point program titled "The Hearst Newspapers Advocate." All the points were national or international, for example, "An agreement of English-speaking peoples to preserve peace among themselves and to promote the peace of the world." A study of editorials in the *Bee-News* and *World-Herald* for 1936, the *Bee-News*'s last full year of publication, demonstrated its editorial indifference to local issues. Less than 20 percent of *Bee-News* editorials were devoted to social problems important to Omaha. Politics, mainly national politics, received three times as much discussion as any other subject.[33]

Hearst's *Bee-News* claimed to be more independent editorially than it had been under its former publisher, Nelson Updike. A grain baron who once plumped for General John J. Pershing as president, Updike had been a "hard-bitten Republican," Hunter said.[34] But Hearst saw the *Bee-News* as one link in a chain of twenty-eight newspapers publishing his views on Americanism to twenty million readers nationwide.

Hearst insisted that Americanism was not tied to one party. Increasingly, however, his Americanism and Republicanism were synonymous. In 1932 he strayed from the Republican fold to endorse Franklin D. Roosevelt for president. In other elections, though, he dismissed the Democratic program as "very imposing . . . to those who are willing to be imposed upon."[35]

Even as Hearst was emphasizing lower-cost, syndicated materials, he reportedly was squandering $15 million a year on himself. He saw himself as a medieval prince, with royal residences on Riverside Drive in New York, at

Palm Beach in Florida, and at San Simeon in California. San Simeon alone was said to have cost him $40 million. While Hearst pressed to extract as much as he could from his papers, they fell victim to the Depression and precipitous drops in advertising.[36]

Shortly after Hearst bought the newspaper in 1928 and the Depression began, management imposed three 10-percent pay cuts to offset losses. "It got to the point where I was down to $36.45 [from $50 a week]," said Stouten, then an editor with nine years' experience. "And the average reporter was down to $27 or $28. That wasn't too damn much money."[37]

Beginning reporters were hired at $15 to $20 for a six-day, sixty-hour week. "On top of that you were subject to call for night work, Sunday work, and everything else," Hunter recalled. "There was no such thing as over-time."[38] The news staff sought protection.

Local unions of reporters, copy editors, and other journalists formed in many cities as early as August 1933.[39] Newspaper representatives from twenty cities met in Washington, D.C., on December 15, 1933. They established the American Newspaper Guild "to improve the conditions under which they work by collective bargaining." Though Hearst, in his earlier, more liberal days, had professed support for organized labor, he judged the Guild improper for journalists. "I have always regarded our business as a profession," he said, "and not as a trade union."[40]

Despite Hearst's views, Hollenbeck and other editors and reporters founded the Omaha and Council Bluffs Newspaper Guild in 1934.[41] In an unpublished semiautobiographical novel written a decade later, Hollenbeck's protagonist says, "I joined the Newspaper Guild, and got on the working man's side; not really because I felt that way, but the people I was working with felt that way, and it was easier."[42]

Whatever the depth of Hollenbeck's real-life commitment, he learned lessons about the modern media conglomerate that would inform his *CBS Views the Press* criticism of New York's newspapers (including two Hearst dailies), and he contributed to the Guild. Stouten, president of the Omaha Guild in 1936–37, said Hollenbeck "was in there at the start with all of us. He did write a good bit and direct the first [Guild] show—the customary roasting thing."[43]

In reaction to the Guild, Hearst increased many *Bee-News* employees' salaries to former levels. But he took his revenge, too. Salaries of some higher-paid reporters and editors were kept low, to make up in part for the raises to entry-level reporters. Hearst also attacked the proposed Wagner Act, which would protect Guild organizing efforts. He labeled the measure "one of the most vicious pieces of class legislation that could be conceived—un-American to the core."[44]

Hearst sought government abolition of all strikes and compulsory arbitration of all labor disputes: "It all depends on whether we hold to the American or have adopted the Russian system."[45] Despite Hearst's opposition, the Wagner Act became law in 1935. It protected the right of workers to form unions and bargain collectively with employers. It also created the National Labor Relations Board to investigate and judge charges of unfair labor practices.

The beginning of the end for the *Bee-News* was the Hearst-mandated support of Alf Landon for president in 1936. Hearst regularly Red-baited Landon's opponent, Franklin D. Roosevelt. In a signed editorial Hearst said the Democratic Party "should not have its honored name stolen by the imported, autocratic, Asiatic Socialist party of Karl Marx and Franklin Delano Roosevelt."[46]

Hearst's correspondents in Washington were discouraged from reporting anything that might suggest the possibility of Roosevelt's reelection. The *Bee-News* repeated almost daily in headline type: "The fact that Communism—nurtured by Soviet Russia—is seeking to destroy the free institutions of America is not to be denied. Neither is the shameful fact to be denied that Communists are supporting Franklin D. Roosevelt for re-election in 1936 IN ORDER TO BUILD A REVOLUTIONARY 'PEOPLES FRONT' IN 1940."[47]

Landon's speeches were published in their entirety, Roosevelt's ignored or buried inside the paper. The "absolutely impartial" poll conducted for Hearst newspapers found Landon only 19 electoral votes short of victory. But Landon lost to Roosevelt in an electoral landslide, 523–8. "That's what partly killed the *Bee-News*," said Mindell. "Hearst was so pro-Landon, anti-Roosevelt. He was a maniac. It became obvious to the people of Omaha. They wanted a change."[48]

In the fall of 1937 the news staff heard that the *Bee-News* was about to be sold. The *Bee-News* was running 17 percent fewer pages than when Hearst bought it.[49] Subscribers and advertisers were fleeing. The paper was starting to publish advertisements as news.

The *Bee-News* also expected each editor to do the work of two or three editors. Hollenbeck performed as "Sunday editor, book editor, every damn editor you can think of," said Mindell.[50]

Given the rumors about the *Bee-News*'s being for sale, the photographer John Savage, Hollenbeck, and other employees formed a committee to buy the newspaper. The committee contacted Hearst, who in nine years had reportedly lost almost $7 million on the paper. Hearst wired: "The *Bee-News* is not for sale." Later the committee learned that Hearst had already sold the paper to its Omaha competitor, the *World-Herald*, for $750,000. On September 28, 1937, the *Bee-News* published its last edition.[51]

Hollenbeck was one of the few *Bee-News* staffers hired by the *World-Herald*. He continued to bring humor to his reporting. He began a front-page story about a visit to rural towns, at 70 miles per hour, by Postmaster General James Farley: "La Platte, Neb. (pop. 79), Fort Crook, Neb. (pop. 211), had their big moments Saturday, and moments they were indeed." Farley's entourage had stopped at every town's post office and "grabbed a lot of hands," spending as little as two minutes in each town before Farley dashed back to his car.[52]

At least one person at the *World-Herald* was not overjoyed with Hollenbeck's writing. Ben H. Cowdery, husband of the granddaughter of Gilbert Hitchcock, the paper's founder, had moved from selling classified ads to working in the newsroom preparatory to becoming publisher in 1950. Cowdery stopped at Hollenbeck's desk one day, peered over his shoulder at the article he was typing, and offered a few suggestions. Hollenbeck, who in his few weeks at the *World-Herald* had developed a strong dislike for the paper, fired back, "You write it yourself."[53] He quit the *World-Herald*.

Hollenbeck's resignation from the Omaha paper was less dramatic than it seemed. Ed Stanley, a friend from Hollenbeck's university days and executive news photo editor for the Associated Press, had been badgering Hollenbeck to join the AP's photo department in New York. "News photos were the cutting edge of the whole business, but I don't know how interested Don was in news photos per se," Stanley recalled. "What he wanted to do in 1937 was to get out of Omaha. What I was after was the quality of the man."[54]

Hollenbeck moved to the AP photo department in New York on October 18, 1937. His selection by the photo department made sense. "He was a bug on photography and a good photographer. He was great at anything he tried," said Mindell, who believed Hollenbeck saw photography as "an avenue to the big time." Savage said, "That was the trend—going into pictures." Mindell added, "The photos were just getting to be big [in newspapers and magazines]. *Life* [the photo magazine first published on November 23, 1936] was becoming popular then."[55]

Hollenbeck performed well at AP headquarters in New York, monitoring the wire photo network and writing captions. Al Resch, the photo service's news editor, said the job "requires a guy who can put down in fifty words what most people take five hundred to do." Hollenbeck could do that. "Don was a tremendously bright guy, tremendously competent in everything he did," Resch said.[56]

James Crayhon, who supervised Hollenbeck at the AP, felt he was a misplaced big-league intellect stuck in a job that required only a farm-team mentality. "He had much wider capabilities. They called him 'the Walking Encyclopedia.'" When a report came of an attack on the Dodecanese Islands in the Aegean Sea, "he was the only guy who knew where the islands were," Crayhon recalled.[57]

Years later Hollenbeck acknowledged his real reason for joining the AP. His dream was not to move from words to pictures, although when he was hired in October 1937, he wrote to Kent Cooper, the AP's general manager, "saying how thrilled I was to be a member of such a far-flung . . . organization, and that my greatest ambition in life was to see pictures increasingly important in the news report, and myself growing greater and better with etc. Stanley helped me with the letter, and I looked at him and grinned and he grinned back. Christ, that I ever wrote such crap."

Hollenbeck said that "I was working for the AP because my other job caved in on me. I would much rather be writing stories about the love life of cucumbers than asking Dallas to get a picture of that set of quadruplets, and please watch the caption. Jesus, was I ever miserable."[58]

Hollenbeck was as miserable in his second marriage as he was in his job. Mildred, his wife, was overwhelmed by New York and by Hollenbeck—by dealing daily with, as a friend described Hollenbeck, "a cultivated intelligence." In June 1939, less than two years after their arrival in New York, they moved to San Francisco. Hollenbeck became the AP bureau's picture editor. "We needed a new boss in San Francisco," Stanley said. "Don really didn't want to go there. I didn't give him an either/or situation, but I persuaded him that it was an interesting position and that he wouldn't be there forever."[59]

Hollenbeck realized he "was sinking slowly into the perfect AP rut," he wrote later. "Pretty fair job, the usual wife, the prospects of meeting other stodgy AP people and living the customary dull round of playing cards or Chinese checkers, getting drunk now and then and feeling lousy about it, because it would be the usual stupid drinking just to be getting drunk, to take off the torpor for a little while, with no high spirits to go with it. And it made me so morose and blue, together with the misery of the AP, that Mildred realized it too, and quite sensibly, in one evening, we decided it was all turning to ashes, and she left the next day. . . . I had got to the saturation point of living a life that I couldn't abide, and after the amputation [Mildred's departure] I got more bitter than ever, decided I was a jinx for anybody."[60]

Then he met Anne Murphy, wife of George Murphy, a photographer who worked with him at the AP. Anne was slender, 5 feet 3 inches tall, with light brown hair—attractive and quick witted. "She was a good match for him," recalled their daughter, Zoë Hollenbeck Barr. Nine years younger than Hollenbeck and a '38 history graduate of the University of California at Berkeley, Anne was smart, spirited, and savvy about poetry and politics, music and media, subjects important to Hollenbeck. He told Anne that they met as equals, "which is something . . . [that] has never happened to me, and which means that we . . . allow each other the floor (it's yours if you can get it)."[61]

The first time Hollenbeck talked with Anne they discussed moral rearmament. The world worried about Germany's remilitarization after the devastation its military had caused in World War I. An international moral rearmament group, basing its teachings on the "Four Absolutes" (honesty, purity, unselfishness, love), called for world moral rearmament as a response to Germany's military buildup. Hollenbeck defended moral rearmament "out of sheer perversity."

"You thought I was an awful burp," he wrote to Anne a month later, describing their first meeting on February 17, 1940, "and I wondered how and where Murphy got himself such a clever wife."[62]

Though the Murphys had separated and were close to divorce, Hollenbeck felt extremely uncomfortable working with George at the AP while dating Anne and talking to her about marriage. Hollenbeck resigned suddenly from the AP on March 5, 1940, and headed east by train to find a job in New York. "He absolutely—literally overnight—just threw up the job," Anne said. "That was my Don. Throw it over and away he'd go."[63] The man whom fellow Nebraska newsmen described as a natural for New York was quickly rejected by the New York Herald Tribune, the New York World-Telegram, Time, and Life.

"I really haven't had much experience of the cold, cruel world after all; things have always come pretty easy, and when a situation like this demands a shrug and a 'what the hell,' it takes me a round or two to get the old eyes in focus again," Hollenbeck wrote to Anne. "I'm not going to toss myself in front of a subway train by any means; after I've got this off my chest, had a cup of coffee, I'll feel a little better. But I want you to know, if you didn't, how a rabbit punch can rock me."[64]

CHAPTER 3

The Founding of *PM*, a "Newspaperman's Ideal"

The theory of PM has been, since its beginning, that it should be a kind of newspaperman's ideal.

—Marshall Field III, *Freedom Is More Than a Word*

Out of work and money in New York, Hollenbeck took a ten-by-twenty room, toilet and bath down the hall, in a five-story flophouse without an elevator at 309 West 14th Street. He smoked Sensations because his favorite Fatimas were, with tax, 17 cents a pack. He borrowed from his father "for the food I eat, and it is bitter bread," he wrote Anne. A breakfast of tomato juice, toasted English muffin, and coffee cost him 15 cents at a neighborhood diner. He stuck to franks and beans, ham and eggs, and veal stew for dinner.

"Prof. Hollenbeck's next lecture will be on 'The Importance of Fried Foods in the Unemployed Man's Diet' with slides showing their effect on the colon and small intestine (guts to you)," he wrote to Anne. Ballantine beer replaced bourbon and scotch. "I promise myself a whing-ding with my first real paycheck," he told Anne. It would be a special drunk, he added: "Roaring, talkative, bedazzled, stammering, glowing, reeling, singing, shouting tipsy-doodle!"[1]

In another letter to Anne he joked about how the New York papers announced his arrival: "*Daily News*, always exuberant, headlined the story (in 96 pt. Gothic) thus: 'SHIT STORM/HITS CITY.' The *Sun*, customarily conservative, outdid itself with the following headline: 'VISITS N.Y.' See what a splurge I made? Editorial comment varied; *Herald Tribune* (we quote): 'Mr. Hollenbeck has been suspected of Red herring tendencies.' The *Daily Worker*: 'Anybody who likes Mendelssohn is a reactionary.'"[2]

But most of the time Hollenbeck found it difficult to laugh about his pre-dicament. After the first week he had to write to his father for more money. Job interviews brought rejection after rejection. "It is at such times that I discover that fine glittering carapace that I sport so blithely is made of nothing but spun sugar, and that a good haymaker to the emotional midriff smacks it to smithereens, and I'm left bewildered and hurt and grabbing for the ropes," Hollenbeck wrote to Anne.[3]

His main comfort was a daily letter from Anne. He typed three-thou-sand to four-thousand-word letters to her. They saved their correspondence in scrapbooks that she called "Le Livre." She marked pages containing good news from Hollenbeck—the possibility of a job or an inexpensive alimony settlement by Mildred—with red tape along the top border.

But there were also blue-tape days. Anne survived moments of over-whelming—once even suicidal—depression. She struggled with being emo-tionally squeezed between George Murphy, her husband, and Hollenbeck, her lover. She wrote to Hollenbeck about standing on a cliff one night and toying with the idea of jumping.

He responded: "I can understand perfectly your detachment and sus-pension, and your looking on Life and Death with differently focused eyes that night on the cliff. I have never been so close to such 'out-of-myselfness,' but the feeling has hit me, and in somewhat similar circumstances. At such times, it seemed to me, there would be no swift plunge, ending in a smash, but rather a kind of buoyancy, time to regard it all with a new insight, and then a sort of cotton-wool bounce into some kind of Elysium, complete with houris, lotus and Scotch."[4]

A big blue-tape day for Hollenbeck occurred when Anne questioned whether they would ever marry. "There was a time when I decided that I was going to stay with my first husband," she recalled. Despite the importance to Hollenbeck of his correspondence with Anne, he destroyed his book of her letters during the breakup. He explained to her, "I was so shaken with grief and rage that I burned every scrap of paper that had anything to do with you. Silly? Perhaps. But I had gone to Le Livre, and was tearing myself apart reading things—the first letter, the last one—looking at our pictures, just being sick all over."[5]

Hollenbeck kept searching for work. Newspaper mergers and deaths in the 1920s and 1930s had thinned the ranks of potential employers. The *Globe, Advertiser*, and tabloid *Evening Graphic* (nicknamed *Porno Graphic* for its nudity, sex, and sensational crime news) had expired. The thin *Tri-*

bune, founded by Horace Greeley, had bought the larger-circulation *Herald* in 1924, creating the Jonah-swallowed-the-whale *Herald Tribune*.

Roy Howard had combined Joseph Pulitzer's once-successful *New York World* with his struggling *New York Telegram* in 1931 to create the Scripps-Howard flagship newspaper, the *World-Telegram*. William Randolph Hearst had merged his morning *American* and his *Evening Journal* to give birth in 1937 to the chain's afternoon *Journal-American*, leaving the morning to his racy, 800,000-circulation tabloid, the *Daily Mirror*, which promised "90 per cent entertainment, 10 per cent information."[6]

After repeated rejections by newspapers that saw themselves as *news*papers, Hollenbeck sought work at the *Mirror*, which even Hearst acknowledged was, like the movies, pictures to be watched, not news to be read.[7] Selig Adler, a *Mirror* editor, promised Hollenbeck a tryout on the rewrite desk. Adler agreed to a Friday appointment. But he was not present at tryout time on Friday. When Adler finally appeared, he asked Hollenbeck to return on Saturday.

Hollenbeck went back to the *Mirror* on Saturday. A man at the front desk told him to wait for Adler. Almost half an hour passed.

Hollenbeck seethed. Finally, he grabbed the foyer phone and called Adler, recounting the conversation that followed in a letter he wrote that night to Anne:

"It's Hollenbeck," he said. "I was to work for you today."

"Look," Adler said, "this is a tough day for me. I don't see how I can get you in. Why don't you talk to me Monday?"

"Look," Hollenbeck barked. "Look, I want a chance at this job, but I hate to be getting the brush-off like this. You told me to come in Friday, you weren't here, you told me to come today, and you put me off again. Does it mean anything or doesn't it?"

"Well," Adler said, "well, if you feel that way."

"I do feel that way." Hollenbeck hung up and said "that cocksucker" loud enough for Adler, who sat around the corner from the front door, to hear.

The mouth of the man at the front desk dropped open. Hollenbeck shouted at him, "You tell him I said that, will you." Hollenbeck wrote to Anne, "Fate robbed me of my smashing exit by making me wait two minutes for the elevator. Somehow I always louse up my exits."

Hollenbeck described his frustration and anger to Anne: "I am still burning at being treated like a mendicant peddling shoestrings, a guy who can be pushed around and told to come back later if you want to kiss my arse, a guy dependent on the whim of a greasy Levantine to beshit myself at his frown and jump over desks at his command. . . . That guy's father jacked off on a hot rock, and he just hatched. Vicious? Sure I'm vicious! A fine time to flaunt injured dignity, pride of race? I can hear the Philistines now, my father first of the chorus: 'Oh you crazy cock, Hollenbeck! Now what have you done?' Well, I burned a bridge, slammed a door, and if I'm to be tried for arson or disturbing the peace, I'll sentence myself. I'm lucky not to be up for mayhem."[8]

After almost a month—on April 4, 1940—Hollenbeck landed an $80-a-week radio news writing job, 3 p.m. to midnight, at NBC. He described it as the "National Bullshitting Company." He celebrated his first paycheck by downing nine scotches with Ben Grauer (the "lot of fun, perfectly natural" announcer for whom Hollenbeck wrote) and other NBC-ers at a nearby Irish bar.

Hollenbeck's first meetings with other big-name NBC announcers—Bill Stern ("pretty much impressed with Bill Stern, he is") and Hans von Kaltenborn ("paunchy, professorial son of a bitch, with his Phi Beta Kappa key hanging like balls on a Prize Poland China boar")—left him underwhelmed. He wrote to Anne: "I listened, really listened, to a news broadcast tonight, paying especial attention to the subject matter, and if that is all there is to it, it is a pushover."[9]

Heading NBC News was Abel "Abe" A. Schecter. Schecter acted like radio news's P. T. Barnum. Hollenbeck jokingly described him as a "'show bizness' Jew who thinks news should be entertaining." Schecter developed radio contests to determine the best-singing mouse and the champion talking parrot.[10] Hollenbeck thought the medium of radio was more about the comedian Jack Benny and peanut butter commercials, and less about serious news and newscasters.

Hitler's push into Scandinavia produced sundown-to-sunrise shifts from NBC night staffers. "These guys are really proud of the long hours they put in," Hollenbeck said. "They walk around bragging about how little sleep they got! . . . They stay up on the slightest provocation, send out for food when they could just as well go out and eat, and otherwise act like the newspapermen of fiction." They saw themselves as the hard-bitten, hard-working reporters from *The Front Page*, the 1928 play by Ben Hecht and Charles MacArthur. "One or two of them, so help me," Hollenbeck said, "wear their hats to work!"[11]

He wrote to Anne about a traumatic subway ride home from work. A seedy old man had sat next to him, timidly touched his sleeve, offered a hard-luck tale about being an out-of-work engineer, and asked in a husky whisper for a dime. Four boys across the subway aisle laughed. An upset, overcome Hollenbeck slipped the man a quarter and got off the subway a station ahead of his stop. The experience, Hollenbeck told Anne, "hit me in the midriff. . . . Your baby is a softy. . . . That's my trouble; I need an emotional gyroscope."[12]

Less than two months after joining NBC, Hollenbeck received a call from William T. McCleery, who had tried to transfer Hollenbeck from photo editing to features when they had worked at the Associated Press. A graduate of the University of Nebraska at nineteen, McCleery had proved himself as a young AP reporter in Washington by landing an exclusive about a $2-million Public Works Administration project won by Nebraska. Soon he was establishing AP feature bureaus across the country and, at twenty-five, running the AP's national feature department from New York.

Early in 1940, after a brief, miserable time with the "Ivy League crowd" at *Life,* McCleery took a 10 percent pay cut to become picture editor at *PM,* a daring daily that was scheduled to begin publication in New York on June 18, 1940. He made the move, he said, for idealistic reasons. *PM* would fight fascism home and abroad, attack anti-Semitism and racism, support labor, and eliminate business bias by accepting no advertising. *PM* would also transform the use of photos. It would proclaim itself the "only daily picture magazine in the world."[13] McCleery offered Hollenbeck a job as chief caption writer—he would be one of three assistant photo editors—at $85 a week.[14]

Hollenbeck had told Anne that *PM* was definitely not for him. "The venture looks awfully scary to me, and I'd hate to have to leave another sinking ship. Security is what I want now." But the excitement surrounding the launch of *PM*—the first paper born in New York since the *Evening Graphic* and *Mirror* in 1924—eventually seduced him. He was not alone. Many journalists felt *PM* would be, as J. Anthony Lukas later wrote, "the first new idea in American newspapering since the penny press."[15]

Photographers and photo editors were especially excited by the possibility that *PM*—some said the letters stood for *Picture Magazine*[16]—would become the foremost news publication for photojournalists in the world. Founder Ralph Ingersoll, who had leaped in only fifteen years from cub reporter on Hearst's *New York American* to managing editor of the *New Yorker* to managing editor of *Fortune* to publisher of *Time,* spoke of "a way to use pictures so that they often tell the news better than words." *PM* would use photos as "a *primary* means of conveying information."[17]

PM claimed that 11,062 editors, reporters, and photographers applied for about two hundred positions.[18] So McCleery's job offer floored Hollenbeck. "I got off the canvas in time to say 'Yes, sir!'" Hollenbeck wrote to Anne. "Going to be a grand thing I think, I'm really enthusiastic about a job for the first time in a long time. I liked the radio business, but I'll never get over wanting to see what I've done in *print*, you know, inky evidence that you done it good, or bum, as the case may be."[19]

PM would fight for right. In the memorandum that launched the newspaper, Ingersoll wrote, "We are against people who push other people around, just for the fun of it, whether they flourish in this country or abroad. We are against fraud and deceit and cruelty and greed, and will seek to expose their practitioners." Even before its first issue, the paper received a letter from an admiring Mr. and Mrs. Edgar Spinney announcing they had named their firstborn son after *PM*.[20]

Liberal *PM* would support the New Deal, President Franklin D. Roosevelt, and his wife, Eleanor; in the presidential race of 1940 *PM* would be New York City's only daily, other than the *Post*, to back the reelection of FDR. Equally important, FDR and Eleanor would support *PM*. The paper's first issue carried a letter from FDR welcoming *PM* to the American scene and slamming other newspapers' bias "because of front office prejudice or 'business' reasons."[21]

Eleanor Roosevelt's syndicated "My Day" column might run in the Scripps-Howard papers, but she would be photographed carrying *PM* and would promote *PM* in her column: "There is barely a day when some article in it is not worth reading from beginning to end." Scripps-Howard's *New York World-Telegram* deleted her plug for *PM*. The *World-Telegram*'s censorship made news in a gleeful *PM*.[22]

PM would also redefine news. It planned to provide aggressive consumer reporting (good buys in food, clothes, and apartments) and news about education, health, labor, the unemployed, the press, and radio programming (its two-page radio schedule and full page of radio news would break a boycott by other newspapers). News would be useful. Ingersoll promised a financial page with news for 95 percent of readers—rather than for the 5 percent who had the money to play the stock market.

PM would not bow to its advertisers or financial backers. Nineteen investors had waived any right to influence editorial or management policies. There would be no advertiser pressure, because there would be no advertising. But to serve *PM*'s readers the paper would print summaries of advertisements published by other New York dailies. At a time of 2-cent tabloids and 3-cent broadsheets, *PM* would rely on its 5-cent cover price (10 cents on Sunday) for all its income. Ingersoll said he anticipated a circulation of 250,000 by the end of the first year and talked of ultimately reaching five million.[23]

Hollenbeck was excited: "A deluxe five cent daily, printed on heavy stock, in offset. That means more like magazine production, with fine screen engravings. Sixty per cent pictures, part of them done by artists. Reginald Marsh is one of them. Margaret Bourke-White is the chief photographer. Elizabeth Hawes is supposedly quitting the dress bizness cold to write fashions. News will be departmentalized, like *Time*."[24]

PM would also rethink conventional newspaper design, format, and printing technology. The paper planned to use a solid "frozen" ink that would liquefy when heated to 220 degrees. The ink would then solidify instantly when striking the paper and result in sharper outlines and a finer screen in photographic reproduction. *PM* would adopt a magazine format: four-column tabloid pages stapled together. The paper would offer eight pages of spot color daily—its signature burnt red plus a rainbow of other colors.

Ingersoll promised the best and brightest of everything—the most up-to-date printing, the greatest freedom to write in the reporters' own styles, the most generous contract (the Newspaper Guild circulated a sample contract that included a closed shop, handsome minimum, and month's vacation after a year), and the most talented staff.

The playwright Lillian Hellman, best known for *The Children's Hour* (1934) and *The Little Foxes* (1939), covered the 1940 Republican National Convention as *PM*'s "guest writer." The novelist Erskine Caldwell, whose *Tobacco Road* (1932) and *God's Little Acre* (1933) contributed to his reputation as one of the most controversial writers of his time, reported from Moscow. Theodore Geisel (Dr. Seuss) drew searing political cartoons of Hitler, Mussolini, and such domestic targets of *PM* as the noninterventionists Charles A. Lindbergh and Father Charles Coughlin.[25]

The sportswriter Jimmy Cannon, the humorist James Thurber, and the playwright-screenwriter Ben Hecht wrote columns. I. F. (Isador Feinstein) Stone, associate editor of the *Nation*, and James Wechsler, former *Nation* assistant editor, reported from Washington. Walter Winchell, the pioneering *Daily Mirror* gossip columnist–radio commentator who played himself in Hollywood movies, moonlighted secretly under the pseudonym Paul Revere II. The author Dorothy Parker contributed book reviews, and Heywood Hale Broun, son of the Newspaper Guild's founder and a future TV sports personality, wrote sports.

The eminence of such contributors and Ingersoll's persuasiveness also attracted talented young journalists. Ingersoll talked to the Nieman Fellows at Harvard in 1939. When *PM* began hiring, four of the Fellows joined the experiment, including Hodding Carter, owner of the *Delta Democrat-Times* of Greenville, Mississippi. Carter wrote about the press until Ingersoll, dissatisfied with Carter's performance, encouraged his resignation and ended the press page. Ingersoll said a press page was impractical for a daily newspaper. Besides, he added, "*PM* itself was a criticism of the press."[26]

PM regularly bashed Hearst and his newspapers for favoring fascism, publishing discriminatory ads ("The Hate Season Blossoms in the 'Journal-American'"), and forbidding newsboys from delivering a *PM* edition with content critical of Hearst. *PM* printed an ad without charge that the *Times* and *Herald Tribune* had refused. Sponsored by the Friends of Democracy, Inc., the ad accused conservative newspaper bosses—Hearst, Captain Joseph M. Patterson of the *New York Daily News*, and Colonel Robert R. McCormick of the *Chicago Tribune*—of "aiding the enemy" by not enthusiastically supporting the U.S. war effort.[27]

The accused newspapers retaliated. Max Annenberg, the *Daily News* circulation boss with a reputation for gangster tactics, threatened to withhold the *News*, the nation's largest circulation newspaper, from newsdealers and distributors who sold *PM*. Average daily circulation for *PM* dropped from 269,765 for the week of June 18, 1940, to 34,098 for the week ending July 31, 1940. The Associated Press, the most complete of the wire and photo services, denied *PM* membership, influenced by Hearst, Scripps-Howard, and other AP members that were publishing newspapers in New York. *PM* was forced to rely on the United Press and supplementary services.[28]

Before its first issue ever came out, *PM* had dug its own grave with impossible-to-meet expectations, thanks to Ingersoll's oversell. "No newspaper could possibly be as good as *PM* proclaimed before publication that it would be," Carter later wrote.[29]

Hollenbeck ridiculed the *PM* edition printed five days before the first regular issue: "The color register is awful—and the marvelous process that was going to make history in newspaper reproduction needs a first aid squad." The color printing did not improve by the first regular issue. A center spread map "looked like somebody had hit an orange with a baseball bat," Hollenbeck wrote. The map was removed after the issue's first edition, and *PM* soon reduced the number of colors it printed.[30]

There was an unevenness to *PM*'s reporting—brilliance mixed with balderdash.[31] Shortly before Wendell Willkie won the 1940 Republican nomination for president, *PM* reported from the Republican convention that Senator Robert Taft of Ohio had locked up the nomination. Hollenbeck's reaction: "Our able Washington staff, augmented by the hare-brains from this office, had made a highball survey, and figured it all out. Jesus, what dopes."[32]

If the preview issues were "any sample of the Shape of Things to Come, kindly reserve me one of your best straight-jackets, please?" Hollenbeck said. *PM* had collected experts—on politics, fashion, labor, and the arts—but they were not expert at getting out a daily paper. "If they are going to put this sheet out on a forty-hour week," Hollenbeck groused, "they had better begin to make arrangements to put the office in Yankee Stadium for all the staff they will need."[33]

Kenneth Stewart surveyed *PM*'s original recruits. He said they fell into three categories. First, the newsmagazine writers—"professional intellectuals" like John McManus, Leon Svirsky, Robert Neville, and Charles Wertenbaker, all from *Time*. Second, the newspaper and press association journalists—"non-intellectual professionals" like AP-ers McCleery, Volta Torrey, Howard Allaway, and Lorimer Heywood. Third, the pundits—"nonprofessional intellectuals." The abundance of expert writers on special subjects caused Ferdinand Lundberg to write, "Probably no newspaper ever had a staff responsible for [having written] so many books."[34]

Ingersoll "looked at people on the basis of what he thought they could do and less on the basis of their newspaper experience," said Victor Bernstein, *PM*'s foreign editor. Indeed, Ingersoll often regarded newspaper experience as a handicap. The paper first tried operating without copy editors. Every writer was to be his own editor. Ingersoll then installed the mystery writer Dashiell Hammett as a $200-a-week copy editor. "While he figured out whether we used the definite or indefinite article, we missed four editions," said Penn Kimball, who joined the paper as a $40-a-week reporter. Hammett disappeared by the end of *PM*'s first month, replaced by seasoned, green-eyeshade copy editors.[35]

The fashion expert Elizabeth Hawes hired seventeen people to staff her "News for Living" section. None had newspaper experience. Immediately before publication of the first issue, she recognized her mistake and called for the help of Assistant Managing Editor John P. Lewis, a veteran of Scripps-Howard whom Kimball labeled the ultimate green eyeshade. Revered by I. F. Stone for his "ability to handle big-city Jewish intellectual prima donnas," Lewis kept the "News for Living" section from dying.[36]

Dalton Trumbo, author of the successful novel *Johnny Got His Gun* (1939), was sent on special assignment to London. But Trumbo had terrible

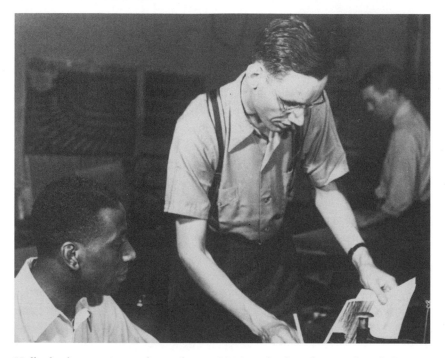

Hollenbeck, an assistant photo editor at *PM* (standing), and an unidentified co-worker in *PM*'s photo department in 1940.

Courtesy Anne Hollenbeck.

news judgment. He had to be backstopped by Ben Robertson Jr., an experienced reporter formerly with the *New York Herald Tribune*.

The energetic, egotistical Ingersoll, a newspaper management novice, ran the paper as if he were Horace Greeley from a century earlier, the publication's indispensable, twenty-four-hour-a-day heart. "*PM* was Ingersoll and Ingersoll was *PM*," wrote the journalist Robert Lasch. Ingersoll raised money; answered letters from angry readers; coordinated mechanical departments; wrote signed editorials; dictated memos to the staff about news, circulation, budget, and production issues; and flew to England and Russia to report on Hitler's foes. Ingersoll's inexperience as a newspaper boss provoked one staff member to describe *PM* as "a school of journalism with 300 highly paid teachers and one pupil."[37]

Ingersoll earned a failing grade from Hollenbeck for everything from hiring to headline writing. "So help me Christ," Hollenbeck wrote to Anne, "the other morning he had a 72-point headline reading 'Fighting continues.'" The bunch of "young fogies" who helped Ingersoll put out the paper caused Hollenbeck to compare *PM* to "the efforts of . . . Eureka High School." Amateurs—"friends of friends," not experts—ran the circulation department. They failed to provide home delivery and lost the list of subscribers. Weeks after *PM*'s opening day, remnants of the list were found near a wastebasket. *PM* lost subscribers' goodwill and at least $100,000 of Ingersoll's $1.5 million seed money.[38]

The newsroom amateurs frustrated Hollenbeck: "I wanted to write captions, good captions, but instead I am nursemaid to a bunch of vague and fubsy woolyheads who haven't the first conception of a newspaper. The announcement about Italy's entering the war came just on the third edition deadline today [for the preview issue of June 10, 1940], but the brain trust spent five minutes standing around screaming at each other instead of hustling into type as they might have been expected to do."[39]

Hollenbeck also despaired about the production challenges that made *PM* a newspaper without the day's news. *PM* was printed on high-quality presses at the *Brooklyn Eagle*, a quarter of a mile from *PM*'s newsroom in a converted Brooklyn factory. To compensate for the time-consuming distance and the peculiarities of the presses—their plates lost sharpness after 200,000 impressions, new plates had to be made—the paper moved up its deadlines.[40]

This infuriated Hollenbeck. He repeated a favorite saying in the *PM* newsroom, "As old as yesterday's news or tomorrow's *PM*."[41] He added, "We are a great newspaper. We had to have Monday's—Monday's mind you—almost made up by six p.m. tonight—Saturday—due to the fact that the press is giving them fits, and has already caved in once or twice. The fresh news our readers get you can imagine. For instance, the first edition for Sunday's paper hasn't one, count them 0, spot news sports stories. Just worked up stuff, all very nice, but a little rough on the guy who wants a baseball score for his dime."[42]

Hollenbeck also had reservations about his duties at *PM*. His job improved, from writing captions to sharing daily supervision of the paper's photos with Howard Allaway, another veteran of the University of Nebraska and the AP. "Each department gets up its own pictures. Allaway and I nurse them along, needle them, see that all the deadlines are met (and there are lots of them), and get out an issue every day." But a month after the first regular issue, Hollenbeck wrote to Anne, "For God's sake, I want to get out of the picture business. I never have liked it, and I don't see why I keep falling for it."[43]

The "picture business" and a $1,000 demand letter from Mildred, Hollenbeck's second wife, led him to indulge in a night of drinking at an appropriately titled Greenwich Village bar, Marie's Crisis Café. "I don't even remember coming home," he wrote to Anne. He was two hours late for work—normally he woke at 3:30 a.m. to arrive on time in *PM*'s Brooklyn newsroom. On another night he blew eleven dollars on round after round of scotch whiskey with Archie Jacobs, the Omaha editor. Hollenbeck wrote to Anne, "Had a hell of a hangover."[44]

The subjective nature of photo selection especially bothered Hollenbeck. The day after Italy entered the war, he chose for page three a photo of the vicar general of Vatican City as he blessed Italian tanks. Hollenbeck wrote to Anne, "Ingersoll thought it stunk. That's what I dislike about the picture business; it's all a matter of personal preference. Almost everybody will agree on a story, almost nobody can agree on a picture."[45]

As much as Hollenbeck disliked picture selection, he was part of one of *PM*'s few professional news divisions. "The photo desk was one of the successes," Kimball said. "All the photographers were great. It was a very happy part of the whole ship." Carter agreed: "*PM*'s pictures and maps were almost always better than the rest of the product and generally better than any other paper's."[46]

Margaret Bourke-White was the photo department's star, paid $233.33 a week, more than three times the salary of other photographers. A pioneering photo essayist for *Life* and *Fortune*, Bourke-White relied on an assistant to carry her equipment. She chafed at newspaper deadlines and requirements. For a Mexican presidential campaign assignment, Bourke-White exposed at least five hundred negatives but failed to provide the information for their captions.[47]

Except for Bourke-White, who would stay less than a year, the photo staff consisted of a dozen newspaper veterans—mostly enthusiastic newspaper veterans. In 1949, when Kenneth Stewart surveyed former *PM* staffers on why they had joined *PM*, he learned that the photo team was "the most starry-eyed of the lot." *PM*, with its emphasis on photos, was their dream newspaper—top-quality images as well as first-rate reporting. Volta Torrey said Hollenbeck too "hoped as did I that *PM* would become a great newspaper."[48]

Managing Editor George Lyon, who was credited with winning the *New York World-Telegram*'s Pulitzer Prize for public service in 1933, pressured Hollenbeck and other editors to overcome *PM*'s dependence on photo agencies' shots and spot-news pictures from the staff to produce what Ingersoll called "story-telling pictures" with "visual kick."[49]

PM needed photos that would "make customers reach for a nickel," Lyon wrote. He called for crusading, social-injustice scoops from *PM*'s photographers as well as reporters: "Every person on *PM*'s staff ought to visualize himself as the people's advocate seven days a week."[50]

The photographers took Lyon's challenge seriously. For the "News of Labor and Unemployed" page on *PM*'s first day, Alan Fisher produced a photo essay on a seventeen-month strike of waiters and cooks at the Brass Rail. Out-of-work strikers, paid fifteen dollars a week during the strike, racked up ninety-five thousand miles as they paced in front of the restaurant. Photos of strikes by coal miners, bus drivers, and steel workers ("State Troopers Ride Down Pickets at Bethlehem; Men and Women Trampled; One Victim Cries 'Is This the American Way?'") established *PM* as the preeminent paper for coverage of labor.[51]

PM's photographers also captured the emotion of discrimination. Irving Haberman photographed white and black schoolchildren who studied blood under a microscope and found no difference based on the donors' skin color; another *PM* investigation revealed that the Red Cross refused blood from blacks and later, under pressure, segregated the blood for use by blacks only.[52]

Sometimes the investigations led to reform. Morris Engel's photos showed one-third of New York schools "unfit for habitation." The board of education said it would replace the schools Engel photographed.[53]

Other photographers spiced *PM* with unusual features. Mary Morris, formerly with the AP, took photos for "Baby Lois"—with information from Dr. Benjamin Spock. "Baby Lois" was a standing feature that followed the growth each week of an infant, born on June 18, 1940, the day of *PM*'s first issue. The photographer David Eisendrath, who came from the *Chicago Times* and *Life*, shot magazine-style features such as "Hitler's Gift to America," a front-page special on Albert Einstein's becoming a U.S. citizen.

Arthur Fellig (professionally known as Weegee), a freelancer who specialized in night photos of fire and crime, cruised the city in his police-radio–equipped 1938 Chevrolet coupe. He stashed a portable darkroom, cameras, and a typewriter in the Chevy's trunk. "With *PM*, anything went," he said. *PM* was the first paper to publish his infrared picture sequences of people in the dark. Arthur Leipzig, hired in 1942 as an assistant photo assignment editor at $25 a week, took photos on the side for *PM*. Soon his pictures of city life were appearing so regularly that he was earning, he recalled, "$75 or $100, depending on the week. They put me on staff at $40 a week, so then they didn't have to pay me for extra pictures."[54]

Hollenbeck and the other photo editors challenged *PM*'s photographers to turn ordinary assignments into originals. Sent to the Waldorf-Astoria hotel to cover a yawner of a blood drive, Leipzig came across a convention of aristocratic, xenophobic Daughters of the American Revolution. His two-page center spread revealed the haughty DAR leadership in full plumage.[55]

The photographers Ray Platnik and Hugh Broderick used zoom lenses to capture base runners stealing home and other sports close-ups that they labeled "Magic Eye Photos." Platnik said, "We enjoyed anything you could do that was new or advanced." The photographers were the first to use 35mm and 2 1/4 x 3 1/4" cameras. They also relied upon multiple-flash bulbs, not singles, and pioneered a "portable" electronic flash unit that weighed one hundred pounds.[56]

There was less excitement for Hollenbeck in his work on the photo desk. He wrote to Anne about how he fought for publication of World War II photos showing triumphant German soldiers entering Paris: "I wanted to toss out a lousy page on Mexico . . . but no—nor could I dislodge a stinking map of Africa that told 0. I finally made it by [Managing Editor] Lyon how the *Mirror* and *News* would smash them, and how very silly we would look with nothing, and he said, 'Do you really think they will?' Did I really think they would! Both papers turned over their double trucks to them. We have a three-column on page four."[57]

In November 1940 Hollenbeck finally escaped the "picture business" forever by returning to NBC at a higher salary, $350 a month, to write news for radio. The more he worked with NBC newscasters, the more he thought of trying to become one. He told Anne that newscasters had the perfect life—"little to do, good pay."[58] He persuaded Abe Schecter, his boss at NBC, to test-record him.

Hollenbeck's test recording eventually led to a successful career as a newscaster at NBC, ABC, and CBS. But he first chose to return to *PM*. He believed the paper, even if it died aborning, occupied a special place in journalism history.

CHAPTER 4

━━━━━━

Politics at *PM*: Commies and "Good Liberals"

> *There were, most obviously, many misfits on PM, including me; not a few card-carrying Communists and fellow travelers, who were waging a class war instead of honestly trying to put out a good newspaper.*
> —Hodding Carter, *Where Main Street Meets the River*

Although ambivalent about *PM* in the summer of 1941, a controversial moment in *PM*'s history, Hollenbeck went back to the paper as a $468-a-month national affairs editor.

The controversy at *PM* involved politics. From the dummy issues before its first day of publication on June 18, 1940, *PM* had made clear its opposition to fascism, especially Nazi Germany's aggressive brand of fascism. But *PM*'s staff was divided about U.S. intervention in the war in Europe.

Some staff members refused to support Britain and France, builders of colonial empires. Others saw Nazi Germany's defeat as the highest priority and sided with Britain and France. The division at *PM* "reflected divisions among liberals and radicals nationwide," wrote the historian Paul Milkman. "Those closest to the American Communist party would continue to see the war as an imperialist conflict being foisted on the people by President Roosevelt."[1]

The *PM* staff's division about U.S. intervention in the war drew attention to the politics of all members of the staff, especially those who were insistently ideological. "There were professional journalists [at *PM*]," said William McLeery, the former AP editor who was a key editor at *PM*. "And there were professional radicals."[2]

The staff broke into three camps politically. The first camp consisted of radicals and, reportedly, a tiny number of Communists. I. F. Stone—

accused six decades later by Ann Coulter, savager of liberals, of being a "paid Soviet agent" as well as a Communist—said the Communists "were really a pain in the ass." Ralph Ingersoll put their number at fewer than ten. Hannah Baker, to whom Hollenbeck paid his four-dollar monthly Newspaper Guild dues, estimated even fewer: "You couldn't fill a broom closet with party members."[3]

Penn Kimball, a reporter who chaired the Newspaper Guild grievance committee at *PM*, doubted the staff had any active Communists: "It's hard to think of any of them on the shortwave taking orders from anybody." Kimball said that the idealistic "so-called party-liners" left over from the thirties "were not unlike the anti-Vietnam zealots in the Sixties—sensitive, somewhat self-righteous, anti-establishment, morally caring about the state of the world."[4]

The *PM* staff members who had signed a Communist Party card or gone to a cell meeting in the thirties had less, if anything, to do with politics, said Kimball, than the "ex-Communists like [James] Wechsler" with "their conspiracy hang-ups." Kimball concluded, "The 'politics' [at *PM*] was the creation of the Red-baiters, not the other way around."[5]

Regardless of whether Kimball was correct, *PM*'s staff included a tiny second camp of anti-Communists—Wechsler and, later, Harold Lavine and Arnold Beichman. The three exaggerated the Communist presence. Wechsler wrote: "In the months that preceded publication, *PM* became the mecca for every Communist and fellow-traveler journalist within traveling distance of New York. An incredible proportion of them got on the payroll."[6]

The staff also included many political independents like Hollenbeck, "good liberals," as they were called. Kimball argued that Ingersoll, Stone, Wechsler, or anyone else who said Communists reported for *PM* should be asked for their names and the "specific example of the story by any one of them which distorted the truth" to push a Communist point.[7] While Kimball contended there were no such Communists at *PM*, a highly inaccurate document, "Communists on *PM*"—reportedly distributed in other New York newsrooms—said Reds controlled *PM*. The document named twenty-two *PM* staffers—thirteen as Communist Party members, nine as Communist sympathizers.

Ingersoll published the document's contents on *PM*'s "Press" page—with photos of the twenty-two journalists named—under the title "Volunteer Gestapo." The title was meant to ridicule the document's distributor. Ingersoll never asked the *PM* staffers pictured how they felt about being Red-baited in their own newspaper. He hoped *PM*'s publication of the "Volunteer Gestapo" would "expose, air and disinfect malicious gossip."[8]

Ingersoll also sent the "Communists on *PM*" document to the FBI, "asking that as soon as they have hunted down all the Fifth Columnists and have some time, they come and investigate us. Or if they wish, they could do it right away."[9]

Ingersoll both praised and pilloried Communists. He believed it difficult for a thinking person not to sympathize with "some but not all" of the Communist Party's domestic agenda—support for trade unionism and opposition to child labor, for example. He declared "right lies to the left" and welcomed everyone on the left—Communists, as well as liberals, New Dealers, socialists, and anarchists—to read *PM* as an "organ of the United Front" against fascism, however much liberals, Communists, and other elements of that United Front might disagree with one another.[10]

But Ingersoll insisted that *PM* remain free of political affiliations. He told *PM* stockholders that, to the best of his knowledge, no staff member took orders from the Communist Party or put "politics ahead of journalism and ahead of the welfare of the organization. . . . If I catch one such [Communist] at work doctoring *PM* dishonestly I will put him out on his ear as fast as I can throw him."[11]

In a convoluted eight-page memo to all *PM* writers and editors, Ingersoll acknowledged he had earlier met the issue of Communists and their influence "elliptically," encouraging misunderstanding. He enclosed what he described as a clarifying editorial—"Communists, Journalism—and *PM*"—that he was about to publish. The editorial called for isolating the Communist influence in progressive movements and learning "what Communists are up to."[12]

Ingersoll had come to believe that Communists were trying to contaminate and control *PM*'s editorial policies. He made staff changes that had the effect of reducing not only costs but also "the left wing's power in the city room," said Wechsler. Hollenbeck, judged by Ingersoll to be "one of the better newsmen" and not seen as a member of what Carter called the "clever, busy Communist minority," survived Ingersoll's early waves of newsroom firings.[13]

A veteran of the Depression, Hollenbeck had once flirted with radical politics. He wrote to Anne: "As far as the Soviets are concerned, any feeling I ever had of fellow traveling is gone with the borscht, and I admit that once I did have such feelings, not to shame either, because it looked like a fair shake for the peepul, of which I admit that I am one." But his flirtation was brief. Communist theory struck him as "crap."[14]

He argued with Henry Ozanne, a friend he described as "an early convert to the theory of communism [who] would defend the acts of the Soviets at the drop of a hat." Hollenbeck could not abide Ozanne's philosophizing, his support of Soviet purges, murders, and mock trials: "I, thinking with my heart of course, would get so God damned mad at him I'd want to pull his mustache out by the roots and stuff it up his anus."[15]

As for Hollenbeck's politics at *PM*, "Don was one of the few I knew who was above ideological considerations," said David Denker, a staff member. Even the anti-Communists attested to nonjoiner Hollenbeck's noninvolvement. "There was a lot of politics on that paper," said Harold Lavine. "And I'm not talking about office politics. Don never participated in it. He never was involved with the Communists. And he never was involved with those that were called the Axis. I was one of them." James Wechsler remembered Hollenbeck as a "thoughtful, serious and warm human being," not as someone involved with the Communists or politics of any kind. Arnold Beichman too observed no Hollenbeck involvement: "None whatsoever."[16]

Repeated efforts to discredit *PM* by labeling it Red annoyed Hollenbeck.[17] Those who painted *PM* Red conveniently overlooked instances when *PM* opposed the Communist line. Before Nazi Germany's invasion of the Soviet Union and before U.S. entry into World War II, for example, when Communists were rejecting the fight against Hitler as an "imperialist war," *PM* was shouting for U.S. intervention.

Or *PM*'s critics dismissed those instances of the paper's disagreement with the Communist Party as clever attempts to conceal *PM*'s Red leanings. Certainly, *PM* did not engage in anti-Communist witch hunting, perhaps the only action that would have mollified its anti-Communist critics.

On balance, *PM* failed to treat Soviet Communism with appropriate skepticism. If the massacres of many millions by the tyrants Joseph Stalin and Adolf Hitler were equally reprehensible, *PM* did not condemn the two mass murderers equally. Ingersoll naively suggested that the "good intentions" of Russian Communists—to educate their people "to a point where they can govern themselves democratically"—justified the Soviet dictatorship.[18]

Hollenbeck said he was judged guilty by association: "I'm accepted as a complete fellow-traveler because I work for *PM*, and I was kept busy [at a party] refuting the charge."[19]

The anti-Communist name-calling against *PM* never ceased. Eugene Lyon claimed the paper was "'colonized'—to use a good Stalinist phrase—by Communists, conscious fellow-travelers, and innocent communist stooges"; Westbrook Pegler—a columnist first syndicated by Scripps-

Howard, then by Hearst—decried what he called the Communist-line "neuro-psycho-journalistic monstrosity, *PM*, otherwise and more fittingly called *PU*." Marion Stern, a major *PM* stockholder, alleged a Communist plot. So did the Reverend Edward L. Curran, who wrote for the *Brooklyn Tablet* and was a supporter of Father Coughlin's. Curran said he reflected the views of *PM*-boycotting Roman Catholic clergy and laity in the Brooklyn diocese.[20]

Kimball, who worked briefly for *PM*, sought a State Department job after his three and one-half years as a marine in World War II. He discovered that he had been secretly classified by the State Department in 1946 as a "dangerous national security risk." His interests and associations as a fledgling Newspaper Guild member at *PM* "were judged to be insufficiently anti-Communist by the government's selected informants."[21]

PM's editors felt the need to prove they were not coddling Communists. Hollenbeck cited *PM*'s rejection of one writer. He wrote to Anne: "She's pink, and she hasn't got a chance, because we have begun energetically to suck the American Legion, the Catholic church, et al., simply because we are being constantly tarred with the pitch of being piped into Moscow. A pesky and dangerous thing, and annoying too."[22]

Less pesky and dangerous was *PM*'s political position on fascism. Ingersoll targeted Hitler and the Nazis in *PM*'s first editorial. News of the war in Europe, Ingersoll wrote, "pitches us, without preparation, into the midst of horror."[23] The Nazis occupied Belgium, Denmark, Holland, Norway, and Poland and threatened Britain and France. Soon Ingersoll called almost daily for the United States to go to war, the faster the better.

PM rejected objectivity as a journalistic standard. Ingersoll did not believe that unbiased journalism exists. *PM* would be, he declared, "unselfconscious about its bias." He said *PM*'s journalists would write in their own style about what they considered important. "Truth," not "objectivity," was their goal.[24] When Hollenbeck rejoined *PM* in the summer of 1941, the domestic targets that the paper deemed important in the months leading up to U.S. entry into World War II were the isolationist, profascist radio priest Father Charles Coughlin, the noninterventionist "Press Axis" (the Hearst press, including the *New York Journal-American* and *Mirror*, and the McCormick-Patterson family's *Chicago Tribune*, *New York Daily News*, and *Washington Times-Herald*), and the isolationist colonel Charles A. Lindbergh.

In 1927 Americans had garlanded Lindbergh, a tall, slender farm boy from near Little Falls, Minnesota, as a hero. His thirty-three-and-a-half-hour, nonstop, transatlantic solo flight in the *Spirit of St. Louis*, a tiny, single-engine monoplane, fired Americans' imaginations. In 1940 Lindbergh became a potential presidential candidate as well as the leading voice of the noninterventionist America First Committee. He opposed U.S. entry into what he regarded as a pointless war with Nazi Germany. (In Philip Roth's novel *The Plot against America*, Lindbergh trounced Franklin D. Roosevelt in the 1940 presidential election; Lindbergh became "the hero of virtually every paper in the country with the exception of *PM*.")[25]

The real *PM* denounced Lindbergh as "Spokesman No. 1 for the Fifth Column," loyal to Nazi Germany. [26] In 1938, shortly before the Nazis began aggressively incinerating the synagogues, residences, and businesses of Jews, Lindbergh had accepted a swastika-studded Service Cross of the Order of the German Eagle, conferred "in the name of the Füehrer" by Field Marshal Hermann Goering. Even when a Roosevelt cabinet member criticized Lindbergh for being a Knight of the German Eagle, Lindbergh refused to return the medal. He saw "nothing constructive gained by returning decorations which were given in periods of peace and good will. The entire idea seems to me too much like a 'child's spitting contest.' "[27]

A turning point in the U.S. public's attitude toward Lindbergh grew out of his September 11, 1941, speech in Des Moines, "Who Are the War Agitators?" Lindbergh named "the Jewish race" and its "large ownership and influence in our motion pictures, our press, our radio, and our government" as one of three key forces pushing the United States toward participation in the war (the British and the Roosevelt administration were Lindbergh's other two forces).[28]

In covering Lindbergh's speech, Hollenbeck wrestled with how to report Lindbergh's accusation without shirking the journalist's ethical obligation to put the accusation in context and explore whether it was true. In a damning lead paragraph Hollenbeck bluntly labeled Lindbergh's address at the America First rally his "dirtiest speech" yet: "For the first time, he came out in the open with the Nazi venom that fits so well with the Nazi medal he has never given up."[29]

The article alternated four excerpts from Lindbergh's speech with four parenthetical, italicized paragraphs of Hollenbeck analysis that pointedly questioned those speech excerpts. Lindbergh, for instance, said the persecuted Jews' experiences abroad should make them proponents of peace, "that they will be the first to feel its consequences." Hollenbeck said in the paragraph that immediately followed: "*(The Jews of Poland, of France, of Germany itself have felt the consequences of peace—Hitler's peace. Lindbergh didn't go into details about their experience.)*"[30]

Hollenbeck monitored the almost daily change in attitude of America Firsters toward Lindbergh. One of Hollenbeck's first follow-ups, on September 15—accompanied by a cartoon that depicted Lindbergh as a Nazi-uniformed, whip-carrying Hitler—reported that the America First Committee "still was whole hog behind" Lindbergh.[31]

PM's managing editor then sent telegrams to members of the America First Committee, asking if they disavowed Lindbergh's anti-Semitism.

Three Hollenbeck articles later that week reported that America First members were beginning to repudiate Lindbergh's remarks. A week later Hollenbeck wrote about the America First Committee's cancellation of a Lindbergh speech in Washington, D.C. Hollenbeck also reported the resignations by members of America First's national committee to protest Lindbergh's "degrading" speech in Des Moines.[32] Lindbergh's political career soon came to an end.

While Lindbergh's views paralleled those of the Nazis, the historian Wayne S. Cole said Lindbergh neither liked Nazism nor favored a Nazi dictatorship for the United States or Germany. But *PM* and other interventionists recalled Lindbergh's annual trips to Germany in the late 1930s and his comments about a German "sense of decency and value which in many ways is far ahead of our own."[33] The interventionist *PM* rarely missed an opportunity to associate Lindbergh with Nazi Germany.

Cole compared the methods used by interventionists in criticizing Lindbergh to those used by McCarthyites in criticizing liberals in the early 1950s: "The McCarthyites discredited their adversaries by associating them with Communist Russia; interventionists discredited their adversaries by associating them with Nazi Germany."[34] The methods in both cases, Cole concluded, destroyed careers.

Once the United States entered World War II, Hollenbeck covered war-related issues, often accompanying his articles with, in *PM*'s evolving style, brassy, brief, bylined editorials. His coverage made clear that *PM* expected Hollenbeck to be more than a beat reporter. He jousted in his editorials with a wide variety of the liberal paper's foes.

Colonel Hamilton Fish, the New York Republican who led a congressional witch hunt for Reds in 1930, worried less about real discrimination against blacks than the fantasy that Communist-influenced blacks in the South would gain the vote and set up "Negro republics of their own."[35]

After Fish asked to command thirty-one hundred black soldiers, Hollenbeck's four-sentence editorial reminded readers that black soldiers were the target of discrimination in the armed forces. Their "very blood has been rejected to save lives of any but Negroes," Hollenbeck wrote. "But for heaven's sake, let's not slap the Negroes with the final insult of giving them Ham Fish to command one of their regiments."[36]

When I. F. Stone reported that Detroit automakers were stopping the production of cars to work on tanks, planes, and guns, Hollenbeck's accompanying editorial reminded readers that U.S. troops were still dying because they were not yet receiving those weapons. "Keep mad," Hollenbeck wrote. "Complacency has put us in the tough spot we're in today. More of it will put us in the spot where we won't be able to punch at all."[37]

The federal government issued regulations requiring a wider variety of biscuits, pemmican, milk tablets, and other emergency rations be carried in lifeboats and life rafts aboard ships. A Hollenbeck editorial commended the requirements but ended with two tart sentences in boldface: "You can't sink a Nazi submarine with an Army biscuit or Navy pemmican, no matter how solid they are. Where in the hell are the guns that the Navy was ordered to put aboard those ships?"[38]

While the critical and self-critical Hollenbeck rarely praised *PM*—one issue, he said with uncharacteristic enthusiasm, had been passable—he vacillated between rooting for *PM* and jumping ship before it sank: "I get blind with rage when crummy sheets like the [*San Francisco*] *Call-Bulletin* get superior and *Editor & Publisher* (Tut-Ankn-Amens) gives us six months. Screw them; at least we are doing something out of the ink-stained tradition, and that they cannot understand. No newspaper has ever been any different . . . [from] any other newspaper, except the *Daily News*, and they judge all prospect of success by the same old yardstick."[39]

Hollenbeck believed *PM*'s position in press history was guaranteed. But he also was a pragmatist: "I simply can't see this thing I'm on as anything but a fantasy that will end in a nice slightly used second-hand press and editorial staff for sale."[40]

The start of U.S. participation in World War II dampened the enthusiasm of *PM*'s investors, boosted the cost of newsprint and other scarce supplies, and robbed the paper of its most imaginative reporters and editors. After receiving a draft notice, the forty-one-year-old Ingersoll enlisted. Kimball, Geisel (Dr. Seuss), and other *PM*ers also enlisted or registered for the draft. A photo story bragged, "These Men Can't Wait to Get into It." Still other staff members, like George Lyon and John A. Sullivan, chose to serve in the Office of War Information.[41]

"Once the war started," Kimball said, "the bloom was off the rose at *PM*." The future of the United States was on the minds of Americans, including *PM* staff members who had not yet enlisted or been drafted. Hollenbeck wrote to Anne about his ride on a Staten Island ferry: "You would be amazed at the thrills I get when I look at the Statue of Liberty, and the Stars and Stripes on the boats. Like you, I am being whipped up into a definite nationalism, only not a jingoistic one, I hope."[42]

PM's operating losses—an average of $200,000 a month during its first four months—pushed the paper toward bankruptcy. Marshall Field III assumed the obligations of *PM's* other stockholders, and cost cutting became a high priority. Features that made *PM* special disappeared. The news crusades by Ingersoll—who "governed with loose reins," Hannah Baker said—gave way to more traditional reporting orchestrated by his successor, John P. Lewis, "a solid middle of the road citizen, smart enough but limited."[43]

The need to penny-pinch forced *PM* to abandon the heavy use of color and other costly innovations. Eventually, *PM* even accepted advertising. But circulation continued to lag well below the first-year's projected break-even of 250,000. An efficiency study by R. A. Lasley, Inc., gave the newsroom a failing grade.[44]

A final problem was that Ingersoll, who originally budgeted for a newsroom staff of 180, had allowed it to swell to 230. The paper was under constant pressure to cut payroll. The prospect of staff reductions made reporters and editors jittery. A management memorandum about an earlier cut did not help: "Until an enterprise whose resources are not limitless is in the black, the survival of the whole is more important than the survival of the individual."[45]

Hollenbeck had another reason to be nervous. Mildred, his wife, wrote demanding $1,200 before she would grant him a divorce. He protested that he lacked the money. She fired back, "You seem to be under the impression that all you have to do after taking up 11 years of a woman's life is to make it possible for her to get a divorce, and you hope there won't be hard feelings."[46]

Finally, in late August, Mildred agreed to $50 a month for nine months, the balance of the $1,200 settlement to be paid to her before the final decree. On May 1, 1941, she obtained a Reno divorce from Hollenbeck and eight months later married Richard F. Jones of Reno.[47] On August 8, 1941, Angelique "Anne" Dean Murphy, who had divorced her husband, George, became the bride of Don Hollenbeck in a ceremony at New York's First Presbyterian Church.

Happy months followed. Hollenbeck shed his $45-a-month, one-room apartment at 55 Morton Street. Anne and he rented a $72.50-a-month, three-room art deco flat, also in the West Village, on tree-lined Grove

Angelique "Anne" Dean Murphy Hollenbeck, a San Franciscoan who was graduated from the University of California at Berkeley and worked in advertising, married Hollenbeck in 1941. In this undated photo she is seated on the bench,
to Hollenbeck's right, at a party in New York City.

Courtesy Zoë Hollenbeck Barr.

Street. Federal-style row houses there dated from the 1820s. "We used to
eat chocolate-covered graham crackers, drink coffee, and play Russian
Bank on an oval-shaped coffee table," Anne said.[48] But within a year World
War II ended the Hollenbecks' honeymoon.

After overrunning much of western Europe, German forces steamrolled
Greece and invaded the Soviet Union. German Field Marshal Erwin Rom-
mel's Afrika Korps drove across northeast Africa for the Suez Canal. "Everything that's worth living for is being swept away," Hollenbeck told Anne.
"Love, music, a little beer, a sense of security—all drowned in blood by a
bunch of maniacs who have gone crazy with shotguns in their hands."[49]

On December 7, 1941, Japan attacked Pearl Harbor and other Hawaiian
and Asian targets by air. At a joint congressional session the next day President Roosevelt called December 7 "a date which will live in infamy." The
United States declared war on Japan. Germany and Italy declared war on

the United States. The United States responded by declaring war on the two Axis powers, and soon World War II engulfed the globe.

Fittingly, many Americans first learned of the Japanese attacks and President Roosevelt's address to Congress by listening to radio. World War II proved to be radio's war, just as Vietnam would prove to be television's war. NBC and CBS competed fiercely to provide up-to-the-minute coverage of the war. "Ubiquitous Max" Jordan, NBC's German-born European representative, used his education and experience in Europe to scoop CBS regularly. In March 1938 a twenty-nine-year-old Edward R. Murrow, CBS's European director, competed with Jordan to report Germany's invasion of Austria. Murrow spent one thousand dollars to fly alone in a twenty-seven-seat plane to reach Vienna before Hitler's arrival. Murrow short-waved an on-the-scene news roundup about the Nazi takeover, the first of five thousand broadcasts during a twenty-three-year career at CBS.[50]

Soon back in London, where he was free of German censorship, Murrow reported with memorable imagery what was being called the bloodless conquest of Austria: "I'd like to forget the tired, futile look of the Austrian army officers, and the thud of hobnail boots and the crash of light tanks in the early hours of the morning. . . . I'd like to forget the sounds of the smashing glass as the Jewish-shop streets were raided; the hoots and jeers at those forced to scrub the sidewalk."[51]

Radio, a storyteller's medium, proved powerful, personal, and to the point. A typical two-minute segment permitted only 250 words. Robert J. Landry, *Variety*'s radio editor, wrote that Murrow's reporting for CBS had more influence "than a ship full of newspapermen."[52] Between the war years of 1938 and 1942, network radio news programming at two major news networks—CBS and NBC Red—almost quadrupled, from an average of 342 hours a year to 1,333 hours a year per network. A 1942 poll showed that, by better than 2.5 to 1, the public put more faith in radio reporting than in newspaper coverage.[53]

The first U.S. troops arrived in Great Britain in January 1942, though six months would pass before they would engage Axis powers in the air war over Europe. In August Hollenbeck, thirty-seven, left *PM*—"not a happy shop," recalled Edward Stanley, an early planner of *PM*—for the Bureau of Pictures and Publications in London. The Bureau was part of Stanley's Overseas Publications Bureau in the U.S. Office of War Information (OWI).[54] Hollenbeck produced illustrated leaflets in Spanish and French. Dropped from bombers, the leaflets reported on resistance to Hitler's push for a worldwide Nazi order. Hollenbeck spent seven-day weeks and ten-hour days preparing the leaflets at the U.S. Embassy and a secret OWI headquarters.

He found the nightly air-raid alerts and blackouts eerie, "with search-lights constantly sweeping the sky, scarcely anyone on the streets, and the ruins you pass every block." The boarded shops and vacant apartments left London looking like a dead city, Hollenbeck wrote. "All those who could afford it, packed up and moved. Those who couldn't stayed and took it."[55]

He wrote to Anne about trying to find time to investigate adoption of a baby from a London orphanage. Appreciative of radio's wartime impor-tance, he also pursued a reporting job with NBC. He arranged a dinner with Robert St. John, NBC's London correspondent, who had just published a best-seller about his two years in the Balkans. A strafing by a Nazi plane had left him with a bullet in his leg. Hollenbeck, who would never return to newspaper journalism, envisioned himself becoming a St. John—a radio war reporter–commentator. Hollenbeck wrote to Anne, "There are so many things that I can think of to get noised abroad."[56]

In other letters to Anne, Hollenbeck complained about every aspect of OWI work, from his $1,000-a-year pay to the dull repetition of writing headlines: "I think if I am ever sent to perdition it will be in the form of sit-ting on the rim of a French copydesk and having nothing to write but one-column heads." The inaccessibility of liquor and the quality of rarely avail-able rot-gut whiskey ($7.50 a bottle) ruined even his off hours. Hollenbeck wrote, "I am getting a fine course of asceticism."[57]

Regardless of Hollenbeck's complaints, he understood what was at stake. He valued the freedoms and "forms of decent living" he experienced at home and in England. He abhorred what Germany and the other Axis powers represented. "I've only got a little Teutonic blood in my veins—and it's Württemberg, where they take life easier—but I hereby renounce it, if you can do that with blood," he wrote to Anne. "Corporal Corpuscle, sur-round those Nazi enzymes and wipe 'em out! It seems to me that the things that we risk losing ARE worth fighting for, even if it's a forlorn hope, and I'd rather leave a few guts waving on the barbed wire than to salute a guttural ubermann with a clipped haircut and red hands."[58]

CHAPTER 5

█████

Covering World War II from Home and Abroad

Murrow . . . What was important in the beginning was the special quality of excellence he and the men he hired set for broadcasting; men who were in his image, and who thereupon brought men to CBS and the other networks in their image.

— David Halberstam, *The Powers That Be*

Everything about wartime London distressed Hollenbeck. His work at the Office of War Information (OWI) and the people there bored him: "It's so damned difficult for me to get along with anybody very long. I'm hypercritical [with people], and I suppose people are with me."[1] In his spare time he read Dorothy Sayers mysteries and Shakespeare, worked Double-Crostic puzzles, played his favorite classical records of the singers Charles Trenet and Maggie Teyte, and wrote letters daily to Anne.

He used the bombings and blackouts as an excuse to jump off the wagon. He regularly downed Drambuie, double scotches, and ale at Manetta's, a neighborhood bar frequented by Americans, until he became "ecclesiasticled," he said. "I have the normal man's horror of saying 'drunk.'"[2]

"You'd be amazed at the solitary life I lead," he wrote Anne. He suggested to her that he become a radio newscaster or bookstore owner: "One thing is sure, I'm not going back into the newspaper business. I've said that before, but this time it's for keeps—I want the rest of my bread-winning days to be quiet ones."[3]

An acquaintance wanted to sell a Manhattan bookstore for $2,000. Hollenbeck fantasized about operating the store. He wrote to Anne, "I'm really nuts about the notion." Anne responded coolly, "And how can we live on 48th Street and have a book business. We'd never be able to pay the rent."[4]

Becoming a radio newscaster was less of a pipe dream. Twenty-one months before leaving New York for London, Hollenbeck had been test-recorded by Abe Schecter, his former boss at the NBC Blue network, which was about to become ABC. Schecter liked the recording. In February 1943 Stanley Richardson of NBC in London, a veteran of the AP, hired Hollenbeck as a $125-a-week war correspondent while he was still working for OWI. Hollenbeck wrote Anne, "I only hope I can say the things that ought to be said."[5] He believed the United States would have known virtually nothing about the Allied effort to drive the Germans out of North Africa without the reporting of CBS's Charles Collingwood and NBC's John MacVane.

Hollenbeck also worried about saying things that ought not to be said. Three years earlier, when he had first joined NBC as a newswriter, he had expressed his misgivings to Anne about perhaps having to go on the air to replace an announcer and "saying balls over the red & blue, and if you ever hear a shaking, quavery voice say, 'This is the National Bullshitting Company,' you will know that is Hollenbeck who USED to work for NBC. . . . Well, it can't last long. I'll screw something up so they'll relieve me."[6]

Hollenbeck loved his military uniform with its green armband and white "C" for correspondent. He was so proud that he had an OWI friend, Sam Boal, take photos of him in his correspondent's uniform—made by Burberry with dark tunic and pants ("Veddy chick")—and then rushed the pictures to Anne.[7]

He judged his first broadcast in London—an anonymous, three-minute news roundup—a success. "I didn't fluff anything," he wrote Anne, "and I got off right on time." He had to sit across the table from a competitor, John Charles Daly of CBS, who would later host *What's My Line?* and serve as ABC's vice president of news, special events, and public affairs. Hollenbeck described Daly as "a professional announcer of the nastiest type, who did his best to turn a freeze on me, a fumbling amateur. Of course, when I got up to leave the studio I tripped over the wires on the headphones, which made me feel like a fool, and drew a 'What kind of barbarian is this?' look from this bastard."[8]

Hollenbeck was given two to three minutes for his *War Journal* reports, barely enough time for straightforward accounts of the air war. The Flying Fortresses, Liberators, and Mosquitoes of the U.S. Army Air Force and the British Royal Air Force were stepping up their bombing of Essen, Dusseldorf, and other German targets. German bombers were retaliating with nightly raids on London and other British targets. Hollenbeck kept score of planes lost, bombs dropped, factories destroyed, and pilots killed. In early April 1943, for instance, he reported the German air force was losing planes at the rate of 2,350 a month, which exceeded Germany's plane production by more than seven hundred planes each month.[9]

But Hollenbeck sought to report more about the war effort than plane and pilot counts. On Easter Sunday he traveled to the U.S. Army Eighth Air Force Composite Command in Northern Ireland to interview ordinary soldiers at work. Sergeant Kermit Iverson of Alta, Iowa, was training to be a bomber radio operator and would, he said, "lay a few eggs for Hitler—big ones." Hollenbeck asked what Iverson thought his family was doing at that moment. "I imagine they're getting ready to put one of those Iowa Sunday dinners on the table—maybe with angel food cake," Iverson said. "I sure hope the hens in Iowa haven't heard about rationing yet."[10]

Hollenbeck also interviewed Welsh miners; Clark Gable, the movie star–turned-captain in the U.S. Army Air Force; and Bernard Marmaduke FitzAlan-Howard, the sixteenth Duke of Norfolk.[11] The duke was promoting the production of food by riding his bicycle 150 miles to obtain front-line updates from rural camps where volunteers from cities were spending their holidays harvesting bumper crops.

Hollenbeck invited Brian Davis, a London secondary school student, to ask him questions about the United States that wartime English students were expected to be able to answer. Hollenbeck answered incorrectly two of the first three questions that Davis asked—about the latitude of the boundary between the United States and Canada and the date that the Santa Fe Trail was opened.[12]

In reporting on the newspaper situation in Britain, Hollenbeck made it clear he favored a press free of government control even in wartime. The Gaullist La Marseillaise, published weekly in London, was forced to suspend publication when the British Ministry of Supply ended its newsprint ration. The ministry insisted it was just a normal step to prevent the unproductive use of paper. Hollenbeck suggested that pressure from Washington had led to the suspension of La Marseillaise, long critical of the United States.[13]

Hollenbeck's radio reports conveyed his sense of humor and his love of music. When explaining why air raid sirens in London sounded much worse than the German bombers whose coming they announced, he tossed in a musical footnote: the sirens wailed "chromatically between C sharp and G natural in an augmented fourth—what they call the devil in music."[14]

Don Hollenbeck (second from left) interviews Clark Gable (third from left), movie-star-turned-U.S.-Army-Air-Force-captain, at Eighth U.S. Army Air Force headquarters in England in 1943. On extreme left is Sergeant Gunner Phillip Hulse of Springfield, Missouri, and on extreme right is Sergeant Gunner Tom Hansbury of Philadelphia, who flew with Gable and took part in the broadcast.

Courtesy AP/Wide World Photos.

As part of an American Week celebration at the schools in Salford, he introduced a forty-five-minute concert of American music, including pieces by Aaron Copland, Victor Herbert, and John Philip Sousa. "Sousa's vitality and his catchy tunes make your feet itch," Hollenbeck said, "you've almost GOT to march when Sousa calls the tune."[15]

Hollenbeck's humor was most evident at the end of broadcasts in his "bright bits." They relieved the reports about deadly destruction. He told stories about the army bugler who added a little boogie-woogie to reveille and rolled out soldiers in swing time, and the town southeast of London that changed its air raid warning to sound like a cuckoo.[16] He also offered miniature portraits of the English:

- "The American movie 'Mission to Moscow' has caused a minor flurry here because of the alleged parody on Lord Chilston, the former British ambassador to Moscow. The *Daily Mail*'s New York correspondent reports he is portrayed as a dull, pompous, billiards-playing person. This was pointed out to Lord Chilston here, and his reply was—'But I'm *not* a billiards player.'"

- When a Polish officer accused of shooting another officer in a dispute about a woman was acquitted, Hollenbeck said, "The judge at Old Bailey, in summing up, said that since both men were foreigners, the jury might have to consider the way in which they looked at things. That's what you mean by insularity."
- "How do the British react to these [German] murder raids? Mostly like Grandma Cass, who's lived in a cottage in one of the coast towns for 50 years. A bomb hit her cottage—she was in it. Out of the wreckage, she called to her grandson. 'Help me out of this Joe,' said Granny Cass. 'I'm not hurt—I'm just mad.'"[17]

At the beginning of August 1943, after about five months of reporting from London, Hollenbeck was assigned by NBC to Algiers, site of Allied headquarters for the Mediterranean theater. The conquest of German-occupied Sicily had almost been completed. The Allies anticipated the invasion of the Italian mainland.

Hollenbeck shared one small room, an ancient Citroën, and an army of mosquitoes and flies with two other NBC correspondents, Ralph Howard and Merrill "Red" Mueller. Reporting ground rules in North Africa were more restrictive than in London. War correspondents were required to submit all copy to field press censors who cut out such lines as, "One high military authority who has just returned from Sicily expressed the opinion that it will all be over there within ten days." Hollenbeck's report from Algiers on August 7 about a U.S. victory in Sicily described heavy Nazi casualties and the capture of 125,000 Germans.[18]

Correspondents in Algiers were expected to attend daily briefings by high-ranking Allied officials. The briefings made Hollenbeck uncomfortable: "My inability or unwillingness to be a joiner may handicap me a little. One sucks up to various supposedly important people here if one wants to do well. I maintain my reserve, and intend to do so."[19]

On August 24 Hollenbeck left behind the briefings in Algiers for the fighting in Sicily by hitching a ride in a general's plane to Palermo, Sicily's administrative center. Hollenbeck reported that day on Palermo's return to life after a thirty-eight-day battle: four-hour-long bread lines, children begging for candy and cigarettes ("it seems most Sicilians start smoking at about the age of four"), and men wearing black lapel patches or black bands around their sleeves, "a reminder that about 9,000 were killed, 25,000 hurt in the air raids that shattered Palermo."[20]

The British Eighth and American Seventh Armies were sweeping forward, the Germans retreating rapidly. Hollenbeck moved with the Allied troops from Palermo and then prepared for the landing at Salerno on Italy's mainland. He wrote to Anne about "shaving out of a steel helmet, sleeping on a bench, eating corned beef twice a day out of a mess tin—never getting a bath—flies and mosquitoes, dirt and sweat! Shit." His first typewriter, an ancient English Smith Premier whose keyboard "rose like a Roxy ballet," died and gave way to a secondhand Hermes. The Hermes slipped overboard from a launch and was replaced by a bulky, borrowed Underwood.[21]

Hollenbeck's griping occasionally turned philosophical: "The more I see of war, the more I realize what a lousy warrior I'd be. It is not a pastime for men of dignity or men of sensibilities, although they must take part in it, and I don't want that to sound stuffy, or upstuck." He reflected on every war's lesson—"that you shed the greater part of your civilization when you participate," he said. "I get to dislike my fellow men a bit more each day."[22]

He reminisced about a 1931 hunting and fishing vacation with his father in Sun Valley, Idaho. Hollenbeck took satisfaction from having failed to catch a fish or shoot a bird or animal: "I admit, it's because I always missed when I cast or when I shot, but the way I feel now I'll never slay anything except flies, and God damn them, they ask for it. 'Grandpa, what did you do for the wild life of this nation?' 'I let it live, durn it.'"[23]

He also drew a connection between the slaughter of humans in war and the mutilation of animals in experimental tests. When he had begun writing newscasts in New York for NBC in 1940, he had put together a piece for the 8 a.m. news about the inventor Lester P. Barlow's testing the potential of his new aerial bomb to kill dozens of goats. "Barlow ties the goats in a field (nice touch, that), sets off his bomb thirty feet in the air above them, and bets the 'shock waves' will kill them. I thought it was a hell of a good story," Hollenbeck wrote to Anne.[24]

But his boss thought the story "too horrible" that early in the morning. "On the same broadcast is a story of six hundred thousand men blasting each other to bloody bits on the Western Front, but that is Historic," Hollenbeck said. "It is awful how you can get to feeling sorry for a smelly goat, but become a grave and impersonal Clio when you write about human life."[25]

Though Hollenbeck hated war, he still proved an effective war correspondent. On September 8, 1943, he filed a pool report for the U.S. press, not just NBC, from an Allied landing craft three days into a rolling, banging, pitching ride to Italy. "There was no going on deck—you got drenched, with no chance to dry off if you did," Hollenbeck reported. So the soldiers sang "Lili Marlene" and drank British "'sergeant major tea'—tea so loaded with sugar that the spoon almost stands unsupported in it."[26]

The next night, when the moon was almost full, Hollenbeck accompanied the British corps of the Allied troops attacking Hitler's "Fortress Europe" at Salerno in "Operation Avalanche."

The day before, General Dwight D. Eisenhower, commander-in-chief of the Allied Expeditionary Force, had announced the surrender of Italy. But the September 9 landing at Salerno by Lieutenant General Mark W. Clark's Fifth Army still met strong resistance from German air attacks. The ferocity of Germany's Luftwaffe, which would fly 450 sorties on September 10 and 11, caused Vice Admiral Henry Kent Hewitt to send a brief, blunt message from the USS *Ancon*: "Air situation here critical."[27]

Hollenbeck rode with the British corps' second assault wave, which was "decidedly more bloody" than the first wave, according to the historian Eric Morris. Hollenbeck said, "We were on a headquarters ship under heavy fire, so had to back off and spend that morning shuttling back and forth in the bay with German aircraft overhead and German 88-mm guns on shore."[28]

In a September 9 pool report Hollenbeck said a "JU88 dive bombed us and planted three bombs in the water not far away. . . . For some time after that things were quiet. The moon went down and the night turned into one of those starlit wonders of the Mediterranean—the Big Dipper over Vesuvius to our left, the path of our little landing craft boiling up in soft phosphorescence."[29]

Under cover of destroyer fire the troops of the British corps finally landed, north of the main U.S. force on the Salerno beaches, accompanied by Hollenbeck and a BBC correspondent who together were carrying a sixty-pound machine that recorded sound on hair-fine threads of steel wire (the wire reels would be transported to Algiers, put on a disc, and shortwaved to the United States on September 17—eight days later). In the late morning, as the troops moved forward off the beaches, the landing craft began to disgorge supply trucks and other vehicles. "A [German] battery chased our landing craft away from the beach. . . . Machine-gun fire forced us to abandon our landing ramp," Hollenbeck reported.[30]

The Luftwaffe kept pounding the Allies. The British Landing Ship Tank (LST) vessels, which carried twenty-five tanks on the lower deck and thirty trucks on top, were such easy prey that they were nicknamed Large

Stationary Targets. As Hollenbeck landed on shore, he reported on his radio wire: "Now we stand, or crouch, rather, because we're under constant fire of German machine gunners. We can see [gunshots drown the words of Hollenbeck's report] smoking in the morning light. Through the glasses we can see Pompeii, eight miles away. Just around the corner, so to speak, is Naples, where we hope and expect to be soon."[31]

Stars and Stripes reported: "Don Hollenbeck of NBC sent back from Italy one of the most dramatic recordings we've ever heard. Against a backdrop of gunfire Don gave a vivid description of the bitter battle raging about him as he stood on the shore with microphone in hand and a portable recorder on his back. Interviews with the boys engaged in the fight were outstanding."[32]

Hollenbeck downplayed the *Stars and Stripes* article. He wrote to his worried wife: "'Battles raging about him' indeed—I was crouched beside a jeep, and all that racket came from our own 105s—your darling doesn't stick his neck out for any kind of kudos, baby."[33]

He trudged away from the shore behind trucks slowly snaking their way up a rugged mountain road. Occasionally, he could hitch a ride. "We all had one thought in our heads, one fear—air attack," Hollenbeck recalled. "We were unable to keep a safe interval between vehicles, and those long strings of trucks moving up from the beach were simply set-ups for bombing and strafing."[34]

The soldiers' fear came true when an Allied driver ahead ran out of gasoline. Every Allied truck in the column stopped dead. "The German planes were on us, drawn like deadly flies to that cluster of men and machinery on the roads," Hollenbeck said.[35]

He joked in a broadcast about the invasion-day truck convoy under attack from German machine-gunners: "In one short trip, I dived into a ditch four times. But you could always reach for a tomato. . . . It got to be a routine. Dive into the ditch, have a tomato, and then crawl back in the truck."[36]

As a pool reporter for the American press, Hollenbeck later covered conditions in the looted city of Salerno. The *Washington Post* and *New York Times* carried his articles about the German devastation: no medical supplies, no water (the Germans had blown up the water plant), and little food. Salerno's seventy-seven thousand residents, who had taken to the caves in the hills north of the city, returned to what Hollenbeck called the "most complete looting job" that the Germans had done in any city. He wrote, "One unconfirmed story is that they drove an armored car down the streets of the city shooting people at random when the news of the armistice came."[37]

On September 13 Hollenbeck reported from a crouched position on a steep, winding mountain trail near the top of Mount Chiunzi "with the most advanced Allied troops in Italy"—Lieutenant Colonel William O. Darby's Third Ranger Battalion, "mostly a tough lot of Midwesterners." The Rangers held the main road to Naples "against great odds—we were under constant fire of German machine gunners, continually raided by German experts in Alpine warfare." The Rangers suffered casualties from a German rope trick: twenty five or thirty Nazis lowered themselves on a one-hundred-yard-long rope to where they could snipe at Rangers, then, after several hours, retreated into impenetrable mountain positions.[38]

On September 15 Hollenbeck accompanied troops to Capri, an island in the Gulf of Naples largely untouched by war. He interviewed an aristocratic British widow in her seventies who had married an Italian, Hollenbeck said, "long ago when that was the romantic thing to do." The war came, but she refused to leave Capri. She complained only about not having had tea in two years. Amid the open tourist trinket shops, ice cream parlors, and bars thronged with sailors, Hollenbeck reported from a tiny table outside a café: "It was very strange to sit and sip a gin and very dry vermouth and remember that only twenty miles away a battle was being fought in the dust, that men were dying, and that Capri itself was one of the stakes of this battle."[39]

A day later Hollenbeck reported from the rocky island of Procida, ten miles southwest of Naples, where invading Allied ships were greeted at 11 p.m. by a full moon, sultry air, a still Mediterranean, and handclapping from small fishing boats filled with men, women, and children. "All we needed," Hollenbeck said, "was music by Puccini to make the occupation completely operatic." One hundred or so disarmed Italian soldiers formally surrendered the island. "Kümmel and cognac went the rounds," Hollenbeck said. "Not even the fact that when the natives first started clapping they thought we were Germans could detract from the triumph."[40]

After Procida, Hollenbeck asked Anne to work for the Red Cross in Rome so they could be together. Anne resisted. She wanted to be with him, but she had a good job with Compton Advertising, and she liked New York. She preferred that Hollenbeck come home.

He acknowledged ambivalence about Anne's career: "Remember now, when Donny comes home, Woman of the Year, Career, and so forth, go out in the garden for fertilizer." Anne said years later, "He was not going to have his wife being self-supporting. . . . When I began to show signs of not walking in his shadow, I think that is when the trouble started. . . . He thought it was absolutely great when the so-called New Look came in, when skirts went down. And I hated it. Then he admitted one time that he did have a Victorian attitude that woman should be in the kitchen and pregnant. And with long skirts."[41]

The discussion about a Red Cross position for Anne ended when Hollenbeck entered a military hospital. Doctors labeled his ailment FUO— fever of undetermined origin. The hospital began treatments for malaria and jaundice. Two weeks later—just as he began to recover from malaria and jaundice—his NBC colleague Ralph Howard also contracted malaria. Howard's illness forced Hollenbeck to return in late September to Algiers to write and air NBC's two-minute morning and evening reports.

"So that means I do all the pieces," he wrote Anne, "which wouldn't be so bad except there's a hell of a lag time between them every day—eleven hours, and the evening program is so damned difficult to fill. These days you mop up every line of the news in the morning period. I dreamed up last night's right out of my own little noggin—and very puny it looked in the clear light of this morning."[42]

He devoted one piece to rehashing his time on Capri. He ended it with a story about the owner of Café Hiddigeigei, named after a cat in an old German verse epic. As Hollenbeck and the soldiers came into town, the café owner was found painting over his sign. "The name he had substituted was Café della Libertà," Hollenbeck reported. "A little crowd of natives watched the new name being put up, and they frowned. What had Capri to do with libertà?"[43]

The days in Algiers dragged. Hollenbeck aired twice-daily updates on the Italian campaign. In a September 21 report he said, "Our air and artillery activity is intense, and German prisoners are coming over in a condition styled by the British and Americans as 'poggled'—a new term for slap-happy." On October 13 he reported that Italy, Germany's ally until the September 8 armistice, was proclaiming itself at war with the Nazis. Marshal Pietro Badoglio, a World War I hero who had been appointed head of Italy by the Italian king, said, "Italians, there will not be peace in Italy as long as a single German remains on our soil. Shoulder to shoulder, we march forward with our friends of the United States, of Great Britain, of Russia, and of all the other United Nations."[44]

Hollenbeck wanted to return to the front. The second phase of "Operation Avalanche" called for the Fifth and Eighth Armies to capture Naples and transform it into a logistical base. Hollenbeck finally managed to get to

Naples, just freed from the Germans, on November 3. Eleven days later he shared in the honor of participating in the first live broadcast from a liberated city in Europe. The radio station's makeshift generator was built from discarded electrical equipment captured from Axis stations at Syracuse and Bari. The transmitter came from the *Seth Parker*, a four-masted schooner that the radio personality Phillips Lord had used during a 1934–35 world tour to send programs by shortwave for broadcast across the United States.

Hollenbeck and other NBC, CBS, Blue, and BBC network correspondents crowded into the closet-sized station to broadcast. The station was so small that Red Mueller, who split the NBC time with Hollenbeck, had to sit on his knee. Hollenbeck told listeners about the historic occasion— the first time in years that free speech had been heard from the continent of Europe.

He described his recent trip around the front with General Clark. Soldiers of the Fifth and Eighth Armies, "who haven't had their shoes and socks off for two weeks," took the mountain towns of Filignano and Pozzilli. Some had been on the front for more than fifty days without sufficient warm clothing, but "none but men with fine morale could have taken those two positions."[45]

On November 17 Hollenbeck filed a two-minute report about an unscheduled reception for Count Carlo Sforza, seventy, an Underground leader who had spent much of the war in exile opposing Benito Mussolini's Black Shirts and their alliance with the Germans. Sforza, who had just returned from the United States, was taking over the Action Party, which was pushing for an Italian republic. He was visiting excavations at the village of Herculaneum on Mount Vesuvius when, Hollenbeck said, "more than a hundred people, mostly women, pressed screaming around him. They yelled for bread. They yelled for justice against Fascist officials who they said were still robbing them of supplies. . . . They tore their hair and exhibited their hungry children."

The aristocratic count mounted a chair and said that, while his heart was touched by their suffering, he could do nothing to help them. Hollenbeck, who identified with the people, ended his report with an ironic touch. He followed Sforza to a villa for lunch. The count, Hollenbeck reported, lunched on the best the black market could provide—eggs with mayonnaise, smoked ham, butter and fettuccine, and steaks two inches thick.[46]

The next day Hollenbeck reported on the first contingent of U.S. women soldiers arriving in Italy. "It gives you a sort of funny feeling—seeing women at war right up there with the men." But he crossed out his final sentence, "Sex and age make no difference." An advocate for equal treatment of minorities, Hollenbeck remained a misogynist. Earlier he had reveled in a *Time* article about the failure of a women's copy desk in Detroit. "Great boost to our manly ego," he wrote to Anne. "Lay off our copy desk!"[47]

Hollenbeck reported from Naples for newspapers as well as for NBC. *PM* hyped his report on Page One ("Hollenbeck from Naples—*PM* Exclusive") about the future of a coalition government in Italy and the presence nationwide of an estimated 300,000 minor fascist officials, some of whom still collected customs at the eight entrance gates to Naples.[48]

On radio he added human-interest touches. He said U.S. soldiers were practicing their Italian syntax and pronunciation by telling local citizens: "I have no fiancée" and "In civilian life in America, I was an honest millionaire." He told about Private M. L. Price of Martinsburg, West Virginia, who was adopting Maria, a five-year-old Neapolitan, the only survivor of a family of five: "She could take the place of the Prices' own baby daughter who died just before he came overseas. Maria's only relation, an aunt, has given permission for the adoption, so now Maria is learning English with a West Virginia accent."[49]

On Thanksgiving, Hollenbeck interviewed two U.S. soldiers recovering in Naples from serious wounds. Private First Class Theodore Q. Butts, a twenty-five-year-old Ranger who had been blown from the ambulance he was driving, wore a head cast with openings for his face and ears. Private Joseph A. Gross, twenty-two, had ridden horseback behind German lines to scout enemy positions. Surrounded by Nazis, he had killed four but "got a slug or two in the back." He expressed thanks that his mare was not hurt: "I'll be able to go out with Girl again."[50]

Also in November, Niles Trammell, the president of NBC, and John Royal, a vice president, visited Naples. Hollenbeck took them on a tour of the front. Later, "Trammell had me up until 2 a.m. writing a perfectly foul piece of crap for him to go home and spout," Hollenbeck said. "He pulls every corny line in the repertoire, and then some. For instance, after the visit, he said it made him proud to be an American—and humble too. People actually say those things with straight faces."[51]

Trammell was, Hollenbeck said, "just a loud-mouthed backslapping small-town handshaker who's got a job much too big for him." But Hollenbeck endured him. "One of my main objectives," Hollenbeck wrote to his wife, "is to sell Trammell the idea that I simply MUST get home in the spring."[52]

Hollenbeck still suffered from malaria and jaundice. "I feel like I am carrying a football just below my ribs, which the doctor says is my liver, *slightly* enlarged," he wrote to Anne. He returned to Algiers at the beginning of December. While he enjoyed the recognition that came to a war correspondent, he was not driven to continue reporting the war. He hoped there wasn't enough "fat between my ears" for that. After a confrontation with a drunk Ernie Pyle, the prize-winning reporter hailed by *Time* as "America's most widely read war correspondent," Hollenbeck wrote to Anne, "The war correspondents all seem so obsessed with their own importance and infallibility, and I just can't put on the act, somehow."[53]

Hollenbeck cabled NBC on December 15, 1943, with an ultimatum. He must be sent home. He mentioned his two serious illnesses: "Rest month or two be able get back on job spring . . . risk complete health breakdown." In the meantime he continued to report the war's progress. On December 27 General Eisenhower suggested the war was winnable in 1944 if Allied soldiers did their "full duty." Hollenbeck's report that day said the general's statement was not reason for optimism, judging from the fighting in Italy: " 'Full duty' in Ortona means the eighth day of street-by-street, hand-to-hand fighting with every house a death trap."[54]

NBC finally returned Hollenbeck to New York in January 1944. He would later tell Zoë, his daughter, that he was "very glad when I could quit being a war correspondent. I never did find much glamour in battle. I detest any kind of a gun. About all it [war reporting] got me was a case of malaria and jaundice, and a sore back from lugging that recording machine around."[55]

George Hicks, who would gain fame for his dramatic broadcast from the USS *Ancon* at the start of the D-Day invasion in June 1944, said that Hollenbeck, the war correspondent, "simply could not believe people were out there trying to shoot each other. He was not afraid, in fact was very brave both physically and mentally, but he felt things too much and seemed too fine-grained. He had a terrific abhorrence of dishonesty, of charlatans, and he was sad about the world, as many idealists are, because it staggered along, run as much by the phonies and self-seekers as by the pure."[56]

On May 6, 1944, Hollenbeck participated in a half-hour NBC special on reporting military invasions, past, present, and anticipated. A month later Hollenbeck called on his reporting from Salerno to enrich NBC's continuous coverage of the Allied invasion of Normandy, perhaps the greatest military mission of all time.

The broadcast historian Elizabeth McLeod said that, although many broadcast historians have a "CBS-centric view," NBC's coverage on June 6–7 of the D-Day invasion of Europe proved superior. While CBS abandoned continuous coverage on the morning of June 6 for regularly scheduled soap operas, Hollenbeck and other NBC network newscasters in New York kept reporting breaking developments and features.[57]

Hollenbeck offered a five-minute feature on the lessons learned for the Normandy invasion from the shortcomings of the amphibious attack on Salerno. First, Salerno, with no landing strip closer than Sicily, had no air cover; an estimated eleven thousand Allied planes provided an air umbrella for the Normandy invasion. Second, the Salerno invasion lacked sea power—"the escort was the barest minimum . . . a few destroyers, a few cruisers," Hollenbeck said.[58] Normandy benefited from an armada of four thousand ships.

Hollenbeck said the soldiers who successfully invaded Normandy should not forget the contribution of the Fifth Army soldiers—"those who didn't come back from the beaches of Salerno, those who came back maimed but alive."[59]

Also in 1944 Hollenbeck succeeded George Putnam on the fifteen-minute weekday news and analysis program at 6 p.m on WEAF, NBC's New York outlet. He drew again on his expertise from the Italian campaign to cover the fighting throughout Europe—in Czechoslovakia, Italy, Greece, Luxembourg, Belgium, and Germany—and the Pacific. His gripping December 20 and 21 reports focused on a powerful, surprise German counteroffensive on the German-Belgian-Luxembourg border. The counteroffensive was designed to slice through Allied forces, capture the strategic port of Antwerp, Belgium, and force a negotiated peace.

Hollenbeck conveyed the big picture, drawing on reporting by the AP's Wes Gallagher. Despite the "confused and serious" situation, the tide appeared to be turning in favor of the Allies. Hollenbeck also detailed Nazi treacheries and triumphs. The Germans machine-gunned at least eighty-six unarmed American prisoners south of Malmédy, Belgium. Nazi troops waved white flags as if they were going to surrender, then advanced to favorable positions, dropped down, and opened fire on Allied soldiers.[60] Germany claimed the capture of more than 10,000 American troops, the most serious U.S. reversal in Europe (later U.S. reports put American casualties during the height of the German counteroffensive—from December 16, 1944, through January 2, 1945—at 41,315, 4,138 of whom were killed in action, 20,231 wounded, and 16,946 reported missing).[61]

Despite the unreliability of Nazi reports and the censorship and delays of at least forty-eight hours in battlefield news required by Supreme Allied Headquarters, Hollenbeck wove together authoritative accounts of the fighting. In the first three months of 1945 Hollenbeck's 6 p.m. reports covered key Allied victories on all fronts: the U.S. invasion of the island of Luzon in the Philippines, which the Japanese had taken three years earlier; the eastern front successes in Poland, Hungary, and Czechoslovakia of the Red Army, and the western front triumph of the Ninth U.S. Army troops. On their way to Berlin the Americans reached the Rhine River, described by a military source as the most significant victory since D-Day.[62]

In a script prepared for broadcast on April 12, Hollenbeck said Germany's defeat was imminent. On the western front a news blackout made it difficult to track the dash of American and British armies across Germany. On the eastern front Moscow radio reported "savage battles west of the Oder," less than one hundred miles from Berlin, Hollenbeck said. "The fact that Soviet censorship permits the story to get out is confirmation that this is it."[63]

Hollenbeck accompanied his accounts of Allied victories with tales of war's tragedies: the major in the Eighth Air Force, with thirty-two-and-a-half German planes to his credit, accidentally shot down on Christmas Day 1944 by American ground gunners, and the thirty-one-year-old air force lieutenant colonel who was court-martialed in Kunming, China, for the mercy killing of a twenty-year-old gunnery sergeant trapped in the flight compartment of a burning B-25 bomber.[64]

Hollenbeck leavened the news of horror with humor. He described the attempt in Washington of a committee of female members of Congress to "get to the bottom" of a diaper shortage. He told of fifteen Nazi prisoners—"super Aryans"—at a Farmingdale, New York, factory who were packing kosher pickles and sauerkraut and, "what's more, every now and then they enjoy a nibble at them." He reported that the wartime need for women workers in Britain caused a member of the House of Commons to recommend that the striptease profession be restricted to women older than fifty.[65]

WEAF listeners appreciated Hollenbeck's reports. C. J. C. Clarke wrote, "You give us the news as simply as though a friend were talking to us in our home." Marion Muller complimented Hollenbeck's honest, straightforward manner: "Your reporting seems to me to be more objective than other commentators.'" Ethel DeForest Moore wrote, "You have everything—voice, speed and clear enunciation." Edith McCabe praised Hollenbeck's breadth of coverage, sense of humor, and presentation: "It was no surprise to us that a poll showed you to be the most listened to."[66]

As World War II's end approached, Hollenbeck narrated some of NBC's most important radio broadcasts. He began an 11:15 p.m. network newscast for NBC over WEAF. He contributed to NBC's election-night coverage. NBC president Trammell congratulated Hollenbeck on "a great job and the surveys indicate we lead over the other networks in listening audience."[67]

After President Roosevelt died in Warm Springs, Georgia, on April 12, 1945, Hollenbeck spent four days in Hyde Park, New York, the president's "first and last home," to interview his friends and neighbors and convey the town's mood leading up to a memorial service at St. James Church, where the president's pew, number four, was left empty.

Hollenbeck began his report: "Franklin Delano Roosevelt is again the Squire of Hyde Park. When the last note of the bugle died away at ten minutes to eleven this morning, and the soldiers marched away from his graveside, he was finished with the cares of state, with the pomp and ceremony of official life in death. Within his hundred-year-old hemlock hedge, he is again as he wished to be, Squire Roosevelt of Hyde Park."

Hollenbeck reported his conversations with Tom Leonard, seventy-five, who had campaigned with Roosevelt in 1910, when he was seeking his first public office as a state senator, and the Reverend Dr. George W. Anthony, seventy-eight, who was judged too old to serve with the military as he wanted but was called out of retirement to direct Roosevelt's service. "We do what we can, don't we?" he said.

Hollenbeck captured the sounds, smells, and sights of the day. Beethoven's Third Symphony (composed, Beethoven wrote, "to celebrate the memory of a great man") played quietly on radios in Hyde Park homes. Mourning bands of purple and black draped the town's buildings. The subtle scent of the violet-carpeted churchyard of St. James, where Roosevelt served as senior warden for fifteen years, lingered in the air. Almost exactly at the funeral hour, the sky darkened, accompanied by a chill and a few drops of rain.

Hollenbeck ended the report in the churchyard with Sexton Arthur E. McConnell: "Sexton McConnell at 4 o'clock yesterday afternoon tolled the bell sixty-three times, once for each year of Franklin D. Roosevelt's life. Sexton McConnell is a bald-headed man with faded blue eyes and New England speech. He looked at the crowd and at the trampled violets in the churchyard and he said: 'Now I know why the president wanted to be buried on his estate. He has been hounded for twelve years. He just wants to be alone for a while.' "[68]

On V-E Day, May 8, 1945, Hollenbeck introduced President Roosevelt's widow, Eleanor, who talked to the nation about what her husband would have wished for the United States. He would have asked Americans to continue the fight with Japan "until the war is fully won," she said, but he also would have asked the country to pursue a permanent peace, the only way to compensate for the thousands who had sacrificed their lives.[69]

Also on V-E Day, Hollenbeck and John W. Vandercook served as lead narrators for *Milestones on the Road to Peace*, NBC's hourlong history of World War II. In one of the program's most powerful segments, Hollenbeck recalled the special wartime role of President Roosevelt, for whom American flags across the country still flew at half-staff. Hollenbeck's voice captured the country's emptiness at Roosevelt's death. The president "had died in battle," he said, "on the threshold of the new world peace which his efforts had engineered."[70]

In a tour de force of a broadcast about the signing of the United Nations charter on June 25, 1945, Hollenbeck mentioned the organization's fifty members in alphabetical order—from Argentina to Yugoslavia—offering an interesting fact about each: "Guatemala, which has the world's lowest crime rate. . . . Haiti, one of the world's two negro republics. . . . Honduras, world's biggest banana producer—never put 'em in the refrigerator. . . . India, half the size of the USA, with three times its population. . . . Iran, fourth largest oil producer in the world. . . . Iraq, only state to develop out of the League of Nations mandate system."[71]

An important part of Hollenbeck's appeal was his willingness to lard his commentaries with side remarks that listeners variously described as "tongue in check," "sage and colorful little jibes," and "pungent cracks." Andrew Moursund wrote, "Here's my bouquet to the deftest and wittiest newscaster on the air." Mrs. S. S. Bliss, a seventy-one-year-old widow who lived alone, wrote to Hollenbeck, "You have such a delicious sense of humor that I often cackle right out."[72]

But NBC executives were not cackling. On one newscast Hollenbeck mentioned a June 24, 1944, *New Yorker* "Talk of the Town" item that referred to the alleged Mutt-and-Jeff complex of Thomas E. Dewey, 5 feet 8 inches tall, the GOP presidential aspirant. If Dewey has such a complex, Hollenbeck said, the Republican Party was in a desperate quandary. The six Republicans being mentioned as vice-presidential candidates to run with Dewey were all six feet or taller.

Hollenbeck repeated the solution suggested by the *New Yorker* writer: Choose the actor Victor Moore, who played Vice President Alexander Throttlebottom in a long-running Broadway musical, *Of Thee I Sing*. Moore was 5 feet 7 inches tall. "His quavering mezzo-soprano would go well with Dewey's concert tenor," Hollenbeck said, reading the *New Yorker* piece. " 'Dewey and

Throttlebottom' ought to sweep the country." Earlier in the same broadcast, according to a media account, "Hollenbeck segued from role of reporter to editorialist for [a] rather lengthy dissertation on [the] action of Navy men sending back $412 for 'money hungry' aircraft plant strikers."[73]

On February 23, 1945, the twenty-seventh anniversary of Red Army Day, Hollenbeck recounted an almost-too-good-to-be-true story from *Pravda*, the propaganda-filled Communist Party paper, about a Red Army Major Sergeyev, who took a German town so quickly that its inhabitants did not know what was happening. Hollenbeck repeated the paper's story: Sergeyev, who spoke German, telephoned ahead to the office of the bürgermeister, the equivalent of the mayor, in Berlin: "This is Major Sergeyev of the Red Army. We'll be seeing you." Hollenbeck noted, without a hint of skepticism, that *Pravda* said the story was true "and 'pravda' is the word for truth."[74]

Then came Hollenbeck's downfall at WEAF and at NBC. Charles Gussman, a friend, attributed it to "an offhand remark about the brigadier generals at Potsdam."[75] David Sarnoff, board chairman of NBC and head of the Radio Corporation of America, returned from duty in the European theater and began to take an interest in WEAF. During World War II Sarnoff, a colonel in the U.S. Army Reserve, had served as communication consultant to General Dwight Eisenhower, implemented electronic news coverage systems for D-Day and the liberation of Paris, and received an appointment as a U.S. Army brigadier general. Sarnoff took that appointment seriously. He preferred to be called General Sarnoff.

Gussman said General Sarnoff telephoned "Ad Schneider, one of the wigs of NBC's news department, and said he'd like to have someone who sounded like the *New York Times* doing the evening news [for WEAF]."[76] Schneider mentioned Hollenbeck.

Sarnoff said he would listen to Hollenbeck for a night or two. "Ad checked after the first night and Sarnoff seemed to like the [broadcast] but said he'd want to listen a few more nights," Gussman recalled. "The second evening, according to Ad, the lead story was about the Potsdam Conference. Don's sidebar was that AP reported 158 generals at the conference, to which he added the comment that 'this probably amounted to having the brigadiers emptying ashtrays.' When Ad checked with Brigadier General Sarnoff next day he wasn't too keen about Don and said he'd like to listen to someone else."[77]

In August 1945, the month atomic bombs were dropped on Hiroshima and Nagasaki and Japan surrendered, NBC sent Hollenbeck to Europe. The assignment was expected to last through the opening of the Nuremberg war crimes trials in the spring of 1946. Hollenbeck did not want to leave New York. But NBC regularly shuttled its newscasters between New York and overseas duty. Hollenbeck knew he was in no position to protest his reassignment. "He was afraid that he was going to be tossed out of his job here," Anne said. After Hollenbeck's indiscreet comments about Tom Dewey, brigadier generals, and other subjects, the assignment abroad would allow the network executives' tempers to cool. Hollenbeck also would have a chance to look for work elsewhere. "This was fighting for time," Anne said.[78]

It did not take long for Hollenbeck to regret his transfer. Shortly after arriving in London, he wrote to Anne about "one of the worst days of my life . . . and I almost said the hell with all this and came right home. . . . I bet I could get a job as a copyreader if I got thrown out of the radio business." He reminded Anne that he had not responded well to his previous wartime assignment in Europe. The killing and looting had disturbed him. Reporting on the Nuremberg trials—recounting the killing and looting—promised to be equally disturbing.[79]

Hollenbeck also feared the overseas assignment would weaken his marriage. Sam Boal, one of his best wartime friends, had returned to Europe as a correspondent. Boal's wife, Margit, was divorcing him. "I don't know all the circumstances of Sam's and Margit's case, but from what Sam hinted, it is going away that touched it off," Hollenbeck wrote Anne. "That case is a constant object lesson, baby." Anne reassured Hollenbeck: "Separations are never good for any marriage, but we've survived before and we always will. . . . You're as complicated a person as Sam is. . . . Margit apparently can't go Sam's duality, but I can go your manic depressiveness."[80]

Hollenbeck also missed one-year-old Zoë, whom Anne and Don had adopted through a private agency shortly after her birth in a New York City hospital. Anne wrote, "Leave the manly sweat if you will, billeting in bad beds and suffering to show how romantic is the profession . . . hell with it. There's more romance in seeing a little girl sucking her thumb. Especially when it's your little girl." Hollenbeck wrote back: "I echo your sentiment: adventurous colorful life be damned: me for you and Zoë and peace and quiet."[81]

Soon after, Hollenbeck discovered that two NBC executives were competing to be his boss and a roving correspondent was trying to take over his Nuremberg trials assignment. "I'm easy to get along with, but the character in question is such an arrogant, self-willed gent that I don't think my mild nature will stand it." Less than a month after arriving in Europe, Hollenbeck told Anne he wanted to quit: "I think it would be a big relief." He contacted one of his newly hired agents, Tom Stix, a partner in Stix and Gude, a firm that specialized in representing newspeople with employers and potential employers. Hollenbeck asked Stix if a position were available in New York so that he and NBC could "simply mutually call . . . the whole thing off."[82]

Stix discouraged him. The opportunities for radio newscasters in New York were disappearing. With the war over, radio news was less interesting than entertainment programming to many listeners and, therefore, to many advertisers. John "Jap" Gude, Hollenbeck's other agent, recalled a conversation with B. F. Goodrich's advertising agency. "They were going to shift to an entertainment program, particularly since they wanted to reach a younger audience," Gude said.[83]

News commentators began to be replaced by lower-cost disc jockeys without news experience who regurgitated bulletins from the news ticker of the Associated Press, United Press, or International News Service. The typical network news executive refused to guarantee commentator positions in New York for returning war correspondents. Stix learned that at CBS Edward R. Murrow felt obligated to find New York positions for the CBS correspondents who had served with him in Europe. At NBC, Stix said, executives were "indefinite" about a position for Hollenbeck in New York.[84]

Stix advised Hollenbeck to continue working for NBC in Nuremberg through the war crimes trials. Anne wrote to Hollenbeck about Stix's advice: "I suppose he is right and then you could come home having accomplished something of distinction."[85] But Hollenbeck had had enough.

In early September 1945 he had just gotten to Berlin on his way to Nuremberg when he received a cable from NBC: "Suggest you London week September 10 for foreign minister conference, check with Richardson status radio correspondents eastern Europe stop think soon thereafter as possible good idea you visit Poland survey situation establish contacts." Hollenbeck wrote Anne, "My God, Poland!... As you say, what the hell next."[86]

Bored, lonely, and "fed up to here with it all . . . fed up with death and destruction," Hollenbeck handed his uniform to another correspondent and flew home. His departure did not surprise Anne. He had written to her two weeks earlier: "I'm not going to be away from you and Zoë any later than Spring, so if things don't look just right here for both of us, then home comes Donny, and the hell with what NBC says or does—we can get along, and will."[87]

Anne said, "That was Don. Precipitous behavior. You know, 'The hell with you, and I'll go back.' He left exactly the way he left the AP in San Francisco. Literally overnight."

"It was the wrong thing for him to do," Gude said. "He just ran out on a very important assignment."[88]

NBC fired Hollenbeck. Gude tried to persuade William F. Brooks, vice president for NBC News, that the impulsive Hollenbeck had been distraught at the thought of what time away from home might do to his marriage and did not deserve to be fired. But Brooks was firm. "I can't let it go," he said. "I have no choice."[89]

CHAPTER 6

■

Getting Fired by NBC and ABC, Then Hired by CBS

Don Hollenbeck . . . just a few weeks ago stunned the radio world by open-ing his news broadcast with a denunciation of the commercial preceding his program.

—Murray Schumach, *New York Times*

Despite the tight market for newscasters when Hollenbeck left NBC, he soon was hired by the American Broadcasting Company. "He was such a good journalist, both as a writer and a reporter," John Gude, his agent, said. "He was as good as the best of them."[1]

ABC assigned Hollenbeck to an unsponsored 7 a.m. newscast on WJZ, the network's New York City station. The newscast provided little oppor-tunity for individuality or innovation. But Hollenbeck's performance delighted ABC executives. Robert E. Kintner, ABC vice president of public relations and radio news, wrote to him in January 1946: "We are extremely pleased by the progress you are making and hope the conditions are satis-factory to you."[2]

In May 1946 ABC invited Hollenbeck to substitute for the vacationing Raymond Gram Swing, the network's evening coast-to-coast commentator on Wednesdays, Thursdays, and Fridays. Hollenbeck chose controversial topics—from illegitimate children born in Europe of American fathers to a hotly contested railroad strike. His commentary on the strike provoked E. A. Clancy, a listener in Alameda, California, to send him a postcard: "I liked your intelligent analysis of the situation and the fairness with which you treated the workers' side. . . . Quite different than those who while commenting on the news attacked workers with bitterness."[3]

On Fridays Hollenbeck continued Swing's practice of addressing U.S. use of the atom bomb. He offered "The Atomic Aesop: The Stupid Giant," a fable about a 170-year-old "fat, sassy and complacent" giant named Sam. The giant possessed "a new type of brass knuckle" and could call his fellow giants and midgets together to act as a committee of custodians of all brass knuckles, including the atomic variety. The giant chose not to make himself heard, "and late in the twentieth century—but that is another fable for another time, and the atomic Aesop ends this inconclusive one with the moral that the bigger they are, the harder they fall."[4]

Listeners wrote to Hollenbeck requesting a copy. Margaret Marshall, deacon of the Little Rock Methodist Council in Arkansas, said: "I feel that it should have value in waking us as individuals and a nation to our responsibility." Listeners also responded to what they called Hollenbeck's "powerful," "eloquent" reading of Hermann Hagedorn's poem, "The Bomb That Fell on America." A stanza began: "The bomb that fell on Hiroshima fell on America too. / It fell on people. / Not a few hundred thousand only, but one hundred and thirty-five million."[5]

The intelligence of Hollenbeck's broadcasts commanded the respect of professional journalists as well as the public. Swing wrote to ABC's Kintner about Hollenbeck's "commendably distinguished job" as his vacation replacement. Carolyn Anspacher, a reporter for the *San Francisco Chronicle*, expressed the views of "a newspaper woman reared to distrust each word emanating from the lips of a radio analyst." She wrote to Hollenbeck, "Your commentaries . . . are unique . . . each one has a third-dimensional quality—a depth of spirit and intellect and concept rarely found [in] these days of too-glib talk."

Listeners like Virginia McAuliffe of Brooklyn wrote to ABC asking that Hollenbeck soon "have a program of his own."[6]

As he became more comfortable at ABC, Hollenbeck let his wit show. While substituting on the *Orson Welles Program* for an ill Welles, Hollenbeck detailed the election of an ostrich queen at a world congress of ostriches in the Libyan desert. As a way of commenting on discussions and disagreements of global leaders, Hollenbeck noted that the ostrich queen, coming across thousands of ostriches with their heads buried in the desert sand, said, "Where in the world *IS* everybody?" Hollenbeck ended his story: "Being ostriches, of course they couldn't tell her."[7]

Another Hollenbeck program greatly amused a listener, reminding her of the satirist Jonathan Swift's "A Modest Proposal for Preventing the Children of Poor People from Being a Burden to Their Parents or the Country, and for Making Them Beneficial to the Public"—by killing the children and serving them cooked as a delicious, nourishing meal.[8]

ABC was less amused. Hollenbeck—always independent, often impulsive—used humor in ways that were guaranteed to worry ABC and the other networks. Newscasters were expected to avoid any controversy that might anger advertisers and threaten the networks' bottom line. The networks preferred marshmallow humor to barbed bon mots. Finally, Hollenbeck's relationship with ABC—like his association with NBC—was destroyed, this time by his old enemy, the candid quip. For three months Hollenbeck had delivered ABC's unsponsored 7 a.m. newscast, preceded each morning, six days a week, by another program that ended with this singing commercial:

SHE: He can hold his cheek close to mine.
HE: And I do.
SHE: Hold me tight. Steal a kiss any time.
HE: Wouldn't you?
SHE: In fact, I'm his most willing slave. The man with the Marlin shave.
HE: I don't know what she sees in me.
SHE: You're a smoothie.
HE: Guess I'm just as lucky as I can be.
SHE: You're for me.
BOTH: He makes all the ladies rave woo-woo! The man with the Marlin shave.[9]

The morning of August 14, 1946, Hollenbeck looked at the script he was about to read. He would report on the death of H. G. Wells, a dispute in the UN, price ceilings, a disagreement among diplomats in Paris, and rioting in Haifa. Then the Marlin Blades commercial started: "He can hold his cheek close to mine." As soon as the commercial ended, Hollenbeck exploded into the microphone, "The atrocity you have just heard is no part of this show."[10]

Three hours later ABC fired him. Kintner, the vice president responsible for news, was furious. Gude tried to explain Hollenbeck's impulsiveness. Kintner remained unsympathetic. He said Hollenbeck "had done something the network couldn't afford—he had criticized the lifeblood of the network, that is, the commercials. It is not the place of the commentator to pass judgment on the sponsor or the contents of the sponsor's message."[11]

Hollenbeck had to have known that ABC would see his comment as treachery. "In those days you did what you were told to do and that was that," Gude said. "I just popped off," Hollenbeck said later. "I knew there would be a reprimand."[12]

But the public sided with Hollenbeck. WJZ heard from his fans:

- "I'll never buy another Marlin blade."
- "Can you imagine WJZ firing a man like Don Hollenbeck for the sake of that loathsome, disgusting, vile, filthy commercial."
- "Somebody sure as hell ought to pound thoroughly on those jokers' heads with a large two-by-four—preferably loaded."
- "By firing Hollenbeck you got rid of the only reason that would cause us to hear Marlin . . . commercials. Excuse me if I sound naive but aren't good programs the thing that draws advertisers to your station? Until Mr. Hollenbeck is reinstated, we will no longer listen to WJZ."[13]

Hollenbeck received 250 fan letters, typically ending with the hope that, as the listener Joseph Lev wrote, "you will be rewarded, not penalized for your conduct." *Time* concluded that "in many a listener's Book of Gold, Don Hollenbeck's name led all the rest." Pro-Hollenbeck letters inundated Marlin Blades, ABC, and Craven and Hedges, Marlin's New York advertising agency. One letter pretended to call on the Bible: "See Matthew 6:24—'Ye cannot serve God and Marlin!'"[14]

The media publicized Hollenbeck's plight. A letter to the editor of *Time* concluded that Hollenbeck had the letter writer's vote for radio's Man of the Year and asked whether Hollenbeck was back on the air. *Time* answered, "He is still out of a job."[15]

ABC wrote noncommittal letters to Hollenbeck's supporters: "We invite your continued interest in ABC programs." Mrs. M. F. Miller of Croton-on-Hudson, New York, responded to one such letter: "May I assure you of my deepest contempt for your action. . . . You should be proud that at least one of your commentators has the guts and honesty to say what every single listener must have felt when he heard the sickening Marlin ditty. If it would really be your policy to serve your listeners and not only your sponsors you should have promoted Don Hollenbeck instead of firing him. I suggest that you reconsider your decision."[16]

The listeners appeared to swing ABC's support to Hollenbeck. A month after his firing Hollenbeck returned to WJZ with a Saturday morning news broadcast sponsored for thirteen weeks by Marlin Blades. Marlin gave up its ditty for a less inane commercial. Murray Schumach, columnist for the *New York Times*, wrote about Marlin's decision to sponsor Hollenbeck's broadcasts. He titled the column "A Modern Miracle."[17]

But the miracle failed to satisfy listeners. Berniece Pidwell, a Hollenbeck fan, wrote to Schumach: "Marlin blades has eaten its words but, why, why, WHY, don't they put him [Hollenbeck] on a daily broadcast of 15 minutes. And at a decent hour!" Mr. and Mrs. Charles J. Suplee, listeners in Bala Cynwyd, Pennsylvania, wrote to Hollenbeck about their delight in his return. But "we feel this is a poor way to use your talents and hope WJZ can find other better spots for you soon."[18] The once-a-week, five-minute newscast at 8:55 a.m. for thirteen weeks was really ABC's way of allowing Hollenbeck to win the battle and lose the full-time-employment war.

Soured by his experiences with NBC and ABC, Hollenbeck sought a better way to use his talents—by writing fiction. "If Don Hollenbeck wanted to be anything that he wasn't, he wanted to be a novelist," said Milton Stern, his close friend. Anne Hollenbeck agreed "that Don was not satisfied just to be a successful newsman."[19]

Hollenbeck was not the only newscaster who in midlife tried becoming a writer of stories that would survive time's test and tell the truth about the pressures on broadcast journalists. Eric Sevareid's short story, "The Meeting in Malaga," was rejected by the *New Yorker*, but Ned Calmer (*The Anchorman*) and William L. Shirer (*Stranger Come Home*) published successful novels about broadcast journalism. In *Stranger Come Home*, an Edward R. Murrow–like wartime radio broadcaster turns network executive and sabotages a liberal foreign correspondent modeled on Shirer.[20]

Fiction writing was not completely new to Hollenbeck. After returning from the Italian campaign, he had tried writing a short story for the *New Yorker* about a Thanksgiving dinner in wartime Naples. Correspondents tear apart, then devour, an undercooked turkey that, in the Neapolitan style, had not been beheaded. Joe, a wounded infantryman invited as a guest, recounts how he once had ambushed German soldiers at lunch, giving them a whistle before he machine-gunned them to death. "I just kind of wanted them to know what was coming—not soon enough so's they'd do anything about it, but just so's they'd get the idea."[21]

William Shawn, editor of the *New Yorker*, recommended that Hollenbeck rewrite the piece and resubmit it. The revised version was gently rejected. Hollenbeck had also written a scenario for a ballet titled "Ulysses at Dublin," based on James Joyce's novel. The choreographer Agnes de Mille said the scenario merited a reworking. She praised the suggestions for music but said the plot and the relationships between characters were too complicated. Again, Hollenbeck's rewrite was rejected.[22]

Nevertheless, in 1946 he undertook an autobiographical novel "about a man who wanted to say something to his generation," Anne said.[23] Simon and Schuster gave him a $25,000 advance and he produced a manuscript that he titled "Give Us Time."

Bart McKenna, the novel's protagonist, sounds familiar. A forty-year-old midwesterner, McKenna provides excellent radio broadcasts from England during the war. His "bell-like voice" charms hordes of adoring old ladies. Not just a voice, he cares about news, ideas, and language. He wants the word *hooligan* used properly, risks a quip about John D. Rockefeller Jr., and cites the German historian and philosopher Oswald Spengler during a broadcast, not to show off but to explain a relevant Spenglerian idea.

When not working, McKenna drinks scotch, buys his ties at Triplers, wears Burberry hats, loves books in Sangorski and Sutcliffe bindings, listens to his favorite recording of Maggie Teyte singing Debussy's "La Chevelure," takes photos with an expensive Rolleiflex, and solves the Sunday *New York Times* crossword puzzle by clipping out the vertical definitions and using only the horizontal ones.

Hollenbeck and McKenna appear to merge. McKenna attacks the aura of fear tied to a broadcaster's job "where you're at the mercy every minute of a guy with a checkbook." McKenna complains that sponsors are permitted to cancel a program with only thirteen-weeks' notice: "It would be nice to have a job where the threat of losing it wasn't always so immediate."[24] McKenna criticizes the promilitary, antiunion bias of reactionary network executives, ad agencies, and sponsors.

Simon and Schuster rejected "Give Us Time." Hollenbeck revealed little about his private thoughts and emotions in the novel. Perhaps he sensed that if he looked below the surface—if he examined his innermost self—he might find something that would improve his novel but help destroy him. "I had the feeling that Don was too fragilely poised to be a novelist," said Milton Stern. "So are a lot of writers." Stern mentioned Ross Lockridge Jr., author of *Raintree County*, and Thomas Heggen, author of *Mister Roberts*. Heggen drowned in his bathwater. The medical examiner ruled his death a "probable suicide." Lockridge died by suicide.[25]

While Hollenbeck was writing "Give Us Time," Gude approached T. "Ted" Wells Church, radio news director at CBS, about having Murrow, who was vice president and director of public affairs, hire Hollenbeck: "I said, 'Look, he has been a bad boy [at ABC and NBC] but I think he wants to come over here.' Ted was very interested. Don was awfully good. His stuff was so well written and so well delivered."

Murrow hired Hollenbeck. If Murrow "could get the best newsroom together, he was going to do it," Anne said.[26]

Hollenbeck started at CBS in October 1946. He was elated at his three-year contract. He described Murrow, his boss, as "one of the most rewarding and stimulating people" he knew. Hollenbeck agreed with Jack Walters, a CBS newswriter, who said, "CBS News, in the forties and fifties, was the Camelot of the English-speaking world." Anne recalled, "CBS was going up in the world and the other stars were descending. NBC was getting rid of all its liberal commentators."[27]

But NBC was not alone. Other networks, including CBS, pruned two dozen liberal voices, at least in part to save money as the post–World War II advertising market for news and analysis collapsed. The radio commentator Bryce Oliver suggested that network irresponsibility, not just the advertising market or reactionary listeners or advertisers, caused the cuts: "The networks' brave wartime intentions to enlighten the public and offer adult viewpoints have been succeeded by a return to old-time commercialism of the most blatant sort."[28]

Once at CBS, Hollenbeck began broadcasting the Sunday morning news roundup and appearing regularly on a weekly fifteen-minute Saturday book review program, *Men and Books*, on CBS's New York affiliate, WCBS. He reviewed books that, for the most part, took him to unfamiliar worlds— Renaissance Italy, rural New York, the hill country of Kentucky, and the boxing ring.

He stated his opinions directly—Maurice Samuel's 484-page novel, *Web of Lucifer*, offered flat characterizations and turgid prose. The reviews also made clear Hollenbeck's moral vision. He saw the novelist Percy Winner's *Dario*, about fascist Italy of 1925–45, as the story of many modern politicians: "If they ever had any principles, they have compromised them so often that they have lost any meaning."[29]

He found in Budd Schulberg's novel about boxing, *The Harder They Fall*, an opportunity for readers to examine their own consciences. Hollenbeck's review focused less on the brutality of those inside the ring than of those in the audience who, he said, "yell for gore, contributing to their own delinquency and the delinquency of the age."[30] Can you really be an innocent bystander to evil, Hollenbeck asked, if you allow evil to happen without openly opposing it?

Hollenbeck also delivered five-minute daily news features at 11:10 p.m.

His features were personal essays on everything from the screaming sirens of U.N. dignitaries' automobile processions along 48th Street (which scared Zoë, then two) to Kierkegaard's existentalism, houseboat living, the scents of spring, the death of dining rooms, the health hazards of anthracite coal mining, and the mule capital of America.[31]

Hollenbeck objected to narcissistic newspeople who inserted themselves into their newscasts. But occasionally Hollenbeck's features were stories about people—usually ordinary people—that revealed an iota about him. He told about William Cimillo, thirty-seven, a Bronx bus driver for seventeen years who took a new, forty-four-passenger bus for a trial run one Friday morning and wound up driving it 1,340 miles to Hollywood, Florida.

Arrested by Hollywood police at a local racetrack, Cimillo told them "only that he wanted to get away from it all—scarcely a full explanation, so one may only guess at his motives," Hollenbeck said. Perhaps Cimillo was rebelling against an overdose of odious bus passengers. Or perhaps "he felt the sweet wind of freedom through the windows of his bus . . . and said the heck with it: he was off," Hollenbeck concluded.[32]

When Damon Runyon died in 1946 at age sixty-two, Hollenbeck portrayed him as an exemplar for his generation of journalists. Runyon wrote the short story that was made into *Guys and Dolls*. He had an earlier newspaper career that paralleled Hollenbeck's. Runyon was born in Manhattan, Kansas, mixed alcoholism with a devil's view of the world ("All of life is 6 to 5 against"), and wrote with an angel's touch for Hearst's *New York American* and other dailies, small and large.

It was that earlier newspaper career Hollenbeck celebrated—the wisecracks and wisdom of "the sports stories, the news stories, the pieces which showed that Damon Runyon knew people inside out. He could unbutton a stuffed shirt faster than anybody else. . . . Runyon seemed to take nothing very seriously, not even death."[33]

Hollenbeck recalled a Runyon column two years before he died in which the columnist interviewed Death, an uninvited visitor who wore a big smile and tailored white flannels. Runyon asked Death to do what he called a scrammola: "Your visit is sure to get noised about, and cause gossip." A weeping Death left. Hollenbeck ended his radio feature: "Tonight death came once more unbidden to Damon Runyon, and in black cerements this time, without the big smile."[34]

At Christmas Hollenbeck told of Joseph Bonavita, a Brooklyn restaurant owner who tried to play Santa to the hungry and thirsty on the Bowery by handing out fifteen hundred dollars' worth of bills. But the derelicts rejected the money, believing Bonavita crazy and his money phony. So Bonavita went to the police with his problem.

Two detectives accompanied Bonavita and reassured the skeptical derelicts. They took Bonavita's money, which was offered with no strings attached. Hollenbeck said: "Nobody had to sing any hymns, or put on any phony thankful act, because, unlike a lot of the do-gooders and Santa Clauses who venture down into the Bowery's world of shadows, Joseph Bonavita didn't present his bounty with any conditions."[35]

A similar interest in ordinary people dominated Hollenbeck's innovative, hourlong radio review of 1946, *Moments Make the Year.* From the CBS Radio Playhouse on Times Square, Hollenbeck re-created the tragic and triumphant moments of sixteen people "whose everyday lives were small but memorable parts of the passing year."[36]

First was Herbert Lamoureaux, a riveter from Gardner, Massachusetts, who reminded Hollenbeck of Leander from Greek mythology. Leander swam across the Hellespont each evening to spend the night with his lover Hero; one wintry night he lost his way and drowned. Lamoureaux, who had signed on the merchant ship *Rushville* to see his English bride, was frustrated when the ship docked in Plymouth, England, but did not allow the crew ashore. When the ship headed for France, Lamoureaux jumped into the icy English Channel and started swimming toward England.

A lighthouse dory picked him up, and a ship carried him to France. Lamoureaux refused to see his swim as a failure: "Eighteen days later another ship and another captain landed me in Liverpool where I saw my wife, Veronica, and—for the first time—my baby Elaine. Right now they are here with me in our home in Gardner. . . . If my wife were still in England and I were on a ship carrying me away from her, I would jump into the sea again to get to her."[37]

Nick Fetsko, a Pennsylvania coal miner, recounted being aboard twenty-five overloaded coal cars traveling fast inside the mine where he worked: "The load began to shake. . . . It was like riding a crack-the-whip." Fearing for his life, Fetsko jumped on mine gravel, crashed into a timber, and lost consciousness. But he did not view his experience as special: "It's not unusual to get hurt in a mine. . . . But we like it. There's an old saying, 'Once a coal miner, always a coal miner,' and it's true. I've been at it for seventeen years. 1946 was just another year."[38]

Helen Ruth Henderson, a Girl Scouts official from Richmond, Virginia, recalled her rescue from a transatlantic plane crash that killed twenty-six in a Newfoundland spruce forest and the teamwork of the fifteen survivors of different nationalities and religions: "I can still see the lovely patterns of the spruce and the silver birch trees, those same trees that cut us off from help; and I can almost hear the noise of the hunters plunging toward us, through the density of that forest." Henderson said she would approach the New Year with great hope and a renewed recognition "that the sky is universal—it covers all continents and all peoples; it transcends all national boundaries."[39]

Almost immediately, Hollenbeck established himself as one of the best of CBS's postwar newscasters. The news team included Murrow, Eric Sevareid, Charles Collingwood, William L. Shirer, Howard K. Smith, and Ned Calmer. Calmer, whose morning radio newscast preceded Hollenbeck's, said: "Without ever sounding like an announcer or one of these commercialized voices, Don had a deep and rather beautiful sound in his voice—he didn't push it at all—which made him very distinctive."[40]

Hollenbeck's voice on radio reminded Calmer of the television voice of the Reverend Fulton J. Sheen, the Roman Catholic auxiliary bishop of New York. Sheen was host to the Emmy-winning *Life Is Worth Living* in the 1950s. Hollenbeck and Sheen "looked quite a bit alike and they both had that rather quietly electric—if you can use such a combination of words—quality of riveting the listener or the viewer with a blunt, honest kind of approach to things," Calmer said.[41]

Hollenbeck also began to demonstrate an ability to make his point without precipitating his dismissal for editorializing. His first evening feature for CBS was about Franco's Spain. Joseph Wershba, the editor on duty that night, reviewed Hollenbeck's script. "By the time it was finished, you wanted Franco out of office. And fast. So I said, 'Mr. Hollenbeck, I happen to agree with this piece completely, but we'll never get on the air again if this goes on. We just don't do that here at CBS.'"[42]

Hollenbeck responded, "Oh, now, aren't you being a little silly about that." But he finally relented. He "de-editorialized and still came out with what he wanted to say," recalled Wershba. "It was my first meeting with him and I said, 'Boy, this guy is something. He's got a brain. Glad to have him here.'"[43]

Murrow too appreciated Hollenbeck's intelligence and seriousness. The two were kindred spirits—talented, honest, well-read loners. They became friends. Wershba said Murrow "had more affection for Don than for anyone else he worked with." Both Hollenbeck and Murrow were typecast as standoffish and somber. But they shared a droll sense of humor. On an evening news program they happily bantered about *The Decline and Fall of Practically Everybody*, a mock history book by Will Cuppy.[44]

Murrow read a Cuppy comment about Lady Godiva or another famous person, and Hollenbeck followed with one of Cuppy's fine-print footnotes. Murrow resisted laughing until they got to Henry VIII. Murrow explained that Henry VIII was, as Cuppy said, "fond of tennis and pole vaulting and wrestling and jousting, and he always won because he made his rules as he went along. He finally developed athlete's head." Hollenbeck followed with a Cuppy footnote on Henry VIII: "He was especially fond of dressing up in armor and beating the Duke of Suffolk over the head with a heavy spear. He had an Aunt Cicely, too."[45]

Murrow struggled to continue, fully regaining his composure for a last Cuppy history lesson, about the Pilgrims: If the Pilgrims were looking for freedom of conscience, "they came to just the right place. In America, everybody's conscience is unusually free." Hollenbeck added: "If it isn't, we fix it. We're funny that way."[46]

Both Hollenbeck and Murrow also infused the news with ideas from the Bible, Shakespeare, and Greek literature. Hollenbeck began a commentary on a new book, *Modern Woman: The Lost Sex*, by paraphrasing Euripides' *Alcamaeon*: Woman brings to man his greatest blessing and his greatest plague. To end an essay on an Illinois governor's call to investigate a deadly mine disaster after the governor had ignored a union's plea to enforce safety laws at that mine, Hollenbeck recalled a line from the *Iliad*: After the event, even a fool is wise.[47]

Murrow and Hollenbeck were both idealistic, if pessimistic, reformers. What the CBS correspondent Richard Hottelet said about Murrow could be said of Hollenbeck: "He expected things to turn out badly, that the curve of history was down." In 1946 Hollenbeck's post-Christmas features tackled the malnourishment of one-quarter of the world's population and continuing racial discrimination in the United States.[48]

He turned what could have been a lighthearted essay on *New York Times*–sponsored fashion shows into a serious critique of the *Times*'s fashion coverage. The *Times*'s fashion editor Virginia Pope—helped by the paper's promotion, advertising, and circulation departments—had started "Fashions of the Times," fashion shows intended to assist area textile manufacturers and boost national apparel advertising in the *Times* (it would jump more than sevenfold between 1940 and 1950).[49]

Times fashion coverage offered, Hollenbeck said, "some of the more ecstatic adjectives which can be squeezed out of a Linotype machine." Hollenbeck also criticized such "Fashions of the Times" clothes as mink bathing suits and coats made from the hair of baby guanaco. He said the "shy little

South American animal" now had not only guanaco-devouring Indians and pumas as its enemies but also kill-for-baby-hair Fifth Avenue fashionistas.[50]

A year after the United States dropped atomic bombs on Hiroshima and Nagasaki, Hollenbeck repeatedly worried aloud about the atomic threat. He ended a radio feature on a New York court's decision that an Edmund Wilson novel was obscene by questioning the U.S.-developed atomic bomb, "which in its use, up to now, might qualify for the definition of obscenity." Hollenbeck's essay on Halloween focused on scientific black magic: the Nobel Prize–winning geneticist Hermann J. Muller's conclusion that "some Japanese exposed to the gamma rays of the atomic bomb may transmit hereditary ill effects to their generations for centuries."[51]

Hollenbeck's essay on the fourth anniversary of atomic energy's creation made a telling, troubling comparison. He called humankind's lighting of the first atomic fire by bombarding uranium 235 with neutrons the twentieth-century equivalent of Prometheus's endowing humans with fire. Hollenbeck then reminded listeners of the world's fate in Greek mythology during the time of Prometheus's son, Deucalion. Zeus, supreme ruler of gods and humans, destroyed Earth, leaving it "a dismal desert, a silent waste."[52]

Murrow admired Hollenbeck's ability as a reporter "with a fine eye for detail" and enjoyed working with him, whether the story was slightly silly or life-and-death serious. Murrow, a baseball fan, gave Hollenbeck his three-dollar ticket to a Dodgers-Giants season opener at Brooklyn's Ebbets Field. Hollenbeck, a baseball illiterate, had never attended a major league game.[53]

In a lighthearted program segment Murrow grilled Hollenbeck, who assured listeners that he had taken careful notes about the game on an empty peanut sack. At the segment's end Murrow asked Hollenbeck for his advice to the nation's youth after twenty years in the news business and one afternoon in a ballpark. Hollenbeck advised them to study baseball, not journalism, especially "how to steal home like Jackie Robinson, and I'd never worry about being out of a job."[54]

A more serious collaboration occurred after the murder in Greece of George W. Polk, CBS's Middle East correspondent, while he was pursuing an interview with a leader of Communist guerrillas. Hollenbeck and Murrow, the only CBS newscasters who had regularly kept in touch with Polk by cable, letter, and telephone, enlisted the help of other CBS journalists to produce four hard-nosed, half-hour broadcasts that investigated who was responsible for Polk's murder.

The final broadcast in April 1949 included Hollenbeck's report on investigations of the murder of Polk—who had been shot through the back of his head at close range—and a report by the CBS correspondent Winston Burdett on the Athens trial of Gregory Staktopoulos (and two Greek Communists in absentia) for Polk's murder. Though Staktopoulos was convicted of being an accessory after the fact and given a life sentence, Burdett concluded, "The whole truth about Polk's death has not yet been told." Murrow ended the broadcast by describing Polk in words that he also felt described Hollenbeck: "One of those reporters who believed that the pursuit of truth will set you free even if you never catch up with it."[55]

Murrow's admiration for Hollenbeck soon showed itself in the choice assignments that Murrow awarded him. When CBS introduced *News of America*, a fifteen-minute weekday program, Murrow selected Hollenbeck as the program's inaugural anchor. *Pathfinder* magazine called Hollenbeck "the first newscaster to put the spotlight on drama from small towns." Hollenbeck reported how a Laredo, Texas, political machine controlled the local daily and the area's AP reporter, preventing news of Laredo from reaching the outside. Gene De Poris, editor of Laredo's independent weekly, *South Texas Citizen*, said Hollenbeck reported on Laredo, in part, because he could not resist the mayor's name, Huey Cluck.[56]

On a later *News of America* Hollenbeck covered the tragedy of three-year-old Kathy Fiscus, who fell ninety-four feet into a fourteen-inch-wide abandoned well in San Marino, California. About twenty-five thousand people gathered to watch fifty rescuers try unsuccessfully for fifty-two hours to save the child's life. The rescue attempt made media history. Though only a few thousand Los Angeles–area homes had television sets, KTLA broadcast live continuously from the well site for 27.5 hours.

But Hollenbeck focused on two out-of-work rescuers, Homer Blickensdefer, a coal miner from Rosemead, and O. A. Kelly, a machinist from Temple City, who collapsed from exhaustion: "Friends are hoping that their heroism and disregard of their own safety will bring rewards in the form of jobs." Hollenbeck ended by noting that the abandoned well had finally been sealed, "too late for Kathy Fiscus."[57]

Beginning with "The Assassination of Abraham Lincoln," the first show in the *CBS Is There* series (later named *You Are There*, for television as well as radio), Hollenbeck regularly played an at-the-scene reporter on the weekly half-hour radio re-creation of important historical events. He also served as a writer on a broadcast about the fall of Troy in 1184 B.C. In "Joan of Arc Is Burned at the Stake," Hollenbeck's favorite *CBS Is There*, he narrated the final hours of Joan of Arc on May 30, 1431. Urged to live, she chose to die "rather than renounce her blessed saints and angels," he said.[58]

After auditioning several CBS newscasters, Murrow chose Hollenbeck to take charge of one of radio's boldest experiments ever, *CBS Views the Press.* In 1947 the newspaper was the mature adult of news media, television was no more than a toddler, and radio an insecure teenager. Newspapers, which had existed in the United States for more than 250 years, could be expected to roast a radio program of press criticism.

"You just didn't criticize newspapers," explained the CBS correspondent Edmund Scott. "They just happened. That was it."[59] Hollenbeck's prize-winning program was broadcasting's declaration of independence from newspapers—the first time a network dared trade roles with newspapers and become criticizer, not merely the criticized.

Only a decade earlier network radio had been a non-news medium beholden to major advertising agencies. The agencies produced the entertainment programs and passed along the advertising revenue that made the networks wealthy. In return, the networks allowed the agencies to control the program distribution and scheduling. To maximize profits, minimize controversy, and reduce the possibility of government regulation, the networks deemphasized news and current affairs commentary for years.

CBS Views the Press risked the wrath of CBS, as well as New York's newspapers. Press criticism inevitably required the expression of opinion. But radio executives had long been working to establish a set of first principles that virtually outlawed opinion. "We must never have an editorial page," William Paley, chairman of the board of CBS, had said. "We must never try to further either side of any debatable question."[60]

Radio's reluctance to provide opinion was reinforced by the code of the National Association of Broadcasters (NAB) and the doctrine of the Federal Communications Commission (FCC). The 1939 NAB code, intended to forestall stronger government regulation of the industry, said news and public affairs broadcasts should not include bias or editorial judgments. In addition, controversial views should not be presented, except in broadcasts airing the opinions of political candidates.

The FCC made its position clear in a 1940 decision involving WAAB, a Boston station owned by the Mayflower Broadcasting Corporation: the broadcaster should not be an advocate. Even when the FCC lifted its ban on editorializing as long as dissenting views were presented ("the fairness doctrine"), the networks fought the expression of opinion.

Of the three networks, CBS had the most formalized guidelines for news analysts. Edward Klauber, a vice president at CBS and former night city editor at the *New York Times*, drafted the network's policy. Paley said Klauber and he "agreed there would be no editorializing during news broadcasts, commentaries would be kept completely separate from the news itself, CBS news would be . . . objective."[61]

News analysts from outside and inside CBS disputed the network's position. NBC's John W. Vandercook said, "Each of us out of his experience, out of his personal knowledge and out of his constant study of all available opinion, out of all available so-called facts, seeks to tell you, his listeners, that truth as he sees it in his own way."[62]

Inside CBS, news analysts found that to question the network's policy was to risk reprisal. Hans von Kaltenborn, who had come to CBS as a $100-a-week news analyst in 1930, said: "No news analyst worth his salt could or would be completely neutral or objective. . . . Every exercise of his editorial judgment constitutes an expression of opinion."[63]

Kaltenborn felt uncomfortable with CBS's suggestion that he use such phrases as "it is said" or "there are those who believe," instead of openly expressing his opinion. In 1940, accompanied by not-so-silent sighs of relief at CBS, he moved to NBC.

Three years later Cecil Brown, a CBS correspondent, returned from a tour of thirteen cities and broadcast a piece in which he questioned Americans' enthusiasm for the war. Paul White, the head of CBS News, chided Brown for presenting his "defeatist" views "under the guise of news analysis." Brown's involuntary resignation followed. Publicly, White talked about how CBS would eliminate correspondents and analysts who expressed opinions. Privately, he said, "We have got rid of the last one."[64]

In this atmosphere the move at CBS in 1947 to broadcast criticism of newspapers and other media was an act of daring—an act supported, crucially, by Murrow. *CBS Views the Press* was the program in which Murrow "took the sharpest interest, and for which he had felt the greatest need," the CBS correspondent Alexander Kendrick said. Murrow had become interested in criticism of the media's performance while covering World War II from Europe. Murrow wanted *CBS Views the Press*, Wershba said, "to be careful about what we did" but to be critical.[65]

Murrow suggested to Paley that the press—which critiqued drama, film, books, and ballet, not to mention radio—deserved to be critiqued itself. Paley recalled, perhaps overstating his own role in the decision, that Murrow and he "both finally came to the conclusion that it [press criticism] would be very useful and serviceable."[66]

Murrow's choice of Hollenbeck to run *CBS Views the Press* was not surprising. Hollenbeck knew newspapers. He sounded under control, however emotional the topic. He had an authoritative, velvety voice, sufficiently deep that it could be "the voice of someone who weighed 190 pounds, not 130," quipped James Crayhon of the AP. And, in Wershba's words, "Don was one of the finest writers, one of the finest essayists, in the country. Ed was picking the best."[67]

Murrow saw something else in Hollenbeck as well, the determination of a journalist committed to pursuing the truth. *CBS Views the Press*, Murrow announced, would be not only "an objective examination" but also a "critical analysis" of the press.[68] That required someone willing to say what needed to be said—willing to critique honestly—regardless of CBS's policy about opinion and regardless of the reactions of powerful media companies.

But the more forthright Hollenbeck's evaluation of the press, the more return fire he would draw, and the more he would face personal as well as professional peril.

CHAPTER 7

The Invention of
CBS Views the Press

Long ago, when Murrow was active at CBS News, he did not see why broadcasters should not turn about and examine what newspapers do. The result was a radio series called CBS Views the Press. There has been nothing quite like it since.

—Edward Bliss Jr., *TV Guide*, July 15, 1978

Whatever personal and professional risks Don Hollenbeck may have anticipated from narrating and writing *CBS Views the Press*, he also understood the historic significance of the program. He knew that in 1947 criticism of newspapers by a radio program represented a revolutionary act.

CBS was asking Hollenbeck, one of its most experienced newscasters, backed by every member of the CBS news staff, to put radio on a par with newspapers and to raise the possibility of an important new role for radio nationwide. The *Washington Post* editorialized: "Newspapers all over the country need the prodding of this sort of inquiry from the outside, need to be jogged for sins of omission as well as for sins of commission."[1]

Hollenbeck and T. "Ted" Wells Church, news director of CBS Radio, selected two experienced journalists, the Brooklynites Joe Wershba and Edmund Scott, to report for the program.

Wershba, twenty-six years old, was striking—6 feet 1 inch tall, 180 pounds, blue eyes, blond-brown curly hair, and ruddy checks. He already was a veteran of almost a decade in journalism.

Beginning at age fifteen, he wrote about high school sports for the *Brooklyn Times Union* ("they always printed everything . . . and never paid me a nickel"), the *Brooklyn Eagle*, and the *New York World-Telegram*.[2]

Edmund Scott (left), Don Hollenbeck, and Joseph Wershba review a script for a
1947 broadcast of *CBS Views the Press.*

Courtesy Anne Hollenbeck.

In 1937 Wershba entered Brooklyn College. On Friday and Saturday
nights he worked on the *World-Telegram* schoolboy sports desk for $10 a
night. "That was a lot of money in those days," Wershba said. Meanwhile,
geology and other subjects were proving to be a problem. "I was an A student in history . . . English and French," he said. "And an F in everything
else. I was interested only in writing."[3]

After his sophomore year, at age eighteen, he and four other young New
York idealists drove 15,150 miles in ninety-two days to write a book, *The
"Argonauts,"* about "the America that could not be found in the textbooks."[4]
The five were associate members of the American Newspaper Guild (guild
chapters donated $122.95 to their trip) and made sure to attend a guild con-
vention in San Francisco. They also walked picket lines in Cleveland and
Chicago, experienced race prejudice in the South, met with capitalists and
Communists, visited West Coast migratory worker camps, and interviewed
John Steinbeck.

The author of *The Grapes of Wrath* advised them, "If you want to write,
you've got to *feel* more. Don't look, *feel.*"[5] When they ran out of money on

the road, Wershba's college friends contributed eight dollars in pennies and nickels to a "Bring Wershba Back Campaign."

Wershba returned to Brooklyn College but left after his junior year, spent two years in the army, and, in 1944, took a writing job at CBS Radio on the midnight-to-eight-a.m. shift.

Church, CBS Radio's news director, liked the way Wershba worked. Wershba was promoted to editor and began spending more time on special projects for Church. They became close personal friends. "He talked my wife, Shirley, into marrying me," Wershba joked. "And he taught us how to drink."[6]

The thirty-eight-year-old Scott had the looks of a reporter from a Hollywood movie—slender and slightly rumpled, five feet nine inches tall, square jawed, with dark, slicked-back, center-parted hair. He had gotten into newspaper work by accident. After graduation from Erasmus Hall High School in Brooklyn and City College of New York, he was hired as a clerk by M. J. Meehan, a Wall Street brokerage house. But he lost his job to the Depression.

He heard on the street that people were needed to help move to the offices of the *Evening Telegram* the news and photo files of the *World*, which the Pulitzer family had recently sold to Scripps-Howard. The *World-Telegram*, the merged paper created by Scripps-Howard in 1931, hired Scott as a library clerk and, after he had filed clippings for three years, advanced him to reporter. In 1940 he and other *World-Telegram* reporters were lured to *PM* by that newspaper's city editor, Elmer Roessner, a former *World-Telegram* editor.

At *PM* Scott was an imaginative legman. He disclosed the possibility of enemy sabotage on the SS *Normandie*, a French luxury liner seized by the U.S. Navy for conversion into a U.S. troop transport: "I went to the [union] local where the *Normandie* was docked, walked in and said, 'I want a job.' The guy was allegedly on the take. Anyway, he took my dough. The next morning I was hired. Worked there three or four days. Didn't do much. Just walked around and planted thick pencils."[7]

The story of the damage Scott could have done to the *Normandie* (renamed the USS *Lafayette*) if he had been a saboteur was held from publication by *PM*. Scott said, "They feared the story would demoralize the public or do something else. Held, that is, until the ship went up in flames."[8] During the ship's conversion to a troop transport, sparks from a welding torch ignited kapok-filled life vests. The flames spread. The ship capsized. Scott's coverage won journalism awards.

In 1947, with *PM* on the verge of being sold or dying, Scott wrote to Hollenbeck about a job. "Everybody had a high regard for Eddie's ability to ferret out stories," Wershba said. "He would get his teeth into something and he wouldn't let go. He was not the radio type that we had. . . . He was very methodical. Very methodical. I think that's why Don wanted him."[9]

Murrow publicly previewed *CBS Views the Press* on May 26, 1947. He said WCBS, the network's flagship station, would broadcast a fifteen-minute program that would critically examine the New York press: "We firmly believe that freedom of press and freedom of radio are inseparable and that mutual criticism will benefit both."[10]

The choice of a subject for the first broadcast of *CBS Views the Press* was extremely important. "In this business," Wershba said, "if your first broadcast is dynamite, they remember you. Then, if you're able to keep that going, then, oh, yeah, that's a great program." Awaiting the first broadcast, the *Washington Post* editorialized, "The criticism will be useful in direct ratio to its disregard for decorum." John T. McManus, a *PM* columnist, wrote, "'CBS Views the Press' figures to become far and away the most popular radio program on the air with newspaper men and women if it criticizes the medium without pulling its punches."[11]

Hollenbeck chose to tackle the treatment by the New York press of thirty-seven welfare families temporarily placed by the city in clean, inelegant, inexpensive hotels because of a shortage of suitable municipal housing. The story had made all the papers, even the comedian Jack Benny's stage routine at the Roxy. Benny was being treated so royally at the Sherry-Netherland Hotel, he quipped, that people assumed he was on relief.

Hollenbeck wrote a draft of what he planned to say about press coverage of the welfare families' placement in hotels. Murrow suggested he send the draft to John Crosby, the *Herald Tribune* columnist, for his comment. Crosby, a friend of both Murrow's and Hollenbeck's, recommended that Hollenbeck make the broadcast tougher.[12]

He did. In the pilot for *CBS Views the Press* he called the press coverage of the welfare families' temporary residence in hotels a "newspaper lynching party." The New York newspapers emphasized the hotels' radios and maids to give "the impression of some extremely fancy living by the relief clients," Hollenbeck said.[13] As a result, the city welfare department reversed itself and moved the relief clients out of the hotels.

"The lynching was a success—if you can call a lynching a success," Hollenbeck continued. The city hustled the families into lodging houses and condemned tenements. "All in all," Hollenbeck said, "it was about as sorry an exhibition as the press—or a section of it—is capable of putting on."[14]

Hollenbeck's first broadcast on May 31, 1947, also critiqued other aspects of the papers' coverage. The papers did not report the statements by private welfare agencies that came to the defense of the welfare department. The papers remained silent about the thirty-seven relief families removed to substandard or condemned housing and the vast majority of the 233,000 people on welfare, each of whom was surviving on an average of $1.31 a day. The *Sun* and the *Journal-American* laced their reporting with Red-baiting. The two papers said Communists played important roles in the welfare department.

The first broadcast also examined coverage of a dispute between the Transport Workers Union and the city's Board of Transportation that caused a slowdown of service on one of the city's subway lines. In its first edition the *Daily News* printed a statement allegedly by William J. Daly, secretary of the Board of Transportation: If the board could prove an intentional slowdown, eight hundred conductors and other subway employees might be fired under a state law that banned strikes by public employees. After he read the first edition, Daly denied he had made the statement and demanded the story and his picture be withdrawn.

In later editions the *Daily News* removed Daly's name and picture but continued to print the statement, attributing it to an "unidentified board official."[15] The *Times* and *Mirror* quoted the same unidentified official as denying *any* firings were being considered, almost exactly the opposite of what the unidentified official was quoted as saying in the *Daily News*.

PM and the *Daily Worker*, the Communist Party paper, also published the statement attributed to Daly by the *Daily News*. Hollenbeck questioned how the two papers obtained the story: "*PM* said it came from the Associated Press, which disclaims all knowledge of it, so the suspicion must remain that *PM* lifted its story from the early edition of the *News*, and since its [*PM*'s] final edition goes to press much earlier, had no chance to change it. We've called the *Daily Worker* four times about their piece, but so far, they haven't told us where it came from."[16]

Hollenbeck ended his first broadcast with five brief notes—two laurels and three darts. After reporting that the serialization of Winston Churchill's memoirs by *Life* and the *New York Times* would net Churchill more than $1 million, Hollenbeck said some of journalism's less prominent toilers "turn in some fine work for a lot less money."[17] He praised the reports by the *Herald Tribune*'s Robert S. Byrd about a lynching trial in Greenville, South

Carolina, and by *PM*'s Billy Rose—better known as a lyricist, Broadway producer, and nightclub owner—about a glamorous war correspondent who was trying to make the transition to peacetime writing.

Two notes foreshadowed concerns about injustice and inaccuracy that would be central to Hollenbeck's *CBS Views the Press*. He frowned upon a column by the vitriolic, anti-Semitic Westbrook Pegler in Hearst's *Journal-American* that made fun of the labor leaders Sidney Hillman and David Dubinsky. Pegler had described them as "dialect unioneers."[18]

Hollenbeck began his last note by declaring the importance to journalism of accuracy: "The conscientious reporter's main concern is that names are correct and facts straight." He reported a sequel to a story about the CBS radio sportscaster Clem McCarthy. McCarthy had announced the wrong horse as the winner of the Preakness. Jack Gould, in his *Times* radio column, said the error would not hurt McCarthy's career. But Gould said incorrectly that the error had occurred at the Kentucky Derby, not the Preakness. Hollenbeck concluded, "Clem and Mr. Gould would now appear to have finished in a dead heat, so far as slips of tongue and typewriter are concerned."[19]

Reaction to Hollenbeck's program ranged from raves to a Red-baiting rebuke. John P. Lewis, editor of *PM*, praised the press's new police officer: "*PM* itself came in for a mild bit of dusting off . . . when Hollenbeck caught us passing on to our readers a bit of phony information which had originated with the *Daily News*. It's a healthy thing and *PM* welcomes it, even in the knowledge that bits of our own hide may be tacked up on the radio tower along with the others."[20]

Crosby, the *Herald Tribune* columnist, was, understandably perhaps, no less enthusiastic about a program he had read in an earlier form: "It took courage to put it on the air and the first program showed evidence of both zeal and discretion." *Variety*'s review—crowned by the headline "Man-Bites-Dog Act Slays N. Y. Press: Dailies' Reaction Big $64 Question"—also gave five stars to *CBS Views the Press*. The review said Hollenbeck's "first stanza went off like a howitzer with Hollenbeck lobbing the critical shells squarely at the editorial mastheads of the country's most powerful dailies."[21]

Walter Winchell, the *Mirror*'s columnist, and Saul Carson, writing in the *New Republic*, called on CBS to go national in reach and content with Hollenbeck's program. Another commentator suggested that radio stations nationwide follow Hollenbeck's lead and tackle the press in their markets. But *Broadcasting*, the trade magazine, warned that " 'editorializing' about the press" could lead to editorializing about state and local events, "which should be done only by able and experienced heads."[22]

Frontpage, the New York Newspaper Guild's monthly, acclaimed his program as "a refreshing departure from the usual squeamishness that characterizes many radio programs of opinion." *Billboard's* Jerry Franken cheered Hollenbeck's "well-rounded job," concluding, "Let's hope that other broadcasters will get their feet wet in the same water." *Editor and Publisher*, the newspaper trade magazine, praised Hollenbeck's flaying of the papers for their handling of the hotel relief story and reprinted the program's text.[23]

The liberal *New York Post* also applauded the program. Three conservative dailies—the *Journal-American*, *Daily News*, and *Sun*—locked their lips. But Nick Kenny, radio columnist for Hearst's *Mirror*, may have reflected the silent fuming inside Hearst's *Journal-American* when he wrote a "Dear Bud" letter to the *Journal-American's* Pegler, a subject of Hollenbeck's criticism. Kenny mailed transcripts of Hollenbeck's first *CBS Views the Press* broadcasts to Pegler as "grist for your mill." Kenny called Hollenbeck "one of the biggest reds in radio (or should I say REDio?). He hates everything American and plugs all Commie*rot*." In a postscript Kenny wrote, "It's getting so people see Red when they CBS."[24]

Editors of the two other silent papers made their views known in *Editor and Publisher*. Keats Speed, executive editor of the *Sun*, said, "Several newspapers follow the Communist line, so why shouldn't a radio station?" Richard Clarke, executive editor of the *Daily News*, said, "CBS has to strain pretty hard in its critical review of New York papers. The papers could do a better job on radio any week."[25]

Harriet Van Horne, the radio and television critic for Scripps-Howard's *New York World-Telegram*, huffed that "the program rings with a smug righteousness that bothers me. I'd like to see what sort of paper the CBS news staff would put out. It might raise a point as to who should cast the first stone." A testy William S. Paley, chairman of CBS, memoed Murrow about Van Horne's comment: "This sounds a little bit like 'If you don't like it here why don't you go back where you came from.' I'm sure that according to Miss Van Horne a music critic would have to be a great composer or conductor . . . and certainly a radio critic one who could run a radio station—or why not a national network."[26]

A few out-of-town papers echoed a maxim of Arthur Hays Sulzberger of the *New York Times*: "I don't believe it's the business of papers to attack each other." Newspapers had no trouble in broadening Sulzberger's prohibition to include a radio program of press criticism. One paper's editorial included a misquotation of the sixth chapter of St. Luke, complete with a

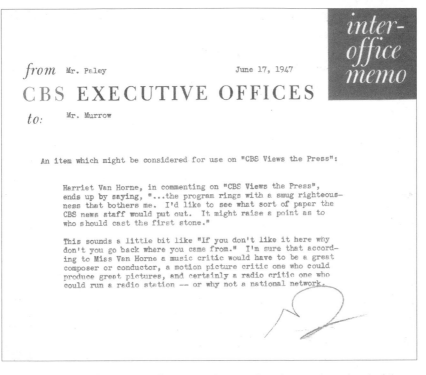

from Mr. Paley   June 17, 1947

CBS EXECUTIVE OFFICES

to: Mr. Murrow

An item which might be considered for use on "CBS Views the Press":

Harriet Van Horne, in commenting on "CBS Views the Press", ends up by saying, "...the program rings with a smug righteousness that bothers me. I'd like to see what sort of paper the CBS news staff would put out. It might raise a point as to who should cast the first stone."

This sounds a little bit like "If you don't like it here why don't you go back where you came from." I'm sure that according to Miss Van Horne a music critic would have to be a great composer or conductor, a motion picture critic one who could produce great pictures, and certainly a radio critic one who could run a radio station -- or why not a national network.

inter-office memo

Memo from CBS chairman Williams S. Paley to Edward R. Murrow, head of the network's news operation, shortly after *CBS Views the Press* first aired.

charming typographical error: "Thou hypocrite, cast out first the bean [*sic*] out of thine own eyes."[27]

Jack Gould, writing in the *Times*, occupied the middle ground. He said the first broadcast indicated that CBS "does not intend to pussyfoot in its analysis and that it is serious about its newfound role of referee of the news columns." But Gould described Hollenbeck's review of the relief story as not evenhanded enough and his coverage of the transit dispute as "a somewhat superficial analysis of 'the unidentified spokesman' who crops up in news stories."[28]

Officials commonly give out news but refuse to allow use of their names, Gould noted, sounding a bit defensive. "Were CBS to have its own reporters covering the news of New York, it might be illuminating to see how they would cope with the situation, particularly when the news so provided is of obvious and urgent importance." Gould closed by acknowledging that CBS had caught him misnaming the race in which Clem McCarthy identified the wrong horse as the winner: "Touché, CBS!"[29]

The public, for the most part, responded enthusiastically to the program. Thirty people telephoned CBS immediately after the first broadcast to praise *CBS Views the Press*. Two said Hollenbeck seemed to be "pushing the *Post* and *PM* in preference to the other papers." CBS received 350 fan letters about the program the first week, which was surprising, said *PM*'s John T. McManus, because "most of New York was away for the Memorial Day weekend."[30]

CBS had not expected Hollenbeck's program to compete with *Arthur Godfrey and His Talent Scouts* or *Lux Radio Theatre* in the ratings race. The typical *CBS Views the Press* broadcast—Hollenbeck talking for fifteen minutes straight—stood for solid, sober reporting.

Seymour Peck, who had served as *PM*'s radio editor, said: "The program was intended to be honorable—to make the network look good in the eyes of those who were concerned with opinion." Saturday at 6:15 p.m. was not "the most convenient hour in the world," Paley said, but "almost everybody connected with a newspaper would tune in to Hollenbeck." Paley said CBS was surprised by "the degree of interest, the seriousness of it—this was a must for newspaper people—and the fact that we got some very strong reactions."[31]

Murrow announced that the program would continue indefinitely: "I think we'll get a mass audience for this one." Hollenbeck promised to turn a detached eye on wire services, advertising, newsmagazines, newspaper columnists, comics, editorial pages, slanted news, and bad writing—everything that had anything to do with the New York press.[32] Hollenbeck, Scott, and Wershba developed a time-consuming technique for locating the best stories each week. On Monday and Tuesday they hunted for topics. They read all editions of ten New York daily papers, from the *Daily News* to the *Wall Street Journal*. They solicited other CBS correspondents for ideas. They encouraged letters and telephone tips from reporters and editors.

But, Wershba said, *CBS Views the Press* refused to repeat trade gossip or inside memos or conversations—such as one reporter's saying, "That son-of-a-bitch editor told me, 'If you don't fake this story I'm going to have your ass.'" The program was going to criticize what was unquestionably fair game—material as published, material to which the listeners of *CBS Views the Press* could have already been exposed. The kind of lead that Hollenbeck, Scott, and Wershba wanted from reporters and editors, recalled Wershba, was, "'Take a look at page 74 in the first edition, then see what happened in the second edition, and in the third. You see three different stories.'"[33]

The *CBS Views the Press* team also wanted leads from reporters and editors about contradictory reports in New York papers. Richard Strouse of the *New York Times* wrote to Hollenbeck about reports that the nationalized mines in England were out of the red: Fred Kuh, in the *Star* [*PM*'s successor], "carried a fine quote ... that the British mines were in such bad shape due to private ownership, they *had* to be nationalized. On the same day, the *Sun* has a by-lined piece by Wendy MacGowan screaming about how much dough the nationalized mines have lost, and suggesting that the Labor Gov't is going slow on nationalization for that reason!!!"[34]

Hollenbeck also received from Strouse a clipping of a feature in the *Star* about a police officer who supposedly had found John Barrymore's runaway son, John Drew Barrymore, because his profile was a carbon copy of his father's. Actually, wrote Strouse, "The lad's stepfather recognized the boy, as well he might, and pointed him out to the cop. Incidentally, . . . the kid looks almost exactly as much like his father as Wershba looks like that midget who sat on J. P. Morgan's lap."[35]

Every Wednesday Hollenbeck, Wershba, and Scott sifted through the prospects for Saturday's broadcast. They picked a half-dozen topics as finalists. Then, while Hollenbeck began clipping and pulling together newspaper articles to compare on the air, Wershba and Scott interviewed the reporters and editors responsible for those articles. "We'd go after both sides," Scott said. "We'd talk to anybody we could."[36]

Wershba and Scott each wrote up the material collected from their interviews to create drafts that were five to fifteen minutes long. Hollenbeck spent Thursdays editing their drafts, adding his own material, and giving the text life. "Don would write the thing for voicing—to fit his own style," Scott said.[37]

Hollenbeck knew the rules of radio writing. He understated, rather than jeweled, his writing. He subscribed to Robert Frost's philosophy: "Anything more than the truth would have seemed too weak."[38] Hollenbeck also enjoyed occasionally breaking the rules. He knew sentences should be short and simple—subject, then predicate.

But sometimes "he hated to bring a sentence or paragraph to an end," Wershba said.[39] Hollenbeck also loved to play with language. He searched for precisely the right word to convey the intended meaning, feeling, and sound. So he occasionally used French phrases and five-dollar words like *casuistry*, flouting radio's rule against foreign and dictionary words.

Once Hollenbeck had written a broadcast, he took it back to his staff. "We debated the matter, content, and style of the pieces," said George

Herman, then twenty-seven, a bright, bespectacled, pipe-smoking graduate of Dartmouth College and Columbia's Graduate School of Journalism who had joined CBS as a radio news writer in 1944 and occasionally worked on the program. Herman had grown up on East Seventy-third Street and may have known more about New York and its press than Hollenbeck. But, Herman said, "Don always was the chief, and what he said went on the air in the end."[40]

Hollenbeck, assisted by Wershba, kept polishing the script right up to airtime on Saturday evening or, often, right up to an earlier taping that gave them, Hollenbeck said, "somewhat more of a weekend, and a permanent record of the broadcasts." The final script was not reviewed by anyone. That practice reflected Hollenbeck's personality. "His relationship with CBS was a trifle prickly," Herman said. "He was a touchy, independent man, unpredictable, and therefore worrisome to the company. His fierce independence made the show what it was."[41]

"At the outset we got a pretty cool reception at newspaper offices when we sought information," Hollenbeck wrote. There was, he added, a bit of the "silent treatment—the don't-look-and-maybe-they'll-go-away technique. That Gibraltar-like blankness and deafness have served before against adverse comment."[42]

Two factors helped end the silent treatment. First, listeners admired *CBS Views the Press*. Reporters, editors, and publishers felt it necessary to treat the program with some degree of respect.

Second, Hollenbeck appeared to be striving for fairness in his criticism. "We loved newspapers," Wershba said. "It was our lives. If we went after a paper, we didn't want to hurt the paper. We just wanted to get out the sinner." Hollenbeck seemed much more interested in pursuing the truth than a political agenda. The CBS newscaster Ned Calmer called Hollenbeck, who was registered in New York as a Democrat, a politically inactive "[Franklin Delano] Roosevelt liberal." The CBS producer Fred Friendly labeled Hollenbeck an "unreconstructed progressive from Nebraska in the Senator [George] Norris tradition [who] always went his own way; anyone who tried to get him to join anything took his life in his hands."[43]

Hollenbeck critiqued the liberal *PM*, his former employer, about as enthusiastically as he critiqued conservative papers. *PM* published a major portion of the *CBS Views the Press* transcript as a Monday feature. In February 1948 Hollenbeck caught *PM* deleting from its published version comments he had broadcast that were critical of *PM*—"a discussion of *PM*'s problem with an advertiser was completely ignored." Hollenbeck recommended that *PM* publish his broadcasts "more nearly as read" or not at all.[44]

In March 1948 *PM* appeared near death. To avoid the appearance of a conflict of interest, Hollenbeck, the *PM* alumnus, had Richard C. Hottelet, a CBS correspondent, deliver the newspaper's obituary. Hottelet began by acknowledging that the obit might be premature. Then he candidly assessed *PM*'s idealistic but often "ineffectual and muddled" brand of journalism, including its naïveté about Soviet and Communist policy. Six weeks later, when *PM* continued publication under new ownership and a new name, the *Star*, Hollenbeck asked with equal candor whether the paper might evolve "from a journal of comment to something it has never really been—actually a newspaper."[45]

Hollenbeck also was unusually evenhanded in his treatment of publishers, bêtes noires of press critics. The Workers Fellowship of the Society of Ethical Culture invited him to speak on distortion of the news. The press critics A. J. Liebling and George Seldes were describing publishers as moneymaniacal reactionaries. The Workers Fellowship heard a different description from Hollenbeck.

"Don got up and made his position very clear, that he didn't think that publishers are wicked people," Wershba recalled. "Everybody's trying to do a job. All he wants is that they do an honest job. Lots of times they represent the moneyed interest, but they're not villainous people or wicked. He didn't play to the audience." About halfway through Hollenbeck's speech, members of the Workers Fellowship began to boo. Hollenbeck walked out.[46]

"We've tried to do an honest job," Hollenbeck wrote in 1948, only months after *CBS Views the Press* began, "and it has paid off. Even those high-level practitioners of journalism who find our guts distasteful will answer our questions and help us clear up confusing points. As for the working press below the level of the brass, the response has been enthusiastic."[47]

For the December 27, 1947, program Hollenbeck offered humorous holiday greetings to a dozen journalists who had been targets of the program that year, including Westbrook Pegler, "whose Christmas card has not yet arrived." Cabell Greet, the Barnard College professor of English who served as CBS's consultant on pronunciation, complimented Hollenbeck: "It was the wittiest broadcast I have heard in lo these many years." His postscript, though, warned Hollenbeck, "But perhaps on other programs wit would be taken as editorializing."[48]

Murrow, however, continued to support *CBS Views the Press*. In July 1947, when he resigned as vice president and director of public affairs, he extracted a promise from CBS president Frank Stanton that he would back *CBS Views the Press*. Murrow also wrote a column for the *Herald Tribune* in which he said that listeners' mail about *CBS Views the Press* was running almost 100 to 1 in favor. To those who said, "It can't last," Murrow insisted, "The program will remain on the air." So Hollenbeck, Scott, and Wershba felt free to report on any aspect of the press the way they wanted to report on it. "The backing Don was getting from upstairs, from Murrow," Scott said, "only added to his enthusiasm."[49]

Furthermore, *CBS Views the Press* had no sponsor. That was by design. The absence of a sponsor meant—at least during Murrow's reign as head of CBS's news operation—one less potential source of pressure. Wershba recalled, "Ted Church, who was my boss, might come across and growl at me, saying, 'Boy, you guys.' But we were not answerable to Ted. We were answerable to no one."[50]

"We were neither muckrakers nor crusaders," Hollenbeck wrote of *CBS Views the Press*, labeling it a program of reporting on good and bad journalism. He devoted the 1948 and 1949 Christmas programs to good journalism. "With indulgent eye" he described what newspaper editors and wire service managers listed as their newsrooms' best work of the year.[51]

Occasionally, *CBS Views the Press* explained how an extraordinary reporter uncovered a great story—for instance, how William Laurence of the *Times* discovered an African plant that yielded an inexpensive cortisone base to help those suffering from arthritis and other chronic ills.[52]

A major focus of Hollenbeck's two and a half years with the program was bad reporting, especially press abuse of the vulnerable and defenseless. Hollenbeck came back again and again to the reporting of the hotel relief story—the subject of his first broadcast.

He showed how national newsmagazines, which supposedly had more time to sort facts, did no better than New York dailies in placing the story in perspective: *Newsweek*'s article "was headlined 'luxury on the dole,' the phrases 'luxurious life,' 'luxury relief' and 'luxury on the dole' occurred in the story, and as a clincher, a photograph was printed alongside. It showed two fat youngsters stuffing themselves with food over a cutline that read, 'Relief families in nine-dollars-a-day hotel suites stir New York.' "[53]

Six months later Hollenbeck documented how newspapers used *mink*, *divorcee*, and other highly charged words to sensationalize relief hearings, suggest that welfare money was going to the rich, and provoke envy and anger. In fact, the mink-attired divorcee in question was flat broke and clearly entitled to relief. Her coat was bedraggled, an old rag that many women would reject.

Hollenbeck said that "by going gunning for mink, the newspapers had given the impression that to live on relief was to indulge in a sort of Lucullan life at the expense of the taxpayers." Equally important, the newspapers' coverage encouraged the public to ignore the larger picture—"the tens of thousands of genuinely needy children, cripples and infirm aged, who are being cheated by inadequate relief budgets."[54]

In a series of broadcasts over fifteen months Hollenbeck carefully tracked the reappearance of inaccurate reports about the lady in mink: first, to the editorial pages of the *Asbury Park (N.J.) Evening Press* and *Chicago Daily News*, then to the *Sunday Standard* of Bombay, India, and *Sunday Telegraph* of Sydney, Australia. Finally, he reported on the story's appearance in *Monica's Monthly*, a magazine published in British Guinea [today the Cooperative Republic of Guyana] that was distributed worldwide to mail-order customers. All of which reminded Hollenbeck of an item in Pudd'n'head Wilson's calendar: "One of the striking differences between a cat and a lie is that a cat has only nine lives."[55]

In all, Hollenbeck devoted parts of eleven broadcasts to the relief stories. He contrasted the way most New York papers flocked to the woman-in-mink story with how they ignored a *New York Post* exposé about the delays in getting help to thousands of poor people who needed housing. He reported that, after the woman-in-mink story, the women and children thrown out of hotels were deposited in flophouses for "drunks, wrecks, the lost-of-the-world." He noted the newspapers' almost total silence about welfare department cuts in monthly relief payments—cuts that affected more than 300,000 people—at a time when private welfare agencies saw the need to boost their stipends to families.[56]

His concern with press treatment of the vulnerable and defenseless also showed in his examination of two blind spots in newspapers' coverage—how they reported on business and race. He critiqued coverage of a city commissioner's charge in 1948 that New York milk companies were price fixing and of a 1949 civil antitrust suit against the Great Atlantic and Pacific Tea Company (A&P) for conspiracy to monopolize the food industry in restraint of trade. "Haphazard and inexpert" business reporting, he suggested, was only part of the problem.[57]

Another part was see-no-evil reporting. When the milk companies immediately denied the charge of price fixing (although milk prices were at record highs), "no attempt was made by any of the newspapers to pursue the story," Hollenbeck said. The milk companies' profits went unexamined. To convey the profits of companies accurately a newspaper needed to report their net worth and their profits on investments, not just on sales. The effect of shoddy, skimpy business reporting, Hollenbeck suggested, was to " 'blank out any criticism of our economic system and the way it works.' "[58]

Hollenbeck's concern about press coverage of the A&P antitrust suit focused on the one-sidedness of the coverage. The food giant A&P spent an estimated $5 million in full-page newspaper ads, the first ad asking, "Do you want your A&P put out of business?" A Justice Department response, sent by the AP from Washington, could be found "in none of the New York papers," Hollenbeck reported. The *Sun* pulled a column by David Law-rence that gave the Justice Department's side. "Both sides ought to get a fair shake," Hollenbeck said.[59]

When the National Federation of Independent Business tried to test-run anti–A&P ads in four Washington, D.C., newspapers, three of them refused to publish the ads. Only Scripps-Howard's tabloid *Daily News* accepted the ads. An anonymous *Daily News* ad executive said, "The other three get [advertising] copy from A&P every week. We don't get any. I have no doubt whatever that if we carried A&P ads regularly, we would also have refused the reply." Hollenbeck said that, despite full AP and UP stories about the Washington brouhaha, only two New York newspapers—the *Post* and the *Herald Tribune*—published a story.[60]

Hollenbeck devoted two broadcasts to another disturbing example of see-no-evil business journalism—the "erratic, incomplete and sloppy" reporting about the war crimes trial of I. G. Farbenindustrie.[61] The corpo-rate chemical giant first bankrolled Hitler and the Nazis, then provided the trained technocrats and weapons for Germany to fight World War II. The *Herald Tribune* and the *Times*, the New York papers most widely known for their international coverage, editorialized about throwing more light on Farben's relationship with U.S. companies.

Neither paper, however, identified the fifty-three U.S. firms linked to Farben. Only the *World-Telegram* and the *Sun* (where the story took sixteen column inches) did. But the *Herald Tribune* and *Times* each devoted about forty column inches the same day to the opening of a branch of Macy's, a major advertiser, Hollenbeck noted. He then read a self-congratulatory *Times* ad about providing readers with the facts they needed to form intelli-gent opinions. "Judging from what has been printed about the Farben trial," Hollenbeck concluded, "no reader could be expected to form any opinion except perhaps to decide that the thing couldn't be very important."[62]

In a half-dozen other programs Hollenbeck concentrated on another press failing: discriminatory coverage. He was not ahead of his time about all forms of discrimination. He either failed to notice or chose to ignore newsroom discrimination against women, ethnic minorities, gays and lesbians, and religious minorities. His personal correspondence contains examples, though infrequent, of the era's sexism, homophobia, and anti-Semitism.

But on the air he bristled at the condescension of New York writers, self-anointed city sophisticates, toward outsiders. He critiqued the stereotypical coverage of Elwin "Preacher" Roe, the Brooklyn Dodgers pitcher from Ash Flat, Arkansas, who shut out the Yankees in the 1949 World Series. Sports reporters wrote of catfish, corncobs, and cotton patches. Instead of writers' "fun and games," Hollenbeck preferred Stanley Woodward's straightforward description of Roe in the *Compass,* successor to *PM* and the *Star,* as "the slim Brooklyn left-hander."[63]

Hollenbeck focused especially on racial discrimination. He was greatly influenced by Margaret "Peg" Halsey, a next-door neighbor and close friend, who wrote *Color Blind: A White Woman Looks at the Negro,* based on her wartime work at the interracial Stage Door Canteen just off Times Square. Published in 1946, the book examined two prime causes of racism—the sexual bogeyman and the search for low-cost labor—and offered a commonsense solution. Everyone should fight discrimination in his or her own way, Halsey wrote: "The main thing is to select something that is in line with your own personality and something that falls within the framework of your life."[64]

In line with Halsey's advice Hollenbeck resigned from his racially discriminatory university fraternity, Phi Kappa Psi. He also squelched racist comments. His style was not to attack the subject of his anger directly. "He would look blank or incredulous and make a remark to somebody else," Milton Stern said. One day Hollenbeck was introduced to Stewart Strand, a CBS director who had just moved to New York from Washington, D.C. Strand told Hollenbeck he was thinking of living on Long Island. But he had one reservation: "There are too many niggers there." Hollenbeck turned to Ted Marvel, another CBS director who had been talking with them, and said with scorn, "Who is this Stew Strand?"[65]

On *CBS Views the Press* Hollenbeck repeatedly criticized discriminatory journalism. His third broadcast began powerfully: "Jim Crow is a journalist, as we learn from reading the daily press. Jim Crow is a journalist, not only in the section of the country where the law gives him full sanction, but right here in New York City, where it does not. Jim Crow has one drinking fountain for whites, another for Negroes; the front of the bus for whites, the rear for Negroes. It also has one code of ethics for writing about white people, and another for Negro people."[66]

About ten years earlier the NAACP had recommended a reporting policy to newspapers: color or race should not be mentioned in describing a person involved in a crime unless it is an essential element in the story. Only the *New York Post* had adopted the policy.

Hollenbeck showed that, in the decade since the NAACP's recommendation, reporting about race had not improved greatly. While three New York papers avoided mentioning race in a story about a Brooklyn minister's rescue of his wife from a black attacker, six did not. "The opening paragraph of the *Daily News* story, in heavy type, identified the accused man as a Negro—not by a name, which he has as we all have, but simply by his color."[67]

Hollenbeck cited the equally deplorable practices of the AP in the South. Black victims of an Arkansas tornado were not identified by name but only by color. Godwin Bush, a black man who escaped a North Carolina lynch mob, was repeatedly described as "almost illiterate." Hollenbeck said, "The fact of Godwin Bush's literacy was no more pertinent to the story than would have been the fact of his left-handedness, if he had been left-handed. As used, it was simply a slur."[68]

Hollenbeck asked at the beginning of another program, "When is an ape man not an ape man? One answer, perhaps, is: when he appears in New York newspaper headlines."[69] A black man who had committed a murder in New York was referred to in headlines as an early form of man, *Pithe-canthropus erectus*, or "ape man." The description had nothing to do with the criminal's actual appearance, only with his skin color.

Hollenbeck balanced his criticism of discriminatory reporting about race with applause for exemplary reporting. He devoted most of a 1948 program to "In the Land of Jim Crow," a twenty-one-part series by Ray Sprigle of the *Pittsburgh Post-Gazette* that had been syndicated in the *New York Herald Tribune* and fourteen other U.S. newspapers. Sprigle, a white, sixty-one-year-old reporter with forty-three years in journalism, had shaved his head and mustache, drawn up a fresh will, tanned his skin for three weeks in the Florida sun, and then traveled four thousand miles through the Deep South as James R. Crawford, a black man.

Hollenbeck portrayed Sprigle as "a sort of reportorial ideal." Winner of a Pulitzer Prize in 1938 for revealing the Ku Klux Klan membership of Supreme Court Justice Hugo Black, Sprigle would do almost anything to get a significant story. By disguising himself as a butcher, he uncovered a black market in meat that prompted a grand jury investigation. To report other important stories he posed as a coal miner, a patient in a hospital for psychopaths, and an illegal gambler.[70]

In praising Sprigle and suggesting he deserved a second Pulitzer Prize for "In the Land of Jim Crow," Hollenbeck also questioned why the series could not have been written by a black journalist who "probably would have collected many times the material the *Post-Gazette* reporter did." Hollenbeck addressed the issue of discrimination against black journalists more directly in a 1949 *CBS Views the Press*. The report told about a prize-winning series by the *New York Post*'s Ted Poston, forty-three, who was said to be the only black reporter working at a New York metropolitan daily.[71]

Born in the South, Poston had asked to cover the Tavares, Florida, trial of three black youths accused of raping a seventeen-year old white housewife. (A fourth black suspect, Poston later reported, had been shot to death in the woods before the trial by a mob of "deputies.") *Post* editors, fearing for Poston's life, thrice rejected his request to cover the trial, then reluctantly granted him the assignment. During the trial Tavares whites learned that Poston, a *Post* reporter since 1937, worked for a predominantly white newspaper. Poston overheard one man snarl: "He ain't working for one of them nigger papers. He's sending lies to one of them Communist sheets up North."[72] Whites' harassment of Poston began. They jostled him, knocked loose his glasses, and stomped them.

The judge warned Poston to leave the county as soon as the all-white jury offered its verdict—death for two of the accused men, life imprisonment for the third. Two black NAACP lawyers, a black *Chicago Defender* reporter, and Poston fled town at 85 to 90 mph, pursued by three cars filled with bloodthirsty whites. Poston's coverage resulted in a federal investigation of the trial. His stories also helped raise more than $20,000 to finance an appeal by two of the accused to the U.S. Supreme Court, which reversed their convictions on the ground of race discrimination in jury selection.[73]

In his criticism of Jim Crow journalism and praise for the reporting by Ray Sprigle and Ted Poston, Hollenbeck made clear that he judged the press responsible to all the people. He agreed with the call by the columnist Bob Considine for "What this means to you" articles to explain to the public war, taxes, the U.N., Congress, and other complex subjects. Hollenbeck said that newspapers needed to bring "the language of the gods down to the jargon of the average working stiff."[74]

When a strike left few New York buses running, he examined the coverage through the eyes of a mythical Sam Swindlefoot, who lived in the Bronx and rode the Bronx–Van Cortlandt bus and a subway to get to work.[75] Swindlefoot needed what the press was not providing—a complete list of bus routes being struck.

Harry Truman's election to the presidency in 1948 caught many dailies by surprise. Hollenbeck questioned whether reporters and analysts still talked with the people—"the grass roots and the lower east side." The press, he worried, "had delegated the journalists' job to the pollsters" and "seemed to have lost all contact with the people for whom [a newspaper] is published."[76]

Hollenbeck's tough criticism of the press made fans out of a wide variety of media. *Vogue*'s "People Are Talking About . . ." section praised his "pleasant-voiced but hard-boiled criticism of newspapers." A *Writer's Digest* column cheered the candor of his program: "Its policy seems to be 'CBS "Phews!" the Press.'" *Editor and Publisher* commended the "much-honored radio program" for winning five of the year's top national radio awards, "though it is still strictly a local show."[77]

One of the awards, a prestigious George Foster Peabody, cited the program's "hard-hitting, frequently witty and always stimulating criticism of the New York press." But another Peabody winner for 1947, the prescient ABC commentator Elmer Davis, forecast trouble. He told Hollenbeck that he would be greatly surprised if CBS "is not put under pressure . . . to stop the show."[78] Indeed, Hollenbeck's prominent role in the invention and production of *CBS Views the Press* made him the target for years of conservative critics who sought to have him fired by the network.

CHAPTER 8

■■■■

Jack O'Brian:
Buffalo Dock-Walloper to
Broadway Drama Critic

Don Hollenbeck's toughest critic was Jack O'Brian, radio and television col-
umnist for Hearst's Journal-American *and a middleweight boxer in build*
and brawny writing style. O'Brian's pro–Joe McCarthy mauling of Hollenbeck
and other broadcasters skeptical of the Wisconsin senator began in 1950, the
year McCarthy established himself as the voice of anti-Communism and after
Hollenbeck left CBS Views the Press. *O'Brian's contempt for Hollenbeck and*
love for McCarthy can be explained, in part, by the columnist's conservative,
anti-intellectual, working-class roots.

He was born John Dennis Patrick O'Brian on August 16, 1914, in the First
Ward of South Buffalo, New York, to an alcoholic railroad conductor and a
mother who would die while he was a teenager.[1] *O'Brian lived in a weathered,*
wood-frame two-family at 198 O'Connell Avenue, less than three blocks from
Our Lady of Perpetual Help, the gothic sandstone Catholic church that still
serves as the First Ward's soul.

Settled by Irish immigrants in the 1840s and 1850s, the neighborhood
remains relatively unchanged—poor, pugnacious, and walk-to-work. Tower-
ing concrete grain elevators on the nearby Buffalo River, and factories, freight
yards, pubs, and one- and two-story clapboard houses symbolize the hard-
working, hardscrabble Irish immigrant life. Donald J. Lutz, pastor of Our
Lady of Perpetual Help, describes the parish today as German, Polish, and
Puerto Rican but still "basically Irish."[2] *His rectory's flagpole flies an Ameri-*
can flag and a faded Irish flag.

O'Brian attended "Pets," the local nickname for the Our Lady of Perpetual
Help school. In June 1927, at age twelve, O'Brian earned acceptable grades.[3]

This 1953 photo of Jack O'Brian accompanied his radio-television column in the New York Journal-American.

But only a year later—after graduation from grammar school—he left the classroom forever.

If Hollenbeck saw education as crucial, O'Brian necessarily viewed it as less essential. Following his mother's death and his father's "long alcoholic decline," he became, he told an interviewer, a homeless street kid who frequented South Buffalo saloons (both his grandfathers had been saloon keepers) and worked as a $10.91-a-week roller-skating messenger boy for the Larkin Soap Company. O'Brian joked, "I was too busy getting an education to go to school."[4]

While Hollenbeck said he had little experience as a boy with the "cold, cruel world," O'Brian said his early years were dominated by that world. "From the time I was a lad, I don't remember a job I ever held—except journalism—that didn't involve sweat and muscle, and pick and shovel," O'Brian said.[5]

At sixteen, the age at which Hollenbeck entered the University of Nebraska, O'Brian joined the Bricklayers, Hod Carriers and Common Laborers Union. He worked hundreds of jobs as a day laborer—as construction worker, sailor, or 47-cents-an-hour dock-walloper.[6] He loaded one-hundred-pound and two-hundred-pound bags of limestone into freight cars for ten hours a day.

He rose to foreman, he said, "due to my superior intelligence, my exquisite capacity for executive perspiration, and the fact that I was the only white man in a gang of forty-five laborers. At least a dozen were better equipped for the job than I."[7]

O'Brian also dug graves. (Decades later, as a columnist syndicated to 250 newspapers, he said of his earlier job digging graves: "Some people claim I never lost the habit.")[8]

For amusement as a teenager, Hollenbeck played the violin. O'Brian played football and brawled. Stocky and "strong as a bull," he was said to have put a couple of men in the hospital, recalled Bridget, his older daughter.[9] He tried three times to join the army, Bridget added, but bad eyesight, perforated eardrums, and other physical ailments prevented his service.

"I was pretty much on my own, a teenager out of work more than not," O'Brian said. "I didn't even know I was homeless—I just knew I often for months was dead broke [and] I actually fainted three times, at least, from hunger."[10]

At seventeen O'Brian started writing for Buffalo-area weeklies, including the South Buffalo News *and the* Catholic Union and Times. *His journalism career began in earnest when he accompanied a First Ward friend, George "Yicka" Hahn, to meet Bill Roseberry, editor of the weekly* Bugle, *best known for printing scandalous details of Buffalo divorces.*

O'Brian said he cajoled Roseberry, "a wildly inspired, talented misfit who'd been fired by all the local daily papers," into letting him write at 10 cents per printed inch.[11] "Within months I was writing a good portion of the Bugle's spirited trivialities," O'Brian said. "When my dime an inch brought me $31 a week, Roseberry offered me the steady weekly salary of $18. I leapt at it. It meant I was for the first time a regularly employed journalist."[12]

O'Brian usually refused to call himself a journalist. He dismissed the word as pretentious. He still saw himself as "Kegga" O'Brian, grammar-school-educated street reporter, barstool Irishman, and friend of First Ward cops and saloon waiters. "A journalist," O'Brian said, "was a double-breasted, vested elegante from the Buffalo News who carried a cane, a gent of considerable façade and super-elegance."[13]

In 1938 John P. Lewis, managing editor of the Buffalo Times, the last Democratic daily in Buffalo, offered O'Brian a six-week stint covering labor, which led to a regular city-room reporting position. The long-suffering Times, a Scripps-Howard paper, died in 1939. O'Brian moved to the New York World-Telegram, also owned by Scripps-Howard. O'Brian said, "I was raised in salary from the Times' starting pittance of $22 to the Telly's similarly thrifty sendoff salary of $25 and glad to get it." He returned to Buffalo in 1940 to report for the News and then the Courier-Express for three years "to get more experience writing," he said.[14]

At the Courier-Express O'Brian uncovered a black market in wartime rationing coupons for meat, butter, and nylon stockings. He said his reporting led to "forty-seven convictions and confessions," the closing of restaurants, clubs, and saloons, and a Pulitzer Prize nomination for his exposé.[15]

He also tried writing reviews, showing signs, Time magazine wrote, "of an incisive critical taste."[16] A guest appearance of juvenile accordionists with the local philharmonic orchestra incensed O'Brian. He damned the selection of the accordionists so devastatingly that their performance with the philharmonic provoked a civic squabble. The orchestra soon changed musical directors. O'Brian claimed credit.

O'Brian moved to the New York headquarters of the Associated Press in 1943, eventually to write drama, movie, and radio reviews. In doing so he escaped Buffalo forever, which reminded him years later of a line from the play A Chorus Line. "One of the chorus boys confessed that he had attempted suicide in Buffalo," O'Brian said. "The response to his revelation was the cruncher, 'Suicide in Buffalo is a redundancy.'"[17]

CHAPTER 9

Press Criticism:
From Name-calling to Nuance

A great newspaper is a public service institution. It occupies a position in public life fully as important as the school system or the church or the organs of government. It is entitled to criticism, and subject to criticism, as they are. The value of such criticism is directly proportionate to the steadiness with which the ultimate end of a better news system is clearly and dispassionately kept in mind.

  —Walter Lippmann and Charles Merz, "A Test of the News"

In the history of journalism Hollenbeck's *CBS Views the Press* represented an important idea whose time had finally come. Criticism of the media, once primarily partisan and political, was entering what Max Lerner, *PM's* editor and later a syndicated columnist for the *New York Post*, called a new phase of more nuanced, more ambitious, and sometimes more entertaining media criticism.[1]

Of the new-phase critics, Hollenbeck was the most ambitious. H*e criticized the writing style of reporters, not just the content of their articles. He used the medium of radio to take listeners to the scene, conveying the emotion of newspaper closings and other events. His ferociously independent, intensely local criticism earned credibility for *CBS Views the Press* and made possible its influence on the behavior of New York City's newspapers. The old-phase criticism had had virtually no influence.

The Brass Check, a 1919 screed by the radical muckraker Upton Sinclair, symbolized the old-phase criticism. A pious idealist with, as he said of himself, "Puritanical fervor," Sinclair labeled American newspapers class institutions: "They value a man, not because he is great, or good, or wise, or useful, but because he is wealthy, or of service to vested wealth." Sinclair viewed newsrooms as battlegrounds between exploitative owners and exploited workers. A socialist, he believed that the capitalist press never would serve the public: "I would say that to expect justice and truth-telling of a capitalist newspaper is to expect asceticism at a cannibal feast."[2]

Newspaper owners offered low wages, required seventy-two-hour work-weeks, and provided no job security. In 1903, when Moses Koenigsberg became city editor of the *Chicago Evening American*, he was the twenty-seventh person to occupy that chair in thirty-seven months. Journalists' short tenure, their pitiful wages, and the per-column-inch system of paying writers encouraged wordy sensationalism, payola, and moonlighting rife with conflicts of interest.

Sinclair self-published *The Brass Check* after commercial book publishers, afraid of libel suits, rejected it. Most newspapers did not review *The Brass Check*. Some, including the *New York Times*, even declined to publish paid advertisements for the book. Others smeared the book, which portrayed them as capitalism's pimps, luring "the virgin hopes of mankind into the loathsome brothel of Big Business." Despite—or thanks to—the smears, Sinclair sold 155,000 copies of *The Brass Check* in the United States alone.[3]

Sinclair's simplistic, moralistic recommendations for reform recall Lewis Mumford's conclusion about the muckrakers: "In attack, in criticism, they did able work; but when it came to offering a genuine alternative, their picture became a negative one: industry without millionaires, cities without graft, art without luxury, love without sordid calculation." Sinclair proposed newspapers without capitalism. His dream paper, the *National News*, would be an ad-free, editorial-free weekly that reported the truth.[4]

Sinclair embraced state-owned, city-owned, and endowed newspapers— any kind of ownership that would transfer newspapers' power from the wealthy to all the people. The acerbic H. L. Mencken pronounced Sinclair's remedy for "the reptile press" to be "simple, clear, bold and idiotic."[5]

With his love for reform through legislation, Sinclair paid little attention to the First Amendment's prohibition against laws restricting press freedom. To prevent newspaper inaccuracy and lying he suggested laws requiring prepublication review by the subjects of articles. He also favored laws requiring publication of corrections or payment to each injured person of at least $5,000. Newspapers would be prevented by law from faking telegraph or cable dispatches. The news monopoly of the Associated Press, operated as a cooperative by the country's major papers, would be made illegal.[6]

Max Lerner said this new phase of press criticism was best found in 1947 in four forums decidedly less naive than Sinclair's book: Hollenbeck's weekly radio critiques of the press; A. J. Liebling's "Wayward Press" articles for the *New Yorker* magazine; *Your Newspaper, Blueprint for a Better Press*, a book by nine of Harvard's Nieman Fellows; and *A Free and Responsible Press*, the report by the Hutchins Commission, a private group of scholars. The new criticism, said Lerner, "is less strident, more sophisticated, more concrete and scholarly, more humorous at times than the old. What it has lost in sheer power and passion it gains in . . . persuasiveness."[7]

Hollenbeck not only reported on the writings of Liebling, the Nieman Fellows, and the Hutchins Commission, but he also endorsed the premise behind their criticism of the press—that journalists and news organizations needed to engage in mutual criticism. The new phase of press criticism in 1947 derived its power, in part, from the interplay of the various critics and the distinctiveness of their voices and ideas, which continue to shape press criticism today.

For Liebling, the most widely read and most entertaining of the new-phase press critics, 1947 was a banner year. He published more "Wayward Press" articles than in any other year. He turned out two books, including *The Wayward Pressman*. The son of a prosperous New York furrier, Liebling had attended Dartmouth College, where he dreamed of reporting for Joseph Pulitzer's *New York World*. Liebling became a stringer for the *Sunday World* after five years at the *New York Times* and *Providence Journal*.

He was still pursuing his dream, a staff position on the *World*, when the paper was sold by Pulitzer's heirs in February 1931 and folded into Roy Howard's *Telegram*. After four years at the *World-Telegram* Liebling requested his first raise. When his request was refused, he quit. Liebling went to the *New Yorker* in 1935 and started writing its "Wayward Press" column (the humorist Robert Benchley had begun the column in 1927).[8]

Liebling saw himself as "a chronic, incurable, recidivist reporter." He read New York's newspapers each day, compared their competing accounts of an event, and then reported on the discrepancies, omissions, contradictions, and failures of journalistic technique that made the accounts less than his ideal. Though he judged the interpretative reporter as second class—below the reporter "who writes what he sees"—Liebling himself went beyond facts and firsthand observations.[9]

He overlaid his reporting of the facts with analysis, humor, and hyperbole. In a revenge piece on Howard and his *World-Telegram*, Liebling explained why readers had stopped buying the paper in the 1920s: "Many of them . . . had developed hallucinations from reading its prose and were dragged from subway trains slapping at adjectives they said they saw crawling over them."[10]

The publication of *The Wayward Pressman* provoked reviewers to compare the criticism of the *New Yorker* columnist to that of Hollenbeck. A *New Republic* review of Liebling's book began, "Thanks to A.J. Liebling in the *New Yorker* and Don Hollenbeck on the radio, the American press, which is more experienced in handing out criticism than in taking it, is currently being subjected to a regular course of measured, chastening and extremely valuable examination by experts." John Hersey's review in the *New York Herald Tribune* touted Liebling's articles as "the best continuing criticism of the press appearing anywhere today—the only competition being Dan [*sic*] Hollenbeck's radio program 'C.B.S. Views the Press.' "[11]

Writing for the *Saturday Review of Literature* magazine, Hollenbeck saluted Liebling's "penetrating and readable" book. He also revealed a good deal about his own perception of the limitations of press criticism. Liebling was fond of saying, "The more I criticized the press, the more it disimproved." Hollenbeck began his book review by declaring that being a press critic is "like hunting water in an empty well. You don't seem to get many tangible results, but, somehow, you've got to keep trying."[12]

Liebling sprinkled his press criticism with recommendations: the hiring of more good reporters for better local, Washington, and foreign coverage; "a school for publishers, failing which, no school of journalism can have meaning"; and the creation of a control newspaper as suggested by Albert Camus. The paper would come out an hour or two after the other papers and estimate the extent of their prejudice. Hollenbeck called some Liebling recommendations unrealistic, including Liebling's call for states to establish "newspaper commissions, like racing commissions, which would set down writers for lying, and rule off habitual offenders." Hollenbeck responded with a commonsense chuckle, "Well, a man can dream can't he?"[13]

But Hollenbeck said Liebling's book and columns served a larger purpose of press criticism—to inform the public. Liebling's criticism avoided a major weakness of scholarly critiques of the press: "The learned and sobersided gentlemen of academic and public life may sermonize and preach all they please about what is the matter with the American press," Hollenbeck wrote. "They are perfectly right in what they say, of course, but the trouble is nobody reads them."[14]

In a *CBS Views the Press* broadcast Hollenbeck amplified on what he found attractive about Liebling's witty writing—it wrapped "some lethal punches in extremely suave and sardonic prose." Hollenbeck also noted that only one of New York's major dailies, the *Herald Tribune*, had so far reviewed Liebling's book: "One way of dealing with a critic is to pretend that he isn't there."[15]

A prime example of an unread academic critique of the press, Hollenbeck said, was the 1947 Hutchins Commission report—Lerner's second example of a new phase in press criticism. The commission was headed by the precocious Robert M. Hutchins, chancellor of the University of Chicago, who had become dean of Yale Law School at twenty-eight and president of the University of Chicago at thirty. He was used to challenging the established order, which may explain why he abolished the university's football program. (He is often cited for the aphorism, "Whenever I feel like exercising, I lie down until that feeling goes away.")[16]

Hutchins led a two-year inquiry into the state of press freedom, funded by $215,000 in grants from Time, Inc., and Encyclopaedia Britannica, Inc. He released a 106-page report, *A Free and Responsible Press*, in March 1947. The report of the highbrow commission read like a treatise—small wonder, given that the commission included nine academics of the caliber of Reinhold Niebuhr, philosophy professor at Union Theological Seminary; Archibald MacLeish, the poet and former assistant secretary of state; and the Harvard historian Arthur Schlesinger.

The report began with a section headlined "The Problem and the Principles." It ended, after a series of generalities that sometimes bordered on the obvious, with thirteen recommendations. A key recommendation was the establishment of an independent agency to evaluate and report annually on the performance of the press.

The independent agency would help the media define workable standards of performance, identify communities in need of alternatives to press monopoly, inquire about the exclusion of minorities from the press, examine the picture of American life presented abroad by the U.S. press, investigate press lying, appraise industry and government action affecting communications, and encourage universities to establish centers of advanced communication study.

As if the Hutchins Commission's call for an agency of press evaluation were not enough to alarm defensive editors and publishers, it also recommended government regulation to improve the press—for example, a law requiring publication of retractions and replies.[17]

Newspapers responded predictably to the commission's report—with silence or name-calling about pie-in-the-sky eggheads. Wilbur Forrest, president of the American Society of Newspaper Editors (ASNE), said the commission was under the influence of forces "long designed to undermine the public confidence in the press." Harry Ashmore, an ASNE member, recalled that the membership huddled, "rumps together, horns out, in the immemorial manner of, say, the National Association of Manufacturers faced by a threat of regulated prices."[18]

Journalists who bothered to read the Hutchins report before judging it concluded that it was, in I. F. Stone's words, "a lot of high-class crap." Frank Hughes, a reporter for the *Chicago Tribune*, which was owned by the reactionary Colonel Robert R. McCormick, devoted a 642-page book to bashing the report as scholarship-free, propaganda-heavy "ignorance" and the Hutchins Commission as "men who have left-wing, Socialist convictions ranging from New Deal 'pink' to Communist 'red.'" Liebling wrote that he was "inclined to wonder uncharitably as I read the book what they had spent the $200,000 on: It contains some sound, unoriginal reflections, but nothing worth over one grand even at *Ladies Home Journal* rates."[19]

Hollenbeck, however, repeatedly emphasized where the commission was on target. He said in a 1947 *CBS Views the Press* broadcast, shortly before *PM* abandoned its press page, that the commission's idea of mutual criticism by the press "is largely the monopoly of the newspaper *PM*" in New York. He devoted a December 1948 program to the commission's call for an independent team to evaluate press performance. *Editor and Publisher* had just proposed that Hutchins select six people to serve on that team and *Editor and Publisher* select another six. The dozen members of the team would meet regularly to discuss the problems and duties of the press.[20]

Except for the *Herald Tribune*, New York's newspapers were silent about Hutchins's speech and *Editor and Publisher*'s proposal. Appearing on *CBS Views the Press*, Hutchins said of the proposed press evaluation team: "If the press pays as much attention to it, or distributes either no information or misinformation about it, as was the case of the Commission on the Freedom of The Press, what do you gain?" Hollenbeck suggested that the public and press might be ready for a continuing press evaluation panel, with a half-dozen independent newspeople and a half-dozen lay people as members. Hutchins joked that Hollenbeck was romantic and unrealistic.[21]

Hollenbeck followed in April 1949 with a *CBS Views the Press* program about the first meeting of the Hutchins/*Editor and Publisher* press panel. "We have yet to see an adequate story about it in the papers," he said.[22] The panel consisted of four educators who had served on the original Hutchins Commission (Hutchins could not attend because of illness), Robert U. Brown, editor of *Editor and Publisher*, and five eminent newspapermen: Turner Catledge of the *New York Times*, Barry Bingham of the *Louisville Courier-Journal*, Gideon Seymour of the *Minneapolis Star and Tribune*, Philip Graham of the *Washington Post*, and Erwin Canham of the *Christian Science Monitor* who was also president of ASNE.

The historic panel criticized the omission of the Arab side in news reports about the Palestine story and noted other problems with press coverage. It also proposed to study how U.S. newspapers could improve and better inform the public about the press. A committee on responsibility would be proposed at the coming ASNE convention.[23]

Toward the end of April 1949 Hollenbeck's *CBS Views the Press* reported again on the Hutchins Commission's efforts. Hollenbeck questioned ASNE's response to the notion of a committee on responsibility and quoted Tom Hanes of the *Norfolk Ledger-Dispatch*, who said, "We have taken the smug position that there isn't anything wrong with us that can't be hidden by a thick coat of whitewash."[24]

ASNE, bent on delay, authorized a committee to spend a year studying the advisability of sponsoring "an appraisal of the self-improvement possibilities of American newspapers." As for a recommendation by Hanes that ASNE require every member newspaper to abide by the society's code of ethics and throw out members in violation, "That will be the day," said Hollenbeck.[25]

Hollenbeck returned to the subject of the Hutchins Commission for one of his last *CBS Views the Press* broadcasts. A January 1950 program ended with the CBS newscaster Quincy Howe—who had been examining journalism that week in a nightly series titled "You and the Press"—hoping the Hutchins Commission "might lead to some self-regulation coupled with some advice from outstanding private citizens."[26]

Advice from outstanding journalists was not mentioned, but it was readily available. In 1947 a group of Harvard's Nieman Fellows—nine journalists who had spent 1945–46 on leave at the university[27]—published *Your Newspaper: Blueprint for a Better Press*, the fourth critique that Lerner had cited as evidence of a new phase in press criticism.

Louis Lyons, curator of the Nieman program, said the nine Fellows wrote a useful companion to the Hutchins Commission's report "out of their own practical experience . . . while the Commission, being philosophers, stuck to principles."[28]

The Fellows began their book with a three-point indictment. First, the book asserted, the press was irresponsible. It published less news proportionately than in the past. It subordinated journalism's primary function, providing news, to making money. It moved with glacial speed toward the enforcement of an ethics code (the unenforced ASNE canon of ethics was dismissed as "a musty dead letter"). The press, the Fellows said, emphasized conflict, "scare" news, and entertainment.[29]

Second, the press was self-serving. The Fellows labeled as "trite accusations" the charges that advertisers controlled the press and that owners conspired to suppress the news. But the Fellows said the press, while purporting to speak for the people, was overwhelmingly antilabor and proadvertiser.[30]

Third, the press was sliding toward monopoly ownership. Ten states had no city with competing dailies. All but 177 U.S. cities had only monopolies. Twenty-two states had no Sunday newspaper competition. Fourteen companies controlled one-fourth of the country's total daily circulation.

The indictment by *Your Newspaper* was less important than its attempt to create a design for a great daily, a hypothetical morning paper of 250,000 circulation (300,000 on Sunday), in a city of 1.5 million with two competing dailies.

The new paper, which would cost $5 million to start and $6 million a year to operate, could be funded, if necessary, by a municipality, foundation, or an endowment attached to a university. The Nieman Fellows looked first, however, to teachers' associations, labor unions, professional organizations, and grassroots gatherings of readers for the establishment of a stock-subscription newspaper.

The paper's 150-person staff of the best reporters, photographers, and editors would receive salaries of $10,000 to $25,000 (the going rate then was $4,000 to $10,000), health insurance, pensions, sabbatical leaves, and "greater security." The paper would feature three or four Washington correspondents, twelve foreign correspondents, including roving experts in science, diplomacy, and economics, and twenty specialists in such areas as science, movies, homemaking and, of course, the press.[31]

The format recalled the prepublication issues of *PM*: tabloid size "fitting in the hand like a magazine"; squared-off blocks of ads; horizontal layouts; more and better photographs; larger, easy-to-read type; and pages stapled together "so that the paper wouldn't turn into garbage when dropped." News would be departmentalized. Stories would be written compactly and crisply and, whenever possible, with humor. News would be told in terms of people. The paper would comparison shop for both goods and ideas. The Nieman Fellows concluded, "Often it would be more helpful to advise [the consumer] what *not* to do or buy."[32]

Most reviewers dismissed the Niemans' newspaper as fairytale foolishness. Harry Saylor told *Saturday Review of Literature* readers that advertisers who want "position" would not permit their ads to be squared off. "Stack your hypothetical ads neatly," Saylor wrote, "and the ads will remain hypothetical." A *New York Times* reviewer called the Nieman Fellows "naively wrong," representing "biased and not mature thinking." Svirsky, the editor of *Your Newspaper*, answered that the caustic *Times* review "was not too surprising—so many of our examples of bad stories were from the *Times*."[33]

Other reviewers offered more balance. Richard Watts Jr. of the *New Republic* called the book "valuable and provocative, although occasionally sketchy," deserving to stand with the "valuable current investigations" by Liebling and Hollenbeck. In the *Herald Tribune* Lewis Gannett said the book was better than the Hutchins Commission report: "At times its voice seems to break into a Boy Scout tremolo, but most of its criticism is professional."[34]

Hollenbeck said the book offered "something of an elementary course in newspaper criticism, and as such, will prove useful." But he felt the authors' "blanket indictment" was not supported by enough evidence from a variety of newspapers to prove their points, nor had they summoned sufficient passion—"the fire necessary to burn up the people it's aimed at."[35]

At the heart of postwar press criticism was the desire to be the interpreter, reporter, and evaluator of the big picture. The targets of the criticism—the trend toward chain ownership, the bias of a capitalist press, the death of newspaper competition—were almost always national, if not international. But Hollenbeck and, to a lesser extent, Liebling developed a distinctive form of press criticism, the local watchdog.

Hollenbeck wanted to evaluate every aspect of the New York news media—foreign-language dailies, obituary writing, letters to the editor, gossip columns, sports reporting, financial columns, even the prose of the *Weekly Block*, a neighborhood paper published by two boys, one nine years old, the other ten. Hollenbeck made the New York press feel that every edition of every issue of every paper was under scrutiny.

He praised a puckishly written account of flying saucers that appeared in the *Sun*'s first edition. The city desk replaced the first-edition story with another—"not half as entertaining," said Hollenbeck—about what some admiral thought of the flying disks. The *Sun* reporter thought he had written a good story, but doubt overcame him when the story ran for only the first edition with a small headline and no byline. "Your kind words made me feel a lot better," he wrote to Hollenbeck. "Incidentally, you must really be on the ball to spot a feature that runs for one edition."[36]

In an important sense Hollenbeck, by systematically reviewing the performance of New York's press each week, set an example for the local journalism reviews, local ombudsmen, local public editors, and other institutional watchdogs that began in the 1960s and continue today. Marion T. Marzolf, historian of press criticism, argues that Hollenbeck and Liebling "laid the groundwork for what could become a professional genre of journalism criticism."

Marzolf concludes: "What they chose to examine—content, form and style, motives, ethics, social worth, and responsibility—suggested a direction for future critics." A stronger case can be made for Hollenbeck's exemplary role than for Liebling's. *Slate*'s Jack Shafer, who labels Liebling the patron saint of press criticism, also calls him a press critic who "made no effort to hide his liberal politics. . . . Far from daring, he was a conformist, reinforcing the majority culture views of *New Yorker* readers."[37]

Liebling's adherence to the liberal line made it more difficult for him than for Hollenbeck to pursue the truth. To Hollenbeck "the question of 'What is truth?'" loomed large and justified the journalist's independence. The less independent Liebling was missing "the biggest story of his time—the Cold War—and allow[ing] himself to get too close to Alger Hiss to see his deceit," Shafer writes.[38]

Hollenbeck, while never free of his liberal roots, neither missed the Cold War story nor got too close to Hiss. *CBS Views the Press* reflected Hollenbeck's independence, his sense of fairness, and his belief in "permitting the other side to have its say." He embraced the notion that CBS correspondents for *CBS Views the Press* would provide evenhanded reporting. During one broadcast Hollenbeck even used the word *objectivity*. He was not so naive as to believe in journalists' ability to report and write uninfluenced by their own values and experiences. But he saw the need to avoid falling victim to propaganda, public relations, and popular opinion—the need "to maintain objectivity . . . in the face of pressure and information from non-objective sources."[39]

That stance gave Hollenbeck's program a credibility with journalists that Liebling's articles and books failed to achieve. Hollenbeck critiqued liberal and conservative papers alike. Following the announcement of a national food-saving drive, Senator Robert A. Taft, a Republican candidate for president in 1948, trumpeted his support for eating less and then immediately began a cross-country campaign trip. The liberal *New York Post* detailed the menu each day and, where possible, the cost of Taft's campaign-trip meals. Designed to show Taft was hypocritical, the *Post's* coverage downplayed a reality that Hollenbeck made clear: "Meals for him had been planned in advance by his hosts . . . it would have been boorish in the extreme—besides being politically unwise—to have made an issue of it among the people whose votes he was interested in."[40]

So *CBS Views the Press*, more than Liebling's "Wayward Press," became the conscience of the city's newspapers, said George Herman, "at a time when there were no magazines [of press criticism] like . . . the *Columbia Journalism Review*. The papers listened to us."[41]

Establishment and nonestablishment papers genuinely cared how Hollenbeck characterized their performance. The managing editor of the *New York Times* and the executive editor of the left-wing *National Guardian* both responded with alacrity to what Hollenbeck had to say about their papers. *Nieman Reports* noted that newspaper people were "reversing their field and doing an honest job after he'd exposed their slippery stories."[42]

Furthermore, Hollenbeck developed to a high art the studying and restudying of editorials and articles. During one broadcast, for example, he demonstrated how a significant error had made its way into the *World-Telegram*. The anti-Communist reporter Frederick Woltman, of all people, had relied on a report in the Communist *Daily Worker*. The *Daily Worker's* report, in turn, had come from an organization that assumed the information was correct because "it had happened that way before."[43]

Hollenbeck also examined press bias—whether the editorial viewpoint of New York City's newspapers influenced the news coverage they gave to a hotly contested issue. When the New York papers covered a referendum on whether to repeal proportional representation in city council elections, Hollenbeck measured the column inches of news reports about the issue.

He found papers that were editorially opposed to proportional representation had printed in their news columns "more than twice as much material arguing against the system" as had those papers that were editorially in favor of proportional representation. Papers that supported proportional representation in their editorials gave ten times as much space in their news columns to reports in favor of proportional representation as did those papers that were against it. Hollenbeck added a fascinating footnote: The *Daily Worker*, "which wrote editorials in its news columns," ran sixty times as many column inches of news in favor of proportional representation as it did column inches against proportional representation.[44]

Hollenbeck's column-inch analysis questioned news-coverage bias in a more subtle, less flashy, fashion than Liebling's criticism. Anne Hollenbeck said, "Don was always very subtle in the way he phrased things because there was always someone waiting in the wings with the poison arrow."[45]

Hollenbeck's careful reading of newspapers proved most provocative when it led him to compare the newspapers' contradictory reports about significant world events. In 1949 he contrasted guesswork reporting about the Soviet Union's replacement of Foreign Minister Vyacheslav M. Molotov with Andrei Y. Vishinsky: "In the *Times* next morning, for instance, Molotov has been sacked; in the *Tribune*, he's been promoted." After reviewing, pundit by pundit, a full week of the New York press, Hollenbeck summarized what the papers' readers could conclude about the change in foreign ministers: "A tougher Soviet policy toward the West, a softer Soviet policy toward the West."[46]

Unlike most press critics before him, Hollenbeck focused on writing style as well as on the substance of what was written. Hutchins, chair of the Hutchins Commission, once told Hollenbeck he was really an academic. "That's the worst insult I can hurl at you," Hutchins teased.[47] The moniker fit. Hollenbeck closely studied literature, especially the works of James Joyce and other innovative writers who took chances with language. He hated newspaper hacks' abuse of language.

In a 1949 broadcast Hollenbeck contrasted the convoluted, confusing writing in *Herald Tribune*, *Times*, and *Daily News* articles to the straightforward prose of David MacDougall, nine, and Billy Weidlich, ten, editors of the *Weekly Block*, which reported on the news of their 115 East 89th Street neighborhood. MacDougall, today an ethnographic filmmaker and professor in Australia, and Weidlich, a retired lawyer living in New York, recall that the *Block*, which began as a free, hand-lettered sheet, evolved into a five-cent, hectorgraphed publication with a paid circulation of fifty and penny-for-two-line ads ("Silverstein's for magazines and jelly beans").[48]

Hollenbeck quoted from a *Block* article about Keats Speed, executive editor of the *New York Sun*, who lived near the boys. The article ended: "Mr. Speed asked us if we thought our paper was fun. We said 'Yes.' Then he said, 'It would not be so much fun if we had eleven labor unions to deal with.'"

(opposite page) Hollenbeck vowed to evaluate every aspect of New York journalism for *CBS Views the Press*. He even commented on the *Weekly Block*, published by David MacDougall (left), nine, and Billy Weidlich, ten. This edition contained an exclusive: "We met Mrs. [Don] Hollenbeck this week. She said that she and her husben [*sic*] both like the *Weekly Block* better than any other city newspaper."

WEEKLY BLOCK

VOL. 1   NO. 9   MARCH 14, 1949

ABANDONED CAR

THERE IS AN OLD DODGE CAR ON 89th ST. IT
HAS BEEN THERE SINCE THE LAST BIG SN OW
STORM. ALL THE WINDOWS ARE SMASHED AND
THE FRONT FENDERS ARE BENT. IT HAS A 1948
license and the number of it is N.Y.2R-393
IT HAS AN ATLANTIC CITY STICKER ON THE
WIND SHIELD AND TWO PAIRS OF SHOES IN THE
BACK SEAT. IT LOOKS AS IF IT HAD BEEN IN
AN AXIDENT. WE WONDER IF IT HAS BEEN STOLEN
AND LEFT HERE.

ALLEYS

THERE ARE THREE MAIN ALLEYS ON THIS BLOCK.
WE EXPLORED THE ONE ON 90thST. AND HAD TO
GO UNDER AN IRON BAR TO GET IN. THERE IS A
COVERED TUNNEL AND A HIGH WALL THAT WE
CLIMBED. WE USED TO GO THERE WITH OUR FRIEND
GEORGE. THE ALLEY BEHIND THE BIG WHITE HOUSE
HAS 5 BACK YARDS WITH FENCES. BOYS LIKE TO
CLIMB ON THE HIGH WALLS WITH THE IRON SPIKES.
LARRY ROCKWELL HAD A HOMEMADE SWIMMING POOL.
MADE OF CANVAS. IT WAS FUN TO GO IN.

INTERVIEW WITH MRS. DON HOLLENBECK

WE MET MRS. HOLLENBECK THIS WEEK. SHE SAID
THAT SHE AND HER HUSBEN BOTH LIKE THE
WEEKLY BLOCK BETTER THAN ANY OTHER CITY
NEWSPAPER.

STORE NEWS

THE LEXINGTON BOOKSHOP HAS STARTED SELLING
ARTISTS SUPLIES. LOOK AT THE WINDOW.

THE MODERNAGE BOOKSHOP TOLD US A HOLE GRADE
OF CHILDREN CAME IN THIS WEEK TO BUY ROGET'S
POCKET THESAURUS. IT SAYS ON IT "This famous
book will end your word troubles." WE BOUGHT
THE LAST COPY.
F

FRANK IN ELMER'S MEAT MARKET TOLD US THE
BEST KINDS OF MEAT STILL COAST A LOT. HE
SAID "UTILITARIAN"KINDS ARE GETTING CHEAPER.

THINGS SOMETIMES COST MORE IN ONE STORE.
AT THE BAKERY ON THE CORNER ECLAIRS COST 10¢
BUT AT THE FRENCH ONE NEXT TO TO ELMER'S
THEY COST 12¢   WE LIKE THEM BETTER.

              DAVID MACDOUGALL &
              BILLY WEIDLICH

          * EDITORS*

IT LOOKED AS IF THE DALTON
SCHOOL HAD A NEW FLAG THIS
WEEK. BUT WE ASKED MRS. GOODWIN
AND SHE SAID SHE THOUGHT THAT
THE OLD ONE HAD BEEN WASHED
FROM THE WINDOW OF THE WEEKLY
BLOCK OFFICE YOU CAN SEE RAY
STANDING ON THE OUTSIDE WINDOW
SILLPUTTING UP THE FLAG IN
MORNING AND TAKING IT DOWN
IN THE AFTERNOON. EXEPT ON
SUNDAY AND SATERDAY.

On the sidewalk on the cor-
NER OF LEX. AND 89th THERE
IS THIS SIGN SOMEBODY PAINT
ED IN WHITE PAINT THAT
POINTS TO THE CURB:
     DOGS ————

ANS. TO LAST WEEKS QUESTION:
     BECAUSE IT TAKES 5 HOURS
FOR THE SUN TO TRAVEL FROM
LONDON TO NEW YORK. SO WHEN
OUR REPORTER WHIT KNAPP CALL-
ED ON THE TELEPHONE TO A
MAN IN LONDON IN THE MORNING
IT WAS AFTERNOON OVER THERE

SOME PEOPLE ON THE BLOCK WHO
LISTEN TO THE RADIO HAVE
HEARD LOUD RINGING NOISES SO
THAT THEY CANNOT HEAR THE
PROGRAM BETWEEN 10 & 10:30
AT NIGHT. IF YOUR RADIO HAS
THE SAME NOISE PLEASE WRITE
TO THE WEEKLY BLOCK AND WE
WILL INVESTAGATE. IT SPOILS
ALL THE STATIONS.

       ADV ADV ADV
  GO TO HAHN'S FOR GOOD SALADS
ROAST BEEF & TURKEY, FROZEN
FOOD & GROCERIES. YOU CAN EAT
THERE AT A TABLE IF YOU WANT
TO. A CHEERFUL PLACE TO BUY
THINGS.
  --*-*-*-*-*-*
  116 EAST 89TH ST.
  NEW YORK, N.Y.

Hollenbeck concluded by complimenting the story's simple charm—no parentheses within parentheses: "We hope Editors MacDougall and Weidlich never lose that simplicity if they . . . join the staff of a daily newspaper."[49]

Hollenbeck's favorite language targets in newspapers were:

- *Giddy goo*. Ruth Brigham, a reporter for the International News Service, wrote that the night of Winthrop Rockefeller's wedding was so "thick with stars that it seemed the Milky Way must have exploded across the heavens—the ecstatic happiness radiated from Palm Beach to take in practically the whole country." On the birth of a son, Charles, to Princess Elizabeth, a *Times* editorialist treacled: "One could hear above the voice of the crowds of London the vast susurrus of the seven seas that wash the shores of what was once the British empire."[50]

- *Clichés*. A Hollywood shooting, Hollenbeck wrote, "brings out all the overworked, outdated, side-of-the-mouth jargon of the trade. In the *News*, this: 'Gangland put the finger on Mickey Cohen, a mobster, who sang, in a burst of gunfire today. . . . The shooting took place in front of Sherry's, a swank filmland restaurant.'" After quoting similar passages in other papers, Hollenbeck concluded, "Somehow, the purple persists."[51]

- *Ten-dollar words*. Few things in journalism irked Hollenbeck more than pretentious writing. He chided editorial writers at the *Times* and *Herald Tribune* for using such words as *aposiopesis* and *susurrus*. He firmly believed shorter, simpler words were more powerful.[52]

- *Wordiness*. Reporters preferred "a lone bandit" (*Times*) or "a lone gunman" (*Daily News*) to a bandit or a gunman. Hollenbeck said: "It reminds us of a story we read once: A solitary horseman shows up on the horizon. Then another one shows up, and pretty soon the place is simply alive with solitary horsemen."[53]

- *Stop-sign participials*. *Times* coverage of the perjury trial of Alger Hiss suffered from many sentences that began with participial phrases— "Testifying for the second day" and "Admitting that he knew." Hollenbeck rejected such phrasing as "the survival of the unfittest."[54] The popular form delayed the reader in getting to the subject of the sentence.

- *Bloated Leads*. To criticize a *Times* article that had crammed everything into the first sentence, Hollenbeck simply read it aloud: "An empire of apartment holdings, stretching from Brooklyn to Mount

Vernon and including choice Manhattan residences, was disclosed yesterday to be controlled by a family whose head was alleged, according
to papers on file in Federal Court, to have milked the properties at the
expense of bankers, tradesmen and mortgage holders."[55]

Hollenbeck's criticism had a therapeutic effect on Charles Grutzner, the
Times reporter responsible for the fifty-one-word lead. He wrote to Hollenbeck, "I was right proud of that Ansonia Apartments lead when it rolled off
the typewriter. But when you read the goddam thing on the radio without
pause for breath, I realized I didn't have to draw the whole picture. I've gone
back to counting words in leads that look fat, and I'm keeping them as far
below twenty-five words as is possible."[56]

Hollenbeck especially enjoyed stories with a trifecta of transgressions.
Clichés, inconsistencies, and muddy writing filled stories about a jewel
robbery involving a beautiful woman, a penthouse, a fortune in gems, and
café-society names. The *Mirror* said the robber was six feet tall, the *Times*
said five feet seven. The *Herald Tribune*'s account offered confusing clauses
within clauses: " 'You are a young man,' Mrs. Hilton, estranged from Conrad
N. Hilton, president of the Hilton Hotels Corporation and Miss Hungary of
1936, recalled telling the intruder." Hollenbeck said, "That would make Mr.
Hilton Miss Hungary of 1936, which is interesting."[57]

That *radio*'s first critic of newspapers was Hollenbeck has a certain irony.
Hollenbeck's brand of local criticism—as proved by the writings today of
newspaper ombudsmen, public editors, and alternative newspaper press
critics—belonged in newspapers. But in 1947 newspapers, except for *PM*,
were not yet ready to report their failings. Hollenbeck's radio program—
and to a lesser extent Liebling's *New Yorker* column—performed the role
that newspapers would not.

Radio permitted Hollenbeck to reach beyond the press critic's normal
audience of journalists and well-educated cognoscenti. *CBS Views the Press*
found more of a mass audience. One poll placed *CBS Views the Press* first in
the ratings for its Saturday evening time slot.[58]

Radio also gave the program a sense of New York and its press that was
unavailable to readers of print—the angry, election-night shouts of a victo-
rious mayor William O'Dwyer about an unprecedented "campaign of filth"
against him that was "supported wholeheartedly by practically all the newspapers"; the sound of a wire-service machine transmitting a photograph;
and the horn honks of a *Mirror* photographer as he raced an ambulance to
get to the scene of a woman injured in a one-story fall. The photographer

won the race, shot a close-up of the woman as she was placed in the ambulance, and drove to the *Mirror* with his photo exclusive.[59]

In 1949 and 1950 *CBS Views the Press* took its listeners to the offices of the *Star* and the *Sun* as they published for the last time. The report on the death of the 117-year-old *Sun* began with the yell of George Pine, a newsboy, at the corner of Broadway and Chambers: "Get your last copy of the *Sun*. Over a thousand out of work." Then Hollenbeck visited the *Sun*'s newsroom, with its worn suggestion box and "a very definite flavor of the past."[60]

There, George Gaston, a makeup editor and forty-six-year veteran of the *Sun*, talked about surviving the *Sun*'s mergers with the *Press* and then the *Herald* and being devastated by the *Sun*'s death: "This has come as such a shock to me and come so suddenly that I'm really without feeling. I don't know exactly what foot I stand on."[61]

Hollenbeck and his *CBS Views the Press* team also reported from the Duane Street office of the *Star* on that paper's last night in 1949. Heywood Hale Broun, a *Star* sports columnist, told Hollenbeck's audience that "working on . . . the *Star* has been a little bit like working on one of those shows that's struggling to get ready for Broadway, except that they just do it for weeks, and we did it for years. When it folds up, and the critics say it was lousy, maybe they were right, and maybe they weren't, but you feel pretty sore . . . anyway, because you've been all wrapped up in it."[62]

CBS Views the Press's listeners heard bell and buzzer announce the beginning of the *Star*'s last three-hour press run and then the newsprint racing through the presses at high speed, a sweet sound to newspaper people. Four months later *CBS Views the Press* returned to the Duane Street office to capture the birth of the *Daily Compass*. Publisher T. O. Thackrey took a break from cutting the length of his front-page editorial to explain that a circulation of sixty-five thousand for the 10-cent, twenty-four-page tabloid would permit it to break even.[63] The presses in the subbasement roared as the first issue's run began.

Hollenbeck's listeners were exposed to what the sociologist Paul Lazarsfeld called, in the argot of the social scientist, "the expressive surplus value of the human voice." Broadcasts of *CBS Views the Press* were more powerful and persuasive because they were heard, not read. The inflections and emphases Hollenbeck placed on words added extra layers of meaning. Marshall McLuhan explained: "Radio affects most people intimately, person-to-person, offering a world of unspoken communication between writer-speaker and the listener."[64] The pauses, the silences between words,

the background sounds, the sound effects—all communicated in important, immediate ways to Hollenbeck's audience.

Hollenbeck had once written that press criticism is "pretty much
like fighting a feather bed." Tangible results were virtually impossible to
achieve. But he showed by example what the press could do. He regularly
aired corrections of mistakes that *CBS Views the Press* had made. On the
second anniversary of the program he listed its shortcomings: not getting
to important stories; not giving sufficient credit to other reporters' work;
not providing critiques of columnists, sports journalism, business reporting, new publications, and gossip columnists; and not covering the growth
in tawdry articles about sex.[65]

"If . . . more and more latitude is being taken in what is fit to print, the
newspapers of the future may be a sight for smoked glasses," Hollenbeck
said. "But we hope there'll always be the *Times* with a big enough wastebasket for all the trash."[66]

Hollenbeck's press criticism asked newspapers to do only the possible.
Report honestly about the truly newsworthy. Avoid publishing propaganda,
phony photos, and slanted press releases. Write clearly. Be fair. Monitor one
another. Live by the ethical standards for journalists that were proudly proclaimed once a year, during National Newspaper Week.

In a *Town Meeting of the Air* Hollenbeck said, "As never before in history,
the people should be looking to the press for leadership and example." Press
mistakes, he insisted, required immediate correction. The denial needed
to catch up with the critical error, "in order that the record may be kept
entirely straight."[67]

By concentrating on the possible, he succeeded where other press critics failed. He focused attention on important stories that editors had overlooked, and in the process he influenced press behavior. For example,
six black men from Trenton, New Jersey, were sentenced to death after a
questionable trial. "New York newspapers virtually ignored the case," the
Louisville Courier-Journal editorialized. "And it was not until Don Hollenbeck . . . called attention to their silence, and to the outrageous character of
the whole case, that it began receiving national attention."[68]

Hollenbeck's criticism also helped change the newspapers' convention of
not naming news media accused of villainy—"the cautious code of journalistic etiquette at work." In at least one instance his criticism had influence
even before he broadcast it. *Time* magazine announced to its employees a
policy restricting their outside writing to material consistent with *Time*'s
editorial views. Outraged employees objected. They charged censorship.

"Don Hollenbeck . . . began to prepare a broadcast touching on the dispute and interviewed a *Time* executive about it," A. J. Liebling reported. "The *Time* management . . . then hedged and told CBS that *Time* 'had never had a policy,' so how could anybody be expected to conform to it?"[69]

But being an honest, outspoken press critic was dangerous, and Hollenbeck provided perhaps the most dramatic example in American journalism of the perils. Hollenbeck acknowledged that listeners, while pleased with his "Don Quixote at the windmills" pursuit of truth, also worried about the consequences for him. He said the public feared "that to discuss with honesty an institution so venerable and so powerful as the press is suicidal."[70]

An independent soul who insisted on telling the truth about the press made himself a target. No issue proved that quite as profoundly as the Red Scare that gripped postwar America.

CHAPTER 10

Jack O'Brian: Championing Decency, Fighting Soft-on-Communism Liberals

In 1947, the year Hollenbeck began broadcasting CBS Views the Press, Jack O'Brian married Agnes Yvonne Johnston, one of ten children of Jimmy "Boy Bandit" Johnston. Johnston managed the world heavyweight boxing champion Jack Sharkey, directed boxing at Madison Square Garden, and exhibited mastery of, in the words of the New York Times, *"colorful invective and lashing sarcasm."*[1]

Perhaps life with her father, the boxing impresario with a verbal punch, had helped prepare Yvonne for life with O'Brian, the pugnacious columnist. In 1943 O'Brian had left Buffalo to join the AP in New York as a crime features reporter. Within six months he was also the AP's drama editor; he claimed more than fourteen hundred newspapers carried "Broadway," his daily column for the AP. Two years after his marriage to Yvonne, O'Brian landed a job at the New York Journal-American *as the paper's radio-television critic. He saw himself as a triple threat: voice of the common folk, champion of decency, and fighter against soft-on-Communism liberals.*

The seven-day-a-week columnist reached out to what he called rank-and-file people by devoting his Saturday column to listener and viewer gripes. He expressed a preference for boxing coverage and low-brow humor by Art Carney, Bert Lahr, Joe Smith, and Charles Dale. A Smith and Dale joke: "I'm sick as a dog." "You came to the right place—I'm also a veterinarian."[2]

O'Brian also attacked symbols of the cerebral and clearly regarded doing so to be part of his brief as radio-television critic. He dismissed David Susskind, host of a television discussion program, as "Little David," CBS newscaster Howard K. Smith as an "apprentice egghead," and Edward R. Murrow as an intellectual stuffed shirt. O'Brian said, "I'm no intellectual. I have the popular mind." He insisted he was *"very happy in the Toy Department of Journalism, covering show business"* and judging even newscasters by a show-business standard: *"Leave 'em laughing" or at least entertain them. So he named the lively, gossipy Walter Winchell, not "drone . . . of doom" Murrow, radio's best reporter.*[3]

As a champion of decency, O'Brian cheered the television programs of Father James Keller and Bishop Fulton J. Sheen (*"simply amazing"*). The columnist also campaigned against *"smut and overly gamey insinuation"* on evening television shows and the plunging necklines of Faye Emerson, Dagmar, and Mary McCarty (O'Brian dubbed them *"frontal epidermis," "fantastic facades,"* and *"down-to-here talents"*).[4]

To combat soft-on-Communism liberals O'Brian wrote us-against-them columns that John Crosby, the television critic for the Herald Tribune, *called "ill-tempered diatribes." The "us" consisted of the anti-Communist William Randolph Hearst, who owned the* Journal-American *(O'Brian called him "a genius"), and O'Brian's Red-hunting* Journal-American *brethren—Westbrook Pegler, Fulton Lewis Jr., Dorothy Kilgallen, and Igor "Cholly Knickerbocker" Cassini. When Cassini, the paper's syndicated society columnist, began a radio program from his East Side living room, O'Brian cheered his slaps at "the pinkish ambitions of Social Register 'intellectuals' and too-obviously portsided 'liberals.'"*[5]

In a column headlined *"Berle, Silvers, Bergen, First in Anti-Red Line,"* O'Brian proudly patted himself on the back for contacting television stars to appear at an anti-Communist May Day demonstration in Union Square. Organizers of the demonstration intended, O'Brian said, *"to reclaim that piece of fine Manhattan real estate from the Commies who thought they had squatters' rights there forever."* O'Brian said he invited no *"bleeding leftwing hearts"* who might try to use their appearance to gain public acceptance for their performance: *"Friends of America only are welcome."*[6]

In his column O'Brian also applauded entertainers like the movie actor Robert Montgomery who publicly identified themselves with anti-Communism. O'Brian quoted Montgomery: *"The Commies are yelling in Hollywood that there's a blacklist against any writer or creative worker who voices liberal tendencies. That's hogwash. But there is some sort of sinister blacklist against some truly talented people who are opposed to the Commies."*[7]

O'Brian rhapsodized about such radio programs as the anti-Communist John Flynn's newscasts, the I Was a Communist for the FBI series (*"the season's sensation"*), and Richard English's Last Man Out series about Elizabeth Bentley, Howard Rushmore, and other disillusioned Communists

Yvonne and Jack O'Brian (left) with the New York Journal-American *columnist Dorothy Kilgallen and her husband, Richard Kollmar, at the Stork Club in 1956. Kilgallen, like O'Brian and other Hearst columnists, hunted for Communists. She wrote about a Communist "espionage-by-blondes" plot deeply embedded "like veins in marble" within a café society vice case.*

Courtesy New York Journal-American Photo Archive, Harry Ransom Center, University of Texas at Austin.

who turned anti-Communist and then named Communists. O'Brian called English's series "brilliant"—the best documentary drama of the 1953–54 season—but others saw it as agitprop designed to make informers of dubious value into heroes.[8]

O'Brian repeatedly praised the work of the anti-Communist newsletter Counterattack: *"Lenin said the capitalist class would supply its own gravediggers: 'Counterattack' backs up Lenin's prophesy by citing the case of two men named as Communists by witnesses in government probes—William Pomerance and David Hilberman—who own a film firm (Tempo Productions) producing TV commercials. . . . The firm makes $250,000 a year off the earnings of you good Americans. Disgusting."[9]*

But O'Brian was not satisfied with just criticizing Communists and Communist sympathizers in his column. One evening around midnight he and his wife met Winchell, the Broadway gossip columnist for Hearst's Mirror, at the Stork Club and, as they often did, went cruising in Winchell's car for police calls. Around 4:15 a.m., as they drove along East 55th Street, they spotted the broadcaster Barry Gray, whom Winchell labeled "Borey Pink," because he "might have once been a member of the Young Communist League and might have contributed articles to the Daily Worker."[10]

"I'm going to get this sonofabitch," O'Brian boasted, screaming taunts at Gray. Yvonne O'Brian grabbed her husband's coat and momentarily prevented him from pursuing Gray. Realizing his life might be in danger, Gray hopped into his car and sped off at what Winchell called "supersonic speed." Winchell and O'Brian resumed pursuit. They chased Gray in and out of the pillars of the elevated train "like the old movies," O'Brian recalled, but lost him.[11]

O'Brian thought Hollenbeck was a liberal like Gray and worth "getting." Hollenbeck was not a Communist, O'Brian said, just "sympathetic to anything on the left and very antagonistic to anything on the right."[12]

CHAPTER 11

▬

The Obsession with Subversives and Communist Spies

The McCarthy era does not date from 1950, when Joseph McCarthy made his first charges. It dates from 1947, from the joint efforts of Truman, Attorney General Tom Clark, and J. Edgar Hoover.
—Garry Wills, introduction to Lillian Hellman, *Scoundrel Time*

In 1947, when Hollenbeck began *CBS Views the Press*, the nation's obsession with subversives and Communist spies received a big boost from President Harry Truman. Truman signed Executive Order 9835 into law on March 21, 1947, initiating a federal loyalty program. The executive order not only expanded the federal role in combating Communism, but it also became a model for state, local, and private anti-Communism initiatives.

To root out Communists and other subversives the office of Truman's attorney general, Tom Clark, screened current and prospective federal employees. At loyalty hearings the sources of accusations could be kept secret, and accusers could not be cross-examined. Those accused could not confront their accusers unless they agreed to appear. Daniel Lang, a reporter who covered loyalty cases, wrote that proving loyalty could be "as difficult and as embarrassing as proving kindness or patience or any other intangible virtue."[1]

The attorney general's office relied on a list of dozens of organizations designated subversive, primarily the Communist Party and its "fronts." But other organizations deemed sympathetic to radical causes also were included. The list legitimized guilt by association. The historian David Caute wrote, "From the outset the list was used to intimidate and morally outlaw the Left, to pillory and ostracize critics of the Truman administration, and to deter potential critics."[2]

Dissent became disloyalty. Attorney General Clark told a congressional subcommittee in 1948 of efforts by the Justice Department "to remove from among us those who believe in a foreign ideology." A national debate focused on whether the American Communist Party should be outlawed. FBI Director J. Edgar Hoover branded the American Communist Party a "fifth column"—a clandestine group of subversives spying for the Soviet Union. Clark worried aloud that for every Communist Party member there were ten fellow travelers "in the shadow ready to fight for the party."[3]

Conservatives in both the Democratic and Republican parties fulminated. The House Committee on Un-American Activities (HUAC), headed by J. Parnell Thomas, a New Jersey Republican, conducted public hearings on Communism in the film industry in 1947. Representative John Rankin, a Democrat from Mississippi who served on the committee, demanded that it investigate "pink professors" who were "trying to indoctrinate our college students with Communistic ideals." Journalists were also suspect. Milton Murray, president of the American Newspaper Guild, testified before a House Labor Committee that Communists had "virtual control" of the New York and Los Angeles Guild locals.[4]

Also in 1947 three former FBI agents—John G. Keenan, Kenneth M. Bierly, and Theodore C. Kirkpatrick—established a weekly, four-page newsletter titled *Counterattack* to expose Communists and other subversives. *Counterattack* focused on radio and other media, labeled its targets "dupes," "stooges," and "appeasers," and used innuendo and inaccuracy as weapons. Helen Rogers Reid, publisher of the *New York Herald Tribune*, inquired about the financial backers of *Counterattack* "because its pages are strangely crowded with misstatements of fact."[5]

Misstatements of fact also appeared in the writings of New York journalists, some of whom saw a Red tide washing over the world in the late 1940s. Hollenbeck's press criticism offered an antidote to the hype and hysteria. He reported on coverage of a medical journal article about three hundred frontal-lobotomy experiments that neutralized anxiety and chronic depression. He called a *Daily News* headline—"Surgeon Claims 'Cure' for Reds"— a phony. Hollenbeck said the article's "tricked-out lead" contributed to distrust of medical reporting. The article began: "A world-renowned brain specialist came up yesterday with a sure way to rid the world of Communists. Make a hole in their heads, but by surgery, not bullets."[6]

Hollenbeck also critiqued coverage of hearings held by the House Committee on Un-American Activities. While the *Times* and the *Herald Tribune* provided the "fairest, most unbiased account" of HUAC hearings on Communism in Hollywood, he said news reports by *PM* and the *Post* were biased against the committee, whereas reports by the *World-Telegram*, *Journal-American*, *Sun*, *News*, and *Mirror* were biased in favor of it. Front-page stories with banner headlines in procommittee papers promised that HUAC would produce great exposés, with Hearst's *Journal-American* declaring: "Evidence will be conclusive." The *Sun* hedged its bet only slightly: "Chairman Thomas indicates new revelations will shock nation." Hollenbeck said, "The story has not lived up to the advance billing."[7]

He also contrasted the extensive coverage given to HUAC hearings about Communism in Hollywood—prompted in part by the testimony of Lauren Bacall, Humphrey Bogart, and other movie stars—to the less prominent coverage given to the report of a presidentially appointed committee on the state of civil liberties in America. While that committee denounced Communism and fascism, Hollenbeck noted, it also spoke to the need to maintain the right to free expression and to avoid "a state of near-hysteria about Communists."[8]

Hollenbeck found the *Herald Tribune*'s coverage of the 1948 political party conventions by the British journalist-novelist Rebecca West, a writer he had previously applauded, to be troublingly warped by her anti-Communism.[9]

West wrote that she could make a good guess about which candidate a convention delegate would support by looking at the delegate's face. While the young, "tall and forthright and healthy" followers of Republican Harold Stassen had "attractive" faces, the "very horrible" young followers of Henry Wallace, the Progressive Party candidate, often "wore on their faces the signs of . . . maladjustment," West wrote. "I never saw so many boys with the sullen eyes and the dropped chins which mean a brain just good enough to grasp the complexities of life and to realize that it would never be able to master them."[10]

West argued that the Progressive Party convention, filled with dead-eyed dimwits, "was Communist-controlled." Hollenbeck suggested that reporters make their assessment of people at least "on the basis of what was said and done." He added, "A careful reporter would hesitate to generalize about the caliber of intelligence behind the facade of a face."[11]

Hollenbeck, not to his credit, did unto West what she had done to the convention delegates—focused on physical appearance. In the process of praising a Stassen delegate as a woman of "happy and hopeful face," West also called her "broad in the beam." Hollenbeck described West as "middle fifties, graying and stout."[12]

Two weeks later *CBS Views the Press* disclosed that West's reporting on the U.S. political conventions for the British press "went further" than her coverage for the *Herald Tribune* and other American papers. West told British readers that Wallace delegates, while they "hated England, they hated America more, and weren't worth much anyway," Hollenbeck reported.[13]

West complained about Hollenbeck's criticism to Doris Stevens, an American friend who was in the habit of feeding West information from HUAC files. West, an FBI informant who corresponded with Director J. Edgar Hoover, asked Stevens, with her HUAC sources, how they could retaliate against Hollenbeck: "Can we put the heat on him?"[14]

Hollenbeck also reported on the paranoia about Communists evident in foreign news coverage. He repeatedly documented the scare tactics used by those who believed war with Russia was inevitable and who sought support for increased funding of the U.S. military.[15] Among Hollenbeck's examples were:

- A "very secret document"—allegedly Moscow's order to German Communists to take over Berlin if relations between Russia and the Western powers worsened—that was reported in the press but later declared a fake
- The *Mirror's* front-page headline for a Drew Pearson story—"U.S. Ship Fired on off Siberia"—that was never corrected, even though the airplanes involved were only dropping identification flares, not firing on the ship
- An AP report that turned out to be false but led to such headlines as "Russians Fire in Berlin Air Lane, Yanks Fly On"
- Stories about "Russia arming for war"—allegedly based on intelligence reports—that proved to be phony and apparently were designed to back President Truman's request for a $1.45 billion arms aid program
- An ominous United Press bulletin reporting that Russian troops had opened fire inside the U.S. section of Berlin. The incident turned out to be about an inebriated Russian Romeo, spurned by an American-sector Juliet and chased by her neighbors. The Russian had shot one of the pursuers in his legs.[16]

Hollenbeck said too much reporting of such incidents was based on unofficial, unverifiable word of mouth and "Don't quote me" sources. He proposed that newspapers and wire services take a National Newspaper Week vow: "When they've been in error they'll say so loud and clear—to assure that the denial catches up with the original error."[17]

But writers at Hearst's *Journal-American* and *Mirror*, who led the anti-Communist attack, continued to foam at the mouth. A *Journal-American* editorial demanded an end to the treasonous Communist Party fifth column in the United States. The *Mirror* columnist Sidney Fields profiled J. B. Matthews, an ardent anti-Communist, who suggested that seventy-five thousand U.S. Communist Party members and 750,000 fellow travelers could act as a potent fifth column in a war with Russia: "Communists are strategically placed in every important industrial plant in America, in every factory from atom bombs to toasters."[18]

Matthews and his fellow anti-Communist watchdogs were equally convinced that Communists and Communist sympathizers were cleverly planted in the news media. In watching the watchdogs Hollenbeck needed to report evenhandedly and to be especially careful not to suggest what he could not know—the guilt or innocence of the person being investigated by the watchdogs.

The case of William Remington, an official in the Department of Commerce, proved the point. In listing journalists' work that he should have "given credit where credit was due," Hollenbeck commended Daniel Lang's "magnificent" ten-thousand-word 1949 article in the *New Yorker* "on the ordeal of William Remington, smeared as disloyal to his country, cleared after agonizing months."[19]

Hollenbeck was not aware that Lang's article, "The Days of Suspicion," relied heavily on information provided by Remington and therefore, as the historian Gary May demonstrated in a 1994 book, "produced an inaccurate account that omitted most of Remington's past."[20]

Remington's story did not end until long after Lang's article and Hollenbeck's mention of it on *CBS Views the Press*. In 1950, despite a Loyalty Review Board's decision in favor of Remington two years earlier, HUAC, the FBI, and a New York grand jury went after Remington.

Remington's ex-wife—May portrayed her as Remington's browbeaten ex-wife—acknowledged that she and Remington had been Communists of a kind. After one of Remington's jury convictions was overturned on appeal, he was convicted of perjury and began serving a three-year prison sentence. On November 22, 1954, two inmates beat him to death. While May declined to label Remington a Soviet agent (a charge made by a KGB-agent-turned-informer and the FBI), the historian concluded that "Remington was no political innocent duped by the Communists, and his conviction for perjury seems justified."[21]

So it was important for Hollenbeck, accused of liberal-left bias, to critique coverage of espionage cases carefully. The accused might be victims of prosecutorial and press misconduct, but they might also be Soviet agents.

Hollenbeck devoted major parts of a half-dozen broadcasts to the controversial cases of Edward U. Condon, Alger Hiss, and Paul Robeson.

Newspaper reports of charges by the Thomas committee against Condon, an expert in quantum mechanics and radioactivity who pioneered nuclear research during the early 1940s, provided a dramatic opportunity to evaluate the press coverage of HUAC's allegations.

Condon had spearheaded a campaign among scientists to place atomic energy under civilian, not military, authority. The McMahon Act, passed in August 1946, put atomic energy under the civilian Atomic Energy Commission.

Two years later the State Department prevented Condon from attending the Soviet Union's celebration of the 220th anniversary of the Russian Academy of Sciences in Moscow by withdrawing his passport at the last minute. Condon, who eventually was named president of the American Physical Society as well as director of the National Bureau of Standards, said: "What is going on? Prominent scientists are denied the privilege of traveling abroad. . . . Let us cast this isolationist, chauvinist poison from our minds before we corrode our hearts."[22]

Other atomic scientists also complained about the Cold War fear that gripped the nation. "Perhaps the greatest impediment to the scientist," warned Hans Bethe, the Manhattan Project's director of theoretical physics and eventually a winner of a Nobel Prize in physics, "is the political climate of the country." Lee A. DuBridge, president of Cal Tech, cautioned against "police-state methods."[23]

Truman's loyalty program made those viewpoints dangerous. The Industrial Employment Review Board started to investigate not only scientists' "subversive activities" but also their "subversive associations." The HUAC's Thomas, bitter that the Atomic Energy Act of 1946 ended military management of nuclear development and ceded it to a civilian Atomic Energy Commission, questioned the loyalty of the commission's five members and of atomic scientists, including Condon. In 1948 Thomas charged that Condon, who had helped draft the Atomic Energy Act, was "one of the weakest links in our atomic security."[24]

The historian Robert K. Carr characterized Thomas's attack on Condon as "a masterpiece of unfair innuendo." Newspapers, some wittingly, some unwittingly, played along with Thomas. Hollenbeck cited the coverage of the *Herald Tribune*, which appeared to link Condon to an extensive Soviet espionage ring operating in the United States. Hollenbeck noted later revelations: The Commerce Department's loyalty review agency had cleared the scientist of any taint of disloyalty, and an important sentence from an FBI report on Condon had been omitted from Thomas's published statement.

"The missing sentence was the assertion by the FBI that in Dr. Condon's reported association with an alleged but unidentified Soviet espionage agent, there was no evidence to show anything illegal or disloyal in Dr. Condon's conduct," Hollenbeck said. "Mr. Thomas' explanation of the missing sentence was interesting: He said first that an investigator had simply failed to copy it from the FBI report—later he said that in the light of the entire FBI report on Dr. Condon, the sentence had no significance anyway."[25]

Toward the end of his broadcast about the coverage of Condon, Hollenbeck moved from describing the specific smear techniques of certain papers to stating the real danger. Hysteria and repression as weapons against Communists were self-defeating. "Communists want nothing more than to be lumped with freedom-loving non-Communists," Hollenbeck said. "This simply makes it easier for them to conceal their true nature, and to allege that the term 'Communist' is meaningless. . . . At the same time, we cannot let abuses deter us from the legitimate exposing of real Communists."[26]

Hollenbeck concluded by saying, "This reporter is very much aware of the full force of these words. As spokesman for 'CBS View the Press,' he has had to take the clothes-brush now and then to some Red smears as well as to some from the other direction. 'CBS Views the Press' has done and is doing its level best to keep a level head in a slanted world."[27]

Counterattack had smeared Hollenbeck less than three weeks earlier, using the same techniques that he examined in his *CBS Views the Press* broadcasts. *Counterattack* said: "The Communists love Don Hollenbeck."[28] As proof, *Counterattck* noted that the *Daily Worker*, the Communist Party newspaper, praised *CBS Views the Press*. *Counterattack* argued that praise by the Communist Party newspaper of Hollenbeck's program meant that he must be pro-Communist.

The newsletter also characterized Hollenbeck as snake-in-the-grass sneaky: His program employed "a strategy of indirection" and "use of camouflage," and he was "adept in innuendo." *Counterattack* called on CBS officials to "look into the matter, take corrective action, for the sake of the public, the press and radio."[29]

Hollenbeck devoted major parts of three broadcasts to coverage of the case of the liberal icon Alger Hiss, president of the Carnegie Endowment for International Peace and a former State Department official. Whittaker Chambers, a senior editor at *Time*, had accused Hiss of passing government secrets to the Soviets.

Hollenbeck avoided portraying Hiss as a wronged innocent. Other press critics were not as careful. A. J. Liebling depicted Hiss as a lamb being led to journalistic slaughter—trial by newspaper. The historian Allen Weinstein, author of *Perjury: The Hiss-Chambers Case* (1978), said Liebling was "an adviser and tipster for Hiss's lawyers." Weinstein felt that Liebling's role raised the question of whether he had "abandoned his normal role of recording events for his column on 'the press' for an advocate's position in the case."[30]

Hiss himself said, "The difference was that Joe [Liebling] was a personal friend and didn't try to hide it, whereas Hollenbeck was very definitely being an objective reporter. I never actually met him. But I respected him. He was, if not unique, certainly extremely unusual in his objectivity and his fairness . . . and courage. It took courage to be fair then."[31]

Hollenbeck's sense of fairness played a role in his decision to ask Wershba, then a CBS correspondent in Washington, to contact Bert Andrews of the *Herald Tribune*, an expert on Hiss-Chambers. Andrews told Wershba, "Look, you better tell Don, 'Be careful with this thing. There's a lot that Chambers knows about Hiss.'" Wershba recalled, "That was the first time I had heard somebody in authority as a reporter say that the people who think Chambers is full of shit have got some big surprises in store for them."[32]

Hollenbeck and his coverage of the reporting of Hiss-Chambers did not take sides on Hiss's guilt or innocence. The writer Charles Gussman recalled, "I've often asked myself if Don, by the subtlest shade of anything he ever said to me, ever betrayed a current or regretted past affinity for the Communist Party. The answer then and now is firmly No." One specific recollection, Gussman said, involved Hiss: "Don believed Hiss to have been guilty. Most [Communist] Party members of the time, in and out of the closet, publicly declared otherwise."[33]

After Hiss's first perjury trial in 1949, Hollenbeck said, "It's a good thing the jury of ten men and two women weren't obliged to reach their decision on the basis of what they read in the newspapers, because if they had, an already complex case would have been rendered downright incomprehensible to them." Hollenbeck reviewed articles and headlines for balance and fairness. The headlines in the *Herald Tribune*, *Times*, *News*, and *Mirror* appeared contradictory: "You might not think it was practically the same story all these headlines were advertising."[34]

Hollenbeck then focused on a lead paragraph in the *Journal-American*: "The government ended its cross-examination of Alger Hiss at 3:01 p.m. today after forcing him to admit he was an associate of Mrs. Carol King, prominent legal defender of Communists, and a friend of Nathan Witt, ex–New Deal lawyer who was fired because of his Communist activities."

Hollenbeck compared the *Journal-American*'s lead with the transcript: "'Question: Did you know Mrs. Carol King at the time? Answer: I think I met her once or twice during that period. Question: So I think your answer is that you knew her? Answer: I said I think I met her once or twice; that is my answer. Question: Was Nathan Witt one of the people in the association? Answer: I'm not sure whether he was or not. If so, that's how I met him. If not, I met him later while I was with the Department of Agriculture.' Now that question and answer transcript adds up to something rather different than what the *Journal-American* made of it in the opening paragraph of its story."[35]

Hollenbeck reported on guilt-by-association writing, including the comment by the *Journal-American* columnist Westbrook Pegler: "Although of course there is no charge of perjury against Mrs. [Eleanor] Roosevelt in the Hiss case, she is co-defendant in a figurative sense because Hiss is a protégé of Felix Frankfurter who has been a power behind the throne ever since the New Deal began." Hollenbeck advocated balance and "enough background or explanatory material to provide fair perspective."[36]

Hollenbeck also used humor in his criticism of Pegler. The *Journal-American* columnist wrote regularly about Mr. and Mrs. George Spelvin, fictional average Americans who expressed Pegler's anti-Roosevelt, country-club views. For a 1948 broadcast Hollenbeck created another set of fictional characters, Mr. and Mrs. George Spavin. He played George Spavin; the actor Julie Bennett played Mary Spavin. Responding with great innocence to Pegler's attack on Bert Andrews, the *Herald Tribune*'s Pulitzer Prize–winning reporter, Mary Spavin said to George Spavin, "Golly, I guess old Peg is just about the last *honest* reporter in America, isn't he?"[37]

Hollenbeck devoted an entire broadcast in 1949 to newspapers' role in perhaps the most dramatic physical confrontation of the domestic Cold

War, which was memorialized in the E. L. Doctorow novel *The Book of Daniel* and the Pete Seeger/Lee Hays song "Hold the Line."

Paul Robeson had scheduled a concert near Peekskill, New York, for August 27, 1949.[38] Until 1947 U.S. labor unions had treated Robeson, the legendary black athlete, lawyer, actor, civil rights activist, and singer, as a champion of the working person. They had honored him with life memberships and invited him to march on their picket lines and perform at their national conventions.

But, by the end of the 1940s, President Truman's loyalty oath, his Cold War foreign policy, and the pressure on labor unions to expel radicals made Robeson's militant unionism unacceptable. His recording contracts and eighty of his U.S. concerts were canceled. So he toured in Europe and lobbed verbal hand grenades toward home.

He said he would testify upon his return in support of Communist leaders on trial in New York City. He criticized U.S. government racism, labeled President Truman's Point Four Program for colonial development a "new imperialist slavery" for Africans, and expressed his support for the Soviet Union, where people had welcomed him warmly, beginning with his first visit in 1934.[39]

He also was quoted (Robeson and his biographer Martin B. Duberman insisted inaccurately) as saying to the April 1949 Congress of the World Partisans of Peace in Paris that the colonial people denounced the U.S. government's policy, "which is similar to that of Hitler and Goebbels. . . . It is unthinkable that American Negroes could go to war on behalf of those who have oppressed them for generations, against a country [the Soviet Union] which in one generation has raised our people to full human dignity."[40]

The announcement that Robeson would give a benefit concert near Peekskill for the Harlem chapter of the Civil Rights Congress provoked outrage from local veterans groups and the Peekskill Junior Chamber of Commerce. A front-page story in the *Peekskill Evening Star* emphasized that the benefit was sponsored by People's Artists, Inc., which had been tagged as subversive by the California Committee on Un-American Activities, and would aid an organization labeled a Communist front by former attorney general Tom Clark.[41]

An *Evening Star* editorial attacked Robeson's political views and the sponsorship of his concert by an un-American political group. A letter to the editor from the commander of the local American Legion post intimated that violence was acceptable. The Junior Chamber of Commerce called the concert "Un-American" and requested group action to "discourage" it.[42]

Veterans' groups and their allies blocked the roads leading to the concert grounds. Protesters checked each car, dragging out some occupants. Jeering crowds shouted, "Dirty Commie!" and "Dirty kike!" The police arrested no members of the mob. Realizing the danger, the driver of the car carrying Robeson backed out of a line of automobiles and drove Robeson to safety. Robeson returned to New York City. At a Harlem press conference he described the rioting as "an attack on the whole Negro people" and called for a Justice Department investigation.[43]

Hollenbeck reviewed the news reports and editorials published after the riot. New York City papers exhibited little editorial leadership. The *Daily News* and the *Mirror* suggested that Robeson had been asking for trouble. The rioting veterans were not to blame for the nine people hurt. Only the *Times*, Hollenbeck said, had separated Robeson's political ideas, however misguided, from his right to sing. The *Times* concluded: "Lamenting the twisted thinking that is ruining Paul Robeson's great career, we defend his right to carry his art to whatever peaceably assembled groups of people he wishes. That is the American way."[44]

As for the news reports in New York City papers, Hollenbeck said that, given the riot, the Peekskill correspondents of most of the papers "did an extremely good job." But the *World-Telegram* concentrated on getting its story from anti-Robeson sources, and the *Compass*—the dying successor to *PM*—from pro-Robeson sources. The *Compass* turned the *World-Telegram*'s report upside down, Hollenbeck said, comparing the Peekskill violence to the Nazi violence in Europe: "The budding storm-troopers of Peekskill and surrounding Westchester County," reported the *Compass*, "... staged a Munich-style putsch at Lakeland Acres Saturday night, complete with such native American-Fascist touches as blazing Ku Klux Klan crosses."[45]

Hollenbeck concluded, "In a story involving as much political tinder as the Paul Robeson concert story did, . . . objectivity seems almost impossible. But, alas, objectivity rather seems to be going out of fashion these days, so perhaps it's only a sign of the times."[46]

As the Cold War heated up and the need for cool-headed, evenhanded press criticism increased, CBS suddenly announced that Hollenbeck was no longer to lead *CBS Views the Press*. On February 4, 1950, he made his last broadcast.

Five days later Senator Joseph R. McCarthy warned in a speech at Wheeling, West Virginia, that there was "a list of names" of Communist Party members—accounts varied on McCarthy's number of Communists, 57, 81, 205, 207, or 208—still shaping policy in the State Department.[47] In the following days McCarthy offered the American public equally exciting charges about even more security risks and card-carrying Communists. He was rewarded with front-page newspaper headlines that were to continue for more than four years.

The reasons for Hollenbeck's departure from *CBS Views the Press* are not altogether clear. Frank Stanton, then president of CBS, insisted that the network's top management never buckled or sought to remove Hollenbeck from *CBS Views the Press*. But the CBS newswriter Jack Walters said Hollenbeck's removal was part of "a CBS executive decision to bow to outside pressures. That was quite common knowledge at the time; Murrow knew it, discussed it, and lamented over it, and there was absolutely no doubt about it in anyone's mind."[48]

Even if subjects of Hollenbeck's criticism did not pressure CBS directly, people appeared willing to apply pressure indirectly, by complaining to the FBI. For years the bureau had been compiling a "security index" of suspect Americans and leaking information and innuendo about potentially dangerous individuals. The FBI, based on its past behavior, might be expected to share its file on Hollenbeck with CBS and anti-Communist friends of the bureau. In late 1949, about six months before Hollenbeck's departure from *CBS Views the Press*, the FBI was advised by "a confidential informant of unknown reliability" that Hollenbeck had admitted to the informant he was a Communist Party member.[49] (Before making its Hollenbeck file available to me, the FBI deleted the informant's name.) The informant also claimed that a Communist Party member had hired Hollenbeck to be a radio announcer.

In response the FBI conducted what it called a discreet investigation of Hollenbeck in 1950. The investigation report rehashed the bureau's favorable report about Hollenbeck from 1942, when he sought an Office of War Information job, quoted from the *Daily Worker* and other Communist or allegedly Communist-influenced publications that praised Hollenbeck's *CBS Views the Press*, and interviewed eleven confidential informants in New York. Despite the charge of the accuser of "unknown reliability," the bureau concluded in May 1950, after interviewing all of the confidential informants, that there was "no other indication subject a CP member."[50]

In its report the FBI chose to highlight a *PM* article that Hollenbeck had written in 1942 about the House Special Committee on Un-American Activities, chaired by Representative Martin Dies Jr. of Texas. In 1942 Washington reporters had reacted with contempt to the committee's grandstanding. The commentator Raymond Clapper had said reporters considered the Dies committee "90 per cent hogwash."[51]

Hollenbeck's article, illustrated by a John Piorotti cartoon of a blind-folded Dies picking names from *Who's Who*, mischievously questioned the Dies committee's work. The committee, Hollenbeck wrote, listed organizations as "Communist fronts" without presenting evidence and then smeared their members. After reviewing the organizations' membership lists, Hollenbeck wrote that Dies could just as easily have imputed Communist ties to other members of the organizations that his committee listed as "Communist fronts"—New York City mayor Fiorello La Guardia; Thomas E. Dewey; Helen Keller; Mrs. James Roosevelt, mother of FDR; Supreme Court justices; and other "monuments of conservatism and respectability."[52]

Hollenbeck, for the record, said his departure from *CBS Views the Press* was caused by "an increase of work [that] makes it impossible to do full justice to a program which requires as much concentrated effort as this one does." He talked about taking a break; he recalled fondly a three-week vacation the previous summer on Martha's Vineyard where the local paper, the *Vineyard Gazette*, "comes out once a week and never gets excited."[53]

But he kept working. He continued to play at-the-scene reporter for re-creations of historical events on *You Are There*, including a parody version for the retirement of two staffers in which "Hollenbeck" fought his way through a mob of radio actors shouting for an audition: "Make way, this is a microphone, let me through please . . . goddamnit." Another reporter in the parody described the accidental electrocution of "Hollenbeck" by the actors, who had never gotten close enough to a real microphone to recognize one: "They plugged him in! . . . May he rest in peace."[54]

Hollenbeck began participating in the *Hear It Now* broadcasts of Murrow and Fred Friendly. Hollenbeck also started planning *We Take Your Word*, a radio panel show about the meaning of words. As emcee for *We Take Your Word*, Hollenbeck moderated a program that *Variety* described as "erudite, but with an informal air far removed from the stuffiness of a classroom. In fact, it had as many laughs as some comedy stanzas."[55] During the first show on January 29, 1950, Hollenbeck pitched words—for instance, *gardenia*—to a panel consisting of the comic Abe Burrows, the scholar Lyman Bryson, and the actor Faye Emerson, who was wearing a gardenia.

Listeners learned that gardenias are named for a Dr. Alexander Garden, an eighteenth-century Scottish physician and botanist who first saw the shrub in South Carolina in 1765. The program closed with Hollenbeck saying goodbye. A deep voice of authority, heard regularly on the program, interjected, "Short for 'God be with you.' "[56]

Don Hollenbeck, an amateur photographer who especially enjoyed shooting pictures of his daughter, Zoë, vacations on Martha's Vineyard with his beloved Rolleiflex.

Courtesy Anne Hollenbeck.

Not all critics praised the program. The *World-Telegram*'s Harriet Van Horne applauded Hollenbeck's low, easy voice: "It bespeaks a quiet, firm man." But she accused him of pomposity. Less than two weeks later *Variety* reported that CBS had invited John K. M. McCaffrey, editor, radio commentator, and former English professor, to replace Hollenbeck as emcee. CBS hoped McCaffrey's personality would make the program a commercial success. McCaffrey debuted in the program's third week. The move, *Variety* said, "left Hollenbeck doing a slow burn, especially since Doug Edwards has already moved in on the '[CBS Views the] Press' program."[57]

Edwards's selection to replace Hollenbeck symbolized significant change at CBS. Hollenbeck's *CBS Views the Press* might win prestigious journalism prizes, including a George Foster Peabody Award and in 1950 the first George Polk Award for radio reporting. But bottom-line values were invading CBS—arguably broadcast journalism's setter of standards. CBS cut the original reporting team for *CBS Views the Press* in half. James Burke, a radio-television writer and editor without a background in newspapers, succeeded Wershba and Scott.

Edwards's selection also represented the replacement of a journalist whom Murrow rated first class by one he rated second class. Murrow and his "boys"—Charles Collingwood, Eric Sevareid, Richard Hottelet, and other correspondents who had served with Murrow in Europe—patronized Edwards. Murrow refused to permit Edwards to participate in the year-end roundup that featured CBS's top correspondents, because, said Sig Mickelson, who was president of CBS News from 1954 to 1961, "he felt Doug was unable to perform with the Hottelets and Collingwoods of the world."[58]

As a newsreader, Edwards was a model of proper pronunciation—a conscientious announcer who would look up any unfamiliar word. "I've been in small stations and heard broadcasters talking shop," wrote the CBS news executive Paul W. White. "'I *know* it's 'in-ex'pli-ca-ble,' one will state categorically. 'That's the way Doug Edwards says it.'"[59] But Edwards, the superb newsreader, failed as thoughtful news reporter, investigator, and writer.

He stood for the new medium of commercial television—less news, more show business. His noon newscast was bait to attract listeners to *Wendy Warren*, a soap opera about a fictitious reporter for the *Manhattan Gazette*. After delivering three minutes of news Edwards would ask the actor Florence Freeman, who played Warren, "Now, Wendy, what's the news today for the ladies?" Freeman would deliver a minute of "news reports from the women's world."[60] Then, after a commercial from Maxwell House Coffee or Jell-O, Freeman would move from the news control booth into the soap-opera world of Wendy Warren's two lovers and manipulative, malevolent competitor Nona Marsh.

Edwards represented a certain kind of success in broadcasting—as primarily an announcer. He rose from being a fifteen-year-old part-time announcer for radio station WHET in Troy, Alabama, to network anchor in New York for CBS's evening television news broadcast. In between he announced for radio stations in the South, then headed north to WXYZ in Detroit at the age of twenty-one. There he announced dance band remotes, special events, and news, along with another future CBS correspondent, Mike—then Myron—Wallace.

Wallace, who became a CBS News correspondent in 1963, and Edwards were "Cunningham News Aces" at WXYZ in 1940–41. They appeared on a five-minute newscast sponsored by Cunningham, a Detroit drugstore chain. Sixty-five years later Wallace made a loud "Rrrrr," recalling how the newscast began with the sound of a P-38 Lightning fighter plane at full throttle, after which the announcer would proclaim, in an appropriately stentorian tone, "The Cunningham News Ace is on the air!" Wallace said *CBS Views the Press* was "not made to order for him [Edwards] by any means." Edwards was not willing to risk trouble with CBS and the New York press in pursuit of the truth. "He was," Wallace said, "no trouble."[61]

Edwards moved to CBS in New York on December 1, 1942, to take a non-news announcer's job. Eventually, after briefly serving as a correspondent in Europe during 1945–46, he became the symbol of television news at CBS, anchoring *Douglas Edwards with the News*, which gave him public recognition and a reputation. "They wanted to put someone on there [*CBS Views the Press*] who had a reputation, who was known," Burke said.[62]

But Burke intimated that Edwards's visibility as a television announcer did not contradict the evidence that at least one CBS executive—Edmund A. Chester—was trying to eviscerate *CBS Views the Press*. In September 1947 Murrow had stepped down as vice president in charge of news to do what he really wanted to do—broadcast again. That left news management in the hands of people, Ed Scott said, "who wanted to gut the show. There was pressure after Murrow left."[63]

Chester had a reputation at CBS as a sweet-talking manager, not as a journalist. As the Spanish-speaking director of CBS's shortwave broadcasting operation in 1940, Chester had toured Central and South America with CBS chairman William S. Paley, helping acquire contracts for CBS with sixty-four radio stations.[64] After the merger of CBS's radio and television news divisions in 1949, Chester, then director of news, special events, and sports for CBS television, was elevated to news director for both radio and television. T. Wells Church, who had been news director for CBS Radio, was relegated to being Chester's assistant.[65]

Church had enthusiastically supported creating a radio review of the press. Chester did not share that enthusiasm. "They were as different as day and night," said the CBS news anchor Dallas Townsend. "Church was a good newsman. Chester wasn't basically interested in news. He was a flack, a PR type. As soon as [Cuban President Rubén Fulgencio] Batista regained power [in a coup d'état in 1952], Chester quit CBS and went down there." He wrote a hagiography of Batista that one expert dismissed as propaganda—"a pro-Batista public relations romp." Chester, a twenty-year friend of Batista's, described the dictator as "an exceptionally nice fellow" and "a great American statesman"—"the first dictator who takes his inspiration from the Bible and from Abraham Lincoln."[66]

Now that he was in charge of *CBS Views the Press*, Chester told Burke, the program's writer, to "'featurize' rather than criticize." Chester realized that the criticism of Hollenbeck's *CBS Views the Press* was controversial at a time when the network was attempting to avoid controversy. Americans feared Communism. CBS wanted to assuage that fear.[67]

In Edwards's earliest *CBS Views the Press* broadcasts—from February 11, 1950, through the end of March 1950—the trappings of Hollenbeck tradition continued. Edwards reported on press coverage of Senator McCarthy's probe of Communism in the State Department. Following the sentencing of Alger Hiss to the maximum of five years for perjury, Edwards also covered newspapers' reaction to the controversial statement by Secretary of State Dean Acheson that he did not "intend to turn my back on Alger Hiss."[68]

But Chester made clear to Edwards and Burke that they were not to continue discussing such controversial subjects. "I got that from Chester, who used to read my scripts himself," Burke said. "Chester would take whole chunks out. It got so that I knew what he would leave out so I didn't put things in."[69]

Edwards resorted to what he called "constructive criticism," with the stress on *constructive*. The program contained virtually no criticism and little original reporting, especially from the scene. Edwards, who commuted two and a half hours a day between his home in New Canaan, Connecticut, and New York, appeared less knowledgeable about the city's press than Hollenbeck, who lived in Manhattan. Edwards rehashed articles and speeches about journalism, featured softball interviews with CBS correspondents, and offered frequent congratulations to journalism prize winners, media celebrating anniversaries, and the *New York Times* for "aiding Princeton University to publish the papers of Thomas Jefferson."[70]

Hollenbeck's program, by contrast, was the work of a brave iconoclast. The news commentator Ned Calmer said, "Don was very courageous in expressing his views on all the issues at a time when everybody was frightened." Hollenbeck reported on the efforts of the American Medical Association to scuttle a national compulsory health insurance plan by purchasing ads in newspapers to influence the editorial positions of those newspapers.

His report led Clem Whitaker, an executive at the AMA's public relations firm, to cancel all radio time contracted with CBS. Whitaker also told CBS that, as *Editor and Publisher* reported, "no further time would be sought by any Whitaker & Baxter accounts until Mr. Hollenbeck's statement had been retracted." Hollenbeck did not retract his statement.[71]

George Herman recalled reporting for *CBS Views the Press* about "a tavern which, anachronistically, was selling five-cent beer and was being cut off by its beer companies. I pointed out that the *New York Times* story had every detail—names, ages, addresses of all persons, everything except the names of the beer companies cutting off the supply." Herman investigated. He learned the companies' names. "One of them called CBS and started putting on a little pressure about canceling their sponsorship of the baseball games," Herman said. Hollenbeck and the CBS news department refused to buckle. "We did the story and listed the names of the beer companies that the *Times* did not see fit to print," Herman said. "The beer company did not cancel."[72]

Hollenbeck's courage was perhaps best exhibited in July 1947. He questioned a banner-headline story in the *Sun*: "Secret A-Bomb Files Are Stolen from Oak Ridge."

He said the *Sun*'s article was unusually vague: It gave no dates, no names, and few details for a story of such significance. It said only that unknown agents—presumably unknown Communist agents—had filched files of top-secret data about the atom bomb from atomic energy facilities at Oak Ridge, Tennessee.

The *Sun*'s story about the theft of secret A-bomb data brought denials from President Truman and Senator Bourke B. Hickenlooper, chair of the Joint Committee on Atomic Energy. Hollenbeck said the *Sun* reporter disclosed that some of his information came from Parnell Thomas, the HUAC chair, a curious coincidence of timing.[73]

The day before publication of the *Sun*'s article, the congressional atomic energy committee had considered five bills that would have abolished civilian control of atomic energy. One of the bills, strongly supported by Thomas, had called for military control of Oak Ridge and other atomic energy facilities. The story in the *Sun* seemed to support such a shift in control. In the second paragraph the reporter noted that the disclosure of the theft of atomic secrets was expected to lead to a new command for the nation's atomic energy.

Hollenbeck reported the views of Keats Speed, the *Sun*'s executive editor. "We know the [theft] story is true," Speed said. "We . . . will stick by the story from beginning to end." But Hollenbeck also conveyed his doubts about the story. For him to criticize the *Sun*'s reporting was to invite attacks from the *Sun*'s management—as well as concern from CBS's management—and to perhaps endanger the life of *CBS Views the Press*. "We were always very, very careful," said Wershba. "But we did have the right to be critical and we were that." [74]

Hollenbeck's broadcast incensed the *Sun*'s management, which demanded time on the next program for rebuttal. Murrow, vice president in charge of news, at first wanted to turn over the whole broadcast to the *Sun*. But Hollenbeck felt the entire program should not be sacrificed to a rebuttal. Murrow insisted. Hollenbeck became despondent. He told Anne that night, "Oh, well, the hell with it," as if to write an end to his involvement with the program and CBS. She looked at him pleadingly, "Don, we're running out of networks." [75]

Wershba tried to convince Murrow that Hollenbeck was right about responding briefly to the *Sun*'s rebuttal. "Ed was very big on fair broadcasts, equal time, and the right of reply—'What right do we have to use the full power of the network to go against one guy?'—so later he was eager to give McCarthy time to reply. . . . I touched Ed where it hurt," Wershba recalled. "I said, 'This is typical Goebbels, a Joseph Goebbels trick, to demand full time. The *New York Times* wouldn't give them the whole issue. Give him fourteen minutes, but we have the right of the thirty seconds at the end to rebut.'" [76]

Murrow finally capitulated to Hollenbeck and Wershba. Colonel Gilbert T. Hodges, chair of the *Sun*'s executive committee, spent the first fourteen minutes of the next week's broadcast reading a prepared statement. "If you see it in the *Sun*, it's so," Hodges said. He closed with a bit of Communist name-calling directed at Hollenbeck: "You are an alumnus of the newspaper *PM* as is your assistant Edmund Scott, who helped prepare the outburst against the *Sun*. Far be it from me to imply that the *PM* newspaper has any Socialistic or Communistic leanings. It claims, I think, to be an independent paper following the liberal line." [77]

Hodges said Hollenbeck, whose "affection for *PM* continues strong," was a liberal who followed "the party line which such liberals invariably pursue," implying that the party line Hollenbeck followed was the Communist Party line. [78]

Hollenbeck responded concisely. First, he said, Colonel Hodges had presented nothing substantially new. *CBS Views the Press* had previously told the *Sun*'s story "from all points, including its own," Hollenbeck said.

Second, Hollenbeck asked, if President Truman's and Senator Hickenlooper's denial of the *Sun*'s story were true, what purpose was served by the *Sun*'s article, "except to rub nerves already raw, to worsen relations with Russia already bad enough"?

Third, in the polite patois of journalism, where liars are rarely called liars, Hollenbeck said Colonel Hodges's insinuation that Scott and he were Communists was "a gross disservice to the interests of the truth."

Hollenbeck concluded by suggesting that if you saw it in the *Sun*, it wasn't necessarily so: "The *Sun*, a week ago Thursday, quoted David Lilienthal, chairman of the Atomic Energy Commission, as having said, 'Nothing of importance has been taken from Oak Ridge.' Colonel Hodges stressed that same point tonight. The fact is, Mr. Lilienthal has told CBS that he made no such statement."[79]

As the program ended, Colonel Hodges got up slowly to leave Studio 9, the seventeenth-floor studio at 485 Madison Avenue from which *CBS Views the Press* was broadcast. "I don't know who let me in for this," Hodges said. "I'm going to find out." Wershba later said, "We cut his balls off."[80]

That broadcast well could have left CBS executives yearning for three years to replace Hollenbeck with someone who was less of a lightning rod, someone like Edwards. A change was difficult to make in the early years of Hollenbeck's *CBS Views the Press*; the program kept winning top journalism awards; Murrow had pushed Stanton not to kill the program. But Jack Gould of the *New York Times* recalled years later that the *Sun*, for one, "according to well-founded reports at the time," threatened to stop publishing its daily schedule of radio programs in retaliation for Hollenbeck's critique of the *Sun*'s coverage.[81]

Whatever Edwards's abilities, his version of *CBS Views the Press* failed. A *Variety* review concluded that his "bloodless" broadcasts missed "any critical insight." A *New Republic* review a month after Edwards took over said he lacked Hollenbeck's "trenchant judgments, his convictions that a newspaper should reflect society's needs, his ability to bite with loving care or caress with a kick." Edwards provided only what another reviewer called "a mere rehash of some of the activities of the New York press—the less significant activities at that."[82]

In June 1950, CBS announced that Edwards's *CBS Views the Press* would disappear for the summer, to be replaced by *Correspondents' Scratchpad*, a program of voice-recorded interviews by top CBS correspondents worldwide that Hollenbeck would pull together. The irony of Hollenbeck's replacing *CBS Views the Press* was not lost on *Variety*, the trade newspaper. *Variety* said that once "CBS yanked Don Hollenbeck" from *CBS Views the*

Press, "the program went into a decline from which it never recovered. But CBS stood pat in keeping Hollenbeck off the show."[83]

At the end of the summer Edwards returned for another season of *CBS Views the Press.* But *CBS Views the Press* without Hollenbeck was not *CBS Views the Press.* Edwards understood. "We went all out—Jim Burke and I— but we had a hard act to follow," he said. In "Myopia at CBS," an editorial for a New York University student newspaper, one writer criticized the shallowness that allowed Edwards to say things like "Ah me, there's only one Winchell." The writer concluded, "Yes, and there's only one Hollenbeck."[84]

In June 1951—a little more than a year after Edwards replaced Hollenbeck—*CBS Views the Press* quietly died. One question remained: Did the powerful Hearst Corporation, owner of two New York papers that had been subjected to some of Hollenbeck's toughest criticism, play a role in ending his version of *CBS Views the Press*?

CHAPTER 12

█████

Jack O'Brian:
Traveling with the Conservative,
Anti-Commie Crowd

Hearst columnist Jack O'Brian called himself a political independent with "no affiliation." But he traveled in a circle of conservative, anti-Communist, pro–J. Edgar Hoover and Joe McCarthy New Yorkers. The American Jewish League Against Communism, headed by Roy M. Cohn, a young lawyer who had served as chief counsel to McCarthy's Permanent Subcommittee on Investigations, awarded its first George E. Sokolsky Awards to O'Brian and Francis Cardinal Spellman. Sokolsky, Hearst's far-right syndicated columnist, had gotten Cohn, then only twenty-five, the highly visible position with McCarthy. Spellman had defended McCarthy's investigations. "No American uncontaminated by Communism has lost his good name because of congressional hearings on un-American activities," Spellman said.[1]

O'Brian's service to McCarthy, Cohn, and Hoover took many forms over many years. In his Journal-American *column O'Brian championed all three avid anti-Communists. When Cohn appeared on television, O'Brian described his friend as "articulate, poised, informed, brilliant and even humble"—not all virtues usually associated with McCarthy's mouthpiece. Before Cohn's disbarment, O'Brian testified as a character witness at Cohn's 1964 retrial in federal court on perjury and obstruction of justice charges (O'Brian acknowledged, under questioning from an assistant U.S. attorney, that he and his wife had a financial interest with Cohn in a private hospital in Nevada and in other businesses).*[2]

More surprising, perhaps, a lawyer associated with Cohn recalled that O'Brian allowed an item of questionable ethics and accuracy in his column. The item suggested that Cohn (who was gay and died of AIDS in 1986) was heterosexual: "Something like, 'Rumors are circulating that Roy Cohn may be

Roy M. Cohn (left), head of the American Jewish League Against Communism and former chief counsel to Senator Joseph McCarthy's Permanent Subcommittee on Investigations, awards one of the league's first two George E. Sokolsky Awards to Jack O'Brian (right), as Paul Schoenstein, managing editor of the *Journal-American,* holds the plaque. The black crop marks on the photo indicate that the *Journal-American* published the picture without Cohn in it.

Courtesy Harry Ransom Humanities Research Center, University of Texas at Austin.

tying the knot with So-and-so.' Miss So-and-so would be calling the office to talk to him [Cohn] because she didn't know anything about it. He'd dodge her. His secretary would say, 'So-and-so is calling. She's called four times this morning. She wants to know about the Jack O'Brian column.'" Cohn would say, "'Tell her I'll talk to her tomorrow. I gotta run.' And it was he who planted the item!"[3]

O'Brian's relationship with Hoover and the FBI was warm and rewarding. It continued well into the 1960s. As a fan of Hoover's and a personal friend of FBI agents' since Buffalo, O'Brian gave his private home telephone number to FBI officials in New York City.[4] The columnist made the FBI's Special Correspondents' List. O'Brian put items in his column that applauded the alarmist anti-Communism of Hoover.

After O'Brian warned in a Journal-American *column that a few actors, writers, and directors sympathetic to Communism were assuming strategic positions in the television industry in 1960, Hoover thanked O'Brian, who wrote back: "Anything I can do to step on the Communists, be assured I will do."[5] In other columns O'Brian defended Hoover and the bureau's television series,* The FBI, *against critics. A 1965 "Dear Jack" letter from Hoover accompanied an autographed copy of his* A Study of Communism.[6]

When O'Brian vacationed in England and Italy (where he kept a villa near Rome for many years), Hoover had legal attachés in London and Rome meet O'Brian and "extend courtesies and assistance where possible." They gave O'Brian the names of a London doctor to vaccinate one of his daughters and a Rome dentist to repair his bridgework. The columnist fawned in return. He said he was "an ardent admirer of the Director" and, an attaché dutifully reported, "praised highly the smooth working relations he enjoyed with Assistant Director John F. Malone and the agents of the New York Office" in the fight against subversives and spies.[7]

But O'Brian's idol was McCarthy, whom the columnist even resembled in several respects. Both celebrated their Irish Catholic roots, though O'Brian insisted he was far from devout. Both were working class and hardworking. Both were early dropouts from school (though McCarthy would return). Both were talkers and what O'Brian called "tipplers."[8]

O'Brian was only too happy to use his column to tout the senator's efforts to keep the nation safe from Communism. McCarthy's projected "delicate" probe of the Federal Communications Commission "won't be so delicate," O'Brian promised readers. McCarthy deserved the nation's thanks. O'Brian ended one column by applauding a reader who wrote that McCarthy "alerted us to the most fearsome menace in modern history—the Reds scheming against us, from inside the government."[9]

The snooping by McCarthy's Senate committee and other congressional investigations revealed "pinkos" and "pro-Commies," not as idealistic "starry-eyed dopes" but as "sly and superior-sounding wise-guy[s]," O'Brian said. "It's a good time to chase the irritation out of the public's eyes and ears for good." A critic of "too damn slanted" journalists who failed to applaud McCarthy's anti-Commie crusade earned an O'Brian "Gripe-A-Day" award.[10]

Both O'Brian and McCarthy were also brawling bullies. In verbally assaulting leftists and liberals, they relied more on knee-to-the-groin tactics than on Marquess of Queensberry rules. Following a dinner dance at Washington's Sulgrave Club, McCarthy ended a verbal fracas with Drew Pearson, who had been disparaging McCarthy in his "Washington Merry-Go-Round" column and weekly radio program, by literally kicking Pearson in the groin.[11]

As for O'Brian, Variety's Nat Kahn labeled him a "very vitriolic and hateful" kind of browbeater.[12] Steve Allen, the creator and first host of The Tonight Show, wrote a column for the Village Voice about O'Brian that began, "At least fifty times during the past several years I have heard TV people say 'Something really ought to be done about Jack O'Brian.'"

Allen accused O'Brian of being a cruel, bloodthirsty liar who assumed "the role of neighborhood bully." Allen said O'Brian reveled in attacking "egghead" television and psychiatrists. "The circumstance whereby the individual most in need of psychiatric aid is discovered to be he who denounces it most vigorously is too classic to require further emphasis," Allen said.[13]

An excellent example of the tactics that Allen abhorred was O'Brian's treatment of the actor Howard da Silva. Da Silva was listed in Red Channels and blacklisted after he invoked the Fifth Amendment privilege against self-incrimination before the House Committee on Un-American Activities in 1951. As a result he could find no movie and television work for most of the 1950s. By 1960 Washington investigators had cleared da Silva. He performed at a capital dinner sponsored by the Republican Women's Conference and attended by President Dwight D. Eisenhower and Vice President Richard M. Nixon.

On July 6, 1960, O'Brian recounted da Silva's past and attacked him as a "many-times identified Communist" in a column that invited NBC to disinvite da Silva to host a television program about presidential politics on July 10, the Sunday preceding the opening of the Democratic National Convention. Two days later, in his July 8 column, O'Brian bragged, "The Sunday Gallery 'political' performance of showbiz pinko Howard da Silva all of a sudden won't be on NBC-TV this Sabbath after all."[14]

The New York Times reporter Les Brown would later write: "It was . . . generally understood at the time that the blacklisting activities of the networks had ended several years earlier. Nevertheless, two days after Mr. O'Brian's article appeared, WNBC-TV replaced the program . . . with a political interview conducted by Gabe Pressman. . . . 'The word came down from somewhere—we didn't know from whom—that we were pre-empted; there was no explanation,' said Gordon Hyatt, who conceived and wrote the program."[15]

Apparently, O'Brian's bullying had succeeded again.

CHAPTER 13

The Hearsts Versus Hollenbeck

*If Senator Joe McCarthy was the best-known individual representative of
the post–World War II heresy hunt, its leading media representative was
the Hearst publishing empire.. . . . For Hearst's anti-Communist crusaders,
New York was a headquarters.. . . . The local Hearst papers were the flagship*
Journal-American *and the tabloid* Mirror.. . . . The massive files of J. B. Matthews, Red fronter turned Red hunter, were stored in the Hearst Building.*
—Jim Tuck, McCarthyism and New York's Hearst Press

In criticizing Hearst's New York newspapers, Don Hollenbeck took on two
popular powerhouses. The tabloid *Daily Mirror* had 919,000 circulation,
second largest in the nation to the New York *Daily News's* 2.4 million. The
700,000-circulation *Journal-American*, which Hollenbeck described in 1949
as "the city's most widely circulated evening newspaper [and] of great influence," saw itself as an exceptional metropolitan daily. The publisher, William
Randolph Hearst Jr., who was known as Bill, said no paper covered New York
as well as the *Journal-American* covered the city: "We kicked hell out of every
other paper on a regular basis." The *Journal-American*, he said, made "New
York laugh and cry—but most of all look at itself in the mirror every day."[1]

Hollenbeck's *CBS Views the Press* suggested that the *Journal-American* in the late 1940s was something less than a magnificent mirror to the
city. Judging from his reports, the paper was short on original reporting
and long on made-up news, exaggeration, anti-Communist slanting, and
self-congratulation.

In a 1947 *CBS Views the Press* on the growing number of argumentative letters to the editor in New York newspapers, Hollenbeck said that

the "Hearst way" of selecting and editing letters differed markedly from that of other papers: Almost without exception, the letters selected for publication supported the *Journal-American*'s editorial policies—"anti-Communism, pro-military training, anti-vivisection and so on." Hollenbeck concluded: "Over a recent six-week period, the *Journal-American* printed about fifty letters to the editor; not one of them opposed to Hearst policy."[2]

The Hearst way of reporting political campaigns also was different. During the *CBS Views the Press* years the voice of the *Journal-American* was still that of Bill Hearst's father, William Randolph Hearst, owner of newspapers and magazines with tens of millions of circulation. On March 1, 1948, Hearst's front-page editorial in the *Journal-American* and his other papers called on America to draft General Douglas MacArthur for the presidency. When MacArthur expressed a willingness to run, assuming public support, the euphoric *Journal-American* celebrated on more than half of its front page and in a five-inch-high banner headline.

An AP survey said newspapers nationwide questioned the volume of public support for MacArthur and called him an enigmatic dark-horse candidate at best. But the rhapsodic *Journal-American*, Hollenbeck noted, reported a different reality: "'In a mighty crescendo of popular acclaim which has reached across the nation people in all walks of life and of every political creed have joined the great spontaneous movement to make General Douglas MacArthur the next President of the United States'"[3]

Hollenbeck's treatment of the *Journal-American*'s campaign for MacArthur provoked telephone calls from twenty-one upset "MacArthur for President" fans. An internal CBS memo about the callers to Davidson Taylor, a CBS news executive who would succeed Edward R. Murrow as head of news, said: "Among their comments [about Hollenbeck] were: 'He must be sponsored by the American Veterans' Committee or the Reds,' and 'Just an anti-MacArthur political blast instead of an impartial analysis of press news.'"[4]

CBS Views the Press also caught the *Journal-American* making up news. The paper reported that Mariella Lotti, an Italian film actor and ex-lover of the former king Michael of Rumania (who was about to wed another woman), planned to enter a convent. Hollenbeck dispatched the CBS correspondent Peter Tompkins in Rome to learn the facts and then reported: "(1) Signorina Lotti is engaged in making the movie 'Guarany' for Universalia. (2) She will soon go to Brazil for location shots. (3) She has no plans for entering a convent. (4) She never had a love affair with former King

Michael." Hollenbeck scolded the *Journal-American*: "While the facts may often spoil a good story, outright fiction really ought to be labeled as such."[5]

Hollenbeck also reported on *Journal-American* exaggeration. A front-page headline screamed: "100,000 here to protest pro-Red peace parley." The *Journal-American*'s story was as bold as its headline, promising "one of the greatest picket lines for freedom that New York had ever seen." But only two thousand people showed up, and, Hollenbeck said, "most of those who did were sightseers." The paper's hysteria, Hollenbeck said, gave the event an importance it did not really have and recalled William Randolph Hearst's admonition to staffers decades earlier: "Don't allow exaggeration. It is a cheap and ineffective substitute for real interest."[6]

The pattern of the *Journal-American*'s exaggerations raised the question of when the unwary subscriber might, in Hollenbeck's words, "read something as news that is straight propaganda."[7] The antiunion, anti-Soviet, anti–New Deal agenda of Hearst often turned news into propaganda or a baffling blend of news and propaganda.

The *Journal-American* published the columnists who most enthusiastically applauded McCarthy and attacked Murrow and Hollenbeck. Having sacrificed the role of watchdog for FBI lapdog, Hearst's reporters received derogatory information from the bureau about individuals and organizations and, in return, provided the bureau with anti-Communist rumors and fabrications. Hearst's employees acted as researchers and private investigators for McCarthy.

Hollenbeck reported in 1949 on two examples of the *Journal-American*'s rewriting of the first draft of history as partisan propaganda. Government officials and many newspapers greeted with skepticism the astounding charge by former major G. Racey Jordan that in 1944 the Soviet Union obtained atomic bomb secrets, plans, and uranium through White House orders, not through espionage. Jordan claimed the late Harry Hopkins, who acted as President Roosevelt's unofficial emissary to British prime minister Winston Churchill and the Soviet leader Joseph Stalin, "gave Reds Atom in 1944," to quote a *Journal-American* headline.[8]

Also in 1949 the Associated Press retracted a story that had made banner headlines in the *Journal-American* six years earlier. In 1943 the *Journal-American* had reported that the AP said U.S. troops fighting on Guadalcanal were forced to unload their own supplies because of the refusal by crews of the National Maritime Union (NMU) to work on Sunday. The AP account, although denied, ducked, or debunked by other New York papers, had led the *Journal-American* not only to hype the story on Page

One ("Union Crew on Holiday; Ill Marines Unload Ships") but also to add its own story, which cited Martin Dies Jr., the first chair of the House Un-American Activities Committee: "Dies said Reds Dominated Union."[9]

The NMU had sued AP and the *Journal-American* for libel in 1943. Six years later, as part of a settlement before trial, the NMU received $8,500 from the AP and Hearst and a retraction from the AP. The *Journal-American*, which was not required by the settlement to publish a retraction, printed none. The newspaper also did not publish the AP's retraction. Hollenbeck recalled the Jonathan Swift line, that "falsehood flies and truth comes limping after it."[10]

Bill Hearst could be expected to pay particular attention to Hollenbeck's criticism of the *Journal-American*'s political coverage, especially of its reporting of the 1948 Democratic convention in Philadelphia. Hollenbeck noted that the columnist John O'Donnell of the *Daily News*, a critic of the late President Franklin D. Roosevelt's, blamed the chaos of the Democratic Party on Roosevelt, "whose overweening passion for one-man rule. . . . impelled him to scythe off the head of every Democrat who seemed to threaten even distantly Roosevelt's preeminence on the national scene."[11]

Then Hollenbeck tweaked Bill Hearst: "Mr. Hearst Junior sharpened his pencil, took off for Philadelphia as a reporter, and on Wednesday, two days after John O'Donnell's column appeared in the *News*, he came up with a story placed right smack on the top of page one with a big, black four-column, two-line head which said: 'FDR's "One-Man Rule" Caused Party Chaos.' "[12]

If there was one area of Hollenbeck's reporting on the *Journal-American*'s political coverage most likely to annoy Bill Hearst, it was the examination by *CBS Views the Press* of the anti-Communism in the *Journal-American* and other Hearst newspapers. Anti-Communism was enshrined in the family bible, *The Speeches and Writings of William Randolph Hearst.*

The anti-Communism found expression in reporting that demonized liberals as "anti-anti-Communists"—enemies of those who would protect the United States from Communism. A cartoon in Hearst's *Journal-American* showed "The Soviet Spider," with "Communism" written across its belly, weaving a web of "Liberalism." Editorials that ran in all Hearst newspapers denounced liberal, fellow-traveling pals of Communism. These "weak-willed citizens, including some of the highly educated," had to be exorcised from the media as well as from the government, military, and arts.[13]

Bill Hearst was raised to be respectful, not independent, of his father, the media magnate. The son absorbed his father's values and lifestyle. The senior Hearst, who was fond of saying, "It takes a good mind to resist education," had flunked out of Harvard after three years and discouraged his sons from completing college. Bill survived only two years at the University of California–Berkeley. Though his father disdained the playboy life for his children, he provided Bill and his four brothers with the fast cars, speedboats, and other toys that encouraged the young men to adopt lives of hard play rather than hard work. Bill said, "We never did a goddamned thing. We never worked because we never had to."[14]

In 1937 Bill assumed a figurehead position, publisher of the *Journal-American*. He was less manager and more "baby-kisser, palm-presser, frontman for the paper," write the biographers Lindsay Chaney and Michael Cieply. "The *Journal-American* set him up; it put Bill at the center of all its promotions, stroked his ego, kept him in the news, never letting a week go by without running a photo or a flattering item." Tall and balding, with sandy hair, the congenial, patrician-looking publisher flew light planes, rode Arabian horses, and greeted presidents, kings, and prime ministers at white-tie dinners. His father said Bill was to "represent the [family] name in New York."[15]

Bill knew that meant supporting Joe McCarthy–style anti-Communism. Bill Hearst's soon-to-be third wife, Austine "Bootsie" Cassini, introduced him to Joe McCarthy in 1947. A year later the Republican senator from Wisconsin attended their wedding. In 1950, when McCarthy said in his famous speech in Wheeling, West Virginia, that he had in his hand a list of Communist Party members still shaping policy in the State Department, Senate colleagues demanded that he identify the subversives.

Bill Hearst said: "Joe gave us a call not long after the speech. And you know what—he didn't have a damned thing on that list. Nothing. He said, 'My God, I'm in a jam. . . . I shot my mouth off. So what am I gonna do now?' Well, I guess we fixed him up with a few good reporters." Bill Hearst drew upon "that little band of anti-red zealots who made their nest at the *Journal-American*," including J. B. "Doc" Matthews.[16]

Matthews, large, rotund, and bedecked with a doctoral degree and bow tie, had developed a list of 100,000 people accused of "Communist front" affiliations and a cross-indexed file of 500,000 cards about the activities of people in "Communist front" and related organizations. Matthews used his list and card file to perform three vital functions for the Hearst Corporation: he strived to keep the company free of Communists, provided ammunition about subversives to anti-Communists everywhere, and encouraged a consistent brand of hard-line anti-Communism among Hearst writers.

In 1950 the managing editor of *Counterattack*, the anti-Communist newsletter, wrote to Bill Hearst applauding his family's papers for their "anti-Communist editorial position" but questioning their favorable publicity for entertainers who are "Communists and Communist sympathizers." Worried about his papers' purity, Bill Hearst asked Matthews the next day for a list of entertainers "we pretty definitely know to be toned with the Red brush. . . . Our papers look kind of silly giving important publicity to Left-Wingers." Two days later Matthews sent him a list of eighty-two entertainers (with more promised for the next week).[17]

Asked to name "Communists and pro-Communist writers in Hearst magazines," Matthews identified eleven, claimed the number with Communist leanings or pro-Communist affiliations came to thirty-five or forty in all, and charged that the company's *Cosmopolitan* magazine harbored more Reds than any other major U.S. magazine.[18] From then on Hearst executives had Matthews vet each week a list of writers and illustrators scheduled to be paid for contributing to the company's magazines.

Matthews consulted his files on subversives to advise Hearst's stable of anti-Communist columnists and even anti-Communist writers at media that competed with Hearst's. Joseph McCarthy also called Matthews regularly for advice. FBI agents, immigration agents, and *Time* magazine and Treasury Department officials visited him at the Hearst building in New York to solicit his opinion about the loyalty of Americans in every field, including journalism.[19]

Matthews was regularly asked to check his three-by-five cards for journalists. Could he provide Westbrook Pegler, the *Journal-American*'s syndicated columnist, with information on writers who had attended a New York meeting that Hearst management judged Communistic? "For instance, Thackrey of the New York *Post* [the *Journal-American*'s competition in the afternoon] made a beautiful Communistic speech. I would like to see Pegler give him a nice treatment. . . . and expose him as he should be exposed." Could Matthews investigate ABC's Chet Huntley? Someone had complained to a Hearst executive about Huntley's questioning the value to America of Hearst's Fulton Lewis Jr. and other conservative radio commentators.[20]

Matthews had three-by-five file cards on CBS correspondents too, from thirty-eight file cards on William L. Shirer to nine on Edward R. Murrow to six on Hollenbeck. The earliest of Matthews's six cards on Hollenbeck identified him as "Liberal newscaster who has been cut by radio's reactionary trend." But Hollenbeck's 1946 departure from ABC, following his ad lib in response to a Marlin Blades commercial, could not be blamed on "radio's reactionary trend." Nevertheless, Matthews's file card sought to tie Hollenbeck's name to the Communist Party by citing only the party's December 28, 1946, edition of the *Daily Worker*—no other newspapers—as the source for information about Hollenbeck's departure from ABC.[21]

Another file card gave as its source the *Daily Worker*, October 20, 1947. The card said that Hollenbeck "charged NY dailies didn't give as fair coverage as *DW* [*Daily Worker*] and *PM*. . . . to fraud charges in PR [proportional representation] issue."[22]

Actually, Hollenbeck's *CBS Views the Press* report had not singled out the Communist Party's paper for praise. Hollenbeck had said the three New York newspapers that editorially supported keeping proportional representation—the Communist Party's *Daily Worker*, the *Herald Tribune*, and *PM*—reported that the petitions circulated to get proportional representation's repeal on the ballot may have contained fraudulent signatures. New York's other major newspapers waited until a council member asked for an official investigation before they reported the possibility of fraud. Hollenbeck's conclusion: The reporting zeal of the three papers that supported proportional representation "coincided with their editorial position! They were happy to raise the suggestion that the enemies of something they were supporting had pulled a fast one."[23]

Counterattack, the anti-Communist weekly newsletter, was listed as the source for information on other Matthews file cards about Hollenbeck. Each card sought by innuendo to tie Hollenbeck to Communists. One noted that the Communist Party's *Daily Worker* of December 25, 1947, praised Hollenbeck for his "excellent survey of the newspapers."[24] But the card did not note that critics and columnists for five other New York dailies—the *Herald Tribune*, *Mirror*, *PM*, *Post*, and *Times*—also praised Hollenbeck for *CBS Views the Press.*

Matthews relied on *Counterattack* for a card that said Hollenbeck "plugged Geo. Seldes' Communist newsletter '*In fact*,' Dec. 20, 1947." Seldes's *In fact* (its motto: "An antidote for falsehood in the daily press") was really a sometimes irresponsible, always irrepressible and irreverent newsletter—liberal definitely, radical perhaps, but Communist not likely, given its helter-skelter, idiosyncratic views. It muckraked weekly on everything from smoking to fake medicines to the National Association of Manufacturers to press Red-baiting. Hollenbeck credited *In fact* for stories it broke but also criticized its "shrill voice" about press evils, and its "swing a little wild" exaggerations and errors.[25]

Another Matthews file card cited *Counterattack* as the source for the Communist Party's praising Hollenbeck "for causing the NY *Herald Tribune* to override Otis L. Guernsey, Jr., movie critic who had refused to review Russian movies in a theater that catered to the Communist trade."[26] The description of the theater as one "that catered to the Communist trade" was another attempt to smear Hollenbeck by linking him to Communists.

What Hollenbeck had covered in November 1947 was something more than Guernsey's refusal to review Russian movies. The CBS news staff had heard that *Herald Tribune* policy—after five years of listing and reviewing Russian movies—was now "to snub Russian movies." But George Cornish, managing editor of the *Herald Tribune*, told Hollenbeck it was not the paper's policy. Hollenbeck reported: "Mr. Cornish says it apparently was a decision within the [newspaper's] movie department—the pictures had been objected to as minor movies that were straight propaganda. Mr. Cornish says he doesn't agree with the decision not to review them, however, and that in the future they will be noted in advance and reviewed."[27]

Finally, after Hollenbeck's *CBS Views the Press* won a George Foster Peabody Award for outstanding journalism in 1948, Matthews depended on *Counterattack* for a card that said: "Nat'l Advisory Board [of Peabody awards] headed by Edward Weeks. Hollenbeck is CP [Communist Party] front supporter."[28] What was the connection between Hollenbeck's being identified as a Communist Party "front supporter" and the Peabody board's leadership by Weeks, who was editor of the *Atlantic Monthly* from 1938 to 1966?

Counterattack frothed about prestigious Peabody awards going to broadcasters and news organizations that it judged to be liberal.[29] In a feature headlined "What Can You Do" the newsletter implored its readers: "Write to Edward Weeks, editor of the *Atlantic Monthly*, and chairman of the Peabody Award Committee and ask why such a large number of individuals they have honored have front records or are obviously biased or have a confused attitude about Communism."[30]

Both *Counterattack* and Matthews seemed to adopt an anti-Communist syllogism: Conservatives were not Communists or Communist front supporters; liberals were not conservatives; therefore, those like Hollenbeck who were identified as liberals qualified as Communists or Communist front supporters.

That logic was reflected in Hearst editorials that attacked liberals who associated with Communists as being as dangerous as—if not more dangerous than—Communists. Hearst helped redefine the meaning of the word *liberal*. *Liberal* and *leftist*, once contrasting terms, became interchangeable.

Hollenbeck criticized the Communist Party's *Daily Worker* as well as New York's mainstream dailies. He made clear in reviewing *Daily Worker* coverage that it was "questionable if the term newspaper may be applied to what is almost entirely a party publication." But that perspective was insufficiently anti-Communist for Bill Hearst to categorize Hollenbeck as anything other than a leftist Communist sympathizer. Bill Hearst even berated Dwight Eisenhower and other Republican leaders for throwing away the "Commies-in-Government issue" and selling out to the "Get McCarthy faction."[31]

Bill Hearst's father, in failing health, was not pleased by the stridency of his son's anti-Communism. William Randolph Hearst's had long been among the strongest voices against Communism, fueled by mid-1930s strikes of the Newspaper Guild against his papers in Seattle and Milwaukee. But he directed a cable be sent to all Hearst editors: "The Chief instructs not, repeat not, to press the campaign against Communism any further. . . . Chief says 'All papers must be careful not to use any editorials against Communism unless specifically ordered. Communism is not to be displayed too much in the news. . . . When we stress a point too strongly it loses its effectiveness. . . . These instructions must be obeyed to the letter."[32]

Soon Hearst editors received a letter of clarification about the intentions of the eighty-seven-year-old William Randolph Hearst. Bill Hearst appeared to have stiffened the anti-Communist spine of his father: editors were to know "that no fundamental change in our news or editorial policy on Communism is intended or implied."[33]

Frank Stanton, CBS's president at the time, said that Bill Hearst pushed him to stop airing Hollenbeck's program: "We took a lot of flak on 'CBS Views the Press.' I remember at least once and maybe more than once—maybe as many as three times—I talked with Bill Hearst face to face to try to get some rhyme or reason out of the attitude that Hearst was exhibiting at the time."[34]

Reporters at the city's newspapers, including Hearst's *Journal-American* and *Mirror*, were feeding Hollenbeck stories. "The more Hollenbeck did and the better he got," Stanton said, "the more feeds he got from people within the newspapers, which was the most damaging thing of all. [Bill] Hearst said, 'Tell me who the sons of bitches are.' I told Bill Hearst, 'This kind of thing just sucks right out of newsrooms anything that doesn't look like it's kosher.' "[35]

"There was a personal background there," Stanton said. "There was bad blood between Hearst and CBS long before my day." In 1932 CBS chairman

William S. Paley had married Dorothy Hart, who had been the first wife of Bill Hearst's brother John. "In fact," Stanton recalled, "I think she was still married to [John] Hearst when Paley met her on a trip to Europe. [Paley divorced Dorothy Hart Hearst in 1947 and five days later married Barbara "Babe" Cushing.] Because Bill Hearst talked with me about that when I was meeting with him, and wanted me to know that that had nothing to do with it, and the fact that he led with it, made me think that it had a lot to do with it."[36]

Bill Hearst disputed Stanton's memory: "That I referred to any of my co-workers on the *Journal-American* as sons-of-bitches is completely untrue. If I felt that way about any of them, I'd ask them to leave the paper. I wouldn't complain to Frank Stanton whom, incidentally, I have never been close to or thought a helluva lot of." Hearst added, "There certainly was never any bad blood between Bill [Paley] and me."[37]

Paley also maintained there never was bad blood. But he recalled a CBS broadcast from the 1936 presidential campaign: "Communism wasn't talked about as much as it is now, [and was] later. They [the Communists] had a point of view, and I thought their point of view ought to be presented to the American public. So we put aside a fifteen-minute period. And [Communist presidential candidate Earl] Browder went on the air. . . . Well, the Hearst press really went after me, hammer and tongs, even a cartoon showing me getting orders from the Kremlin."[38]

As for *CBS Views the Press*, Bill Hearst said, "I vaguely remember Hollenbeck was doing a hatchet job rather than a constructive one on the press in general and the Hearst press in particular, but I was raised to ignore that kind of criticism as much as I might disagree with it or how offensive I might find it." Whether he really ignored the criticism of *CBS Views the Press*, he certainly hoped the public would ignore it. Hearst's *Journal-American* never identified Hollenbeck and *CBS Views the Press* in its "Radio Log," cryptically referring to the program as "WCBS—Talk."[39]

The Hearst Corporation expected Matthews to perform a third function—help maintain a consistently alarmist, pro-McCarthy, pro–J. Edgar Hoover brand of anti-Communism throughout the company. Matthews's treatment of two left-wingers who became anti-Communists—Harvey Matusow and Howard Rushmore—showed how he worked.

The two men, like Matthews himself, were suspect in the minds of journalists who, as the historian Donald A. Ritchie writes, "found it exasperating to be scolded from the right by the same people who had previously assailed them from the left." The news commentator Elmer Davis said the Communists and

Communist sympathizers who had turned into "extreme reactionaries" saw no middle ground. Evil became good, good became evil.[40]

The anti-Communist Harvey Matusow was Matthews's kind of ideological chameleon. Matusow grew up middle class in the Bronx during the Depression. He joined the army in 1943. When he got out of the army three years later, he looked for something with similar esprit de corps. He found it first in the American Youth for Democracy, which included liberals, Zionists, Socialists, and Communists, and then in the Communist Party, which he joined.

He became disillusioned with the party and went to the FBI in 1950. Soon the FBI was paying him $70 to $75 a month for informing on his Communist friends. In his autobiography, *False Witness*, Matusow writes, "For the first time in our history, the informer was a hero." The Communist Party expelled him from membership as "an enemy agent," Matusow claimed.[41] After he was invited to testify before the House Committee on Un-American Activities in 1952, he sold his story for $750 to the *Journal-American*.

In New York he was subjected to what he called "a systematic and meticulous questioning" by Matthews. After Matthews was satisfied, Matusow helped Howard Rushmore, the *Journal-American's* ex-Communist labor editor, write a four-part "as told to" series. The first part appeared the day before Matusow's HUAC appearance. The *Journal-American's* front-page banner screamed, "Secret FBI Man Reveals: 3,500 Students Recruited Here for Red Fifth-Column."[42] The number 3,500 was a complete fabrication intended to grab readers.

Matusow was welcomed into the Matthews inner circle. Regularly invited to Matthews's penthouse for dinner, he soon became an anti-Communist lecturer, contributor to *American Legion Magazine* (Rushmore wrote the article), assistant to the editor of *Counterattack*, election campaigner for Joe McCarthy, and professional ex-Communist informer. In October 1952 he told a Senate Internal Security Subcommittee that the *New York Times* employed "well over one hundred dues-paying [Communist Party] members" and *Time* magazine employed seventy-six.[43] Later he disavowed those allegations.

Rushmore, the idealistic, Depression-era graduate of St. Brendan's Catholic School in Mexico, Missouri, had thought Communism would help poor and honest people like his parents. He organized farmers in Iowa and the Dakotas for the Communist Party, then moved to New York in the mid-1930s to become a $25-a-week writer for the *Daily Worker*.

But he soon soured on Communism. The reaction to his mixed review of the movie *Gone with the Wind*—the *Daily Worker* had expected him to denounce the film as reactionary and racist—led him to leave the paper and the party in 1939. He told the *New York Times* he "would go back to old-fashioned American Americanism" and joined the *Journal-American* in 1940. He immediately wrote a repentant series about how he had been "duped by false pictures of the Soviet Union."[44]

Theo Wilson, who covered the courts for the *Daily News*, later said, "When Rushmore turned anti-Commie, he did it with a vengeance."[45] He not only reported anti-Communist news and wrote his "Subversive Front" column for the *Journal-American*, he also spied on *Journal-American* colleagues, branded people as Communists in testimony before congressional investigative committees, and joined McCarthy's Permanent Subcommittee on Investigations as research director.

The 1947 testimony of the *Journal-American's* labor editor about Communists in the movies "was so hot. . . . that only actor Robert Taylor managed to get a bigger headline play," said Wilson. Rushmore's 1949 testimony about ten alleged Communists teaching in New York public schools and colleges was the first stage of Rushmore's campaign to remove or ruin the instructors he named. He targeted them in the *Journal-American*, pressured the city's Board of Education to fire them, and gloated over their eventual destruction.[46]

For years Rushmore was the *Journal-American's* leading anti-Communist. He wrote the attacks that attracted, from Bill Hearst's viewpoint, the right kind of criticism. In a 1947 *CBS Views the Press* broadcast, Hollenbeck questioned a Rushmore article about three hundred employees at the Office of International Information and Cultural Affairs, a New York–based State Department project that distributed information abroad about the United States. Rushmore claimed the employees were threatening "virtual mutiny" because they had not been paid for one to three months.[47]

Hollenbeck reported that, despite Rushmore's claims, the three hundred State Department employees apparently were not refusing to work and were not threatening to strike. Every journalist must, Hollenbeck said, "refuse to do a dishonest job." He concluded that the article by Rushmore, a member of the Newspaper Guild, was deserving of an award that a Guildsman once proposed for slanted reporting: "A miniature of the leaning tower of Pisa."[48]

Bill Hearst himself became a critic of Rushmore when the columnist dismissed Roy Cohn and G. David Schine, McCarthy's trusted assistants, as "self-seeking and publicity-grabbing" bumblers.[49] Rushmore's attack in Bill Hearst's *Journal-American* strained the Hearst-McCarthy relationship.

The *Journal-American* fired Rushmore in 1954. When Rushmore asked Matthews for an explanation, Matthews cited two mistakes by Rushmore. First, Rushmore had criticized Roy Cohn, Senator Joseph McCarthy's chief counsel, and Cohn's protégé G. David Schine, chief consultant to McCarthy's staff, for the two men's tour of Europe in 1953. Cohn and Schine, rumored to have had a homosexual relationship, had sought to cleanse the libraries of the United States Information Agency of books by Communists and fellow travelers. Second, Rushmore had associated with Frederick Woltman, a pro-McCarthy, anti-Communist *World-Telegram* columnist who began a five-part July 1954 series about McCarthy with a startling about-face: "Sen. Joseph R. McCarthy has become a major liability to the cause of anti-Communism." Matthews called the effectiveness of Rushmore's service to anti-Communism "greatly diminished" as a result.[50] Matthews's explanation devastated Rushmore.

In 1958, when Rushmore committed suicide after using his .32-caliber Colt pistol to murder his wife, a *Daily News* reporter recalled Rushmore's response to the suicide of a New York schoolteacher. She had been fired after being accused of once having been a Communist Party member. The reporter said, "Rushmore announced happily 'I was responsible for that. That's the second one I testified against that committed suicide.'"[51]

The Hearst family not only showed its unwavering support for McCarthy when even Rushmore's ardor for him cooled, the family showed it when McCarthy failed to convince a Senate Foreign Relations Committee panel chaired by Senator Millard E. Tydings, the Maryland Democrat, of McCarthy's allegations about Communist subversives in the State Department. The panel's majority report on July 17, 1950, labeled McCarthy's allegations "perhaps the most nefarious campaign of half-truths and untruths in the history of the republic." The 313-page report—marred by its own partisan half-truths and untruths—attacked McCarthy's "totalitarian technique of the 'big lie' employed on a sustained basis."[52]

Two days later all sixteen Hearst dailies defended McCarthy in one McCarthy-style tirade. The front-page editorial, titled "A Shameful Performance," said: "The Tydings Committee's majority report on the McCarthy charges of Communist influence in the State Department is probably the most disgracefully partisan document ever to emanate from the Congress of the United States. . . . It verges upon DISLOYALTY."[53]

Journal-American feature writers, reporters, and columnists echoed the editorials of Hearst papers nationwide and practiced McCarthyism well outside the political arena. The gossip columnist Igor "Cholly Knickerbocker" Cassini skewered Mrs. Cornelius Vanderbilt and other "rich parlor pinks, traitors to their class." The columnist Dorothy Kilgallen discovered a Communist "espionage-by-blondes" plot deeply embedded "like veins in marble" within the café society vice case of Minot "Mickey" Jelke, the twenty-three-year-old heir accused of running an international prostitution ring. The columnists Jack O'Brian, Westbrook Pegler, and Fulton Lewis Jr. found Commies conspiring at CBS and elsewhere in the media. Lewis claimed to reveal, as the headline promised, "Leftist plot to use radio for Red propaganda."[54]

At Hearst's *Mirror* the radio columnist Nick Kenny, whom one writer described as looking like a muscle-bound bouncer in a beer hall, made Hollenbeck his target. Kenny produced a newspaper column of birthday mentions (press agents paid $2 per); plugs for song-publisher friends (he made up to $10,000 a year as a lyricist); sentimental verses about his daughters, America, and nature (snow was "God's dandruff"); and occasional rants from the right. Kenny described Hollenbeck as "that Stalinbeck lad who makes listeners see Red when he shoots his weekly arrows at the 'capitalistic press.'"[55]

Kenny smeared Hollenbeck not only in his column but also in communications to the FBI. In 1950 such attacks from Hearst employees took a bizarre turn. CBS, which the FBI's Hoover was calling the Communist Broadcasting System, established its own internal security office and program of loyalty oaths to root out Communist employees.

CHAPTER 14

Jack O'Brian: Attacking the Communist Broadcasting System

Jack O'Brian devoted many columns to promoting his favorites, including the newscaster Walter Winchell, comedians Jack Benny and Eve Arden, and radio and television host Arthur Godfrey, about whom he wrote his only book. O'Brian also regularly used stories, one-liners, and letters from readers of his Journal-American *column to question the politics and performance of CBS, Don Hollenbeck, and Edward R. Murrow.*

O'Brian often insinuated that CBS was the Red network. A temporary ban on producing color television sets during the Korean War gave him the opportunity to suggest that despite the ban, given CBS's preference for Red, "color TV is HERE."[1]

In another column, O'Brian wrote, "CBS fired its popular Madison Ave. doorman, Mike Donovan. For fighting with an elevator man. (But it keeps the lefties who fight the anti-Commies.)"[2]

Occasionally, O'Brian insinuated that CBS was the treasonous Communist Broadcasting System without even mentioning the network's name. In a 1951 column he imagined a nightmare of a telecast: "Its producers, directors, writers and choreographers could be selected from a too-long list of card-carrying Commies; in several cases each job could be filled by Stalinist Reds with morally lavender trimmings." The hero of the telecast could be played by a phony patriot of a comedy star—a blond who "screamed shrilly that he was a homosexual and threatened suicide in order—successfully—to evade the draft." O'Brian ended by asking, "What network would this scream-in-the night [telecast] decorate? One guess!"[3]

The readers whom O'Brian chose to quote in his column—they invariably agreed with his conservative politics—also criticized CBS. One asked: "Why

Jack O'Brian participates in a 1951 grip-and-grin photo to promote the television host Arthur Godfrey's selection by readers of O'Brian's Journal-American *column as television entertainer of the year.*

Courtesy New York Journal-American Photo Archive, Harry Ransom Center,
University of Texas at Austin.

is CBS-TV so available to leftist sympathizers—Philip Loeb [Broadway actor who won fame on an early television series, The Goldbergs], Louis Unter-meyer [the well-known poet who would be removed by CBS as a What's My Line? *panelist and blacklisted when named by a HUAC investigating Com-munist subversion], [the pianist, playwright, and composer] Marc Blitzstein (guested on Faye Emerson's show)? They are not political innocents who joined theatrical organizations which later turned out to be Red fronts."*[4]

O'Brian not only ran anti-CBS letters, he also berated CBS president Frank Stanton and CBS during haranguing calls. Stanton said, "I had angry and endless telephone conversations with him, and he was impossible."[5]

Only once did a network other than CBS earn an equivalent level of O'Brian opprobrium. In 1951 the Peabody awards honored the American Broadcasting Company for its refusal to succumb to the pressure on all networks to blacklist the stripper Gypsy Rose Lee, who had been named in Red Channels *as a Communist sympathizer. O'Brian said the Peabody's special award for ABC ("pink-tinged, no doubt") really called attention "to the fact that a small but furiously efficient cell of sinister citizens" was poisoning radio and television: "It is an invasion of our decency to foist politically unpalatable characters on us."[6]*

O'Brian first targeted Hollenbeck for contributing to the "violently leftist" PM *and directing* CBS Views the Press. *The* Journal-American *columnist dismissed the program as only "criticism of conservative newspapers." In profiling television commentators who were covering the 1952 political conventions, O'Brian cast Hollenbeck as "the stern, intense type, [with] a messianic mien and a habit of baiting Dixiecrats and conservatives with blandly phrased 'loaded' questions."[7]*

O'Brian called Murrow "Egbert" (his first name at birth, dropped in his teens, when he started calling himself Ed) and "Egghead." O'Brian also labeled Murrow a "crack of doom," left-wing editorialist. Following the appearance of the actor Tallulah Bankhead on Murrow's Person to Person *interview program, O'Brian, defender of Senator Joe McCarthy, snipped: "Taloo neatly fended off Edw. R. Murrow's customary slanted query about what La Bankhead thought of 'our Senators today.'"[8]*

O'Brian also cheered the "savagely perceptive" satire of Murrow by the comics Art Carney and Robert Q. Lewis. An O'Brian one-liner noted: "Model Nan Rees figured her 'Person to Person' guesting would bring scads of assignments but E. R. Murrow was too busy puffing ego and cigaret to mention she's with the Eileen Ford pulchritude assembly line."[9]

O'Brian regularly insinuated that people refused to appear on Murrow's programs to avoid being contaminated by a Commie lover. In a 1954 column O'Brian wrote: "One of the most famous crooners of all time turned down Murrow's 'Person to Person' because he didn't wish to be mentioned in the same portsided breath." In another 1954 column O'Brian said: "Gregory Peck did not have to consider more than a moment whether to appear on Edward R. Murrow's 'Person to Person.' He said absolutely no quicker than you could say Malenkov."[10] Georgy Malenkov succeeded Joseph Stalin as premier of the Soviet Union.

CHAPTER 15

Loyalty Oaths, Blacklists, and Joseph McCarthy

The Cold War ruined many careers. . . . But in the tight family of CBS staff employees, particularly those who belonged to the News Division, we defended our own all the way down the line.

—William S. Paley, *As It Happened*

One critic: "Paley was the black knight in the blacklist scandal. He had lunch with J. Edgar Hoover and Hoover called CBS the Communist Broadcasting System. This shook Paley, and he went along with the loyalty oath and all the rest of it."

—Robert Metz, *CBS: Reflections in a Bloodshot Eye*

When Hollenbeck left *CBS Views the Press* in 1950, television news was no longer a novelty. Two million families had installed televisions, and 100,000 more families were putting them in their homes every month. The Korean War, which started that year, would be known as the first war that many Americans learned about primarily from television. Evening news broadcasts, such as Douglas Edwards's fifteen-minute program five nights a week on CBS, were becoming news sources as important to Americans as their hometown newspapers and radio stations.

Hollenbeck was part of the CBS Radio news staff in the early 1950s that Murrow accurately described as "an old team trying to learn a new trade." They were learning to report for television while continuing to work as radio journalists. Hollenbeck kept his national fifteen-minute weekday radio program, *News of America*, in the early 1950s. And he added other radio assignments: coordination of a high-profile weekly program, *Washington, U.S.A.*, and narration of documentaries like the hourlong *Gamblers* and novelty programs like *Candid Microphone* with Allen Funt, the radio version of *Candid Camera.*[1]

But, increasingly, Hollenbeck appeared on television. CBS's hourlong prime-time *Hear It Now*, which first broadcast to 173 affiliated radio stations on December 15, 1950, evolved into CBS's *See It Now* after only one season, symbolizing the substance and speed of the radio-to-television transition.

The Edward R. Murrow–narrated, Fred Friendly–edited *Hear It Now* captured on audiotape the voices of newsmakers (about sixty in the first program) and created what CBS trumpeted as "weekly recorded history." The program, which did not rely on actors and sound effects, won a Peabody award for ambitious, independent reporting with enormous impact. After a broadcast traced the movement of a pint of blood from the United States to a wounded soldier in Korea, listeners donated 500,000 pints of blood.[2]

Hear It Now was not only "recorded history" but also spoken ideas and opinions. Murrow envisioned *Hear It Now* as a broadcast magazine of the intellect. The first three *Hear It Now* broadcasts in December 1950 featured columnists: Abe Burrows on the theater, Bill Leonard on books and movies, Red Barber on sports, and Hollenbeck on the press.

In two-and-a-half- to three-minute essays—too short to provide the information or analysis of his *CBS Views the Press* broadcasts—Hollenbeck addressed controversial subjects, from the coverage of a fracas in which Joe McCarthy kneed the columnist Drew Pearson in the groin to the prose of Hearst's histrionic, hyper-right-wing Westbrook Pegler to the (mis)reading of American newspapers by Soviet propagandists.[3]

The brief commentaries came across less as informative reports and more as pious pronouncements. They sounded to Jack Gould, the *Times* critic, as "self-conscious and somewhat condescending."[4] In the fourth *Hear It Now* broadcast, the first of 1951, Murrow thanked listeners for their encouragement and criticism of the program. He talked about still experimenting. Hollenbeck's pieces and most of the other commentaries instantly disappeared.

In less than six months *Hear It Now* itself disappeared, to be succeeded later that year on television by *See It Now*, where words became less important than pictures. Words also played a different role. In a piece titled "They Talk Too Much," Ben Gross, the radio-TV columnist for the *Daily News*, complimented Hollenbeck for his philosophy of saying more on television by saying less: "All a reporter should do here is to set up the pictures, explain adequately what they are about, . . . and then shut up."[5]

Hollenbeck soon received choice television assignments. He not only appeared on *See It Now* but also narrated editions of *The American Week*, a news review program, and *Westinghouse Studio One*, an hourlong docudrama. He participated in documentaries, re-creations of dozens of historical events titled *You Are There*, and a nightly television roundup, *News in Review*.[6]

Later he interviewed newsmakers on CBS's weekly fifteen-minute *Longines Chronoscope*, competition for NBC's *Meet the Press*. With Murrow he covered the coronation of Queen Elizabeth II.[7] With Howard K. Smith, the chief European correspondent; Eric Sevareid, the chief Washington correspondent; and other CBS correspondents, Hollenbeck addressed trends in world affairs on Murrow's hourlong year-end review.

Hollenbeck was part of Murrow's television team that covered the national elections and party conventions. Walter Cronkite recalled that at one convention Hollenbeck waited in line for the men's room: "He was wearing the man-from-Mars equipment with which CBS had outfitted him—a backpack, earphones, a silly little skullcap with a long antenna rising from it." An inebriated man in line ahead of Hollenbeck looked over his shoulder at the CBS newsman and shouted: "Oh, no, not television in here!"[8]

After leaving *CBS Views the Press*, Hollenbeck also coanchored a local fifteen-minute television news broadcast at six o'clock. Such a local newscast was a revolutionary idea for television in 1950. For the *6 O'Clock Report* Hollenbeck provided five minutes of hard news, the sportswriter Tom Meany reported five minutes of sports, and Bill Leonard had five minutes for features. Leonard said Hollenbeck helped him learn how to write for television: "He showed me what a professional could do to transform ordinary wire-service news copy into broadcast material that almost seemed to sing. Not by making it more complicated but by somehow making it more simple. He was a *writer*."[9]

Meany, with no radio experience, found it difficult to master television. He got through his sports report the first evening but fumbled a live commercial for Kool cigarettes. He lit the wrong end of a cork-tip Kool, coughed at the first puff, and muttered on air, "Switch from Kools to Hots." He soon was replaced by Jim McKay.

Eventually, Hollenbeck and other radio veterans became expert at using film, superimposing sound, and writing for television. For many, however, conscience and conviction came more slowly than technical ability, as one issue proved.

That issue was public anxiety about Communism. Alarm bells had gone off for Americans in 1949, when the Soviet Union detonated its first atomic bomb, marking the beginning of the nuclear arms race. Also that year the U.S. government convicted eleven Communist Party leaders under the Smith Act, which made it unlawful to advocate the violent overthrow of the government. Communists took over mainland China in 1949 and heightened the domino-theory fear of Communists' grabbing other nations, one by one, until they controlled the world.

For Americans fearful of Communism's spread 1950 began with other, equally terrifying events. On January 20 Alger Hiss, the Harvard-trained attorney and former State Department official accused of being a Soviet spy, was found guilty of perjury. A week later Klaus Fuchs, a German theoretical scientist who had become a British citizen in 1942 and had worked on the atomic bomb at the Los Alamos National Laboratory in New Mexico, confessed to being a Soviet spy.

The Korean War began on June 25 and eventually pitted U.S. troops against soldiers from the People's Republic of China and their Soviet combat advisers. School drills in 1950 sent children diving under their desks in anticipation of a Soviet nuclear attack. Julius and Ethel Rosenberg were arrested for conspiracy to commit espionage for the Soviet Union (they would be convicted in 1951 and executed in 1953). The McCarran Internal Security Act of 1950 required Communist and Communist-dominated organizations to register the names of all members and contributors with the U.S. attorney general.

Soon the newly created Senate Subcommittee on Internal Security, the House Committee on Un-American Activities, and Senator Joseph McCarthy's Senate Subcommittee on Investigations, working with sympathetic Justice Department employees and FBI agents, focused public attention on questions of security and Communist spying. The investigators targeted security risks in all branches of government, not just the State Department, and in industry and the media.

Advertisers and advertising agencies sought to make sure the television programs they sponsored and the networks that produced those programs were free of Communists and Communist sympathizers. In June 1950 the three former FBI agents who produced *Counterattack*, the weekly anti-Communist newsletter, published *Red Channels: The Report of Communist Influence in Radio and Television*.

The 213-page book purported to help advertising agencies, advertisers, and the networks smoke out Communists. The book listed 151 people in radio and television and their links, however tenuous, to allegedly pro-

Communist causes or organizations, many out of business for more than a decade. Some people listed were Communists or Communist sympathizers, but others were mainstream liberals or apolitical innocents.

The editors of *Red Channels* claimed the book was not a blacklist. But, in a seven-page introduction written by the former naval intelligence officer Vincent Hartnett, they quoted a *Broadcasting* magazine editorial that said, "Communists and Communist sympathizers have no place on our air."[10] Advertisers agreed and conveyed their message to the networks.

Strange things began to happen to people listed in *Red Channels*. In early 1950 Robert Lewis Shayon, a former CBS *You Are There* writer-director-producer, was offered a position by the Economic Cooperative Administration, which administered the Marshall Plan in Europe. Shayon accepted. But *Red Channels* and the February 17, 1950, issue of *Counterattack* charged that he was active in a Communist front, the Progressive Citizens of America. The overseas job offer was withdrawn.

Taking his wife's advice, Shayon protested his innocence to the FBI and, later, to a coauthor of *Red Channels*. But the mention in *Red Channels* "cost me five years of my life and career," Shayon said. That was a price that those who supported the blacklists were willing to have others pay. Charles E. Martin, a producer-director, could have been speaking for numerous sponsors, networks, and advertising agencies when he testified in a *Red Channels* lawsuit: "We quarantine everybody [mentioned] in the book. We cannot take any chances."[11]

Given CBS's reputation among militant anti-Communists as the Communist Broadcasting System, the network's employees received special attention. A June 1949 internal FBI memo described "Communist infiltration" of CBS. Hearst's *Journal-American* focused on "the employment of Communist fronters by CBS."[12] An April 1950 FBI memo targeted "Edward Roscoe Murrow, CBS News Analyst" and others at CBS "believed to be communistically inclined or fellow travelers." *Red Channels* identified the CBS correspondents Howard K. Smith and Alexander Kendrick as being Communists or Communist sympathizers.[13]

Counterattack officials monitored CBS press releases for mentions of people they deemed to be "members of the Communist Party or fellow travelers" and sought out informants to identify CBS subversives. An unnamed informant—an "executive at CBS"—fingered six CBS employees. *Counterattack* officials also wrote memos about the "Communist-front organization" associations of Murrow, William L. Shirer, John Henry Faulk, and Philip Loeb—though not Hollenbeck.[14]

Loeb played a character on CBS's *The Goldbergs*, a show sponsored by General Foods' Sanka coffee. He was listed in *Red Channels*, along with a page and a half of allegations that Loeb was pro-Communist.[15] The network received only three complaints about Loeb. General Foods received just one. But General Foods panicked. General Foods, CBS, and the Young and Rubicam advertising agency met with Gertrude Berg, the star and owner of *The Goldbergs*. Berg refused to fire Loeb.[16]

Jack O'Brian thrashed CBS in his *Journal-American* column for retaining Loeb and then delighted in reporting that CBS—"never previously at a loss for loyalty before in similar situations parked firmly to the left"—had finally canceled *The Goldbergs*. Berg was unable to find an advertiser to sponsor the show with Loeb acting in it. *The Goldbergs* moved to NBC. O'Brian then publicly bullied NBC about whether it would employ Loeb "in light of objections from all patriotic sides" and gloated when he could write, "Philip Loeb will NOT be on 'The Goldbergs.'"[17]

Depressed and despondent, worried about his mentally ill son, unable to get work in radio or television, and harassed during his theater performances, Loeb took an overdose of sleeping pills and killed himself.

"The country was sort of carried away by this fear of Communism," CBS chairman William S. Paley said years later. "And so everybody was called upon to more or less examine his own shop." In December 1950 Joseph Ream, an executive vice president at CBS, drafted what many network employees called a loyalty oath—Paley called it "an in-house questionnaire"—to "reassure the advertisers we weren't a nest of Commies," Ream said.[18] NBC administered a similar questionnaire, though the network required only new employees to complete and sign it. NBC's rhetoric was almost as alarmist as CBS's. Joseph McConnell, NBC's president, said the network must not only check scripts for subversive material but must also make sure it harbors no traitors: "We propose to keep our house clean." Only ABC refused to administer a loyalty test.[19]

CBS employees were asked to check off whether they had ever been a member of any Communist organization, any fascist organization, or any of the organizations designated subversive from the 1950 list devised by the attorney general and reprinted on the back of the CBS questionnaire. Employees were required to return the signed loyalty questionnaire, with a written explanation of memberships, to Ream's office.

With the Korean War heating up, Ream spoke as if he were expecting a Communist version of the Japanese attack on Pearl Harbor any day. His memo to CBS employees talked about CBS's role "in the last war," adding,

"Today, we are faced with a new crisis in our national life." CBS established its own security operation under a new corporate vice president, Daniel T. O'Shea, a lawyer who had been an executive with Vanguard Films in Hollywood. O'Shea hired Alfred Berry, a former FBI agent, to help him. O'Shea said their job was to track down "Communists and strong friends of the Communists."[20]

O'Shea and Berry used contacts in the FBI, congressional committees, and specialists like J. B. Matthews to learn about the political activities, past and present, of CBS employees and outside writers, directors, and actors seeking employment at CBS. O'Shea said he interviewed anyone "in trouble." O'Shea would check what he knew about the person against what the person volunteered. O'Shea said that anyone who held back was dismissed with the words, "It's been nice talking to you."[21]

Berry recalled that "advertisers were saying, 'You use this guy and I'll take my business elsewhere.'"[22] The anti-Communist crusader Laurence A. Johnson, who owned four grocery stores in Syracuse, New York, prodded corporate sponsors to continue to pressure the networks. Johnson started letter-writing campaigns to sponsors, visited Madison Avenue advertising agencies, and met with network officials. He told CBS president Frank Stanton that Johnson's Syracuse stores were going to display ballot boxes that would permit their customers to vote on the proposition: "Do you want any part of your purchase price of any products advertised on the Columbia Broadcasting System to be used to hire Communist fronters?"[23]

Johnson also asked CBS sponsors how they would feel if he put a sign in his supermarkets over their products that asked: "Would you want to buy this product from a sponsor who hires Communists for his radio and TV shows?" Near those goods, Johnson said, his stores would display competing products with a sign saying the sponsor shunned "Stalin's little creatures." As an officer in the National Association of Supermarkets, Johnson gave the impression that he could mobilize the owners of thousands of supermarkets across the United States.[24]

Thirty years later Paley and other CBS executives remembered the network's loyalty questionnaire program as an innocuous bit of public relations, intended more to placate sponsors and the *Red Channels* people than to oust undesirables. Paley said the in-house questionnaire "took off the heat if someone said, 'What are you doing to protect yourselves against infiltration by Communists, [because] if they get on your air it could do fantastic damage?'"[25]

Berry recalled "a guy from the Ford Foundation, concerned with black-listing, asking O'Shea and me, 'How many people do you keep off the air? Now write the number of people you think are kept off the air.' I wrote nine or ten. O'Shea wrote nine or ten. It really wasn't that bad at all. This guy thought there were close to ninety."[26]

A person who belonged to one of the organizations that *Red Channels* or *Counterattack* had associated with Communism was not automatically dismissed, Paley said. Without mentioning Winston Burdett by name, Paley told a story about a CBS news commentator who, in front of a Washington investigative committee, acknowledged his former Communist Party membership, said he regretted it, and remained at CBS.

Burdett, who had majored in romance languages at Harvard and graduated summa cum laude in only three years, started covering culture for the *Brooklyn Daily Eagle* when he was twenty. Early in 1940 he moved to Scandinavia to report the war there as a stringer for the *Eagle* and then for the Transradio Press news service. CBS eventually hired him as a staff correspondent.

Slight of build, with wavy dark hair, Burdett had the look of a well-dressed college professor. But he was a bulldog of a foreign correspondent. Beginning in 1940, he reported from Norway, Finland, Rumania (where he married the Italian journalist Lea Schiavi), Yugoslavia, Turkey, and Iran. After Schiavi was murdered while reporting from Iran in 1942, Burdett covered the war in North Africa and Italy, spent a postwar stint in Washington, and returned to CBS's Rome bureau.

There, in December 1950, he received the network's loyalty questionnaire. In answering it, he told CBS that he had joined a Communist cell of ten or so people at the *Brooklyn Daily Eagle* and later spied for the Soviet Union. CBS instantly ordered Burdett to move to New York. But the network chose not to punish him so long as he went to the FBI. CBS and the FBI kept his secret for more than four years, and CBS handed Burdett top assignments—U.N. reporter and then Washington correspondent. Concerned that his past might be leaked to the public, Burdett took the initiative. He agreed to testify publicly and to name former party associates as a way of clearing his name and preserving his position at CBS.

On June 28, 1955, Burdett starred as the lead-off witness in a series of public hearings by the Senate Subcommittee on Internal Security about Communist infiltration of New York newspapers and the Newspaper Guild. Burdett said that he joined the Communist Party cell at the *Brooklyn Daily Eagle* in August 1937, grew into "a fanatical and hotly dogmatic" party member, and spied in Finland, Yugoslavia, and Turkey for the Soviets during 1940–42. From his contacts with older, more sophisticated war correspondents, he came to see the Communist Party as "a tool of a cynical power," Russia.[27]

Burdett also testified before the Senate subcommittee that his wife's murder in Soviet-occupied northern Iran was a "deliberate political assassination . . . at the instigation of the Russians." Out of what Burdett called an obligation to do right as he saw it, he named as Communists twenty-one people, primarily from his *Brooklyn Daily Eagle* days fifteen years earlier. Burdett softened his testimony by speculating that the party members he named, "honest idealists," had left the party. But a dozen of the twenty-one he named were required by the Senate subcommittee to testify.[28]

Several months later the Senate subcommittee convened a new round of hearings that appeared to be aimed at smearing the *New York Times*, symbol to some committee members of liberal/left fellow-traveling reporters. Six witnesses, including three *New York Times* employees, were fired. O'Shea, CBS's security boss, arranged Burdett's return to the network's Rome bureau early in 1956. But CBS could not protect Burdett from the disdain of colleagues. Some saw him as a traitor whose testimony had ruined careers and lives. They never spoke to him again.[29]

Even in 1950, four and a half years before Burdett's testimony, the CBS loyalty questionnaire did not have the ring of an innocuous bit of public relations to Hollenbeck and other CBS employees. They believed a job-threatening, security-list mentality pervaded CBS. Sig Mickelson, president of CBS News in the 1950s, carried with him a list of 130 names from the network's high command: "It was suggested at the time that I keep a close eye on it."[30]

Listed were not only entertainers, including Philip Loeb, but also announcers and commentators—Ben Grauer, Charles Irving, William L. Shirer, Johannes Steel, and William S. Gailmore. Mickelson checked job candidates against the list before permitting them to be hired by CBS. "If I hadn't enforced the prohibition at my level," Mickelson said, "it would have been enforced at a higher level."[31]

Chairman Paley acknowledged that he had insisted on establishing CBS's loyalty questionnaire. "My own feelings for personal privacy are so strong that I am astonished that I could have tolerated the invasion of privacy," he said later. He also said Murrow participated in the decision to institute the loyalty questionnaire. "We all discussed it," Paley recalled, "and we all thought that was something we ought to do." Murrow agreed not to talk about the "vexed subject" of the questionnaire in public.[32]

Murrow, perhaps sensing he lacked the power to change Paley's mind, signed the loyalty questionnaire and advised other CBS employees to do the same. Hollenbeck wanted to fight the questionnaire, but Murrow said, "Oh, go ahead and sign it." Murrow told David Shoenbrun, a correspondent: "If you don't sign it, suspicion will hover over you. . . . I'm signing. Do you have more integrity than I do, David?"[33]

Eric Sevareid and William L. Shirer—two of the "Murrow boys," the talented radio correspondents assembled by CBS before and during World War II—had personal reasons for taking opposing views on Murrow's response to CBS's loyalty questionnaire.

After World War II Shirer's best-selling *Berlin Diary* and highly rated Sunday news analysis program made him a celebrity. "It was easy," he said, "to get puffed up about yourself." His 5:45 p.m. program for CBS received the highest Hooper rating of any Sunday program. But a J. Walter Thompson advertising agency executive told Shirer in March 1947 that the J. B. Williams shaving cream company no longer wanted to sponsor his program. Shirer assumed that his liberal views had caused anti-Communist conservatives to write angry, anti-Shirer letters to the Williams company: "Even the vice-president of the ad agency that handled the shaving-cream company account began to hint that I was 'too liberal.'"[34]

Shirer phoned Murrow, who met with Paley to argue for Shirer's keeping the 5:45 p.m. news program, despite the Williams company's decision. But Paley refused Murrow's request. Murrow "caved quickly," recalled Stanton, who told Shirer the bad news. Murrow said CBS would try to find Shirer another time slot and sponsor. Much of the New York press treated the story the way *PM* headlined it on Page One: "William Shirer, Liberal Commentator, Gets Axe." Picketers demonstrated in front of the CBS building to protest Shirer's removal. Murrow and Paley blamed Shirer for organizing the picketers. Despite evidence to the contrary, Shirer insisted he played no role in organizing anyone.[35]

Jack Gould, the *New York Times* radio critic, questioned Murrow's assertion that "the decision to drop Mr. Shirer from the Sunday period was solely that of CBS." Gould wrote that "an advertiser again has figured prominently in a controversy over the presentation of opinion on the air when actually there should be no opportunity whatsoever for him to do so."[36]

In his 1990 memoir Shirer criticized Murrow's role in CBS's new policy of "knuckling under to what it thought was the temper of the times." Murrow, said Shirer, "turned out to be uncharacteristically slick in trying to confuse the public, diffuse the protests, and finish me off at CBS. I was appalled by his disregard for the truth. It was a side of Ed that I didn't suspect existed."[37]

In a prepared statement to the press following his last Sunday program, Shirer said that CBS had made it clear by the public declarations of Paley and Murrow that his usefulness at CBS was over, so he was resigning. In reality, Shirer said later, "I was forced to resign by Paley and Murrow. . . . And in the end Ed got thrown out. It happened to anyone who had any guts." As for Hollenbeck, who Shirer said also had guts and came under attack from the anti-Communist right, "I don't think he got any support from Murrow."[38]

Sevareid, like Shirer, experienced advertiser pressure. In March 1950 Metropolitan Life Insurance canceled its sponsorship of Sevareid's award-winning radio news program. Metropolitan Life had received mail complaining about "Eric the Red" Sevareid and his treatment of Joseph McCarthy. "The idea seemed to be," Sevareid recalled, "that every liberal was a Socialist, every Socialist a Communist, and every Communist a spy; no part of which was true, but that was the feeling."[39]

When CBS moved Sevareid to an unsponsored 11 p.m. news program and replaced him at 6 p.m. with a more compliant Alan Jackson, Metropolitan Life resumed its sponsorship. Sevareid, unlike Shirer, kept quiet and eventually was named anchor of a fifteen-minute Sunday afternoon program of news and commentary. "I didn't have any money. I had a chronically and dreadfully ill wife, two small children," Sevareid said.[40]

Sevareid, unlike Shirer, refused to fault CBS or Murrow, who was also under attack from the anti-Communist right. "Nobody, including Murrow, can spend every day of his life slaying dragons," Sevareid said. He also declined to attach much significance to what he denied was a company loyalty oath: "It was a request that all employees indicate on a form whether they had ever been a member of the Communist Party or any of its auxiliaries such as the Youth Communist League. It was distasteful but did not strike many of us as questioning our integrity. Having nothing to hide, I signed it with the others."[41]

But many CBS staffers disagreed with Sevareid. Joe Wershba called the loyalty questionnaire "the greatest disgrace in the history of this company. I'm ashamed that I didn't fight the oath harder." The newswriter Nat Brandt signed the questionnaire when he joined CBS: "I had to explain in grueling detail why, as a college senior, I had become a member of the Socialist

Party, which was considered in league with the Communist Party. (Out of curiosity, I, together with friends, had attended a political rally for Henry Wallace and responded to an invitation for party literature. Next thing I knew, a membership card came in the mail.)"[42]

John Horn, a CBS publicist assigned to Fred Friendly and Murrow, said, "I took the oath as a bureaucratic piece of nonsense, signed it, and sent it off. At the end of the week, a girl in the office said, 'I'd like to talk to you.' She asked about the loyalty oath. She said, 'It's not nonsense to me.'" Though she had no skeletons in her closet, she believed that the loyalty questionnaire should be opposed. She feared she would be fired if she spoke in opposition and that her husband, a government employee, would lose his job, too.[43]

Several other CBS employees who balked at signing the questionnaire were dismissed or threatened with dismissal. "We only realized too late that the oath was a real issue—that we should have made an issue of it," Horn said. "This was a time when liberals were running, hiding, quaking, not realizing that this was a time to fight."[44]

Arthur Bonner, a newswriter who disliked the questionnaire on principle, finally signed. "The pressure was constantly on us," he said. Bernard Birnbaum, a freelance camera operator who was joining CBS as a lighting director, said, "I had to sign the loyalty oath. You knew you had to do it to get the job." The newswriter Jack Walters, "with a mortgage, a wife, and a second child on the way," said he signed the oath and wrote on the form, "I think this is a lot of bullshit." He said, "We didn't see what we could do individually. Nobody had much guts."[45]

Other CBS employees tried to avoid signing the questionnaire by stalling. Fred Friendly, who became president of CBS News in 1964, said he never pushed or protested, "I just never sent the thing back." Walter Cronkite, who joined CBS in 1950, was assigned to a newscaster's position at WTOP-TV, a Washington station recently purchased by CBS. He believed his relatively anonymous status as a newcomer and his location outside New York worked in his favor. "I thought it was a mistake [to sign]," he said, though he felt pressure. "As I recall, I stalled."[46]

An employee who refused to sign could expect coverage in the press, especially in newspapers that saw themselves as anti-Communist. The *Journal-American* reported that John K.M. McCaffery, master of ceremonies for *We Take Your Word*, would not sign the CBS questionnaire. But the *Journal-American* also reported that McCaffery submitted to Ream a detailed letter disavowing any Communist affiliation and explaining he was a Catholic: "It is . . . impossible for a Catholic to be a Communist." The *Journal-American* noted Ream's acceptance of the letter and mentioned in passing: "Ten days ago CBS dismissed a girl employe who refused to sign the pledge."[47]

CBS and other news media contributed to the early witch-hunting by McCarthy. He took advantage of a traditional rule of reporting: Accusations from a responsible source must be reported. "McCarthy's charges of treason, espionage, corruption, perversion are news which cannot be suppressed or ignored," wrote the Pulitzer Prize–winning columnist Walter Lippmann. "They come from a United States senator . . . in good standing at the headquarters of the Republican party."[48]

It was also news, as the McCarthy biographer Richard Rovere said, that this U.S. senator was lying. The news media, however, rarely caught up with the lies. McCarthy's charges always seemed to be made only minutes before deadline. And much of the news media did not at first denounce the lies for what they were—unfounded charges dressed up in the rhetoric of patriotic anti-Communism. Eliot Fremont-Smith, a magazine editor and a book critic for the *New York Times*, said that in the early McCarthy years the supine news media, even ostensibly liberal journalists, "suffered a prolonged attack of *laryngitis intimidatus*."[49]

CBS was slow to challenge McCarthy. "We're bringing up the rear," Murrow said. At ABC the radio commentators Martin Agronsky and Elmer Davis had begun criticizing McCarthy years earlier. In 1953 Agronsky lost more than half of his 120 sponsors nationwide for his fifteen-minute Washington program because, he said, of pressure from retaliating McCarthyites. They called for ABC president Robert Kintner to fire him. But Kintner told Agronsky to "keep it up."[50]

CBS's first challenge to McCarthy—a *See It Now* broadcast by Murrow and Fred Friendly—occurred three years after McCarthy had begun to charge that the State Department employed Communists. The program, on October 20, 1953, was not advertised by the network. Murrow and Friendly bought a $1,500 ad in the *New York Times* with their own money.[51] But perhaps the absence of network identification with the program was appropriate. *The Case against Milo Radulovich, A0589839* was part editorial, something CBS said it did not tolerate.

The thirty-minute broadcast told the story of a lieutenant in the Air Force Reserve from Dexter, Michigan, who had suddenly been classified as a security risk and asked to resign. Anonymous accusers had alleged that Radulovich's sister and father were radicals. The air force was, in effect, demanding that Radulovich stop "associating with his father and sister."[52] Radulovich refused to do that. He also refused to resign from the air force.

Radulovich was stripped of his commission, though never permitted to learn the source or content of the specific allegations against him. During his *See It Now* broadcast Murrow recommended a reassessment of the personal and legal rights of someone accused of being a threat to national security.[53]

The air force retreated. Secretary of the Air Force Harold E. Talbott, speaking on a subsequent *See It Now* broadcast, said he had determined that Radulovich was not a security risk. Radulovich's position as a lieutenant in the reserve would be restored.

Murrow followed on March 9, 1954, with a *See It Now* broadcast about McCarthy that often has been called television's finest half hour. Again, CBS provided airtime but little more for a program that was as much editorial as news report. Friendly and Murrow took out another advertisement in the *New York Times*, without the CBS eye or other network trademark.[54]

On the morning of the broadcast, Friendly wrote, Paley called Murrow with what Friendly interpreted as a menacing message: "I'll be with you tonight, Ed, and I'll be with you tomorrow as well." Paley insisted he was not threatening Murrow with the loss of his job. Paley recalled saying to Murrow, "I'll wait until everybody sees it," adding, "That was meant as a vote of confidence and was received by him as such."[55]

The broadcast artfully juxtaposed edited film clips—McCarthy attacks refuted by Murrow facts. McCarthy was his own worst witness. Film showed McCarthy scoffing at President Eisenhower; attacking "Alger, I mean Adlai" Stevenson, the former Illinois governor and unsuccessful Democratic presidential candidate, and calling General Ralph Zwicker, who was a hero of Normandy and the Bulge in World War II, "a disgrace to the Army."[56]

In a closing that was more editorial than news report, Murrow acknowledged the need for congressional committees to investigate before legislating: "But the line between investigation and persecuting is a very fine one, and the junior senator from Wisconsin has stepped over it repeatedly. His primary achievement has been in confusing the public mind as between the internal and the external threat of Communism."

Murrow said Americans "must not confuse dissent with disloyalty" and "must remember always that accusation is not proof and that conviction depends upon evidence and due process of law. We will not walk in fear, one of another."

Finally, Murrow called for action, as if he were a president trying to rouse a complacent, slumbering citizenry: "This is no time for men who oppose Senator McCarthy's methods to keep silent, or for those who approve. . . . We proclaim ourselves, as indeed we are, the defenders of freedom—what's left of it—but we cannot defend freedom abroad by deserting it at home."

Murrow seemed to excuse McCarthy for his actions, only to better make the case for the public's responsibility: "The actions of the junior senator from Wisconsin have caused alarm and dismay amongst our allies abroad and given considerable comfort to out enemies. And whose fault is that? Not really his. He didn't create this situation of fear; he merely exploited it, and rather successfully. Cassius was right: 'The fault, dear Brutus, is not in our stars but in ourselves.' Good night, and good luck."[57]

At 11 p.m., a few seconds after Murrow finished, an ecstatic Hollenbeck came on the air in New York for his WCBS newscast. Murrow had just said, "This is no time for men who oppose Senator McCarthy's methods to keep silent." Hollenbeck did not keep silent. He told his WCBS audience, "I don't know whether all of you have seen what I just saw, but I want to associate myself and this program with what Ed Murrow has just said, and I have never been prouder of CBS."[58]

With that sentence Hollenbeck "put himself in a position where he was open to attack," said Friendly. Collingwood recalled the network's reaction to Hollenbeck's extemporaneous remark: "This was taken as a sign of almost unprofessionalism." Collingwood added, "There was a kind of growing tension between Hollenbeck and management: his own personality—not letting anyone kick you around—plus his taking . . . chances." Friendly said Hollenbeck needed to be careful: "CBS was not as courageous as it could have been. Someone made the decision that Don was expendable."[59]

McCarthy and his fans, including Jack O'Brian, the *New York Journal-American* columnist, understood that Hollenbeck was vulnerable at CBS in a way that Murrow was not. Murrow "was God," Friendly said. And CBS was determined to protect its god. After Murrow's broadcast about McCarthy, CBS put together a high-powered team of Cravath, Swaine and Moore lawyers and researchers and consulted Bruce Bromley, a Court of Appeals judge who had been one of the country's best trial lawyers, to develop Murrow's defense in what they called "Matter of M."[60]

They assumed that McCarthy's televised counterattack would call for an investigation of Murrow or the network before a congressional committee. Friendly said, "Murrow would go up to the twentieth-floor conference room, three to four hours a day," to confer with the lawyers about his activities as a student, to review the politics of all people who had ever worked for him, including clerks and secretaries, and to develop a strategy for responding to the anticipated McCarthy smear.[61]

While the *Journal-American* critic did not go after Murrow as doggedly as CBS expected, O'Brian repeatedly used his column to bludgeon the vulnerable Hollenbeck. Friendly said that O'Brian was a bully, and "a bully, just like any predatory animal, always looks for the vulnerable guy."[62]

CHAPTER 16

___

The Walking Wounded

Youngsters read back and they think only one person in broadcasting and the press stood up to McCarthy, and this has made a lot of people feel very upset, including me, because that [Murrow] program came awfully late. But in the meantime, the place was strewn with the walking wounded and the bodies of journalists who'd been under fire.

—Eric Sevareid

Although Jack O'Brian's *Journal-American* column had sniped regularly at Edward R. Murrow and Don Hollenbeck for years, the assaults intensified after Murrow's famous *See It Now* broadcast about Joseph McCarthy and Hollenbeck's extemporaneous remark. O'Brian pummeled Murrow's program in his column—"An Analysis of Murrow's Portsided Political Pitching"—as a "hate-McCarthy telecast" and vilified both Murrow and Hollenbeck.[1]

O'Brian claimed CBS had allowed Murrow to escape its "clean house of lefties" campaign. Murrow's "Sevengali-style influence," said O'Brian, explained CBS's "heckling of publications . . . anywhere to the right of Murrow." O'Brian blamed Murrow for *CBS Views the Press*, in which "Don Hollenbeck, a graduate of the demised pinko publication '*PM*' attacked conservative newspapers with sly and slanted propaganda of the sort Murrow last evening plucked from the content of Sen. Joseph McCarthy's speeches over the last few years." When Murrow finished his slur of McCarthy, O'Brian wrote, Hollenbeck followed "in an obviously gloating mood," with the hope that "viewers had witnessed his patron's triumph from and for the left."[2]

George Herman, a member of the *CBS Views the Press* news team, recalled a *Journal-American* columnist's telling him of a strategy meeting at which Hearst officials planned how they would get back at those responsible for *CBS Views the Press* and paint CBS as "the Red Network." But O'Brian said neither the conservative, anti-Communist William Randolph Hearst Jr. nor anyone else at Hearst's *Journal-American* encouraged him to attack Murrow and Hollenbeck. O'Brian suggested he needed no encouragement to criticize Hollenbeck.[3]

On March 12, 1954, two days after O'Brian's column, Hollenbeck had an additional worry. He experienced severe stomach pains. His doctor, Willis A. Murphy, asked him to enter Doctors Hospital. Murphy thought Hollenbeck might need surgery for a bleeding duodenal ulcer.

Murphy had seen Hollenbeck every six months for sixteen years. The doctor recalled that Hollenbeck's usual physical condition was "fine, really fine. He was a very wiry type. He had no disability. The only thing he had to do was lay off scotch."[4] Hollenbeck was having five or six drinks a day.

Murphy asked a specialist to examine Hollenbeck. The specialist "didn't think it was anything to worry about," recalled Murphy. "No surgery was necessary." Exactly one week after Hollenbeck entered Doctors Hospital, he was released in "improved condition," according to the discharge report.[5]

But he still had not fully recovered. Joe and Shirley Wershba, his friends from CBS, telephoned him the day he returned home from the hospital to announce the birth of their son. "I said, 'Don, your namesake has arrived,'" Shirley recalled. "He said, 'And you're really calling him Don?' He got out of his bed [at home] and came down to the hospital that afternoon to take a look at him. I was so amazed because Don had just gotten home himself and looked so weak."[6]

A month later, on April 21, Hollenbeck reentered Doctors Hospital. He complained of stomach pains. He could not eat. The diagnosis was gastritis and, again, a duodenal ulcer. The doctor noted that Hollenbeck "drinks and smokes (4 packs a day)"—only a month earlier it had been "2 1/2 packs a day or more." Hollenbeck was "very nervous," Murphy said. But he did not know the reasons for Hollenbeck's nervousness. "He was very close-mouthed," Murphy said. "He was definitely uncommunicative. He never opened up to me about CBS or his personal problems."[7]

The personal problems—including Hollenbeck's drinking—tore apart his marriage to Anne. The first years of the marriage had been joyous, romantic ones—probably the happiest of his life. In 1944 they had adopted Zoë. "No child was more adored," said Anne. "I remember right after we brought her

In an undated photo taken toward the end of his life, Hollenbeck sits with an empty liquor bottle in his right hand, a martini glass and a bottle of scotch next to him. In a note accompanying this photo, Zoë Hollenbeck Barr, his daughter, later wrote: "I don't know where this was but I think the rest speaks for itself!"

Courtesy Zoë Hollenbeck Barr.

home from the hospital. She was lying in her crib, crying. Don went in. He said, 'My sweet Zoë, Zoë darling.' And she stopped crying. And he came back and announced this as if, 'Today I'm a father.' He had fallen in love."[8]

His marriage had begun to fall apart when he returned from his Nuremberg trials assignment for NBC in 1945. "They [Don and Anne] wanted to be together," said Sig Mickelson, "but every time they'd get together there would be some kind of split again so they'd separate off." Milton Stern, a friend, described the Hollenbecks' relationship as "a warring equilibrium" not helped by the long hours that Don spent at CBS: "I think we saw that marriage in the process of decline. If he had had more time to give to it, it might have worked out."[9]

Hollenbeck believed he should live alone. He was sure he could never make marriage work. But living alone depressed him. Anne could not be expected to solve that quandary. As Margaret Halsey, a friend of the Hollenbecks', said, "Maybe no woman could have done it all."[10]

In 1946, as Hollenbeck worked to complete a draft of "Give Us Time," his novel about radio broadcasting, Anne took Zoë with her for two weeks in the country. Anne left a note for her husband. In it she wrote that he had given her "a convincing demonstration the other evening . . . that it is quite all right if we go two separate paths—that you are disinterested in any activity not having to do with: 1) your book; 2) your job; 3) your whirl with Scotch."

Anne doubted her ability to help her husband: "It's no use to ask you to try changing things, because of me or Zoë. If it doesn't come from yourself, for yourself, it won't be very good to any of us." Anne ended her note by pleading with her husband to "give some thought to another try with the people who can help you find out the basis for your unhappiness with life, and with me."[11]

Three decades later she said, "Probably if I knew what I know now about people and human relations, I would, of course, have done many things differently."[12] But she did not know what to do except recommend that he see a psychiatrist.

Anne and Don knew a psychiatrist, Marynia F. Farnham, socially. Educated at Bryn Mawr College and trained at the University of Minnesota, Farnham looked at Don from the perspective outlined in *Modern Woman: The Lost Sex*, a controversial book that she wrote with Ferdinand Lundberg in 1947.

Feminists labeled Farnham an antifeminist who argued that an emphasis on equality with men violated women's deepest needs. In feminists' eyes Farnham stereotyped women as seekers of dependence, inwardness, security, and passivity. Betty Friedan charged that *Modern Woman* spread a "feminine mystique" about women: Housewives are the creators and re-creators of culture and civilization; to offer women the same careers and higher education as men, *Modern Woman* declared, would lead to the "masculinization of women with enormously dangerous consequences to the home, the children dependent on it and to the ability of the woman, as well as her husband, to obtain sexual gratification."[13]

Farnham had equally controversial views about men. She believed that male creativity was often abnormal. It was psychically distorted—"creating at the expense of naturalistic self-realization," Farnham and Lundberg wrote. The stereotype of the unhappy male genius was a reality. He achieved his work goals only by denying a large part of himself. "All too often," the authors wrote, "the 'successful' man is not a success as a man."[14]

Farnham concluded that a man should be judged by his success in building a healthy home, not by his acquisition of wealth, distinction, or knowledge. A man who falls prey to those values of acquisition, as Farnham and Lundberg wrote, "can hardly regard himself as more than a disease, perhaps not worthy of his own serious consideration."[15]

Farnham's negativity showed through in her work with patients. The CBS newscaster Ned Calmer, who was a close friend of several of her patients', described Farnham as "a wild woman herself—a screwball." Marie Coleman Nelson, a psychotherapist who practiced in New York at the time, was disappointed by Farnham's response to the psychological condition of a friend. Nelson would only say of Farnham, "She was a monstrously destructive person."[16]

Anne Hollenbeck said Farnham's destructiveness surfaced in her sessions with Don: "He would quote something—this was Don's way of showing his erudition—and then she would come in on the following line. He didn't need her to come in and say, 'Oh, boy, I'm as smart as you, and if you think you are smarter, you're not.' She was competing with him. Well, for Christ's sake, he was always competing with me. He was always competing with his first wife. In a sense competing with his mother. He was always having to top those damn women."[17]

Despite the tension between Hollenbeck and Farnham, counseling improved the Hollenbecks' relationship for a few months in 1948, at a disastrous time in the marriage, Anne recalled. "We really got to the point where the barriers were down," Anne recalled. "We were beginning to like each other again. And then, boom, one time he said, 'I'm not going back [to see Farnham].' And that was it."[18]

Anne telephoned Farnham and asked what she could do for her husband. Anne recalled that Farnham told her to forget him: "He's no good for any woman. He will never do anything for you."[19]

Anne said that her husband had wanted to end the sessions with the psychiatrist about the time he started to understand the truth about himself—"when it began to tear into his gut." She added, "It was getting too close to the bone." Hollenbeck "found the treatments threatening," said Betty Koenig, a close friend.[20] On one level he rejected Farnham simply because he was skeptical about her and about psychiatry. On another level he rejected Farnham because he would not—or could not—confront himself.

Anne knew her husband was drifting away from her. He, like other newscasters, was idolized by the grown-up groupies at CBS. The more uninterested the newscasters, "the deeper ran the women's attraction," recalled Jack Walters, a former senior writer at CBS. "Such palpitating bosoms for passions that probably never penetrated lower."[21]

A gentle man, Hollenbeck possessed a personal charm—what Kay Campbell, Murrow's assistant, called "a dissipated elegance"—that was especially attractive to women.[22] Beyond the moderately deep, cultivated voice; beyond the tasteful Borsalino hats, Brooks Brothers suits, and stylish suspenders; beyond the Lincolnesque frame and piercing green-brown eyes was the aura of the tragic, fragile, misunderstood loner.

On one occasion during the period leading to their separation in 1951, Hollenbeck told Anne he could get standing room for himself at the opening night of the Metropolitan Opera if he waited in line. As he was about to leave for the opera in his tuxedo and homburg, Anne noticed a button loose on his overcoat. She offered to sew it on, but he said somewhat nervously, "It's all right, baby, you don't have the time." Anne wondered, "What is this act that he doesn't want me to sew on the button?"

The next day Anne happened to be at CBS. She noticed that Alice Weel, a young newswriter who worked with Don, was wearing a corsage of gardenias slightly brown at the edges. "When I saw that corsage," Anne said, "something clicked. That he'd taken Alice to the opera." In the evening Anne confronted him. "You took Alice to the opera, didn't you?" Anne recalled that Don stared in disbelief, "Yes, how did you know?"[23] Anne slugged him.

When Don and Anne separated, Anne and Zoë moved into a nearby apartment on Madison Avenue. Hollenbeck rented a small apartment at the Middletowne, a residential hotel on East 48th Street.

Hollenbeck continued to adore Zoë and their special times: Zoë's building sand castles with him on Martha's Vineyard, sitting in his lap at age eight to steer his '50 crimson Ford convertible, and getting up at 4 or 5 a.m. to accompany him to a CBS studio. On those mornings he bought her an English muffin. "To this day, I adore English muffins," she said.[24]

She recalled visiting her father one night a month: "When I was old enough I would take a suitcase and walk the block [from her mother's apartment] to his apartment." Her father enjoyed taking pictures—"thousands and thousands" of pictures, said Anne—of Zoë in her dressiest clothes. He developed the photos in his closet darkroom. He prominently displayed them on his apartment walls and office desk. And he bought his daughter stylish clothes and accessories that, he wrote, "seemed to me worthy of Zoë." There were blue shoes from Paris and a grown-up purse to accompany a floor-length, off-the-shoulder gown that she wore with pearls when she was eight. "I remember feeling like a princess," Zoë said.[25]

In 1950, as a Christmas present for his six-year-old daughter, he had selected his best radio broadcasts—from an interview of Eleanor Roosevelt to his wartime report from Naples to a controversial *CBS Views the Press* program—and created a three-record sampler. The records would, he hoped, "help answer some questions that will come up as to exactly how I spent my erratic life."[26]

Supporting two households increased the financial pressure on Hollenbeck. In 1951 he earned a princely $32,138, but he gave Anne $1,000 a month, made his income tax payments, contributed to his daughter's Dalton School education, and paid a 10 percent commission to his agents, Gude and Stix. Shortly after he separated from Anne, he told Gude on two occasions that he could not pay Stix and Gude their commission. Gude said, "We'll cut the commission in half until you get on your feet."[27]

Hollenbeck's income increased significantly each year. He earned $35,465 in 1952 and $49,244 in 1953. But the increases brought no feeling of satisfaction or security. "He did not enjoy his success," Anne said. "The times were so perilous for liberals, he was sickened by what was happening in this country." Stern believed that Hollenbeck felt trapped. "He didn't have any other resources," Stern said. "He was under pressure to keep that job to be able to support wife and child in a style to which they had all become accustomed."[28]

Hollenbeck sought outside work to supplement his CBS salary. A year before his death he considered narrating two documentaries for $5,000, a large fee then and money he needed. But his decision to narrate the documentaries was complicated by his abhorrence of guns and killing. The first documentary, a half-hour paean to the Seafarers International Union that was directed and photographed by Stanley Kubrick, did not disturb Hollenbeck. At a preliminary screening of the second, an account of the migration of Canada geese, he reacted strongly to a brief closing sequence in which hunters shot at the geese from blinds. "The lights went on," recalled the projectionist, Manfred Kirchheimer, "Mr. Hollenbeck stood up and said, 'I'll have nothing to do with the slaughter of animals,' . . . and he walked out."[29]

In addition to facing financial pressure, Hollenbeck could not control his drinking. "Don wasn't the kind of guy who would deliberately—particularly when he was cold sober—get himself into trouble unless he was doing it for a reason," said Ned Calmer.[30]

Walters recalled an early morning drinking session at Tim Costello's, a watering hole for CBS news staffers. Among the people in the bar was Arthur Bonner, a diminutive, argumentative young newswriter for CBS who dressed like a hippie and wore a Fu Manchu mustache and long hair almost a decade before the hippies. Calmer and a drunk Hollenbeck entered. Bonner, who admired Hollenbeck, complimented him for a recent *You Are There* television program. Hollenbeck turned to Bonner and said, "What the fuck do you know about it, you little son of a bitch?" Walters said, "Bonner was so shaken that he just quietly put down his glass, turned around, and walked out. Don would do this occasionally, turn on people who liked or loved him most. But this was the alcoholism, this wasn't part of Hollenbeck's nature."[31]

Calmer and the humorist Frank Sullivan invited Hollenbeck to the Players, a private, members-only male social club on Gramercy Park for actors and theater people. The occasion was one of the Players' black-tie "pipe nights" to honor theatrical notables. "From the moment he walked into the place, Don bristled because it was too much of the Rotarian atmosphere," Calmer said. "Don drank and drank. Finally, before the evening was even half over, Don suddenly stood up and said, 'I'm going to get the hell out of this goddamned place.'"[32]

Hollenbeck tried not to let his drinking interfere with work. "He was a heavy drinker in his off times," the former CBS writer Robert Rogow said. "But he wasn't the kind of guy who would sneak off for a drink. He never smelled of it. He never acted drunk."[33]

Walters, who described himself as a recovering alcoholic, agreed that Hollenbeck's drinking rarely affected his work. But he said that Hollenbeck "was always suffering from his hangover or a withdrawal, and this was not recognizable to anybody else. They assumed it was a part of his nature—which indeed it was."[34]

To Hollenbeck, drinking helped define the good life. Walters recalled working one night, then having a few drinks one morning in a New York pub with Calmer and Hollenbeck, whose marriages were "cracking wide open," and barreling down the New Jersey Turnpike with them to Bucks County, Pennsylvania, in Hollenbeck's 1950 red Ford convertible. They were joined by Walters's first cousin Leonie and two unmarried sisters, fans of French wines, to enjoy a somnolent summer day picnicking "in a field Matisse might have painted." Walters wrote about the day in a poem that ends with Hollenbeck saying, "My friends, let us remember this day, for there are not too many of them in our lives."[35]

CBS colleagues did not identify Hollenbeck's behavior as that of an alcoholic, Walters said. "I used to be his substitute when he would break down on the air on radio. He didn't do it that frequently but several times. In the middle of a newscast he just simply stumbled over words and was unable to go on. This would be the result, I think, of withdrawal."[36]

Just when Hollenbeck's coworkers thought his marital problems and job pressures had strained him to the breaking point, he would escape to Chile, Cuba, or Martha's Vineyard for two or three weeks on assignment or vacation. He would return tanned and rested. He would have no on-air problems for many months afterward.

But Hollenbeck's drinking continued. He subsisted on an early morning Danish pastry that he did not finish and coffee, black and bitter. At one time, Walters said, Hollenbeck's refrigerator contained one hard-boiled egg and several magnums of champagne. James Crayhon, a friend from their days together at the Associated Press, doubted that Hollenbeck had ever eaten two pieces of chicken at one meal in his life. When Calmer took Hollenbeck to eat at an excellent French restaurant—Hollenbeck had promised he would change his eating habits—"the only thing Don ate was six snails," Calmer said.[37]

Hollenbeck joked about his emaciation. Despite his cane-thin legs and knobby knees, he vowed to walk to work in Bermuda shorts during a summer hot spell. The next day he arrived at work in long pants. "God damn it," he told his coworkers, "I got halfway here and the urchins were pelting me in the street with garbage, so I turned around and changed."[38]

For almost twelve months in 1950–51, recalled the CBS program assistant Betty Koenig, Hollenbeck had stopped drinking entirely. Shirley Wershba, a CBS newswriter and close friend, said, "I can remember him saying, 'It's like suddenly withdrawing from a kind of nourishment that you've been dependent upon. You have definite physical reactions.' "[39]

Hollenbeck had resented being on the wagon. A nauseated Rogow, nursing a massive hangover, bumped into Hollenbeck one morning and said, "Jesus Christ, I feel terrible." Hollenbeck had fixed him with a sour look and said, "You know something, I almost envy you."[40]

Hollenbeck had begun to drink again, consuming as much as a bottle of scotch a day. "Don had taken to drinking Cutty Sark because it was pale," Calmer said. "He could serve a darker scotch to his friends and he could drink the Cutty Sark. It appeared as if it had been mixed with water."[41]

Hollenbeck's drinking problem, his ulcer, the breakup of his marriage, and his financial insecurity—all weighed heavily on him as he awaited release from his second visit to Doctors Hospital in 1954. He did not reveal the extent of his depression to even his closest friends at CBS. With Stern, however, he was more open. "He was very dismal and he talked about suicide," Stern said. "He talked about it fairly directly."[42]

This was not the first time he had discussed suicide. "Don was always suicidal," said Anne Hollenbeck. "When I first knew him in San Francisco, and he and his second wife were separated, he told me, 'Everything I touch turns to dirt.' It's a frightening thing to hear. He just was not happy with his life. Later, when we became very close to one another, he told me he'd often thought of suicide, contemplated it. But I think he sort of got himself locked into that old Dorothy Parker thing, 'Razors pain you; rivers are damp; acids stain you. . . . You might as well live.' "[43]

The deaths by suicide of friends, the famous, and not-so-famous over the years encouraged Hollenbeck to contemplate his own death by suicide.

On a two-month leave from the editorship of the *San Francisco News* after a nervous breakdown, fifty-year-old Wilbur N. Burkhardt, an acquaintance of Hollenbeck's, plunged to his death from the San Francisco–Oakland Bay Bridge. For seventeen years Burkhardt had campaigned for a bridge across the bay. "He considered its completion a personal triumph," the *News* reported. Hollenbeck told Anne: "I think the Golden Gate is the one I'd pick; the tides would make short work of you, and in double quick time you'd belong to the Pacific."[44]

John Boettiger, who met Anna Eleanor Roosevelt, daughter of President Franklin D. Roosevelt, while a *Chicago Tribune* political reporter, married her in 1935. For almost a decade John and Anna served as publisher and associate editor, respectively, of Hearst's *Seattle Post-Intelligencer*. They bought a Phoenix shopping weekly in 1946 and a year later converted it into the daily *Arizona Times*. They sold the struggling newspaper in 1948 and divorced a year later.[45]

John tried to establish himself as a writer. Then he remarried and joined a New York public relations firm. On a Sunday afternoon in October 1950, though friends said he had seemed in "normal spirits," he was found unconscious in his hotel room after an overdose of sleeping pills. While awaiting admission to a hospital for treatment, the 6 feet 2 inch, two-hundred-pound Boettiger overpowered a male nurse and leaped to his death from the hotel's seventh floor. He left two notes to his wife. One was illegible. The other said: "Good night, darling, we love you." Hollenbeck said he could sympathize with Boettiger's impulse.[46]

The Progressive Wisconsin senator Robert "Young Bob" M. La Follette Jr., for twenty-one years a Senate champion of labor reform, social security, and unemployment relief, lost to Joe McCarthy in the Republican Senate primary of 1946. By 1953 La Follette was working in Washington as a business consultant and enduring depression and a variety of physical health problems, from mild diabetes to diverticulitis, though nothing terminal.

On the afternoon of February 24, La Follette's wife found his body, lying face up on the floor of their bedroom and holding a target pistol. Speculating on La Follette's suicide, the biographer Patrick J. Maney wrote that his 1946 defeat "ate away at him like a cancer and, coupled with an unrewarding job as a business consultant and with the destructive activities of his successor, McCarthy, heavily contributed to his depressed state of mind."[47]

In May 1953 Raymond Kaplan, a forty-two-year-old Voice of America (VOA) radio engineer and former army major, killed himself by stepping in front of a truck. Kaplan said in a note to his wife and son that he had been driven to his death by the fear of persecution by McCarthy: "Once the dogs are set on you, everything you have done since the beginning of time is suspect. It will not be good or possible to be continuously harried and harassed for everything that I do in a job."[48]

In executive session Joseph R. McCarthy's Senate investigating subcommittee had heard testimony that two VOA transmitters had been sited in locations that prevented VOA signals from penetrating the Iron Curtain. McCarthy had implied that the siting errors were part of a Commie conspiracy. Kaplan's note made clear that the team for which he was a liaison officer had chosen the locations "not deliberately" because they were bad sites but because of experts' recommendations: "I have not done anything in my job which I did not think was in the best interest of the country."[49]

Two earlier deaths—an apparent suicide in 1948 and a suicide five months later in 1949—could not have escaped Hollenbeck's mind in 1954, the year Jack O'Brian escalated his attacks in the *Journal-American* on the newscaster.

Laurence Duggan fell—or jumped—to his death from a New York office building on December 20, 1948. Ten days earlier Duggan, whose career at the State Department paralleled that of Alger Hiss, had been questioned by the FBI about his contact with Soviet intelligence in the 1930s. After Duggan's death Representative Karl Mundt, a member of the House Committee on Un-American Activities who had accused Duggan of being part of a Communist ring in the State Department, was asked when other "Communist agents" would be identified. "We'll give them out," he quipped, "as they jump out of windows."[50]

Four days after Duggan's death Attorney General Tom Clark said an investigation had found no evidence tying Duggan to espionage. Clark called Duggan a "loyal employee of the United States government." In the 1990s, however, when thousands of decrypted U.S. and Soviet intelligence documents from a half-century earlier were finally made public, the evidence suggested otherwise.

Citing information from KGB archives, the historian Allen Wein-stein and the retired KGB agent Alexander Vassiliev report that Duggan, code-named "Frank," had begun secretly passing sensitive State Depart-ment information to the Soviet Union in 1936, a year after formal U.S. recognition of the USSR. He had refused money and gifts for his work, telling an agent he "was working for our common ideas." Indeed, ideal-ism had brought many Depression-era liberals to Washington, D.C., to work in Franklin Roosevelt's New Deal government. Some romantic anti-fascists, like Duggan, had seen the radical state economic management of the Union of Soviet Socialist Republics as an admirable experiment worth supporting.

The purges of 1936 through 1939, when the Soviets imprisoned, tortured, and executed millions, had caused Duggan to break with his Soviet han-dlers. During World War II, with the USSR and United States fighting on the same side, a Soviet agent had persuaded Duggan "to help your own country by helping us win the all-out war we are waging." In 1943 and 1944, Duggan had told Soviet intelligence officers about Anglo-American plans to invade Italy and perhaps Nazi-occupied Norway.[51]

Then there was the death of James Forrestal. In 1949 the former secretary of defense, suffering at Bethesda Naval Hospital from "a severe psychosis," wrote a suicide note that included lines from Sophocles about the warrior Ajax, "worn by the waste of time." Forrestal tied one end of his dressing-gown sash to a radiator just below a sixteenth-floor window and the other end around his neck. He climbed out the window and jumped or hanged himself until the sash broke and he fell to his death.[52]

Forrestal's mental illness had first been made public by Drew Pearson and Walter Winchell, who inaccurately and maliciously assaulted Forrestal in columns and radio broadcasts. Westbrook Pegler, whose syndicated col-umns ran in the Hearst papers, charged that Forrestal had been "hounded" by Pearson and Winchell "with dirty aspersions [and] insinuations" until he killed himself.[53]

As a prominent press critic, Hollenbeck was asked about the columnists' responsibility for Forrestal's death. "I don't think Forrestal was hounded to death by the columnists," Hollenbeck said. "Winchell, Pearson and Pegler can dish it out, and if you're a tough enough character you can take it."[54] Jack O'Brian, the New York Journal-American columnist, would test whether Hollenbeck was a tough enough character in 1954.

O'Brian repeatedly attacked Hollenbeck in the Journal-American as a soft-on-Communism, hard-on-McCarthy propagandist who deserved to be dismissed by CBS. On May 26, 1954, scarcely more than a month after Hollenbeck had been discharged from the hospital a second time, O'Brian wrote, "Don Hollenbeck's late evening newscast as usual contained the shrewdly selected unflattering film clip of Sen. McCarthy. . . . And right after CBS Board Chairman Bill Paley's noble speech about objectivity and balance in the selection of news. All the news that fits Hollenbeck's view. Meaning, all the news that's left."[55]

On June 7 O'Brian hammered Hollenbeck again: "We're getting lots of mail wondering how Ch.2's Don Hollenbeck gets away with his slanted newscasts." A week later O'Brian devoted almost his entire column to criticizing Hollenbeck. O'Brian quoted from the letters of readers, inevitably anonymous readers, who just happened to hold exactly the same views as O'Brian. A college instructor, identified by O'Brian as a middle-of-the-roader who asked to keep his identity secret, attacked what he called the antiracism, prounion, anti-American leanings of Hollenbeck, "a graduate of the Commie-laden newspaper '*PM*.'"[56]

The letter writer said that Hollenbeck, during a West Point graduation newsreel on his show, "tossed in a sly, softly spoken and entirely biased aside on a routine loyalty check of our service school graduates. It was shrewd, slick and oily, just enough to get over a left-handed swipe at the necessarily cautious study we must make these days of any danger point, and any place where a man of privately treasonable conscience might secretly plot against our county under the patriotic guise of a uniform must satisfy our fears with a reasonable investigation. . . . Think of what Benedict Arnold almost did."[57]

O'Brian ended his column by asking readers to send him more letters pillorying the Hollenbecks of broadcast journalism: "Please write about political slanting you catch anywhere in radio and TV. We'll print as many as we can. It might help."[58]

O'Brian's attacks troubled Hollenbeck. Murrow told him not to worry. CBS's strategy was to avoid getting into a shouting match with the likes of O'Brian. Hollenbeck should try to ride out the storm, Murrow suggested.[59]

Hollenbeck had used the same strategy during his days on *CBS Views the Press*. His standard response then was, "I have only one answer to those who try to brand me with Communism. That is by continuing my course exactly in the way I have been doing." But this turn-the-other-cheek response made it no easier for Hollenbeck to endure O'Brian's tirades. Hollenbeck obsessed about the *Journal-American* columnist. He dreamed of confronting O'Brian in a verbal duel, a high noon of words.[60]

He also worried about being fired. He knew of the fear that gripped CBS. "Everybody was scared," said Fred Friendly, executive producer of *CBS Reports* and later president of CBS News. "And anybody that wasn't scared was a liar. Everybody was scared, and all the corporations were more scared than anybody."[61]

"Don really was desperate," Anne said. "Desperately beside himself. He was so terrified that he was going to lose his last sinecure." Friendly said, "There comes a time in any big organization when you're somebody they want to fight for or they don't want to fight for. They're weary—it's not that they're out to get you. The one place you don't want to make mistakes is when they have crossed over the line and don't want to fight for you anymore."[62]

Hollenbeck had risked being fired by CBS before. At a time when the network had started to worry about refuting its identification as the Communist Broadcasting System, Hollenbeck had refused to remain silent about oversimplified Cold War reporting that blamed Communists for all the world's woes. He had questioned *Herald Tribune* articles from Greece by the playwright Maxwell Anderson, who concluded that Communist guerrillas were the cause of Greece's problems.

Hollenbeck had begun a 1948 *CBS Views the Press* broadcast about Anderson's articles by crediting veteran correspondents with providing "as accurate and unbiased an account of what is going on in Greece as conditions will permit." But Hollenbeck questioned accounts by "visiting firemen, the in-and-outers" who "pay a quick visit to a place and come up with a lot of quick answers."[63]

When Hollenbeck interviewed Anderson for his side of the story, Anderson said his two articles were garbled in transmission and that three other articles, which would have clarified his position, were not published by the *Herald Tribune*. But the playwright defended the Greek government, which some correspondents were calling a dictatorship, as worthy of U.S. support, though "far from perfect." To him "the third world war had begun," and the civilized world needed to defeat the Communist guerrillas.[64]

Hollenbeck noted that full-time correspondents stationed in Greece found the situation more complicated. The Communist problem existed, they felt, because of an inept government, civil war, unemployment, poverty, hunger, and 400,000 homeless refugees. The government's imprisonment of thirty thousand people without warrants, court action, or the right to bail also aggravated the situation.

Hollenbeck reported that the correspondents said Anderson's claim about the Communist guerrillas' being the sole villain "belonged in the realm of simple fiction rather than of fact." The CBS correspondent George Polk wrote to Hollenbeck from Greece: "I . . . read the whole thing [Hollenbeck's script] aloud to the group [of correspondents]. It restored our faith . . . a slick job of dissection. . . . Frankly, I don't see how you get away with such a script."[65]

Throughout Hollenbeck's time at CBS Murrow's support made a crucial difference to him. "Murrow cared terribly about the things that mattered to him," said Calmer. "And one of them was the commercialization and the lack of spine of radio and later television news. I'm sure that Murrow felt so strongly about Hollenbeck, as he always felt about the people that he cared about particularly, [that] he would have said to Paley, because Murrow wouldn't bother with anybody else, 'Look, if you want my resignation, fire Hollenbeck.' "[66]

But Murrow and the rest of Hollenbeck's CBS colleagues could not provide the personal support he needed in 1954. Murrow, especially, was not psychologically suited to offer Hollenbeck the empathic reassurance that he required while enduring O'Brian's salvos. Murrow, like Hollenbeck, was shy, almost reclusive. "Both were very private," recalled George Herman. Murrow knew many important people, but they were really business acquaintances, not close friends. "His only intimates, and with no great intimacy either, were those with whom he worked every day," said Alexander Kendrick, the CBS correspondent and Murrow biographer. "Even with these close associates he maintained a deep reserve." Murrow's distant, somewhat pontifical, manner led Hollenbeck to address him as "Your Grace."[67]

Hollenbeck, for his part, distanced himself from almost everyone. At a *You Are There* rehearsal three days before his death, he sat in the corner of the studio reading a paperback detective story and not encouraging anyone to chat with him, as some of the actors wanted to do. But Calmer recalled that Hollenbeck said to him, " 'Come on over after you do your next show.' He didn't say, 'I want to talk to you.' He just said, casually, indirect approach as always, something like, 'Drop over.' "[68]

Calmer did not accept the invitation. He had to substitute that afternoon for another broadcaster. And that evening he was expected at his Westchester home to entertain guests. "I didn't, at the time, feel any urgency . . . about his suggestion," Calmer said. "But I recognized in retrospect that he had wanted to talk to me."[69]

That afternoon Hollenbeck went to see his dentist, Dr. Isaih Lew. Hollenbeck's diet of scotch and coffee had destroyed his teeth. Five months earlier

Lew had begun capping them. "Don owed me some money," Lew recalled. "I think it was about $500."

Lew was friend, as well as dentist, to a number of CBS newscasters. He admired the honesty of Hollenbeck's broadcasts. During his visits Hollenbeck was unusually candid with Lew about Jack O'Brian. "That's the only time I heard vehemence in his voice," said Lew of Hollenbeck, who talked to him about "the injustice, the inhumanity" of O'Brian, "the McCarthy tactics. How do you fight it? How impossible it is to overcome. That seemed to be the all-pervading preoccupation."

Lew's last meeting with Hollenbeck was brief. Hollenbeck grumbled about his depression and the attacks on him in the *Journal-American*. "That O'Brian is driving me crazy," he said.

Hollenbeck insisted on paying his $500 bill. "I was in a rush," Lew recalled. "I couldn't spend much time with him except to say, 'Don, what the hell is your hurry?'" With the advantage of hindsight, Lew said, "He obviously had already made up his mind that he was going to do away with himself."[70]

CHAPTER 17

The Sermon in the Suicide

We look for the sermon in the suicide.

—Joan Didion, *The White Album*

Usually, Hollenbeck arrived at CBS's television news offices in the Grand Central Terminal Building at 6 p.m., in plenty of time to select the film and write the words he would deliver on the 11 p.m. *Sunday News Special*, the only television news program that CBS broadcast on Sundays.

He knew the routine well. He had been doing the fifteen minute program continuously for three and a half years, since January 1951. He brought with him crossword puzzles from the *Sunday New York Times* and *Times* of London. He looked at a piece of film, completed one of the puzzles using a pen and none of the vertical clues, reviewed another piece of film, and then worked on the other puzzle.

"Don let the pictures tell the story," said Ted Marvel, the program's veteran director. "He never wrote a script for a film." He dropped in a minimum of words and phrases to complement the images, as if he were ad-libbing. "It enhanced rather than took away from the film," Marvel said.[1]

Hollenbeck chain-smoked Gauloises, strong, unfiltered, dark-tobacco French cigarettes. "When someone waved his arms dramatically at the pungently unpleasant odor," recalled George George, then a graphic artist, "Don would join in the general merriment and light another from the stub of the one he had just consumed."[2]

Hollenbeck worked on the broadcast quickly but calmly. As the pace and noise of the newsroom increased, he imitated the sound of the anxious voices around him, "Chip, chip, chip, chip chip, chip," as if to say, "Why are

A CBS promotional photo shows Hollenbeck preparing for a broadcast of *Sunday News Special*, the program during which he broke down two days before his death by suicide on June 22, 1954.

you guys working so hard at being busy?" About 9 p.m. he usually ducked out to his nearby apartment. He would return in time for the 10:30 p.m. dress rehearsal.

Twenty-five-year-old Nat Brandt, a pulled-down-tie, rolled-up-sleeves newswriter, marveled at Hollenbeck's effortless speed: "Words just seemed to flow from his typewriter, words that were conversational in tone, the true talent of a great radio and TV reporter-writer. For Don I did little but lay out the wire copy as per subject, brief him on the film in hand, write the puff pieces, like about the weather, and also did the sports. Don did all the rest—until that last night."[3]

On Sunday, June 20, 1954, Hollenbeck arrived in the early evening as usual to review the film and write the accompanying words. He appeared to be drunk. "That whole year before," Anne Hollenbeck said, "he was not drinking anything."[4] But this night he had had more than one martini, Anne said. He was despondent about Jack O'Brian's attacks on him. His coworkers, sensitive to his feelings, kept the *Journal-American* from him when it contained one of O'Brian's personal strafings.

It was also Father's Day. "Don had been with his daughter, and I guess it all caught up with him," said Brandt. Zoë said her father had taken her to a neighborhood bar. She was allowed to order her first Shirley Temple, topped with a shiny red maraschino cherry—"the best thing since sliced bread," she said a half-century later. "When you're nine years old, you don't ask for much."[5]

Marvel recognized Hollenbeck's condition, ordered black coffee for him, and then moved him to a couch in a quiet office. Hollenbeck went to sleep. Brandt wrote the program. While Sunday was often a slow news day, Brandt had to contend with the emergency surgery that Harry Truman had undergone. Except for a bulletin late Saturday night about the former president's being rushed to a hospital, CBS had not reported the gall bladder operation on television. "So it was an important item for our Sunday night audience," Brandt said, "and brought up to date Truman's condition."[6]

After sleeping for two hours, Hollenbeck seemed his normal self. Marvel helped him drink more coffee and escorted him to Liederkranz Hall at 111 East 58th Street, where the show aired. But Hollenbeck wound down again during the 10:30 p.m. dress rehearsal.

Marvel was frantic. With only a few minutes remaining before the 11 p.m. program, he decided to let Hollenbeck do the broadcast: "We had put the show together, and I thought he was going to be all right. But God Almighty, from the very beginning on the air it was very obvious that this guy was not himself. It was slurred, slightly slurred, speech. It just wasn't the usual Don Hollenbeck at all."[7]

Hollenbeck dropped the page that contained the news about Truman's operation. "So it never got read," Brandt said. "And, worse still, Ted ended up the show with a tight close-up of Don that showed the bleary eyes, every line in his face, all the pain, and more. I died inwardly when I saw that close-up." Hollenbeck saw himself in the monitor beside the television camera in front of him. Brandt believed that Hollenbeck realized the close-up of his face "finished him."[8]

Hollenbeck's performance unnerved CBS executives. James Burke, television news manager at CBS, watched *Sunday News Special* from home. "That night Hollenbeck was obviously under the weather," Burke recalled. "It wasn't so apparent at the beginning of the broadcast. Toward the middle, it became more obvious. By the time he got to the weather, it was extremely obvious."[9]

Burke said he might have telephoned CBS News president Sig Mickelson. Mickelson remembered receiving a call as soon as the broadcast was over: "Something would have to be done, whether to remove him [from that program] or what, and we had to talk to him during the week." Mickelson insisted that no thought was given to firing Hollenbeck. "It would have been impossibles because it [his contract] was a relatively long-term arrangement," Mickelson said.[10]

But other executives might have been more willing than Mickelson to seek an end to Hollenbeck's career at CBS. Brandt recalled learning, as a junior member of the CBS news staff, how office politics worked: "Burke let me take the blame for something he ordered me to do—interrupt a commercial for a bulletin—even though I had questioned him in advance about the necessity of doing so during prime time when I was left in charge of the newsroom."[11]

At least one of Hollenbeck's superiors at CBS had reprimanded him for his extemporaneous on-air remark after Murrow's broadcast about McCarthy, recalled Anne Hollenbeck and Sherry Walters, secretary for *Sunday News Special*. Anne said Hollenbeck was called in and "told in measured words, 'The—sponsor—just—wants—you—to—give—the—news—and—none—of—your—opinions.'" Now Hollenbeck's performance on *Sunday News Special* gave CBS another reason to consider firing him. Hollenbeck and Sherry Walters retired to a neighborhood bar. She tried to comfort him. "He was very down—very depressed," Walters said. "He didn't eat. He talked about his child in a very wistful way."[12]

Walters accompanied him to his apartment. "Nothing I could say could pull him up, or get him out of the despair," Walters said. She left Hollenbeck's apartment. She was concerned, but she thought there was nothing especially unusual about his state of mind. "He was a very moody kind of person," she said, "that was just his way."[13]

Walter Cronkite, who had moved in 1954 to an apartment not far from Hollenbeck's neighborhood, thought he observed a change in Hollenbeck that year. Cronkite later recalled regularly walking part of the way home with him from CBS. "They were wonderful walks across the city," Cronkite said. Hollenbeck railed against architecturally distinctive buildings' falling to the wrecking ball to be replaced by modern, glass-sheathed boxes. "He was very upset about the new architecture," Cronkite said. Hollenbeck would say, "There goes another one of those glass monsters."

Cronkite thought Hollenbeck "took it far too personally. It really wasn't a balanced comment. I'm trying to find the word for it, [it was] an illusion of some kind." Architecture wasn't the only subject, Cronkite suggested, about which Hollenbeck's strongly held opinions began to border on a worrisome irrationality. Cronkite believed Hollenbeck "was losing it a bit."[14]

Milton Stern, who had seen *Sunday News Special,* called Hollenbeck the next morning. Stern was on vacation at his White Plains home and asked Hollenbeck to visit him. Hollenbeck said he could not. Undeterred, Stern volunteered to come into the city that night to be with Hollenbeck. "He was grateful," Stern said.[15]

Hollenbeck canceled his weekly lunch with John Gude, his agent, to meet Anne for lunch. Hollenbeck joined his wife and friends of hers at a midtown restaurant. He wanted to know whether Anne had seen the broadcast.

Anne had not. "It was one of those times when I had gone to bed early," she recalled. "God damn it. If I had seen that broadcast, I would have done something."[16]

Hollenbeck ordered a martini, his wife a scotch. When the waiter brought the drinks, he said to Hollenbeck, "I've seen you somewhere before, haven't I? I know you from somewhere. You're Don Hollenbeck." The recognition made Hollenbeck smile. He sipped his martini and told Anne, "I'm going to miss all this."[17]

Hollenbeck took Anne in a taxi to the front door of her Madison Avenue apartment building. She could not recall their last words. "Did he say, 'May I come up?' and did I say no? Or did I say, 'Would you like to come up now?' and did he say, 'No, not now'?"[18]

Hollenbeck telephoned CBS in the afternoon to say he would not be in that evening for his 11 p.m. newscast. Bob Trout would substitute for him.

Worried about Hollenbeck, Marvel stopped by his apartment for a conversation and a drink. Then Marvel went home.

Betty Koenig, the CBS program assistant who had been dating Hollenbeck, was concerned by his absence from CBS that Monday afternoon. She called him about 8 p.m. to ask if he wanted her to come over to his apartment. He said he did.

When Koenig arrived, she suggested to Hollenbeck that she go out to buy something for him to eat. But he refused to let her leave. He was drinking, and his conversation rambled. She said to him, "If you go on like this, you're going to lose your job." He only laughed.[19]

He started talking about his daughter, Zoë. She was coming to an age when she would be aware that he was drinking too much. "This bothered him," Koenig said. "He was very attached to her."[20] It was not merely the usual desire to have his child think well of him but a premonition about an early death, a death "coming not necessarily as a matter of course," recalled his friend Charles Gussman.

Gussman remembered asking Hollenbeck, when Zoë was only a preschooler, why he had just bought a country place in Bucks County, Pennsylvania, when he was short of money. Hollenbeck said, "Well, I got to worrying about what Zoë would have if something happened to me." Gussman said, "I didn't have to point out the absurdity of leaving a four-year-old-girl with country real estate."[21] Hollenbeck allowed it was pretty ridiculous and sold the property in 1950.

Hollenbeck focused on little but Zoë, his job, and O'Brian. Hollenbeck did not talk about his own health. "It was really a withdrawal, a disillusionment with life. Nothing really mattered," Koenig said, except O'Brian. She recalled that Hollenbeck once said to her, " 'Oh, if I just could get hold of the SOB'—stronger words than that."[22]

Milton Stern arrived at Hollenbeck's apartment between 10:30 and 11 p.m. He did not know Koenig, but he appreciated the challenge she faced. She was trying to get Hollenbeck into bed. "He had obviously had too much to drink," Stern said. "She was just trying to take care of him. He was extremely agitated."[23]

Finally, Koenig left. Interviewed decades later, she could remember little about the two and a half hours she spent with Hollenbeck: "After going over it a thousand times in my mind, for my own sake I've blocked it out. Someone you care for, and you've left him and then he commits suicide, you go through all the feelings—guilt, sorrow, and remorse. You ask yourself if you did all the things you could."[24]

After a lesson on how to steer her father's crimson 1950 Ford convertible Zoë Hollenbeck stands in the driver's seat while her father looks on admiringly.

Courtesy Zoë Hollenbeck Barr.

After Koenig departed, Stern and Hollenbeck went into the living room. Hollenbeck lamented his isolation from his CBS colleagues. "I'm out of touch with these people," he told Stern. "They don't say anything to me. I don't know where I am. Do I have a job? What have they been doing? Are they afraid? What am I supposed to do? There are stories I did that I can't do today."[25]

Stern tried to calm him: "Look, those guys aren't all that bad. In general terms, sure, some of them are chicken. But some of them are just being what people are, self-absorbed. . . . Believe me, a guy like Murrow has his own problems at this point in history. . . . You probably have a point. They're probably, some of them, saying, 'Oh, let Hollenbeck take care of himself. I'm glad I'm not the object of all these attacks.' But maybe there's something to be done about it." Stern assured Hollenbeck that he would call Gude early in the morning and ask him to meet with CBS management.[26]

Hollenbeck continued to despair about the frustrations of his life. His failed marriage. His job. O'Brian. Suicide.

"He talked about his history of suicide," Stern recalled. "He talked about his mother. He talked about one of his wives. So he was surrounded by the idea of suicide, not that it needs much prompting in certain circumstances. In Don's case, what kind of prompting did it need?"[27]

Stern tried to persuade Hollenbeck to take the train with him to White Plains. But Hollenbeck said he wanted to stay in New York. "I didn't spend forever there because I figured it would be better for him to get to sleep," Stern said. "So I must have left there about 1 a.m."[28]

Stern asked Hollenbeck to call him in the morning, before 8:30 a.m. "He didn't call me. I remember very well saying to my wife and Cora Tolliver, our cleaning woman, 'That man worries me. There's something wrong.' "[29]

Stern telephoned Hollenbeck. No answer. Stern returned to the kitchen where Peg, his wife, and Tolliver were standing. He told them, "I believe that man has killed himself."[30] Both were silent.

"Cora said nothing because she did not know Don," recalled Peg, "and I said nothing because I thought Milton was probably right."[31]

Milton Stern waited awhile, then telephoned Hollenbeck again. A police officer answered and asked who Stern was. "You know, usual cop talk, noise in the background," Stern recalled. "Then I knew."[32]

A tenant of Hollenbeck's apartment hotel had complained that morning to John Bell, the building manager, about the smell of gas. Bell and Henry Tobin, a porter, traced the odor to Hollenbeck's two-and-one-half-room apartment. Tobin entered the apartment and found Hollenbeck, wearing shorts and a bathrobe, slumped on a hassock in his kitchenette. The four burners of the stove and the oven jet were open. The hotel staff called Dr. Max David from across the street. He pronounced Hollenbeck dead. The police arrived and, for forty-five minutes, administered almost four tanks of oxygen. But Hollenbeck could not be revived. Emanuel Neuren, the assistant medical examiner, ruled that Hollenbeck's death had resulted from "illuminating gas poisoning."[33]

The New York papers that had been the subject of Hollenbeck's press criticism got the last word, their accounts of his death marred by error after error. Even the article by the authoritative *Times* contained three mistakes.[34] The front-page story ("Don Hollenbeck a Suicide") in Hearst's *Journal-American*, fittingly perhaps, contained the most inaccuracies. The paper not only published four errors, it also reported that Hollenbeck "had been under criticism from supporters of Sen. [Joseph R.] McCarthy," who accused him of slanting the news.[35] Hearst's flagship newspaper failed to acknowledge, however, that it was Hearst columnists, especially the *Journal-American*'s own O'Brian, who were the chief accusers.

The *New York Post*'s Jay Nelson Tuck, recalling that *CBS Views the Press* had "found the weak points of the Hearst papers," suggested that O'Brian and other Hearst writers had never forgotten and still harbored resentment. Tuck asked in his *Post* column whether O'Brian's tirades in the *Journal-American* "counted for anything in those final hours of [Hollenbeck's] darkness."[36]

The *Post* columnist said he had twice almost told the story of O'Brian's "day after day" attacks on Hollenbeck—of the "persistent campaign to drive him off the air"—but that Hollenbeck had asked his friend to withhold the story. Hollenbeck thought it better, Tuck recalled, "not to be enticed into a gutter fight."[37] Hollenbeck said he would try to ride out O'Brian's attacks. With Hollenbeck dead Tuck angrily dissected O'Brian's smear campaign, including his request for letter writers to Red-bait Hollenbeck.

Tuck called the campaign a cowardly act. O'Brian implied, but never quite said, that Hollenbeck was pro-Communist, Tuck wrote. "O'Brian, after all, does not enjoy Senatorial immunity from the libel laws." Tuck also raised the question of whether the smear campaign was O'Brian's idea or "on the boss's orders." Regardless of the role of William Randolph Hearst or his son, Tuck held O'Brian responsible: "It was not a single attack. It had gone on for months.. . . . It was an attack meant to draw blood."[38]

CBS newscasters also blamed O'Brian for causing Hollenbeck's death. Walter Cronkite described O'Brian as "a McCarthyite Red-baiter who had the distinction, as far as we at CBS News were concerned, of having hounded to a suicide's grave one of our most distinguished reporters." O'Brian "was really a very bad man," Cronkite said. Mike Wallace agreed: "O'Brian would never let up. He was a bad guy. He was a really bad guy. He was a mean son of a bitch, a mean-spirited man."[39]

George Clooney's movie *Good Night, and Good Luck* captured a worried, weary Hollenbeck privately seeking reassurance from Edward R. Murrow about O'Brian's attacks in the *Journal-American*. Hollenbeck says to Murrow in the movie, "He is killing me."

In real life, Wallace, who himself once attempted suicide, echoed the line in the Clooney script: "Jack O'Brian just killed him day after day. He wanted that man. That was the scandal back then—that he was the man who caused Don Hollenbeck's suicide."[40] Joe Wershba, who worked with

Hollenbeck as a reporter at *CBS Views the Press*, more than fifty years later raged at O'Brian, calling him "a murderous son of a bitch, a murderous son of a bitch."[41]

O'Brian's venomous attacks in the *Journal-American* well could have represented an emotional tipping point to Hollenbeck. In portraying Hollenbeck as a soft-on-Communism lefty who deserved to be fired, O'Brian invited the corporate brass at CBS to sack him.[42]

One fact is certain, said Anne Hollenbeck: By killing himself, her husband rid himself of O'Brian as well as the self "he pretty much hated."[43] But even in death Hollenbeck was not rid of O'Brian. Decades after Hollenbeck's death O'Brian still smeared him. When I called O'Brian to arrange a face-to-face interview about his coverage of Hollenbeck, which O'Brian refused, he volunteered that Hollenbeck "was called to Washington to testify [by a congressional committee] the day before he committed suicide. It got very hot for him and he took the easy way out."[44]

To read Hollenbeck's FBI file is to question O'Brian's allegations about Hollenbeck. There is no evidence that Hollenbeck was being called to testify before a congressional committee. There is no evidence that Hollenbeck was a Communist sympathizer. Indeed, two detailed FBI investigation reports suggest Hollenbeck was a patriotic American.[45]

J. Edgar Hoover, the FBI's director, said the bureau had burrowed underground with the Communists to locate informants who could identify Communists and other subversives.[46] FBI agents also prided themselves on conducting thorough field investigations. In 1942, when Hollenbeck applied for a job in the Office of War Information, FBI agents in Lincoln, Omaha, New York, and San Francisco interviewed Hollenbeck's landlords, bankers, editors, and employers. They also spoke to "confidential informants," lawyers, and record keepers at credit associations, courts, police departments, Lincoln High School, and the University of Nebraska.

The agents reported Hollenbeck to be, in the words of one interviewee, "a loyal American."[47]

In 1945 the FBI investigated the possibility that Hollenbeck was the "Hollenback (phonetic)" who spoke "Russian like a native" to a Soviet consulate employee in New York. The FBI concluded that Hollenbeck, who had resigned from OWI on April 22, 1943, and spoke no Russian, was not "the individual referred to as Hollenback (phonetic)."[48]

But O'Brian's column the day after Hollenbeck's death ("Continuing Study of the Continuing CBS News 'Slant'") again portrayed him as a Communist sympathizer: "Hollenbeck was one of the most prominent members of the CBS lefties, and he hewed to its incipient pink line without deviation." Hollenbeck qualified as "a reactionary leftist," O'Brian said: The viewer could be certain of his position "every time, and well in advance of his reaction to any specific news item of national, global or sociological content. His method. . . . was to present each item of 'hard' news in a soft, deceptively straight-forward fashion; then drop in delicately some editorial comment which epitomized the usual CBS political partyline."[49]

As a Murrow protégé who "as such, apparently remained beyond criticism or reasonable discipline," Hollenbeck "drew assignments which paid him lush fees, pinkpainting his news items and analysis always with a steady left hand," O'Brian continued. Then the columnist repeated his guilt-by-association charges: "Hollenbeck was a graduate of several suspicious training posts: He was with the Office of War Information when it was loaded with Commies and pinks of every possible persuasion. He did a stretch as a top editor of the Commie-laden newspaper *PM*, whose staff was infiltrated slyly by a slew of sinister types not equaled this side of the *Daily Worker*."[50]

The day after O'Brian's column appeared, several individuals (whose names were blacked out by the FBI in records the bureau only recently made public) called the FBI to draw its attention to O'Brian's allegations. The informants, echoing O'Brian, labeled Hollenbeck a "'revolutionary leftist' and a protégé of Edward R. Murrow, CBS Executive" and slanter of news "in a very subtle fashion carrying out the Communist Party line." The callers described themselves to the FBI as being "strongly anti-Communist and anxious to be of assistance in following Communism in the field of radio and TV."[51]

No evidence exists in the FBI records or in interviews with CBS chairman William S. Paley and other CBS executives that anyone at the bureau or the network acted on the informants' charges. Indeed, Paley said, "Murrow was very upset [about Hollenbeck's suicide], because they were good friends, and he felt he [Hollenbeck] was a first-class newsman." Murrow reacted angrily to the irony that O'Brian, a Hearst writer, had attacked Hollenbeck for his remark following Murrow's *See It Now* McCarthy broadcast. Newsreels for *See It Now* were shot by Hearst–MGM *News of the Day* employees. Within weeks after Hollenbeck's death Murrow, with Paley's support, had ended the Hearst tie. "Every *News of the Day* cameraman, editor and technician working on *See It Now* resigned from Hearst to come to work for us," said Fred Friendly.[52]

The night of Hollenbeck's death, Murrow closed his *See It Now* telecast with a program segment on military training at West Point and the French

École Spéciale Militaire de Saint-Cyr. The segment ended with Murrow quoting lines from the West Point prayer that seemed to apply to Hollenbeck: "Make us to choose the harder right instead of the easier wrong, and never to be content with a half truth when the whole can be won."

Then Murrow asked permission of his viewers to read a thirty-second tribute to Hollenbeck. Glancing down at the words of the script in his left hand and then staring stonily into the camera, Murrow said: "One of the best programs I ever heard was called 'CBS Views the Press.' A great many people liked it; some didn't. No one ever said it was anything but honest. It was the work of an honest reporter, Don Hollenbeck.. . . . He had been sick lately, and he died this morning. The police said it was suicide—gas." When Murrow got to the word *gas*, his stern face momentarily flashed emotion. For a second his lower lip appeared to disappear under his upper lip.

Then Murrow looked straight into the camera as if he were talking to O'Brian, and said, "Not much of an obit," and continued to speak without looking again at his script: "But at least we had our facts straight, and it was brief, and that's all Don Hollenbeck would have asked."[53]

Murrow also aired a longer tribute on CBS Radio during his 7:45 p.m. newscast. He said Hollenbeck never blunted his perception or courage during his twenty-five years in the news business: "He was a friend of truth, an enemy of injustice and intolerance. His language had a cutting edge, but I never heard him employ it against an individual. He was a gentle man with a well-disciplined mind. There was no arrogance in him, but there was considerable steel.. . . . Those of us who worked with him will miss his grace of manner, his devotion to truth and justice. His funny bone and his backbone were both fully developed."[54]

EPILOGUE

The past is never dead. It's not even past.

—William Faulkner, *Requiem for a Nun*

After Hollenbeck killed himself, commentators for the three major networks broadcast eulogies that tried to sum up his tangled, tortured life. Bill Leonard, a CBS News correspondent speaking on WCBS radio's *This Is New York*, offered the most perceptive assessment.

Leonard, who was one of the few CBS colleagues Hollenbeck invited to his apartment to drink and talk, described him as being too sensitive to endure the consequences of his courage: "No man was ever more poorly fitted for public exposure and few were better at it." Leonard said honesty and shyness were Hollenbeck's "in extraordinary proportions, and this is a desperate condition. . . . On the air, the wisdom, the truth, the humor and the courage that was in him overpowered the gauntness of his face and the flat understatement of his voice. And like a halo, these qualities shone around him."[1]

Leonard said passionate idealism and bitter skepticism about the world dueled in Hollenbeck. "His complexity was his power, and it was his tragedy," Leonard said. "He was at once gentle and fearless, dour and warm and so passionately idealistic that bitterness was his only armor against the world's shortcomings and his own. Words alone behaved the way he wanted them to, and they became his world." Leonard, echoing a line from Shakespeare's *Tragedy of Hamlet*, ended, "Here at CBS, we are sad that he is gone, but sadder that he left unhappy. He was a man of principle, and this is a quality never so important as when it has departed."[2]

CBS veterans found it hard to think about Hollenbeck and not consider reviving a version of his principled *CBS Views the Press*. CBS chairman William S. Paley said that he personally persuaded correspondent Charles Collingwood, who was reluctant to move from the network to a local station, to undertake a televised fifteen-minute version of *CBS Views the Press* for New York's WCBS in 1961. The message was, Collingwood recalled, "What we want to do is encourage the five CBS-owned-and-operated stations to look at the press in their own areas and then possibly we'll go to the network with the pattern of Hollenbeck's program."[3]

WCBS-TV Views the Press had a short, unhappy life. Later CBS broadcast a snippet of media criticism nationally during *CBS Morning News*. And Mike Wallace, who saw Hollenbeck as a hero, tried unsuccessfully to sell Don Hewitt, producer of *60 Minutes*, on occasionally running a Hollenbeck-style segment of press commentary on *60 Minutes*. To Paley, Hollenbeck's *CBS Views the Press* represented a golden moment in the network's history. "He set a very high standard," Paley said. "We never could find anybody after that we thought could do such a good job."[4]

Asked to explain Hollenbeck's success, Paley repeatedly mentioned only the broadcaster's neutrality. "He was an honest man who tried to look at things objectively," Paley said. "He wasn't out to get anybody, he was out to do an objective job in reviewing what the press was doing."[5] But some of what also explained Hollenbeck's success—his independence, intellect, and indignation—made Paley and other network bosses nervous.

They worried not only about rancorous partisanship but also about any opinion and analysis by newscasters. Less than a month before Hollenbeck's death, Paley spoke to the National Association of Radio and Television Broadcasters about "the road to responsibility." He insisted that broadcasters had the same right as print journalists to independent expression. In the next breath, however, he said, "I am not urging anyone to exercise this right."[6]

Others understood that an unexercised right inevitably turns into a nonexistent right. John Crosby, the noted radio and television critic, decried the absence of independent expression in television news when it was still in its infancy. He hoped that Hollenbeck's *CBS Views the Press* would be "the forerunner of other programs of the same style and with as much integrity."[7]

The CBS Radio veteran Robert Lewis Shayon, who became a *Saturday Review of Literature* radio and television critic, in 1951 applauded tape recordings and other improvements in broadcast news reporting. "But let the news producers not stop here," Shayon continued. "Let them . . . apply a point of view to them . . . any point of view so long as it is honest, creative, responsible, and courageous."

Shayon made clear that independent judgment by itself was insufficient. Correspondents also required intelligence. "I have in mind," Shayon wrote, "the kind of job Don Hollenbeck used to do on 'CBS Views the Press.' But that kind of job takes not only money and time—it takes thought; and that's a dimension that's sort of scarce around the networks these days."[8] Hollenbeck drew on history, literature, music and other fields to give his journalism a timeless quality, as if he spoke to the human condition, not just about the human peccadilloes of the day.

George Hamilton Combs, a news commentator heard on WABC, spoke of another Hollenbeck quality—his intense devotion to principle. He would "strike no compromises," Combs said. "Hollenbeck was perhaps an oversensitive man of deep conviction whose boldness belied his mild and self-deprecatory manner. There was little in his voice to denote the crusader. But his moral indignation was incandescent and his sense of justice a personal creed."[9]

Hollenbeck's conscience and hair-trigger impetuousness led him to risk controversy and his career. He stretched to its outermost limit the second-class version of the First Amendment tolerated by the networks, which were afraid to allow analysis and opinion that might anger the public and threaten stations' highly profitable licenses to broadcast. He did not blatantly abuse the networks' rules against the broadcasting of opinion. But, recalled the CBS newscaster Alan Jackson, "He said what he wanted to say."[10]

Sometimes Hollenbeck irreverently targeted a trifle. During a heat wave Hollenbeck had a sound engineer play behind his narration a chorus chanting, from *Kiss Me Kate*, the refrain "It's too darned hot." "The word 'darned' came clear and naughty into the living rooms of America," George George said. "There were calls, there were letters, but . . . the whole affair had been so damned right and fitting. In the early days no one ever risked introducing humor of this order."[11]

Hollenbeck introduced more than humor. George Seldes, editor of the muckraking opinion paper *In Fact*, said Hollenbeck made few friends in journalism with his truth-telling, especially with his criticism of New York's powerful press. Hollenbeck endured the newspapers' charges and threats largely in silence. Seldes said that not many people who heard Hollenbeck "realized the great courage this journalist had exposing not only the McCarthyites but also the newspapers and columnists who were much more responsible than the senator himself for blackening a decade."[12]

The broadcast eulogists lacked the boldness and bravery to remind listeners of the attacks on Hollenbeck by Jack O'Brian and other newspaper columnists. The ABC radio news commentator John W. Vandercook, a liberal whose on-air views had contributed to his firing by NBC in 1946, came as close as any of the eulogists. He broadcast a tribute to Hollenbeck that blamed his death on the "tremendous tensions" of the times. "Tragically," Vandercook concluded, "Don Hollenbeck has somehow been destroyed by them."[13]

Those who had worked with Hollenbeck agonized about whether they could have shielded him from those tensions and prevented him from killing himself. Ted Marvel, the director of *Sunday News Special*, the program on which Hollenbeck had broken down two days before his death, wrote a letter to Anne Hollenbeck seeking her forgiveness. Anne answered, "We all could have done more for him if we had known how. He was too bewildered and sick to see his way clearly. . . . There is nothing to forgive."[14]

Murrow, an honorary pallbearer at Hollenbeck's funeral, did not write to Anne, though he told her, "I was very cavalier with Don." Less than a week after Hollenbeck's death Murrow received the annual Freedom House Award. His acceptance speech rang with a recognition of the dangers inherent in McCarthyism and in the attacks on Hollenbeck by O'Brian and others. The award citation to Murrow might also have referred to Hollenbeck: "Free men were heartened by his courage in exposing those who would divide us by exploiting our fears." Murrow talked about "how much freedom we can afford." The hot war, World War II, had given way to the era of the Cold War and McCarthyism—"a fearsome, frightened time," he said.[15]

Murrow worried aloud about the U.S. decision to curb freedoms during the Cold War. He said the decision should hinge on the immediacy of the danger to our democracy. In a cold war, time exists. Then, in words that brought to mind O'Brian's bullying assaults on Hollenbeck in the *Journal-American* and have a special resonance today, Murrow said: "There has been no pressing need for self-appointed crusaders to replace the courts and to prosecute and condemn dissenters in committees, or in the newspapers, or on television or radio. Many individuals have been cruelly punished."[16]

If independent voices and dissenters are penalized, Murrow said, "the tendency of the citizen will be to avoid trouble," to say nothing, to contribute to nationwide conformity. Conformity begets paralysis, Murrow said, and paralysis subverts the society: "Democracy cannot be kept alive by putting it to sleep. We have to be just as much engrossed with promoting its vigor and liveliness as its military security. One freedom that does not make sense, even in a cold war, is the freedom to reduce freedom."[17]

Without referring specifically to Senator Joseph McCarthy, Murrow ended his speech with words that could refer to the present: "We live in a time of fear and prejudice" that requires Americans not to remain silent.[18] The Senate chose not to remain silent about McCarthy. Only three months later a bipartisan Senate committee unanimously recommended censure because of his behavior as committee chair. The full Senate passed a resolution on December 2, 1954, that condemned McCarthy for abusing his power as a senator. He became invisible as well as infamous. President Eisenhower repeated a quip that was making the rounds in Washington—"It's no longer McCarthyism. It's McCarthywasm."[19]

But McCarthyism had not been McCarthywasm for Hollenbeck. Indeed, McCarthyism—smearing people with charges of disloyal opinions or deeds, however out of date, distorted, or make-believe the charges—predated the Republican senator from Wisconsin and still lives. The venomous twenty-first-century versions—partisan polemical blogs, high-decibel talk-show savagery, political attack ads, and propaganda podcasts—blur the line between journalist and nonjournalist. As Jim Squires, former editor of the Chicago Tribune, writes, "Actors, comedians, politicians, lawyers, infamous criminals and some who fit all five categories regularly masquerade as reporters on newscasts and talk shows."[20]

In every era a democracy needs journalists to report the truth, as best they can, with impartiality. "When the evidence on a controversial subject is fairly and calmly presented," Murrow said, "the public recognizes it for what it is, an effort to illuminate rather than to agitate."[21] But a democracy also needs those journalists, when the moment requires, to honor their conscience, as Hollenbeck repeatedly honored his. Journalists must tackle the toughest topics. And they must speak about them with principle and passion, whatever the personal cost.

Acknowledgments

I owe the deepest debt to those closest to Don Hollenbeck: Zoë Hollenbeck Barr, his daughter; and Anne Hollenbeck, his widow, who spoke freely with me and lent me scrapbooks, photos, broadcast transcripts, and personal correspondence; Joseph Wershba, a *CBS Views the Press* coworker, and Shirley Wershba, also a colleague of Hollenbeck's at CBS (the Wershbas thought so much of Hollenbeck that they named their son for him); and Milton Stern, a friend and neighbor from Hollenbeck's days in New York.

For most of those people, remembrances of Don were filled with anguish. At one point in my correspondence with Anne Hollenbeck, I requested answers to questions raised by my interviews with people at CBS. A close friend of hers wrote to me, "The flashing-back to painful and regretted events was depressing Anne so sorely that she's asked me to take over for her." To those who even today deeply feel Hollenbeck's loss, I offer special thanks.

I never met Hollenbeck and am too young to know his era firsthand. In reconstructing his career—student and reporter in Lincoln, Nebraska; reporter and editor in Omaha; war correspondent in Europe and North Africa; editor and broadcast journalist in New York—I relied heavily on more than 120 interviews with those who knew him. Some of the people interviewed did much more than answer my questions, and I am especially indebted to them.

Joe W. Seacrest, Hollenbeck's former brother-in-law and president and publisher the *Lincoln Journal*, conducted a search of the newspaper's records and gave me family photos and letters. Beatrice "Mike" and James C. Seacrest also helped me. Harold Davey, a descendant of the

Davey-Hollenbeck families and their historian, provided early family photos and details about Malcolm, Nebraska, the hometown of Hollenbeck's mother. I also owe a debt to Rayma Shrader of Lincoln City Libraries; Andrea Faling, associate director, library and archives, of the Nebraska State Historical Society; the Lincoln historian James L. McKee; Gilbert M. Savery, retired managing editor of the *Lincoln Journal*; John Gephart, second vice president, Union Central Life Insurance Company; Mary Ellen Ducey, archivist, University of Nebraska–Lincoln; Dean Will Norton Jr., assistant to Dean Mary H. Garbacz, and professors Jerry Renaud and Larry Walklin of the College of Journalism and Mass Communications, University of Nebraska–Lincoln. The Archives and Special Collections of the University of Nebraska–Lincoln Libraries are home to the Hollenbeck papers.

Roy F. Randolph, a member of Hollenbeck's class at Lincoln High School, provided recollections and a fifty-year-reunion address book for the class of 1921 that helped me locate many classmates. Arthur H. Hudson, the reporter who succeeded Hollenbeck when he left the *Lincoln Journal*, wrote a thirty-five-page reminiscence in 1978 that was a starting point for placing Hollenbeck's experience at the *Journal* in perspective.

Sam Mindell and John Savage, who worked with Hollenbeck on the *Omaha Bee-News* in the 1930s, led me to two dozen *Bee-News* alumni and provided photos, clippings, and other memorabilia from Hollenbeck's years in Omaha. Edward Stanley directed me to people who worked with Hollenbeck during his brief interlude at the Associated Press, as well as during his years in Omaha and New York City.

David Crosson, research historian at the American Heritage Center, University of Wyoming, located manuscripts in the Kenneth Stewart Collection about the early years of *PM*. The photographer David Eisendrath tracked down *PM* veterans I would not have met otherwise. Robert H. Giles, curator of the Nieman Foundation at Harvard, provided access to fourteen boxes of *PM* materials (including David D. Denker's 1951 doctoral dissertation, "The Newspaper *PM*, 1937–1942: An Internal Study") housed in the foundation's Bill Kovach Collection of Contemporary Journalism. Paul Milkman, author of *PM: A New Deal in Journalism 1940–1948*, pointed me to relevant *PM* manuscript collections and critiqued my chapters on Hollenbeck's time at *PM*.

John G. Gude, one-half of Stix and Gude, the agency that represented Hollenbeck during his career as a radio and television commentator, detailed Hollenbeck's turbulent years at CBS, 1946 through 1954. Dozens of people at CBS during that period, from William Paley on down, were exceptionally cooperative.

Five people deserve special mention: Ned Calmer, a CBS commentator and Hollenbeck friend, gave me insight into Hollenbeck's personality; Ted Marvel, director of Hollenbeck's last newscast, relived that broadcast and lent me photos, correspondence, and books; Sig Mickelson, former president of CBS News, spoke candidly about the blacklisting at CBS in the early 1950s; Elizabeth (Koenig) Van Bergen, a CBS program assistant in 1954, recounted the thoughts that Hollenbeck expressed to her during the last days of his life; Jack Walters, a self-described recovering alcoholic and former CBS News staff senior writer, went beyond reminiscence to explain how drinking may have become for Hollenbeck a way of living and dying at once.

The writing of this book—by necessity part time—occurred in two stages. I started in the 1970s while I was editor and publisher of the *Evening News* in Southbridge, Massachusetts. The indulgence of everyone at the *News* allowed the writing to continue. Stasia Beach, Sherry Broskey, Diane Krohn, Doris Mittasch, and Helen Rhodes helped with typing and correspondence.

The research and writing resumed in 2004, after a break of almost twenty years. Bridget and Kate O'Brian, daughters of the *New York Journal-American* columnist Jack O'Brian; David Valenzuela, library director of the *Buffalo News*; and Monique Daviau, researcher, and Lauren Gurgiolo, library assistant, both at the Harry Ransom Center, University of Texas at Austin (home to the *New York Journal-American* photo morgue), helped me understand O'Brian, Hollenbeck's toughest critic. My sense of Buffalo, New York, O'Brian's hometown, benefited from contacts with police officers, pub owners, and priests in the First Ward and the research help of the staffs of the Archives and Special Collections, Buffalo State College, and the Buffalo and Erie County Public Library.

My knowledge of 1940s and 1950s politics deepened from inspection of the J. B. Matthews Papers at Duke University, the Edward R. Murrow Papers at Tufts University, the *Counterattack* files at New York University's Tamiment Library and Robert F. Wagner Labor Archives, and the files on Hollenbeck and O'Brian compiled by offices of the Federal Bureau of Investigation. Craig Wright, an archivist of the Herbert Hoover Presidential Library, found letters critical of Hollenbeck in the James Westbrook Pegler Papers.

To hear and see all extant Hollenbeck broadcasts and to review everything available about Hollenbeck and his era, I benefited from the detective work of Ron Simon, curator, television and radio, and his staff at the Paley

Center for Media (formerly the Museum of Television and Radio) in New York City; Jennifer B. Lee, librarian for public services and programs, Rare Book and Manuscript Library, Columbia University; Michael Henry, reference specialist, Library of American Broadcasting; Mike Mashon, head, and Josie Walters-Johnston, reference librarian, Moving Image Section, of the Motion Picture, Broadcasting and Recorded Sound Division, Library of Congress; Dan Einstein, television archivist, and Mark Quigley, manager, Research and Study Center, of the UCLA Film and Television Archive; Ruta Abolins, director, Media Archives and Peabody Awards Collection, University of Georgia Libraries; Dennis Frank, archivist, Douglas Edwards Archives, St. Bonaventure University; Terry Salomonson, Audio Classics Archive, Howell, Michigan; J. Fred MacDonald, MacDonald & Associates, Chicago; Chris Chandler, CNN Radio, Atlanta; and literally dozens of helpful people on the staffs of the CBS News Archives, Northwestern University Library, Boston University Library's Gotlieb Archival Research Center, and the main branch of the New York Public Library.

I consulted Dr. Madelyn S. Gould, professor of psychiatry and public health, Columbia University, and a volunteer on the *Talk to the Experts* Web site of the American Foundation for Suicide Prevention. She made me aware of recent research about suicide risk factors and recommended changes in wording. While I did not accept all of her recommendations, this book benefits greatly from her thoughtful questions and comments. The errors in the book are mine alone.

Juree Sondker and Philip Leventhal, associate editors, Columbia University Press, skillfully guided the manuscript through the many stages of review and editing to publication. Polly Kummel, a talented copy editor with a light touch, spotted gaps that needed to be filled, paragraphs that deserved to die, and questions that remained to be answered.

Northwestern University president Henry S. Bienen and provost Lawrence B. Dumas generously provided a one-year leave of absence, 2006–07, at the end of my term as dean of Northwestern's Medill School of Journalism. I completed the book during that year, with the support of Dean John Lavine and Senior Associate Dean Richard Roth of Medill.

Charles Geraci, Kasandra Lewis, Judy Lindsay-McCoy, Keerana Swastikul, and Liz Zuehlke at Medill typed or photocopied drafts of the book without a whimper. Michael MacMillan, my son-in-law; Greg Schrader, Medill's director of technology; and Jesse Henderson, Jonathan Love, Matt Paolelli, Todd Schanbacher, David Strebel, and Bret Walker saved me from losing the book manuscript from my various computers, including a dying laptop.

The research and editing assistance of Medill students Alessandra Calderin, Elizabeth A. Davidz, Chris Etheridge, Leah Nylen, Brian D. Sabin, Michael Saccone, Sarah Schaale, Meg Tirrell, and Sisi Wei proved invaluable.

Some people shaped my thinking and writing in important ways, long before I heard about Don Hollenbeck: Fred Rodell and Edson Scudder, exceptional teachers and trusted mentors; Herbert Brucker, Victor Navasky, and Martin Weinberger, editors who influenced my vision of what a journalist should be, and my parents, who always supported me in whatever I undertook.

Others were of crucial importance once I focused on Hollenbeck. Edward Alwood, Ben H. Bagdikian, Alfred Balk, Mervin Block, Roger Boye, James Boylan, Nathan Brandt, Chris Chandler, Christine Cipriani, Frances and Theodore Geiger, Donna Kwiatkowski, Lawrence Lichty, Bob Mann, S. Branson Marley, Mike Wallace, Jack Walters, and Joe and Shirley Wershba provided valuable criticism of drafts of this book and asked the questions that helped me to understand, finally, Hollenbeck's significance.

During the first stage of the writing of this book, my daughters, Jessica and Laura, endured my escapes to the attic typewriter on more nights and weekends than I care to admit. Nancy, my wife, is owed the most. She encouraged me when I needed support and read, edited, typed, critiqued, and lived with this book for thirty-five years. Without her understanding, sacrifice, and love I never would have completed this book.

Notes

Unless otherwise noted, all correspondence and all broadcast scripts and transcripts may be found in Don Hollenbeck, Broadcast Papers (MS 319), Archives and Special Collections, University of Nebraska–Lincoln Libraries. Hollenbeck's CBS Views the Press broadcasts were recorded; printed transcripts of the recordings were distributed to the news media for publicity purposes. But it is impossible to determine whether the written versions of Hollenbeck's other broadcasts are transcripts or scripts revised before broadcast. So they are listed as scripts.

Introduction

1. Fred Friendly, interview by author, July 8, 1975.
2. Mike Wallace, speech titled "Confronting the Crisis," at a December 1997 forum sponsored by the *Columbia Journalism Review.* His remarks were quoted in "The Erosion of Values: A Debate among Journalists over How to Cope," *Columbia Journalism Review*, March–April 1998, 47.
3. Edward R. Murrow, foreword to *This I Believe: The Living Philosophies of One Hundred Thoughtful Men and Women in All Walks of Life*, ed. Edward P. Morgan (New York: Simon and Schuster, 1952), xi.
4. Nat Brandt, interview by author, April 24, 1978.
5. Hollenbeck's principled positions earned him the respect of his colleagues. For example, Walter Cronkite, who joined CBS in 1950 and served almost two decades as anchor of the *CBS Evening News*, called Hollenbeck "a brilliant guy," whose critiques of the press exhibited exceptional courage (Walter Cronkite, interview by author, October 11, 2005).

6. Mike Wallace, interview by author, August 15, 2005; "Erosion of Values," 47.

7. Jack Walters, letter to author, July 21, 1977; Robert Lewis Shayon, interview by author, June 3, 2006.

8. Murrow's tribute, and other broadcast tributes to Hollenbeck following his death, can be heard on an eight-minute, twenty-four second recording in Don Hollenbeck, Broadcast Papers (MS 319; hereafter Hollenbeck Broadcast Papers), Archives and Special Collections, University of Nebraska—Lincoln Libraries.

9. George Clooney said that *Good Night and Good Luck* did not repeat "anywhere the worst of what he [O'Brian] said about Hollenbeck, because I felt people wouldn't believe it." Kerry Lauerman, "Salon Interview: George Clooney," September 16, 2005, www.salon.com/ent/feature/2005/09/16/george_clooney/print.html. Clooney also said the Hearst Corporation refused to grant "us rights [to quote O'Brian's *(New York) Journal-American* articles smearing Hollenbeck]. Then . . . I pulled up other papers; the front page of the New York *Post* says 'Don Hollenbeck kills himself,' and just inside it says, 'Jack O'Brian blamed for his death,' which makes [O'Brian] a news story. His articles were now newsworthy because they were part of a story. So as far as I was concerned, I was welcoming a suit from the Hearst Corp. They backed down eventually."

10. John Horn, letter to author, March 6, 1978.

11. Richard Hofstadter, "The Paranoid Style in American Politics," in David Brion Davis, ed., *The Fear of Conspiracy: Images of Un-American Subversion from the Revolution to the Present* (Ithaca, N.Y.: Cornell University Press, 1971), 2; Davis, introduction to *Fear of Conspiracy*, xviii. See also David H. Bennett, *The Party of Fear: From Nativist Movements to the New Right in American History* (Chapel Hill: University of North Carolina Press, 1988); Jean Pfaelzer, *Driven Out: The Forgotten War against Chinese Americans* (New York: Random House, 2007), 65.

12. "Critics: The Man with the Popular Mind," *Time*, November 20, 1964, 50.

13. Lawrence K. Grossman, interview by author, October 16, 2006; Neal Gabler, *Walter Winchell: Gossip, Power and the Culture of Celebrity* (New York: Knopf, 1994), 436; Nat Hentoff, "N.Y. TV Criticism: The Stumbling Eye," *Village Voice*, March 5, 1958, 5; Nat Hentoff, interview by author, July 27, 2005.

14. Hentoff interview; Bob Schieffer, Face the Nation: *My Favorite Stories from the First Fifty Years of the Award-Winning News Broadcast* (New York: Simon and Schuster, 2004), 26.

15. Sally Bedell Smith, *In All His Glory: The Life of William S. Paley—The Legendary Tycoon and His Brilliant Circle* (New York: Simon and Schuster, 1990), 305.

16. See Thomas Doherty, *Cold War, Cool Medium: Television, McCarthyism, and American Culture* (New York: Columbia University Press, 2003), 255–58.

17. Bob Edwards, *Edward R. Murrow and the Birth of Broadcast Journalism* (Hoboken, N.J.: Wiley, 2004), 123. Also see Harriet Van Horne, "The 'Moral Majority' and Us," *Television Quarterly* 18, no. 1 (Spring 1981): 65. Horne called Hollenbeck

one of the "decent, gifted individuals" who committed suicide. In addition, *Fear on Trial*, a television program that aired on October 2, 1975, and was based on the 1964 book by the CBS broadcaster John Henry Faulk, re-created his case and blamed the McCarthyism of O'Brian and others for Hollenbeck's death. Driven off the air by anti-Communist blacklisters, Faulk fought back in a civil lawsuit not only for himself but also, he said in *Fear on Trial*, for "Don Hollenbeck and the others who have been killed by this thing." Faulk is quoted in Doherty, *Cold War, Cool Medium*, 258. See also Michael C. Burton, *John Henry Faulk: A Biography* (Austin, Tex.: Eakin, 1993), 118.

18. For a transcript of *Good Night, and Good Luck*, see George Clooney and Grant Heslov, *Good Night, and Good Luck: The Screenplay and History behind the Landmark Movie* (New York: Newmarket, 2006), and www.script-o-rama.com/movie_scripts/g/good-night-and good-luck-script.html.

19. Hollenbeck refers to himself as an ordinary working stiff in one of his earliest radio broadcasts for CBS. See "UN in Our Street," October 23, 1946, 1, script. In fairness to *Good Night, and Good Luck*, a commentary by Clooney and Heslov (coauthors of the screenplay) that was added to the widescreen DVD edition of the *Good Night, and Good Luck* makes clear that they did not intend to create a biopic but to capture a moment of courage in the career of the broadcast journalist Edward R. Murrow. "To us," said Clooney, "it's not about the life of a man."

20. William Butler Yeats, "To a Friend Whose Work Has Come to Nothing," in *The Collected Poems of W. B. Yeats* (New York: Macmillan, 1956), 107.

21. Milton Stern, interview by author, May 12, 1975.

22. Ned Calmer, letter to author, July 22, 1977.

1. The Boy *from* Lincoln

1. Neale Copple, *Tower on the Plains: Lincoln's Centennial History, 1859–1959* (Lincoln, Neb.: Lincoln Centennial Commission, 1959), 115.

2. Raymond A. McConnell Jr., "The Prairie Capital," in Virginia Faulkner, ed., *Roundup: A Nebraska Reader* (Lincoln: University of Nebraska Press, 1957), 254.

3. In her 1939 novel *Capital City*, Mari Sandoz portrayed the "better" Lincolnites—Franklinites in the novel—as thinking of themselves "as patrons of the arts" (Sandoz, *Capital City* [Boston: Little, Brown, 1939], 213).

4. McConnell, "Prairie Capital," 255.

5. John D. Hicks, "My Nine Years at the University of Nebraska," *Nebraska History* 46, no. 1 (March 1965): 6.

6. John Andrew Rice, *I Came out of the Eighteenth Century* (New York: Harper, 1942), 290, 288.

7. See Eunice M. Willman Williamson, *Malcolm as It Was: The Story of My Hometown of Malcolm, Nebraska, a Most Wonderful Place to Live and Grow, from Its Very Beginning up to 1948* (Lincoln, Neb.: Dageforde, 1995); "Malcolm, Nebraska

USA: Historical Background" at www.lincoln.ne.gov/towns/malcolm/History. htm.

8. Gilbert M. Savery, interview by author, June 26, 2006.

9. Lincoln city directories for 1902 (p. 283), 1907 (271), 1911 (260), 1916 (314), 1917 (265), 1919 (259), 1922 (223), and 1925 (266).

10. Margaret Williams Baker, letter to author, July 10, 1975; John Gephart, interview by author, February 15, 2008.

11. Kathleen Deming Weller, interview by author, July 4, 1975.

12. Monte Kiffin, interview by author, June 27, 1975.

13. William Bogar, principal of Lincoln High School, letter to author, September 11, 1974, accompanied by transcript of Hollenbeck's high school record.

14. Don Hollenbeck, letter to Anne Murphy, March 30, 1940.

15. *The Links*, 1921 Lincoln High School yearbook, 138–39, Jane Pope Geske Heritage Room, Bennett Martin Public Library, Lincoln, Neb.

16. Joe Wershba's recollection of his conversation with Carl Sandburg, as recorded on "A Tribute to Zoë," a three-record set of reminiscences and radio broadcasts created in 1950 by Don Hollenbeck for his six-year-old daughter, Zoë. The "Tribute to Zoë" records may be found in Hollenbeck Broadcast Papers (MS 319; hereafter Hollenbeck Broadcast Papers), Archives and Special Collections, University of Nebraska–Lincoln Libraries.

17. Marion Easterday Kingdom, letter to author, July 14, 1975.

18. Amorette Pardee Page, letter to author, July 5, 1975.

19. Hollenbeck to Murphy, April 15, 1940.

20. *The Links*, 34.

21. Roy F. Randolph, interview by author, April 4, 1975.

22. Hollenbeck to Murphy, May 4, 1940.

23. Ibid.

24. Philip Aitken, letter to author, July 11, 1975.

25. W. E. Bradley, letter to author, April 10, 1975.

26. Ann Raschke Seacrest, "Genealogy and Heritage of the J. C. Seacrest Family," prepared for a Seacrest family gathering at the Broadmoor, Colorado Springs, Colorado, August 7, 1980, Hollenbeck Broadcast Papers.

27. University of Nebraska transcript for Jessica Sniveley Seacrest, who entered the university on June 8, 1924, and was suspended on February 11, 1925.

28. Carol Reeve Burchette, interview by author, January 25, 1975; Arthur H. Hudson, letter to author, May 12, 1978.

29. Burchette interview; Willa Cather, "Nebraska: The End of the First Cycle," in Faulkner, *Roundup*, 7.

30. Joe W. Seacrest, interview by author, January 24, 1975.

31. Betty Stevens, *Thirty: A History of the* Lincoln Journal (Henderson, Neb.: Service Press, 1999), 94; Jettie Seacrest, quoted in Ted C. Seacrest, "J. C. Seacrest Family Orientation Manual, Section 2: History of the J. C. and Jessie E. Seacrest Family,"

37, Hollenbeck Broadcast Papers; James C. Seacrest, interview by author, June 26, 2006.

32. Burchette interview; Joe W. Seacrest interview.

33. Hudson to author, May 12, 1978.

34. Horace Noland, letter to author, April 22, 1975.

35. Margaret Williams Baker, letter to author, July 10, 1975.

36. Burchette interview.

37. "Seacrest-Hollenbeck" in "Weddings and Announcements," front page of the "Society, Clubs and Editorials" section, *(Lincoln, Neb.) Sunday State Journal*, April 11, 1926, and top-of-the-page photo of Mrs. Don Hollenbeck on the front page of the "Society, Clubs and Editorials" section, *(Lincoln, Neb.) Sunday State Journal*, April 18, 1926; Burchette interview.

38. Rice, *I Came out of the Eighteenth Century*, 290.

39. Chancellor Samuel Avery, quoted in R. McLaren Sawyer, *The Modern University*, vol. 2 of *Centennial History of the University of Nebraska* (Lincoln: Centennial Press, 1973), 38.

40. McConnell, "Prairie Capital," 257.

41. "Move Dishar Frank Bartos," *Lincoln (Neb.) Star*, March 17, 1926, 2; "Finds Mor al Turpitude in Bartos' Act," *Lincoln (Neb.) Star*, June 2, 1926, 2; "Cop Is Hooch Sniffer—'Suspicious' Suitcase Yields Three and a Half Pints of Alleged Booze," *Lincoln (Neb.) Evening State Journal*, December 11, 1926, 6.

42. Hollenbeck to Murphy, June 30, 1940.

43. Harold Stebbens, interview by author, May 26, 1975; Noland to author.

44. "Gere Won Race to Start a Newspaper in New Capital," *Lincoln (Neb.) Evening Journal*, November 2, 1967, centennial edition supplement, 6.

45. Stevens, *Thirty*, 14.

46. On Joe C. Seacrest's career see Will Owen Jones, "A Rough Sketch of the Publisher," *Lincoln State Journal*, July 24, 1927, C-2; Copple, *Tower on the Plains*; and "Gere Won Race."

47. Jones, "A Rough Sketch of the Publisher," C-2; H. L. Mencken, *A Gang of Pecksniffs*, ed. Theo Lippman Jr. (New York: Arlington House, 1975), 63.

48. Ann Raschke Seacrest, quoted in Stevens, *Thirty*, 31.

49. Stevens, *Thirty*, 28.

50. "Reporter and News Staff Director for Thirty Years," *Lincoln (Neb.) State Journal*, July 24, 1927, 12F. On Williams also see Stevens, *Thirty*, 45.

51. Hudson to author, May 12, 1978; Stevens, *Thirty*, 22, quotes Seacrest on "shortcomings."

52. Stevens, *Thirty*, 13 (hogs); Copple, *Tower on the Plains*, 84 (parades). On Gere's life see "Charles Gere" in James L. McKee, *Remember When . . . : Memories of Lincoln* (Lincoln, Neb.: Lee, 1998), 87.

53. Hudson to author, May 12, 1978.

54. Art Hudson, letter to author, March 31, 1978.

55.   Savery interview.

56.   "Men and Things," *Lincoln (Neb.) State Journal*, December 8, 1926, 14; "Python Injures Dancer," *Lincoln (Neb.) State Journal*, October 19, 1926, 1.

57.   Savery interview; Wadhams is quoted in Gilbert M. Savery, "They Trod the Wear-Cupped Stairs: Part III," in *As I Used to Say* (Lincoln, Neb.: Aluminum Pica Pole Press, 2002), 64; "Church and Religion," *Lincoln (Neb.) Evening Journal*, November 2, 1967, centennial edition supplement, 14.

58.   "Goes to Spier's" and "With Spier's," *Lincoln (Neb.) State Journal*, October 7, 1926, 14; "Greet Their Governor; Ray Ronald, Head of 19th District, Rotary, Speaks at Noon Luncheon," *Lincoln (Neb.) State Journal*, December 7, 1926, 14.

59.   "Embarrassed Mr. Orr," *Lincoln (Neb.) Evening Journal*, December 8, 1926, 1.

60.   See *Lincoln (Neb.) State Journal*, December 7, 1926, and Stevens, *Thirty*, 32.

61.   Hudson to author, May 12, 1978.

62.   Nell Greer, interview by author, August 11, 1975; Hudson to author, May 12, 1978.

63.   Burchette interview.

64.   Greer interview; Noland to author.

65.   Robert Y. Ross, undated letter to author, typed on the back of author's letter to Ross, March 28, 1975; Anne Hollenbeck, interview by author, October 26, 1974; Burchette interview. Fred Stouten, a copy editor who worked with Hollenbeck at the *Omaha Bee-News*, recalled the story somewhat differently: "His [Don's] wife came to him. 'Don, I'm going to have a baby, and I don't think it's yours'" (Stouten, interview by author, July 13, 1975). J. Wilson Gaddis described Hollenbeck's "sad marriage": "I think she was playing around flagrantly.... He was very much put out by this" (Gaddis, interview by author, May 2, 1975).

66.   Charles E. Oldfather, for the law firm of Cline, Williams, Wright, Johnson and Oldfather, Lincoln, Neb., letter to author, July 29, 1977.

67.   Ibid.; page proof for Hollenbeck's 1952 *Who's Who in America* listing, attached to a form letter to him from Wheeler Sammons, publisher of that biographical reference book, in Hollenbeck's scrapbook, 142, Hollenbeck Broadcast Papers; "Hollenbeck, Don," *Current Biography* 12, no. 2 (February 1951): 28–30.

68.   Anne Hollenbeck interview, October 26, 1974; T. Seacrest, "J. C. Seacrest Family Orientation Manual," 37.

69.   Hollenbeck interview, October 26, 1974; Margaret Halsey, interview by author, August 20, 1974.

70.   Hollenbeck interview, October 26, 1974.

71.   On the early life of Clara Hollenbeck and the lives of her parents, James Ezekial Davey and Rosalie Davey, see the unpublished family genealogy database, "James E. Davey Descendancy Narrative," prepared by Harold L. Davey, Alexandria, Virginia, who is available at hdavey@comcast.net.

72.   *Portrait and Biographical Album of Lancaster County, Nebraska* (Chicago: Chapman, 1888), 326.

73. Frank O'Connell, *Farewell to the Farm* (Caldwell, Idaho: Caxton, 1962), 101; Hollenbeck interview, October 26, 1974.

74. Certificate of death, Nebraska Department of Health, Bureau of Vital Statistics, state file no. 6601669, Clara Genevieve Hollenbeck, 1636 M Street, Lincoln, Nebraska, August 1, 1927. See also "Woman Found Dead in Home," *Lincoln (Neb.) Star*, August 1, 1927, 1.

75. Halsey interview; Harold L. Davey, e-mail to author, July 10, 2006.

76. Joe W. Seacrest interview.

77. "Lincoln Woman Is Found Dead," *Lincoln (Neb.) State Journal*, August 1, 1927, 1, 12; "Woman Found Dead in Home." Though the *Star* reported that Clara Hollenbeck was forty-eight years old at her death, she actually was forty-six.

78. Hollenbeck to Murphy, June 16, 1940.

79. Hollenbeck interview, October 26, 1974.

80. Hollenbeck to Murphy, March 14, 1940.

2. Working for William Randolph Hearst in Omaha

1. Sam Mindell, interview by author, April 23, 1975. On Omaha see Deb Myers, "Omaha," in Virginia Faulkner, ed., *Roundup: A Nebraska Reader* (Lincoln: University of Nebraska Press, 1957), 157, and G. R. Leighton, "Omaha, Nebraska," *Nebraska History* 19, no. 4 (October–December 1938): 322. On the history of Omaha see James W. Savage and John T. Bell, *History of the City of Omaha, Nebraska* (New York: Munsell, 1894); Alfred Sorenson, *The Story of Omaha from the Pioneer Days to the Present Time* (Omaha: n.p., 1923); Orville D. Menard, *Political Bossism in Mid America: Tom Dennison's Omaha, 1900–1933* (Lanham, Md.: University Press of America, 1989); Lawrence H. Larsen and Barbara J. Cottrell, *The Gate City: A History of Omaha* (Lincoln: University of Nebraska Press, 1997); and Lawrence H. Larsen, Barbara J. Cottrell, Harl A. Dalstrom, and Kay Calamé Dalstrom, *Upstream Metropolis: An Urban Biography of Omaha & Council Bluffs* (Lincoln: University of Nebraska, 2007).

2. Archie Jacobs, interview by author, May 23, 1975; Fred Hunter, interview by author, May 23, 1975.

3. Gilbert M. Savery, interview by author, June 26, 2006; William Randolph Hearst, "Entertaining News," in *Selections from the Writings and Speeches of William Randolph Hearst* (San Francisco: n.p., 1948), 306. For an example from the *Omaha Bee-News*, see "Girl Bandits in Daring Raid," *Omaha Bee-News*, October 26, 1928, 1.

4. John K. Winkler, *William Randolph Hearst: A New Appraisal* (New York: Hastings House, 1955), 220.

5. "Hearst Predicts Defeat of Smith on Rum Issue," *Omaha Bee-News*, September 2, 1928, 1.

6. Mindell interview, April 23, 1975. See "Marion Davies and Clark Gable Score in Witwer's 'Cain and Mabel,'" *Omaha Bee-News*, November 13, 1936, 19.

7. "Kills His Bride for Smoking," *Omaha Bee-News*, November 3, 1928, 1; W. A. Swanberg, *Citizen Hearst* (New York: Scribner's, 1961), 59, 195–96; Irving Baker, interview by author, April 24, 1975.

8. "Real Fistic Drama Rips Show Apart," undated *Omaha Bee-News* clipping, and undated note signed "Hunter" to "Stouten" in Hollenbeck scrapbook, 3, Don Hollenbeck, Broadcast Papers (MS 319; hereafter Hollenbeck Broadcast Papers), Archives and Special Collections, University of Nebraska–Lincoln Libraries.

9. "Omahans Set for Opening Excitement," undated *Omaha Bee-News* clipping in Hollenbeck scrapbook, 4.

10. "'Promoter' Gives Warm Beer and Filthy Show for Dollar," *Omaha Bee-News* clipping, April 27, 1937; "Hoppers So-o-o Big Outstate" and "It's Sad, Sad Tale of Zinsky and Jail," undated *Omaha Bee-News* clippings; Peter Johnson, letter to the editor, *Omaha Bee-News*, September 20, 1938, all in Hollenbeck scrapbook, 3–5.

11. Hunter interview.

12. "Total of 110 Years for $1,000,000 Embezzler; Former Nebraska Banker Lost All Speculating," *New York Times*, April 9, 1931, 4.

13. "Boldness Prevented Being Identified, Says Wupper," *Omaha Bee-News*, April 6, 1931, 2.

14. A box of twenty *Omaha Bee-News* clippings from the series, published between January 29 and February 19, 1937, is in the Hollenbeck Broadcast Papers. The article about Miss Emma Fullaway's kindergarten class at Druid Hill School appeared in the *Omaha Bee-News*, January 29, 1937, 6.

15. See, for example, "Weeping Water—Famous for Its Foursquare Bank System," *Omaha Bee-News*, November 22, 1936, sec. A, 10, as reprinted in brochure, included with letter from John S. Savage to author, May 7, 1975. See also "Plattsmouth—A City That Glories in Its Past and Future," *Omaha Bee-News*, November 15, 1936, sec. A, 10; "Louisville—A Friendly, Bustling Town of Contrasts," *Omaha Bee-News*, November 29, 1936, sec. A, 11; "Nebraska City—A Paradox—An Old City Yet Young," *Omaha Bee-News*, December 6, 1936, sec. A, 12; "Young Man—God to Wahoo—It Lacks Eligibles," *Omaha Bee-News*, January 10, 1937, sec. B, 6; "Ashland, Which Lost Capital Because of Mosquitoes," *Omaha Bee-News*, January 17, 1937, sec. B, 6.

16. Byron Reed, interview by author, April 24, 1975; Gaddis interview; Volta Torrey, interview by author, June 25, 1975.

17. Don Hollenbeck to Anne Murphy, April 20 and 23, 1940.

18. Victor Haas, interview by author, April 24, 1975.

19. Anne Hollenbeck, interview by author, October 27, 1974.

20. Fred Stouten, interview by author, July 13, 1975; Don Hollenbeck, "New Book Marks a Signal Advance," *Omaha Bee-News*, August 15, 1937, A-8.

21. Hollenbeck to Murphy, April 23, 1940.

22. Bess Furman, *Washington By-Line: The Personal History of a Newspaperwoman* (New York: Knopf, 1949), 15, 18–22.

23. Mindell interview, April 23, 1975; Hollenbeck to Murphy, May 4, 1940.

24. Hollenbeck to Murphy, May 4, 1940.

25. Arthur H. Hudson, letter to author, May 12, 1978. See also 1930 census listing for Mildred Raleigh, Omaha, Ward 9, Block No. 78, Douglas County, Nebraska, Enumeration District No. 28–99, Supervisor's District No. 7, Sheet No. 16A.

26. Hollenbeck to Murphy, March 30, 1940.

27. Hollenbeck interview, October 27, 1974.

28. "Miss Raleigh Holiday Bride of Hollenbeck," *Omaha Bee-News*, December 21, 1934, 17. See also Douglas County Courthouse, Omaha, Nebraska, Marriage Records, vol. 72, p. 150, containing Hollenbeck-Raleigh marriage license number 80328 for their marriage on December 20, 1934. For more information about "The Logan," which was listed as a Nebraska National Register Site on July 22, 2005, see the Nebraska State Historical Society Webpage "More Nebraska National Register Sites in Douglas County," www.nebraskahistory.org/histpres/nebraska/douglas2. htm.

29. Stouten interview.

30. Hunter interview.

31. Torrey interview.

32. "$2,807 Needed before July 5," *Omaha World-Herald*, June 15, 1939, 1; "Four Thousand Prizes for Best Ideas to Advance Omaha, State," *Omaha World-Herald*, May 3, 1939, 1; "*World-Herald* Wins Pulitzer Prize Medal; Scrap Drive Example Rated Outstanding Service to Public," *Omaha World-Herald*, May 4, 1943, 1. The first Pulitzer won by a *World-Herald* staff member went in 1919 to H. E. Newbranch, the paper's editor, for his "Law and the Jungle" editorial, which dealt with a mob that stormed the county jail to lynch a prisoner, damaging and burning the building and many valuable records.

33. "The Hearst Newspapers Advocate," *Omaha Bee-News*, November 7, 1928, 22; Ira O. Jones, "A Study of the Editorial Policy of the *Omaha Bee-News* and the *Omaha World-Herald* with Regard to Social Problems," master's thesis, University of Omaha, 1937.

34. Hunter interview.

35. "W. R. Hearst Tells Why People Will Elect Roosevelt," *Omaha Bee-News*, October 24, 1932, 1; "A Plain Talk with the Readers of This Paper by the Editor," *Omaha Bee-News*, October 28, 1928, 2.

36. Swanberg, *Citizen Hearst*, 508; David Nasaw, *The Chief: The Life of William Randolph Hearst* (Boston: Houghton Mifflin, 2000), 426.

37. Stouten interview.

38. Hunter interview.

39. There had been one earlier attempt in Omaha to establish a union. In 1919 Upton Sinclair wrote about a "News-Writers' Union" being formed in Omaha (Sinclair,

The Brass Check: A Study of American Journalism [1919; reprint, New York: Arno, 1970], 419). But the unionization effort failed. Daniel Leab wrote, "On August 20, 1919, the bulk of the *Omaha Bee's* editorial staff, 20 reporters and copy editors, went out on strike after having failed for some time to obtain any satisfaction from the publisher concerning their wage and hour demands. Within 24 hours the strike had ended ingloriously. The morning after the walkout, while their fellow strikers picketed, five of the *Bee* men returned to work, and thereafter throughout the day one after another of the reporters and desk men rushed back to work, hoping that it was not too late to get back their old jobs" (Leab, *A Union of Individuals: The Formation of the American Newspaper Guild, 1933–1936* [New York: Columbia University Press, 1970], 18).

40. Leab, *A Union of Individuals*, 46–47; "Hearst, Sailing, Shifts to NRA," *New York Times*, May 27, 1934, 3.

41. Sam Mindell's first Guild card was dated February 6, 1934.

42. Don Hollenbeck, "Give Us Time," unpublished manuscript, 16–17, Hollenbeck Broadcast Papers.

43. Stouten interview.

44. Swanberg, *Citizen Hearst*, 472–73.

45. Hearst, *Selections*, 368.

46. Ibid., 460. As for the front-page editorial that followed in Hearst's papers, see Arthur M. Schlesinger Jr., *The Age of Roosevelt: The Politics of Upheaval* (Boston: Houghton Mifflin, 1960), 619.

47. Leo C. Rosten, "President Roosevelt and the Washington Correspondents," *Public Opinion Quarterly* 1, no. 1 (January 1937): 51; *Omaha Bee-News*, October 7, 1936, 10, and *Omaha Bee-News*, October 5, 1936, 1.

48. "Gov. Landon Is Only 19 Votes Short of Victory, Poll Shows," *Omaha Bee-News*, October 11, 1936, 1; Mindell interview, April 23, 1975.

49. This comparison is based on the number of pages in the issues for the week of September 16, 1928, and the week of September 19, 1937.

50. Mindell interview, April 23, 1975.

51. Torrey interview. See "*Omaha Bee-News* Ceases Publication," *Omaha World-Herald*, September 28, 1937, 1, and "To Readers of the *Omaha World-Herald* and Former Readers of the *Omaha Bee-News*," *Omaha Morning World-Herald*, September 29, 1937, 1.

52. "Farley Makes (Hello There) Flying Visits; La Platte, Fort Creek Have Big Moments with Party Chief," *Omaha World-Herald*, October 3, 1937, 1.

53. Stouten interview.

54. Edward Stanley, interview by author, June 17, 1975.

55. Mindell interview, November 16, 1975; John Savage, interview by author, April 24, 1975.

56. F. A. "Al" Resch, interview by author, June 25, 1975.

57. James Crayhon, interview by author, July 11, 1975.

58. Hollenbeck to Murphy, April 23, 1940.
59. Hudson to author, May 28, 1978; Stanley interview.
60. Hollenbeck to Murphy, April 12, 1940.
61. Zoë Hollenbeck Barr, interview by author, July 15, 2005; Hollenbeck to Murphy, June 7, 1940.
62. Hollenbeck to Murphy, March 24, 1940.
63. Hollenbeck interview, October 27, 1974.
64. Hollenbeck to Murphy, March 28, 1940.

3. The Founding of *PM*, a "Newspaperman's Ideal"

1. Don Hollenbeck, letters to Anne Murphy, March 13, March 26, and March 24, 1940.
2. Ibid., March 20, 1940.
3. Ibid., March 26, 1940.
4. Ibid., March 31, 1940.
5. Anne Hollenbeck, interview by author, October 27, 1974; Hollenbeck to Murphy, May 18, 1940.
6. Neal Gabler, *Walter Winchell: Gossip, Power, and the Culture of Celebrity* (New York: Knopf, 1994), 74.
7. Ibid., 75.
8. Hollenbeck to Murphy, March 30, 1940.
9. Hollenbeck to Murphy, April 4, 1940.
10. Ibid., April 11, 1940; A. A. Schecter with Edward Anthony, *I Live on Air* (New York: Stokes, 1941), 178–91 and 192–201. See also Elizabeth Fones-Wolf and Nathan Gotfried, "Regulating Class Conflict on the Air: NBC's Relationship with Business and Organized Labor," in Michele Hilmes, ed., *NBC: America's Network* (Berkeley: University of California Press, 2007), 72–73.
11. Hollenbeck to Murphy, April 10, 1940.
12. Ibid., April 23, 1940.
13. Paul Milkman, *PM: A New Deal in Journalism, 1940–1948* (New Brunswick, N.J.: Rutgers University Press, 1997), 18; David D. Denker, "The Newspaper *PM*, 1937–1942: An Internal Study," Ph.D. diss., Yale University, 1951, 81, box 4, *PM* Collection, Bill Kovach Collection of Contemporary Journalism, Nieman Foundation, Harvard University; Myra MacPherson, *All Governments Lie! The Life and Times of Rebel Journalist I. F. Stone* (New York: Scribner's, 2006), 196.
14. On *PM* salaries as of June 27, 1940, see "Editorial Payroll," "Operations—Payroll Personnel 6/27/40" file, box 7, *PM* Collection. Hollenbeck was part of a group of "trained news-getters" with AP experience that McCleery brought to *PM*. The group included Howard Allaway, Herbert Yahraes, Volta Torrey, Lorimer Heywood, Russell Countryman, Mary Morris, and Harold Dietje.

15. Hollenbeck to Anne Murphy, March 20, 1940; J. Anthony Lukas, "Where Are You Now, PM Spinney?" *New Republic*, September 9, 1972, 27.

16. Milkman, *PM: A New Deal in Journalism*, 43.

17. "We, the Staff of PM . . . ," advertisement, *New York Herald Tribune*, June 14, 1940, 11; Milkman, *PM: A New Deal in Journalism*, 41.

18. Approximately eleven thousand people applied for jobs there in only two weeks (Ralph Ingersoll, interview by author, October 19, 1972). The ad that began "We, the staff of *PM* . . ." boasted: "11,062 experienced newspaper people from all over the country applied to *PM*. We are the 151 in the Editorial Department who heard the words: 'When can you start?'"

19. Hollenbeck to Murphy, May 26, 1940.

20. Marshall Field, *Freedom Is More Than a Word* (Chicago: University of Chicago Press, 1945), 93–94; for the Spinney letter see Lukas, "Where Are You Now?" 29.

21. *PM*, June 14, 1940 (preview issue), 18; *PM*, June 18, 1940, 19.

22. Milkman, *PM: A New Deal in Journalism*, 58.

23. "To the Readers of *PM*," *PM*, June 18, 1940, 18.

24. Hollenbeck to Murphy, May 26, 1940.

25. See Richard H. Minear, *Dr. Seuss Goes to War: The World War II Editorial Cartoons of Theodor Seuss Geisel* (New York: New Press, 1999).

26. "General Office Memorandum #47," Ralph Ingersoll to the staff on the suspension of *PM*'s Press page, in "Ingersoll memos 1940—July–September" file, box 7, *PM* Collection; Hodding Carter, *Where Main Street Meets the River* (New York: Rinehart, 1953), 119–20.

27. "Hearst Hits a New Low," *PM*, May 1, 1942, 2; "Hearst Keeps up Barrage of Lies," *PM*, May 5, 1942, 15; "How Hearst Kept Step with Axis for Eight Years," *PM*, May 21, 1942, 1; "The Hate Season Blossoms in the 'Journal-American,'" *PM*, May 4, 1942, 3; Volta Torrey, "Hearst Pushes around Newsboys Who Sell *PM*," *PM*, May 22, 1942, 13; Friends of Democracy, Inc., advertisement, *PM*, May 13, 1942, 2.

28. Denker, "Newspaper *PM*," 100, 137; Milkman, *PM: A New Deal in Journalism*, 177–78.

29. Carter, *Where Main Street Meets the River*, 112.

30. Hollenbeck to Murphy, June 13 and 18, 1940.

31. Some writing had "an amateurish flavor," wrote the historian Frank Luther Mott (Mott, *American Journalism, a History: 1690–1960* [New York: Macmillan, 1962], 772).

32. Hollenbeck to Murphy, June 14, 1940 (his first letter of the day to her).

33. Ibid. (his second letter of the day to her).

34. Kenneth Stewart, "The People Who Made *PM* and the *Star*," 14, 15, manuscript, Kenneth Stewart Collection, American Heritage Center, University of Wyoming Library, Laramie.

35. Victor Bernstein, interview by author, July 2, 1975; Kenneth Stewart, *News Is What We Make It: A Running Story of the Working Press* (Westport, Conn.: Greenwood,

1970), 240; Penn Kimball, interview by author, July 4, 1975; "Experiment in Progress," *Time*, July 29, 1940, 58. *Time* insisted the *PM* copy desk was "the biggest one
in New York City, with five divisions for various sections of the paper and five
managing editors."

36. Milkman, *PM: A New Deal in Journalism*, 14–15; I. F. Stone, interview by author,
April 17, 1975.

37. Robert Lasch, "'*PM*'s Post-Mortem," *Atlantic Monthly*, July 1948, 44. The newspaper boss was John Walker, quoted in Kenneth Stewart, "Notes on Interview with
William McCleery," 2, undated manuscript in the Stewart Collection.

38. Hollenbeck to Murphy, June 21, 1940; Wolcott Gibbs, "Ralph Ingersoll—A Very
Active Type Man," *New Yorker*, May 2, 1942, 28 ("young fogies"); memo from Mr.
Baumrucker, September 10, 1940, "Operations—Payroll Personnel 6/27/40" file,
box 7, *PM* Collection; Milkman, *PM: A New Deal in Journalism*, 56.

39. Hollenbeck to Murphy, June 10, 1940.

40. Lukas, "Where Are You Now?" 27; Milkman, *PM: A New Deal in Journalism*,
52.

41. David Eisendrath, interview by author, July 4, 1975.

42. Hollenbeck to Murphy, June 22, 1940.

43. Ibid., June 2 and July 21, 1940.

44. Ibid., June 20 and July 15, 1940.

45. Ibid., June 11, 1940.

46. Kimball interview; Carter, *Where Main Street Meets the River*, 117.

47. See "Editorial Payroll," June 27, 1940, 14, "Operations—Payroll Personnel 6/27/
40" file, box 7, *PM* Collection; on Bourke-White's chafing at newspaper requirements and on her Mexico assignment, see Hollenbeck to Murphy, July 11,
1940.

48. Kenneth Stewart, interview by author, July 24, 1975; Volta Torrey, letter to author, July 3, 1975. Hollenbeck told Stewart that his reason for joining *PM* was the
"usual dream" of being part of a great newspaper. See "No. 20. Don Hollenbeck,"
response to Stewart's June 1, 1949, questionnaire sent to former *PM* and *Star* employees, Stewart Collection.

49. Ralph Ingersoll, "New Plan for Picture-Editing of *PM*," July 15, 1940, memo, "*PM*
June–July 1940" file, box 7, *PM* Collection.

50. George Lyon, memo, June 18, 1941, "*PM* June–July 1940" file, box 7, *PM* Collection.

51. "'Brass Rail' Walkout Begins Its 518th Day," *PM*, June 18, 1940, 14; on *PM*'s
coverage of the Bethlehem strike, see Milkman, *PM: A New Deal in Journalism*, 128–31; on *PM*'s labor coverage see Ralph Steiner, "Pictures Can Report
Labor Strife Better Than Words," in *Picture Stories of the Year* (New York: *PM*,
1941), 49.

52. Milkman, *PM: A New Deal in Journalism*, 155.

53. Ibid., 45.

54. Louis Stettner, ed., *Weegee* (New York: Knopf, 1977), 13; Kay Reese and Mimi Leipzig, "An Interview with Arthur Leipzig," asmp.org, 1996, www.asmp.org/60th/interview_arthur_leipzig.php.
55. See Milkman, *PM: A New Deal in Journalism*, 44.
56. Ray Platnik, interview by author, July 20, 1975.
57. Hollenbeck to Murphy, June 23, 1940.
58. Ibid., July 21, 1940.

4. Politics at *PM*: Commies and "Good Liberals"

1. Paul Milkman, *PM: A New Deal in Journalism, 1940–1948* (New Brunswick, N.J.: Rutgers University Press, 1997), 60–61.
2. William McLeery, interview by author, July 2, 1975.
3. Ann Coulter, *Treason: Liberal Treachery from the Cold War to the War on Terrorism* (New York: Three Rivers, 2003), 97; I. F. Stone, interview by author, April 17, 1975; Ralph Ingersoll, interview by author, June 15, 1975. Baker is quoted in Milkman, *PM: A New Deal in Journalism*, 123.
4. Penn Kimball, interview by author, July 4, 1975; Penn Kimball, letter to author, no date.
5. Kimball to author.
6. James Wechsler, "The Life and Death of *PM*," *Progressive*, March 1949, 10.
7. Kimball to author.
8. Ralph Ingersoll, "Volunteer Gestapo," *PM*, July 12, 1940, 21; Kenneth Stewart, *News Is What We Make It: A Running Story of the Working Press* (Westport, Conn.: Greenwood, 1970), 243.
9. Ingersoll, "Volunteer Gestapo."
10. Confidential memorandum of Ralph Ingersoll, July 26, 1940, quoted in David D. Denker, "The Newspaper *PM*, 1937–1942: An Internal Study," Ph.D. diss., Yale University, 1951, 156, 24–25, box 4, *PM* Collection, Bill Kovach Collection of Contemporary Journalism, Nieman Foundation, Harvard University.
11. Confidential memorandum of Ralph Ingersoll.
12. See Ralph Ingersoll memorandum, December 21, 1940, and accompanying *PM* editorial, "Communists, Journalism—and *PM*," "Ingersoll Memos—December 1940" file, box 7, *PM* Collection, Bill Kovach Collection of Contemporary Journalism, Nieman Foundation, Harvard University.
13. Ibid.; James Wechsler, *The Age of Suspicion* (New York: Random House, 1953), 167; Ralph Ingersoll, letter to author, September 3, 1974; Hodding Carter, *Where Main Street Meets the River* (New York: Rinehart, 1953), 115.
14. Don Hollenbeck, letter to Anne Murphy, June 11, 1940.
15. Ibid., March 24, 1940.
16. David Denker, interview by author, July 2, 1975; Harold Lavine, interview by

author, July 3, 1975; James Wechsler, letter to author, November 4, 1974; Arnold Beichman, interview by author, October 3, 2006.

17. Two weeks before the publication of *PM*'s first issue, when the paper was publishing only preview copies, Hollenbeck wrote to Anne, "Already we are being called Red because of the amount of space we are giving to Labor news, and that Labor department! A bunch of those pinkos, you know, intellectual comrades!" (Hollenbeck to Murphy, June 2, 1940). In another letter he complained about members of the Newspaper Guild who were sympathetic to the Soviet Union: "The outfit is definitely in the hands of the radicals" (Hollenbeck to Murphy, June 8, 1940).

18. Milkman, *PM: A New Deal in Journalism*, 48.

19. Hollenbeck to Murphy, July 23, 1940.

20. Eugene Lyon, "The Strange Case of *PM*," *American Mercury*, August 1940, 485; Westbrook Pegler, "Autopsy on a Weird Journalistic Creation," *New York Journal-American*, August 31, 1949, clipping in J. B. Matthews Papers, Research Correspondence Series, Box 675, Westbrook Pegler file, Rare Book, Manuscript, and Special Collections Library, Duke University; Denker, "Newspaper *PM*," 90, 149.

21. Penn Kimball, *The File* (San Diego: Harcourt Brace Jovanovich, 1983), 8.

22. Hollenbeck to Murphy, July 25, 1940.

23. Ralph Ingersoll, "To the Readers of *PM*," *PM*, June 18, 1940, 18.

24. Ralph Ingersoll, "Editorializing in News," staff memorandum, "Ingersoll memos 1940—July–September" file, box 7, *PM* Collection.

25. Philip Roth, *The Plot against America* (London: Vintage, 2005), 150.

26. Milkman, *PM: A New Deal in Journalism*, 77.

27. Wayne S. Cole, *Charles A. Lindbergh and the Battle against American Intervention in World War II* (New York: Harcourt Brace Jovanovich, 1974), 42, 44.

28. Ibid., 171–72.

29. Don Hollenbeck, "Lindbergh's Dirtiest Speech: Attack on Jews," *PM*, September 12, 1941, 14.

30. Ibid.

31. Don Hollenbeck, "Fifty-eight Americans Demand Spiked Guns against Hitler," *PM*, September 15, 1941, 10.

32. Don Hollenbeck, "America First's Silence Means It Supports Lindbergh," *PM*, September 16, 1941, 10; Don Hollenbeck, "Hugh Johnson Rolls His Own Rap at Lindbergh," *PM*, September 17, 1941, 11; Don Hollenbeck, "Two More Replies to *PM* Query," *PM*, September 18, 1941, 11; Don Hollenbeck, "America First Ducks Lindbergh Washington Speech," *PM*, September 23, 1941, 10; Don Hollenbeck, "America First Committeemen Take Stand on Lindbergh," *PM*, October 1, 1941, 12; Don Hollenbeck, "America First Resignations," *PM*, October 29, 1941, 10.

33. Cole, *Charles A. Lindbergh and the Battle*, 38.

34. Ibid., 152.

35. Hamilton Fish, *The Challenge of World Communism* (Milwaukee: Bruce, 1946), 214.

36. Don Hollenbeck, "On Negroes in the War Effort," *PM*, March 8, 1942, 9.

37. Don Hollenbeck, "Good News, But—," *PM*, February 13, 1942, 12.

38. Don Hollenbeck, "They Ask for Guns, They Get Pemmican," *PM*, January 23, 1942, 3.

39. Hollenbeck to Murphy, June 14, 1940 (second letter of the day).

40. Ibid.

41. Milkman, *PM: A New Deal in Journalism*, 84. James Crayhon, who was with Hollenbeck at the AP, said that Edward Tuck Stanley "got a lot of us into" the OWI (James Crayhon, interview by author, July 11, 1975).

42. Milkman, *PM: A New Deal in Journalism*, 84; Hollenbeck to Murphy, June 3, 1940.

43. Milkman, *PM: A New Deal in Journalism*, 59.

44. Denker, "Newspaper *PM*," 164–70; Harry A. Berk, Inc., "The Process of Making a *PM* Reader," in "Surveys 1940–1941" file, box 10, *PM* Collection; "Editorial Survey for the Newspaper *PM*, Inc., by R. A. Lasley Inc.," file box 5, *PM* Collection.

45. Kenneth Stewart, "The People Who Made *PM* and the *Star*," 38, manuscript, Kenneth Stewart Collection, American Heritage Center, University of Wyoming Library, Laramie.

46. Hollenbeck to Murphy, June 25, 1940.

47. Alex Coon, County Clerk, Washoe County, Reno, Nevada, letter to author, March 25, 1975, accompanied by a copy dated May 1, 1941, of "Findings of Fact, Conclusions of Law and Decree" in the Second Judicial District Court, County of Washoe, State of Nevada, divorce case of Mildred L. Hollenbeck vs. Don Hollenbeck; marriage certificate, Washoe County, Nevada, No. 127225, for the marriage of Richard F. Jones of Reno and Mildred Hollenbeck of Reno, December 31, 1941. See also Mrs. Richard F. Jones, letter to author, April 5, 1975.

48. Anne Hollenbeck, interview by author, October 27, 1974.

49. Hollenbeck to Murphy, May 15, 1940.

50. Alfred Balk, *The Rise of Radio, from Marconi through the Golden Age* (Jefferson, N.C.: McFarland, 2006), 237.

51. Balk, *Rise of Radio*, 237–38.

52. Robert J. Landry, "Edward R. Murrow," *Scribner's*, December 1938, 8.

53. The quadrupling of hours of network news programming is based on Lawrence W. Lichty and Malachi C. Topping, *American Broadcasting: A Source Book on the History of Radio and Television* (New York: Hastings House, 1975), "Network Radio News Programming—World War II," table 30, 434. The 1942 poll, which was government sponsored, is cited in Mark Bernstein and Alex Lubertozzi, *World War II on the Air: Edward R. Murrow and the Broadcasts That Riveted a Nation* (Naperville, Ill.: Sourcebooks, 2003), 219.

54. Edward Stanley, interview by author, June 17, 1975.
55. D. Hollenbeck to A. Hollenbeck, August 28, 1942.
56. Ibid., February 21, 1943.
57. Ibid., October 24 and September 5, 1942.
58. Ibid., May 15, 1940.

5. Covering World War II from Home and Abroad

1. Don Hollenbeck, letter to Anne Hollenbeck, October 4, 1942.
2. Ibid., December 24, 1942.
3. Ibid., October 17 and December 26, 1942.
4. D. Hollenbeck to A. Hollenbeck, January 10; A. Hollenbeck to D. Hollenbeck, January 28, 1943.
5. D. Hollenbeck to A. Hollenbeck, February 21. 1943.
6. Ibid., May 1, 1940.
7. Ibid., March 11, 1943.
8. Ibid., February 27, 1943.
9. *War Journal*, script, April 11, 1943.
10. Ibid., April 25, 1943, 2.
11. On the Welsh miners: *Bridgebuilders*, script, BBC North American Service, July 20, 1943; on Clark Gable: *War Journal*, script, June 5, 1943; on the Duke of Norfolk: *War Journal*, script, July 24, 1943.
12. *Victory Hour*, script, April 27, 1943, 2.
13. *War Journal*, script, July 7, 1943, 4–5.
14. Ibid., script, May 21, 1943, 2.
15. *American Music*, script of program broadcast from Broughton Senior School, Salford, England, June 30, 1943, 4.
16. *War Journal*, undated script, 1.
17. Ibid., scripts, May 1, 2; June 2, 2; May 24, 1943, 2.
18. Ibid., August 7, 1, and August 9, 1943, 2.
19. D. Hollenbeck to A. Hollenbeck, August 11, 1943.
20. *War Journal*, script, August 24, 1943, 1.
21. D. Hollenbeck to A. Hollenbeck, September 6 and August 6, 1943.
22. Ibid., September 10, 1943.
23. Ibid., May 18, 1940.
24. Ibid., May 16, 1940.
25. Ibid.
26. Untitled script, September 8, 1943, 2.
27. Rick Atkinson, *The Day of Battle: The War in Sicily and Italy, 1943–1944* (New York: Holt, 2007), 214.
28. Eric Morris, *Salerno: A Military Fiasco* (New York: Stein and Day, 1983), 71. Hollenbeck is quoted in "Nebraska's War Correspondents: Charles Arnot, Grant Parr,

Walter G. Rundle, William McGaffin, Don Hollenbeck," *Nebraska History* 25, no. 1 (January–March 1944), clipping, in Hollenbeck scrapbook, 14, Don Hollenbeck, Broadcast Papers (MS 319; hereafter Hollenbeck Broadcast Papers), Archives and Special Collections, University of Nebraska–Lincoln Libraries.

29.   Untitled script, September 9, 1943, 11.

30.   Ibid., 13.

31.   Collected in "A Tribute to Zoë," a three-record set of reminiscences and radio broadcasts created in 1950 by Don Hollenbeck for his six-year-old daughter, Zoë, in the Hollenbeck Broadcast Papers.

32.   *Stars and Stripes*, edition unknown, September 20, 1943, clipping in Hollenbeck scrapbook, 18.

33.   D. Hollenbeck to A. Hollenbeck, September 20, 1943.

34.   Ibid.

35.   Ibid.

36.   Untitled script, September 20, 1943 (22:20–23:23), 2.

37.   "Newsman Finds Angry Nazis Left Salerno Completely Looted," undated *Washington Post* clipping, and "Salerno Thoroughly Looted," undated *New York Times* clipping, Hollenbeck scrapbook, 16.

38.   Untitled scripts, September 13, 1943, 1; September 20, 1943 (12:02:15–12:04:15), 1.

39.   Ibid., September 15, 1943 (Capri), 1, 3.

40.   Ibid., September 15, 1943 (Procida), 1, 5.

41.   D. Hollenbeck to A. Hollenbeck, October 4, 1942; Anne Hollenbeck, interview by author, October 27, 1974.

42.   D. Hollenbeck to A. Hollenbeck, October 13, 1943.

43.   Untitled script, September 19, 1943, 4.

44.   Ibid., September 21 (2320–2322), 2, and October 13, 1943 (after 4 p.m.), 1.

45.   Ibid., November 14, 1943, 1.

46.   Ibid., November 17, 1943, 1.

47.   Ibid., November 18, 1943, 3; D. Hollenbeck to A. Hollenbeck, November 4, 1942.

48.   Don Hollenbeck, "Badoglio Coalition Plan Doesn't Satisfy," *PM*, November 1, 1943, 8.

49.   Untitled scripts, November 22, 2; November 19, 1943, 2.

50.   Ibid., November 25, 1943, 2.

51.   D. Hollenbeck to A. Hollenbeck, November 11, 1943.

52.   D. Hollenbeck to A. Hollenbeck, December 4 and November 5, 1943.

53.   Ibid., December 10, March 9, 1943; "Man about the World," *Time*, May 31, 1943, 44; D. Hollenbeck to A. Hollenbeck, December 4, 1943.

54.   D. Hollenbeck to A. Hollenbeck, December 15, 1943.

55.   "A Tribute to Zoë."

56.   Broadcast tribute to Hollenbeck, June 22, 1954, Hollenbeck Broadcast Papers.

57.   Elizabeth McLeod and Harlan Zinck, "D-Day Documented: A Broadcast Time

Capsule," introductory liner notes to Radio Archives' *D-Day: History as It Happened*, a collection of seventy-two CDs of NBC and CBS radio coverage.

58. Radio Archives' "NBC D-Day Coverage," 1:30–2:30 p.m., June 6, 1944, CD.

59. Ibid.

60. December 20 and 21, 1944, broadcasts.

61. March 2, 1945, broadcast.

62. Hugh M. Cole, *The Ardennes: Battle of the Bulge* (Washington, D.C.: U.S. Department of the Army, Office of the Chief of Military History, 1965), 674.

63. Untitled script, April 12, 1945, 6.

64. Ibid., January 15 and March 7, 1945, broadcasts.

65. January 15 and March 7, 1945, broadcasts.

66. C. J. C. Clarke, letter to Don Hollenbeck, October 5, 1944; Marion Muller, letter to Don Hollenbeck, December 23, 1944; Ethel DeForest Moore, letter to Don Hollenbeck, November 22, 1945; Edith McCabe, letter to Don Hollenbeck, July 9, 1945.

67. Niles Trammell, letter to Don Hollenbeck, November 13, 1944.

68. *World News on Parade*, script, April 15, 1945, 7.

69. May 8, 1945, broadcast.

70. *Milestones on the Road to Peace*, script, May 8, 1945, 23.

71. Untitled script, June 26, 1945, 2.

72. Montana X. Menard, postcard to Don Hollenbeck, January 13, 1947; Mary Elizabeth Forrest, letter to Don Hollenbeck, January 25, 1945; Mary Wye, letter to Don Hollenbeck, January 29, 1945; Andrew Moursund, postcard to Don Hollenbeck, February 1, 1946; Mrs. S. S. Bliss, letter to Don Hollenbeck, July 2, 1945.

73. "The Talk of the Town," *New Yorker*, June 24, 1944, 17; "Inside Stuff Radio," undated *Variety* clipping, Hollenbeck scrapbook, 16.

74. February 23, 1945, broadcast.

75. Charles Gussman, interview by author, September 29, 1973.

76. Charles Gussman, letter to author, May 15, 1977.

77. Ibid.

78. Hollenbeck interview, October 27, 1974.

79. D. Hollenbeck to A. Hollenbeck, August 12, 1945.

80. Ibid., September 15, 1945; A. Hollenbeck to D. Hollenbeck, August 31, 1945.

81. A. Hollenbeck to D. Hollenbeck, September 4, 1945; D. Hollenbeck to A. Hollenbeck, September 15, 1945. The Hollenbeck correspondence and other materials do not make clear why the two executives were competing to be Hollenbeck's boss.

82. D. Hollenbeck to A. Hollenbeck, August 31 and September 7, 1945.

83. John Gude, interview by author, June 16, 1975.

84. Erik Barnouw, *The Golden Web*, vol. 2, *1933 to 1953*, of *A History of Broadcasting in the United States* (New York: Oxford University Press, 1968), 219; Anne Hollenbeck quotes Stix in her letter to Don of September 11, 1945.

85. A. Hollenbeck to D. Hollenbeck, September 17, 1945.

86. D. Hollenbeck to A. Hollenbeck, September 9, 1945.

87. Ibid., August 26 and 30, 1945.

88. Hollenbeck interview, October 27, 1974; Gude interview.

89. Gude interview.

6. Getting Fired by NBC and ABC, Then Hired by CBS

1.   John Gude, interview by author, June 16, 1975.

2.   Robert E. Kintner, letter to Don Hollenbeck, January 30, 1946.

3.   E. A. Clancy, postcard to Don Hollenbeck, May 24, 1946.

4.   "The Atomic Aesop: The Stupid Giant," script, May 21, 1946, in Hollenbeck scrapbook, 94, Don Hollenbeck, Broadcast Papers (MS 319; hereafter Hollenbeck Broadcast Papers), Archives and Special Collections, University of Nebraska–Lincoln Libraries.

5.   Margaret Marshall, letter to Don Hollenbeck, May 25, 1946; J. F. Quinn, letter to Don Hollenbeck, June 3, 1946, on Hollenbeck's powerful delivery; H. Loy Sumner, letter to Don Hollenbeck, May 31, 1946, on Hollenbeck's eloquence; Hermann Hagedorn, *The Bomb That Fell on America* (Santa Barbara, Calif.: Pacific Coast Publishing, 1946), 29.

6.   Raymond Swing, letter to Robert E. Kintner, July 2, 1946; Carolyn Anspacher, letter to Don Hollenbeck, May 30, 1946; Virginia McAuliffe, letter to ABC, with copy to Don Hollenbeck, June 1, 1946.

7.   "Queen Two-Toes," script, July 21, 1946, 5.

8.   Mari Sandoz, letter to Don Hollenbeck , August 26, 1946.

9.   "Off Pitch," *Time*, August 26, 1946, 56.

10. Ibid.

11. Kinter's reaction was described by Gude when I interviewed him.

12. Ibid.; Murray Schumach, "A Modern Miracle," *New York Times*, October 13, 1946, sect. 2, 9.

13. Mary Gill, letter to WJC, August 27, 1946; Berniece Pidwell, letter to Murray Schumach, copy to Don Hollenbeck, October 13, 1946; Harvey Schatzkin, letter to Don Hollenbeck, August 27, 1946; Roland Wehrhein, letter to WJZ, September 6, 1946.

14. Joseph Lev, letter to Don Hollenbeck, September 4, 1946; "Off Pitch," 56; Mrs. Wilma M. Cope, letter to Don Hollenbeck, September 4, 1946.

15. "Blurt v. Blurb," *Time*, September 16, 1946, 8.

16. Ibid.; Mrs. M. F. Miller, letter to George Olenslager, ABC, August 29, 1946.

17. Roger Kenna, vice president, Martin Firearms Co., razor blade division, letter to Louise Gable, September 26, 1946; Schumach, "A Modern Miracle."

18. Pidwell to Schumach; Mr. and Mrs. C. J. Suplee, letter to Don Hollenbeck, September 30, 1946.

19. Milton Stern, interview by author, May 12, 1975; Anne Hollenbeck, interview by author, October 27, 1974.

20. Raymond A. Schroth, *The American Journey of Eric Sevareid* (South Royalston, Vt.: Steerforth, 1995), 338; Ned Calmer, *The Anchorman* (New York: Doubleday, 1970); William L. Shirer, *Stranger Come Home* (Boston: Little, Brown, 1954).

21. "Holiday," undated manuscript attached to August 31, 1944, letter from William Shawn of the *New Yorker*, Hollenbeck Broadcast Papers.

22. Scenario for a ballet titled "Ulysses at Dublin," accompanied by a letter of rejection from Agnes de Mille, May 11, 1945, Hollenbeck Broadcast Papers.

23. Hollenbeck interview, October 27, 1974.

24. "Give Us Time," bound manuscript, Hollenbeck Broadcast Papers.

25. Stern interview; John Leggett, *Ross and Tom: Two American Tragedies* (New York: Simon and Schuster, 1974), 430.

26. Gude interview; Hollenbeck interview, October 27, 1974.

27. Don Hollenbeck on "A Tribute to Zoë," a three-record set of reminiscences and radio broadcasts created in 1950 by Hollenbeck for his six-year-old daughter, Zoë —the quotation is from Hollenbeck's introduction to his April 19, 1949, broadcast with Edward R. Murrow; Jack Walters, interview by author, August 5, 1975; Hollenbeck interview, October 26, 1974. The "Tribute to Zoë" records may be found in the Hollenbeck Broadcast Papers.

28. Bryce Oliver, "Thought Control—American Style," *New Republic*, January 13, 1947, 12, 13.

29. *Men and Books*, script, April 12, 1947, 5, 8.

30. Ibid., August 30, 1947, 7–13.

31. "UN in Our Street," script, October 23, 1946, 4; Don Hollenbeck, "Existentialism: Fashionable Despondency," *Talks: A Quarterly Digest of Addresses in the Public Interest by the Columbia Network*, January 1947, 41–42; "Home Sweet Mal de Mer," script, November 18, 1946; untitled broadcast, script, March 20, 1947; "A Room with a Doom," script, November 15, 1946; untitled broadcasts, scripts, March 27 and April 7, 1947.

32. Untitled broadcast, script, March 31, 1947, 2, 3.

33. Ibid., December 9, 1946, 1–2.

34. Ibid., 3.

35. Ibid., December 25, 1946, 3.

36. *Moments Make the Year*, script, December 31, 1946, 2.

37. Ibid., 5.

38. Ibid., 22.

39. Ibid., 32–33.

40. Ned Calmer, interview by author, August 4, 1975.

41. Ibid.

42. Joseph Wershba, interview by author, November 10, 1974.

43. Ibid.

44. Wershba interview, August 10, 2006. A copy of the 1950 Hollenbeck-Murrow broadcast was made available by the radio newscast collector Chris Chandler of Atlanta. For a written description of the Hollenbeck-Murrow broadcast, see Thomas Maeder, afterword in Will Cuppy, *The Decline and Fall of Practically Everybody*, ed. Fred Feldkamp (Jaffrey, N.J.: Godine, 1984), 230.

45. Cuppy, *The Decline and Fall of Practically Everybody*, 1st ed., ed. Fred Feldkamp (New York: Holt, 1950), 170–71.

46. Ibid., 213.

47. The quote from *Alcamaeon* begins Hollenbeck's January 7, 1947, broadcast. The quote from the *Iliad* ends Hollenbeck's March 27, 1947, broadcast, Hollenbeck Broadcast Papers.

48. Richard Hottelet is quoted in Joseph E. Persico, *Edward R. Murrow: An American Original* (New York: McGraw-Hill, 1988), 233. Malnourishment and racial discrimination were the topics of Hollenbeck's untitled December 28, 1946, radio feature; the script is in his papers.

49. Meyer Berger, *The Story of the* New York Times: *The First 100 Years, 1851–1951* (1951; reprint, New York: Arno, 1970), 495.

50. "A La Mode," script, October 30, 1946, 1, 2.

51. "The Princess with the Criminal Record," script, November 28, 1946, 4; "Modern Witchcraft," script, October 31, 1946, 3.

52. "The Great God K," script, December 2, 1946, 3.

53. Untitled broadcast, script, April 19, 1949, 3.

54. Ibid., 5.

55. *CBS Reports: The Murder of George Polk*, April 27, 1949, in the collection of MacDonald and Associates, Chicago.

56. *Pathfinder* magazine, March 22, 1950, is quoted in "Hollenbeck, Don," *Current Biography* 12, no. 2 (February 1951): 29; Gene De Poris, interview by author, July 10, 1975.

57. *News of America*, April 11, 1949, broadcast, in the collection of MacDonald and Associates, Chicago.

58. "Joan of Arc Is Burned at the Stake," *CBS Is There*, February 29, 1948, on "A Tribute to Zoë."

59. Edmund Scott, interview by author, November 10, 1974.

60. William S. Paley, "Keeping the Editorial Page Out of Radio," *Broadcasting*, December 15, 1937, 20.

61. William S. Paley, *As It Happened: A Memoir* (New York: Doubleday, 1979), 120. See also John K. Hutchens, "Quiet, Please: The Columbia Network Tells Its Analysts to Keep Their Opinions to Themselves," *New York Times*, September 26, 1943, X9.

62. John W. Vandercook is quoted in Edward Bliss Jr., *Now the News: The Story of Broadcast Journalism* (New York: Columbia University Press, 1991), 140.

63. Ibid., 141.

64. Alexander Kendrick, *Prime Time: The Life of Edward R. Murrow* (Boston: Little, Brown, 1969), 264.

65. Ibid., 299; Wershba interview, November 10, 1974.

66. William S. Paley, interview by author, February 16, 1977.

67. James Crayhon, interview by author, July 11,1975; Wershba interview, November 10, 1974.

68. "Critical Analyses of New York Press Scheduled to Start May 31 on WCBS," WCBS press release, May 26, 1947, Hollenbeck Broadcast Papers.

7. The Invention of *CBS Views the Press*

1. "Viewing the Press," *Washington Post*, May 29, 1947, 14.

2. Joseph Wershba, interview by author, November 10, 1974.

3. Ibid.

4. Lillian E. Ross, George Whitman, Joe Wershba, Helen Ross, and Mel Fiske, *The "Argonauts"* (New York: Modern Age Books, 1940), 1.

5. Ibid., 165.

6. Wershba interview, November 10, 1974.

7. Edmund Scott, interview by author, November 10, 1974.

8. Ibid.

9. Wershba interview, November 10, 1974.

10. "Critical Analyses of New York Press Scheduled to Start May 31 on WCBS," CBS press release, May 26, 1957, Don Hollenbeck, Broadcast Papers (MS 319; hereafter Hollenbeck Broadcast Papers), Archives and Special Collections, University of Nebraska–Lincoln Libraries.

11. Wershba interview, November 10, 1974; "Viewing the Press," 14; John T. McManus, "New CBS Program Will Criticize New York Press," *PM*, May 26, 1947, 19.

12. Wershba interview, September 7, 2006.

13. *CBS Views the Press*, broadcast transcript, May 31, 1947, 2.

14. Ibid., 1.

15. Ibid., 8.

16. Ibid.

17. Ibid., 9.

18. Ibid.

19. Ibid., 10

20. John P. Lewis, "The Press Gets a Policeman," *PM*, June 3, 1947, 25.

21. John Crosby, "The Press in Review," *New York Herald Tribune*, June 9, 1947, 15; Herman Schoenfeld, "Man-Bites-Dog Act Slays N.Y. Press: Dailies' Reaction Big $64 Question," *Variety*, June 4, 1947, 29.

22. Walter Winchell, "In New York," *New York Mirror*, undated clipping, in Hollenbeck scrapbook, 28, Hollenbeck Broadcast Papers; Saul Carson, "Doldrums," *New*

Republic, June 16, 1947, 35; "Affiliates Would Copy 'CBS Views,'" undated and un-identified clipping, Hollenbeck scrapbook, 55; "CBS Wind Sock," *Broadcasting*, June 9, 1947, clipping, in Hollenbeck scrapbook, 38.

23. "Radio Takes a Look at the Press—It's Mostly a Mess,'" *Frontpage*, June 1947, 5; Jerry Franken, "CBS Views the Press," undated *Billboard* clipping, 15, in Hollen-beck scrapbook, 37; "CBS Station in New York Starts Criticism of Press," *Editor and Publisher*, June 7, 1947, 11, 95, in Hollenbeck scrapbook, 31.

24. Nick Kenny, letter to Westbrook Pegler, December 5, 1947, Herbert Hoover Presi-dential Library, West Branch, Iowa.

25. "CBS Station in New York Starts Criticism of Press," 11.

26. William S. Paley, CBS interoffice memo to Edward R. Murrow, June 17, 1947, in Hollenbeck scrapbook, 25.

27. Sulzberger is quoted in Lewis, "Press Gets a Policeman," *PM*, 25; *Jamaica (N.Y.) Leader-Observer*, June 5, 1947, clipping in Hollenbeck scrapbook, 29.

28. Jack Gould, "CBS and the Press: New Program Appraises Performance of New York Newspapers," *New York Times*, June 8, 1947, sec. 2, 9.

29. Ibid.

30. Arthur Perles, CBS office communication to Edward R. Murrow, June 2, 1947, in Hollenbeck scrapbook, 26; John T. McManus, "Listeners Cry for More CBS Views on the News," *PM*, June 3, 1947, 23.

31. Seymour Peck, interview by author, July 21, 1977; William S. Paley, interview by author, February 16, 1977.

32. "Look Who's Talking," *Time*, June 16, 1947, 54; Don Hollenbeck, "CBS Views the Press," *Atlantic*, September 1948; for other Hollenbeck self-criticism, see *CBS Views the Press*, broadcast transcript, June 4, 1949, 1–10.

33. Wershba interview, November 10, 1974.

34. Richard Strouse, letter to Don Hollenbeck, July 20, 1948.

35. Ibid.

36. Scott interview.

37. Ibid.

38. Robert Frost, "Mowing," in *Complete Poems of Robert Frost* (New York: Holt, 1949), 25.

39. Wershba interview, November 10, 1974.

40. George Herman, letter to author, September 29, 1974.

41. Don Hollenbeck, "'Dear Mr. Hollenbeck'—," undated clipping (with 1948 pen-ciled on it) from *Page One* in Hollenbeck scrapbook, 93; Herman to author.

42. Hollenbeck, "'Dear Mr. Hollenbeck.'"

43. Wershba interview, November 10, 1974; Ned Calmer, interview by author, August 4, 1975; Fred Friendly, *Due to Circumstances beyond Our Control . . .* (New York: Vintage, 1967), 63.

44. *CBS Views the Press*, broadcast transcript, February 14, 1948, 9.

45. For Hottelet's assessment of *PM* see *CBS Views the Press*, broadcast transcript, March 20, 1948, 1–9; for Hollenbeck's assessment of the *Star*, *CBS Views the Press*, broadcast transcript, May 1, 1948, 1.

46. Wershba interview, November 10, 1974.

47. Hollenbeck, " 'Dear Mr. Hollenbeck.' "

48. *CBS Views the Press*, broadcast transcript, December 27, 1947, 1; Cabell Greet, memo to Don Hollenbeck, December 30, 1947, in Hollenbeck scrapbook, 81.

49. A. M. Sperber, *Murrow: His Life and Times* (New York: Freundlich, 1986), 294; Edward R. Murrow, "Notes on the News," *New York Herald Tribune*, September 5, 1947, clipping in Hollenbeck scrapbook, 56; Scott interview.

50. Wershba interview, November 10, 1974.

51. "Man with a View," *Cue*, December 18, 1948, 17; *CBS Views the Press*, broadcast transcript, December 25, 1948, 1.

52. *CBS Views the Press*, broadcast transcript, September 10, 1949, 1–5.

53. Ibid., June 7, 1947, 5.

54. Ibid., November 8, 1947, 6, 7.

55. Ibid., November 22, 1947, 4; May 24, 1948, 4–6; August 28, 1948, 9–11; May 29, 1948, 4.

56. Ibid., May 29, 1948, 10; December 17, 1949, 3–10.

57. Ibid., July 10, 1948, 8.

58. Ibid., 2, 3. Here Hollenbeck is quoting the freelance journalist Nathan Robertson.

59. *CBS Views the Press*, broadcast transcript, October 22, 1949, 3, 4, 9.

60. Ibid., November 26, 1949, 3, 6.

61. Ibid., September 29, 1947, 9.

62. Ibid.

63. Ibid., October 15, 1949, 4, 5.

64. Margaret Halsey, *Color Blind: A White Woman Looks at the Negro* (New York: Simon and Schuster, 1946), 150.

65. Milton Stern, interview by author, May 12, 1975; Ted Marvel, interview by author, August 9, 1975.

66. *CBS Views the Press*, broadcast transcript, June 14, 1947, 1.

67. Ibid., 2.

68. Ibid., 4

69. Ibid., June 19, 1948, 1.

70. Ibid., August 21, 1948, 4; Bill Steigerwald, "Sprigle's Secret Journey," *Pittsburgh Post-Gazette*, undated, www.post-gazette.com/sprigle/Sprigleintroduction.asp.

71. Ibid., 5; December 3, 1949, 6–7.

72. Ted Poston, "Horror in Sunny Florida: Negro Reporter from Up North Put in 'His Place' by the South," *New York Post*, September 7, 1949, reprinted in Ted Poston, *A First Draft of History*, ed. Kathleen A. Hauke (Athens: University of Georgia

Press, 2000), 65. On Poston see Kathleen A. Hauke, *Ted Poston: Pioneer American Journalist* (Athens: University of Georgia Press, 1998).

73. *CBS Views the Press*, broadcast transcript, December 3, 1949, 7; for the Supreme Court's decision see *Shepherd v. Florida*, 341 U.S. 50 (1951).

74. Ibid., September 17, 1949, 8.

75. Ibid., November 6, 1948, 2.

76. Ibid., November 13, 1948, 2–4.

77. "People Are Talking About . . . ," *Vogue*, September 1947, 181; Helen Rowland, "Radio and Television," *Writer's Digest*, October 1947, 75; Jerry Walker, "Don Hollenbeck Views Much-Honored Show," *Editor and Publisher*, May 15, 1948, 44.

78. CBS press release about 1948 Peabody award winners, April 14, 1948, 2, in Hollenbeck scrapbook, 88; Elmer Davis, letter to Don Hollenbeck, April 26, 1948, Hollenbeck scrapbook, 92.

8. Jack O'Brian: Buffalo Dock-Walloper to Broadway Drama Critic

1. For six weeks in 1991 Gladys K. Drewelow, chair of the Room Dedication Committee of the Buffalo Convention Center, interviewed Jack O'Brian by telephone. She shared her eleven-page summary of those interviews with him. He added corrections and personal notes. The summary, "Jack O'Brian Reminisces about Buffalo," accompanied Drewelow's December 10, 1991, letter to Elliott Shapiro of the library at the *Buffalo (N.Y.) News*. The interviews with O'Brian were in anticipation of his October 1991 visit to Buffalo for the unveiling of a public room at the Buffalo Convention Center bearing his name. The description of O'Brian's parents appears on page 2A of "Jack O'Brian Reminisces about Buffalo."

2. The Reverend Donald J. Lutz, interview by author, June 29, 2006. On the early First Ward see Mark Goldman, *City on the Lake: The Challenge of Change in Buffalo, New York* (Buffalo, N.Y.: Prometheus, 1990), 56. See also Goldman, *High Hopes: The Rise and Decline of Buffalo, New York* (Albany: State University of New York Press, 1983), 73, 78–79, 84.

3. Erik Brady, "Bdwy.'s Favorite Scribe Is Buflo.'s Favorite Son," *Buffalo Courier-Express*, May 18, 1979, 3; Annette Bitterman, records secretary of the Department of Catholic Education, Diocese of Buffalo, Buffalo, New York, letter to author, June 12, 2006.

4. Drewelow, "Jack O'Brian Reminisces about Buffalo," 2A, 7; Dick Christian, "Jack O'Brian Hailed for Successful Career," *Buffalo News*, October 30, 1991, B-12 (O'Brian on education).

5. Don Hollenbeck to Anne Murphy, March 26, 1940; Christian, "Jack O'Brian Hailed."

6. Drewelow, "Jack O'Brian Reminisces about Buffalo," 2A.

7. "O'Brian, Jack," in Frances C. Locher, ed., *Contemporary Authors* (Detroit: Gale Research, 1982), 370–71.

8. Marty O'Neill, "Columnist Jack O'Brian Enthralls Advertising Women with Star Tales," *Buffalo Courier-Express*, April 26, 1978, 19.

9. Bridget O'Brian, interview by author, June 8, 2005.

10. Drewelow, "Jack O'Brian Reminisces about Buffalo," 10.

11. Ibid., 8.

12. Ibid.

13. Ibid.

14. Ibid., 9, 3.

15. Ibid.

16. "The Man with the Popular Mind," *Time*, November 20, 1964, 50.

17. "O'Brian, Jack," 371.

9. Press Criticism: From Name-calling to Nuance

1. Max Lerner, "The Six Deadly Press Sins," *PM*, December 4, 1947, 12.

2. Leon Harris, *Upton Sinclair: American Rebel* (New York: Crowell, 1975), 37, 178; Upton Sinclair, *The Brass Check: A Study of American Journalism* (1919; reprint, New York: Arno, 1970), 125.

3. On the *New York Times* and socialists, see Sinclair, *Brass Check*, 330, 436; on the sales of *The Brass Check*, see Judson Grenier, "Upton Sinclair and the Press: *The Brass Check* Reconsidered," *Journalism Quarterly* 49, no. 3 (Autumn 1972): 430.

4. Lewis Mumford, *The Golden Day: A Study in American Literature and Culture* (Boston: Beacon, 1957), 124; Sinclair, *Brass Check*, 438–39.

5. H. L. Mencken, *A Gang of Pecksniffs*, ed. Theo Lippman Jr. (New York: Arlington House, 1975), 61.

6. Sinclair, *Brass Check*, 406–7.

7. Lerner, "Six Deadly Press Sins," 12.

8. Raymond Sokolov, *Wayward Reporter: The Life of A. J. Liebling* (New York: Harper and Row, 1980), 177.

9. Ibid., 177; A. J. Liebling, *The Press*, 2d rev. ed. (New York: Ballantine, 1975), 317.

10. Sokolov, *Wayward Reporter*, 142.

11. "School for Publishers," *New Republic*, undated clipping in Hollenbeck scrapbook, 77; John Hersey, "Books and Things," *New York Herald Tribune*, November 7, 1947, clipping in Hollenbeck scrapbook, 77, both in Don Hollenbeck, Broadcast Papers (MS 319; hereafter Hollenbeck Broadcast Papers), Archives and Special Collections, University of Nebraska–Lincoln Libraries.

12. Don Hollenbeck, "Swinging at a Feather Bed," *Saturday Review of Literature*, November 8, 1947, clipping in Hollenbeck scrapbook, 76; Liebling is quoted in Sokolov, *Wayward Reporter*, 33.

13. Liebling, *Press*, 35, 22n9; Hollenbeck, "Swinging at a Feather Bed."

14. Hollenbeck, "Swinging at a Feather Bed."

15. *CBS Views the Press*, broadcast transcripts, November 22, 1947, 10; January 10, 1948, 4.

16. For Hutchins's attitude on exercise and athletics, see Milton Mayer, *Robert Maynard Hutchins: A Memoir* (Berkeley: University of California Press, 1993), 139–40.

17. Commission on Freedom of the Press, "What Can Be Done," in *A Free and Responsible Press* (Chicago: University of Chicago Press, 1947), 79–106.

18. Alice Fox Pitts, *Read All about It! Fifty Years of ASNE* (Easton, Pa.: American Society of Newspaper Editors, 1974), 17; "The Hutchins Report: A Twenty-Year Review," *Columbia Journalism Review*, Summer 1967, 20.

19. I. F. Stone, interview by author, April 17, 1975; Frank Hughes, *Prejudice and the Press: A Restatement of the Principle of Freedom of the Press with Specific Reference to the Hutchins-Luce Commission* (New York: Devin-Adair, 1950), 25, 62; A. J. Liebling, *The Wayward Pressman* (New York: Doubleday, 1948), 280. See also Liebling, "Some Reflections on the American Press," *Nation*, April 12, 1947, 427.

20. *CBS Views the Press*, broadcast transcripts, August 30, 1947, 3; December 4, 1948, 1–9.

21. Ibid., December 4, 1948, 5, 7.

22. Ibid., April 9, 1949, 2.

23. Ibid., April 30, 1949, 2.

24. *CBS Views the Press*, broadcast transcript, April 9, 1949, 7.

25. Ibid., 4.

26. Ibid., January 21, 1950, 9.

27. The nine Nieman Fellows were James Batal, Charlotte FitzHenry, Arthur W. Hepner, Frank Hewlett, Frank K. Kelly, Mary Ellen Leary, Cary Robertson, Ben Yablonky, and Leon Svirsky. Svirsky was the editor of *Your Newspaper: Blueprint for a Better Press* (New York: Macmillan, 1947).

28. Svirsky, *Your Newspaper*, xii.

29. Ibid., 12–20, esp. 13–14.

30. Ibid., viii, 14–17.

31. Ibid., 180, 176.

32. Ibid., 162, 164–65, 167.

33. Harry T. Saylor, "A Newspaperman's Newspaper," *Saturday Review of Literature*, December 6, 1947, 74; Charles McD. Puckette, "Nine Newspapermen Consider Their Profession," *New York Times Book Review*, December 21, 1947, 7; Leon Svirsky, letter to author, October 21, 1972, in the files of Nieman Foundation for Journalism, Harvard University.

34. Richard Watts Jr., "Which Paper D'Ya Read?" *New Republic*, December 15, 1947, 28; Lewis Gannett, "Books and Things," *New York Herald Tribune*, December 10, 1947, clipping in Hollenbeck scrapbook, 56.

35. *CBS Views the Press*, broadcast transcript, November 22, 1947, 9.

36. Ibid., July 12, 1947, 9; "Invisible Man," letter to Don Hollenbeck, July 16, 1947.

37. Marion T. Marzolf, *Civilizing Voices: American Press Criticism, 1880–1950* (New York: Longman, 1991), 177; Jack Shafer, "The Church of Liebling," *Slate*, August 25, 2004, www.slate.com/id/2105627.

38. *CBS Views the Press*, broadcast transcript, September 6, 1947, 11; Shafer, "Church of Liebling."

39. *CBS Views the Press*, broadcast transcripts, June 21, 1947, 4; February 12, 1949, 7.

40. Don Hollenbeck, "CBS Views the Press," *Atlantic Monthly*, September 1948, 50.

41. George Herman, letter to author, September 29, 1974.

42. "CBS Rides Herd on New York Papers," *Nieman Reports*, October 1947, 25. On the response of the *Times*, see Edwin L. James, letter to Don Hollenbeck, January 17, 1949, and Herman to author. On the *National Guardian* see James Aronson, letter to Don Hollenbeck, April 19, 1949, and John T. McManus, letter to Don Hollenbeck, April 19, 1949. McManus, who was general manager of the *National Guardian*, wrote, "Nobody, except yourself, has ever mentioned the *Guardian's* role in the [Trenton Six] case although all used our basic coverage." (The Trenton Six were black men sentenced to death after a questionable trial.) In a two-year-review edition of *CBS Views the Press*, Hollenbeck again credited the *National Guardian*. See *CBS Views the Press*, broadcast transcript, June 4, 1949, 7.

43. *CBS Views the Press*, broadcast transcript, May 15, 1948, 4.

44. Ibid., October 18, 1947, 9.

45. Anne Hollenbeck, interview by author, October 27, 1974.

46. *CBS Views the Press*, broadcast transcript, March 12, 1949, 1, 9.

47. Ibid., December 4, 1948, 7.

48. *CBS Views the Press*, broadcast transcript, February 26, 1949, 8–9; David MacDougall, interview by author, January 30, 2008; William Weidlich, interview by author, January 29, 2008; "New Paper Out; 'Weekly Block' Has All the News," *New York Herald Tribune*, January 29, 1949, 13.

49. *CBS Views the Press*, broadcast transcript, February 26, 1949, 9.

50. *CBS Views the Press*, broadcast transcript, June 4, 1949, 3.

51. Ibid., July 23, 1949, 6, 7.

52. On the use of *aposiopesis* see *CBS Views the Press*, broadcast transcript, September 27, 1947, 10, and on the use of *susurrus*, see June 4, 1949, 3.

53. *CBS Views the Press*, broadcast transcript, October 11, 1947, 11.

54. Ibid., July 9, 1949, 3, 4.

55. Ibid., February 26, 1949, 8.

56. Charles Grutzner, letter to Don Hollenbeck, March 1, 1949, in Hollenbeck scrapbook, 126.

57. *CBS Views the Press*, broadcast transcript, October 11, 1947, 10.

58. Jerry Walker, "Don Hollenbeck Views Much-Honored Show," *Editor and Publisher*, May 15, 1948, 44.

59. *CBS Views the Press*, broadcast transcripts, November 12, 1949, 1; June 5, 1948, 3; August 21, 1948, 9–11.

60. Ibid., June 7, 1950, 2, 3.

61. Ibid., 8.

62. Ibid., January 29, 1949, 4.

63. Ibid., May 21, 1949, 5.

64. Paul Lazersfeld, *Radio and the Printed Page: An Introduction to the Study of Radio and Its Role in the Communication of Ideas* (New York: Duell, Sloan and Pearce, 1940), 178; Marshall McLuhan, *Understanding Media: The Extensions of Man* (New York: McGraw-Hill, 1965), 299. On Hollenbeck's use of sound effects to create mood, see Giraud Chester and Garnet R. Garrison, *Radio and Television: An Introduction* (New York: Appleton-Century-Crofts, 1950), 421–22.

65. Hollenbeck, "Swinging at a Feather Bed."; *CBS Views the Press*, broadcast transcript, June 4, 1949, 1–10.

66. *CBS Views the Press*, June 4, 1949, 9.

67. Don Hollenbeck, "Is the American Press Doing Its Job Today?" *Town Meeting of the Air*, May 9, 1950, broadcast transcript, 5.

68. *Louisville Courier-Journal*, May 17, 1949, 4.

69. *CBS Views the Press*, broadcast transcripts, July 26, 1947, 2, and September 20, 1947, 1–10; A. J. Liebling, *Mink and Red Herring: The Wayward Pressman's Casebook* (New York: Doubleday, 1949), 46.

70. Don Hollenbeck, "CBS Views the Press," *Atlantic Monthly*, September 1948, 50.

10. Jack O'Brian: Championing Decency, Fighting Soft-on-Communism Liberals

1. "Jack O'Brian Takes Bride," *New York Times*, January 16, 1947, 31; "J. J. Johnston Dies; Ring Promoter, 70," *New York Times*, May 8, 1946, 25.

2. Jack O'Brian, "It's Wonderful They're Always So Wonderful," *New York Journal-American*, March 12, 1951, 26.

3. Jack O'Brian, "Liberace Lives in a Grand Piano; Well, Darned Near!" *New York Journal-American*, February 19, 1954, 26; Jack O'Brian, "A Happy 1961 to Blydens," *New York Journal-American*, July 8, 1960, 20; "Critics: The Man with the Popular Mind," *Time*, November 20, 1964, 50; Jack O'Brian, "Don't Tell Us You Missed This One!" *New York Journal-American*, June 16, 1953, 36; Jack O'Brian, "The Best: Bing, Benny, Cole, Eve, Jo M.M.McB., Groucho," *New York Journal-American*, April 16, 1953, 34. As for O'Brian's being "very happy in the Toy Department of Journalism," see Anne McIlhenney Matthews, "Jack O'Brian: A Real Puncher," *Buffalo Courier-Express*, May 4, 1973, 27.

4. On the "simply amazing" Bishop Sheen, see Jack O'Brian, "Critic's Aunt Sends Letter by Aerial Mail," *New York Journal-American*, June 3, 1952, 31. The "smut and . . . insinuation" quote is from Jack O'Brian, "Story of Radio Free Europe on

Video Tonight," *New York Journal-American*, October 23, 1951, 32. On "frontal epidermis," "fantastic facades," and "down-to-here talents," see Jack O'Brian, "Mary McCarthy Denies Cleavage Ambitions on TV," *New York Journal-American*, October 30, 1951, 34; Jack O'Brian, "Mary and Dag Are Mighty Purty Bad Examples," *New York Journal-American*, October 24, 1951, 40; and Jack O'Brian, "What Medium Needs Is to Be Not So Medium," *New York Journal-American*, September 29, 1952, 23.

5. John Crosby, "Some Irritability Around," *New York Herald Tribune*, April 25, 1958, sec. 2, 1; Jack O'Brian, "'Cholly' Starts New WJZ Radio Show on Monday," *New York Journal-American*, March 31, 1951, 18. On Hearst as "the only real newspaper genius of his era," see Jack O'Brian, "Hearst Vision Traced through Radio and TV," *New York Journal-American*, August 15, 1951, 34.

6. Jack O'Brian, "Berle, Silvers, Bergen, First in Anti-Red Line," *New York Journal-American*, April 30, 1954, 35.

7. Jack O'Brian, "Bob Montgomery Not Too Busy to Belt at Reds," *New York Journal-American*, November 4, 1950, 18.

8. Jack O'Brian, "Check Grabber Has Ripping Time for $10,000," *New York Journal-American*, February 23, 1952, 23; Jack O'Brian, "'The Continental' Has Fanciest Sets on Video," *New York Journal-American*, April 3, 1952, 35; Jack O'Brian, "Eve Arden, Jack Benny Are JO'B's Radio Bests," *New York Journal-American*, March 18, 1954, 36. For a critical view of the *Last Man Out* series, see Victor S. Navasky, *Naming Names* (New York: Hill and Wang, 1991), 41–42.

9. O'Brian, "'Continental' Has Fanciest Sets."

10. Neal Gabler, *Walter Winchell: Gossip, Power, and the Culture of Celebrity* (New York: Knopf, 1994), 443.

11. Ibid.

12. Jack O'Brian, interview by author, February 3, 1975.

11. The Obsession with Subversives and Communist Spies

1. Daniel Lang, "The Days of Suspicion," *New Yorker*, May 21, 1949, 37.

2. David Caute, *The Great Fear: The Anti-Communist Purge under Truman and Eisenhower* (New York: Simon and Schuster, 1978), 169.

3. U.S. Congress, House, Subcommittee on Legislation of the Committee on Un-American Activities, *Hearings on Proposed Legislation to Curb or Control the Communist Party of the United States*, 80th Cong., 2d sess., on H.R. 4422 and H.R. 4581, February 5, 6, 9, 10, 11, 19, and 20, 1948 (Washington, D.C.: U.S. Government Printing Office, 1948), 17; U.S. Congress, House, Committee on Un-American Activities, *Hearings on Bills to Curb or Outlaw the Communist Party of the United States*, 80th Cong., 1st sess., on H.R. 1884 and H.R. 2122, March 26, 1947 (Washington, D.C.: U.S. Government Printing Office, 1947), pt. 2, 43, 16.

4. "Promises Quiz of 'Pink Profs,'" *New York Journal-American*, January 12, 1947, L6;

Julien Steinberg, "Ferment in the New York Newspaper Guild," *New Leader*, May 10, 1947, 5; "Guild Here Red-Run, Says National Head," *New York Times*, March 16, 1947, in American Business Consultants, Inc., *Counterattack* files, box 23, folder 13–54, Tamiment Library and Robert F. Wagner Labor Archives, Elmer Holmes Bobst Library, New York University, hereafter, *Counterattack* files.

5.   Helen Rogers Reid, letter to Ernest L. Klein, Chicago, January 26, 1948, *Counterattack* files, box 24, F14–0–284.

6.   *CBS Views the Press*, broadcast transcript, December 20, 1947, 2–3; November 1, 1947, 6, 8.

7.   Ibid., November 1, 1947, 9, 10.

8.   Ibid., 10.

9.   Ibid., June 21, 1947, 11; November 22, 1947, 6.

10.   Rebecca West, "British Observer Is Impressed Most by Stassen's Following," *New York Herald Tribune*, June 23, 1948, 3; Rebecca West, "Rebecca West Says Communists Controlled Wallace Convention," *New York Herald Tribune*, July 26, 1948, 2.

11.   West, "Rebecca West Says Communists Controlled Wallace Convention"; *CBS Views the Press*, broadcast transcript, August 7, 1948, 9, 8. For a later attack on Communism and defense of Joseph McCarthy, see West, "A Briton Looks at 'McCarthyism,'" *U.S. News and World Report*, May 22, 1953, 60–81.

12.   West, "British Observer Is Impressed"; *CBS Views the Press*, broadcast transcript, August 7, 1948, 2.

13.   *CBS Views the Press*, broadcast transcript, August 21, 1948, 6, and corrected version of transcript, 7.

14.   Carl Rollyson, "Rebecca West and the FBI," *New Criterion*, February 1998, 15; Rebecca West, letter to Doris Stevens, August 29, 1948, in "The Rebecca West–Doris Stevens file, 1947–1959," appendix to Rollyson, "Rebecca West and the FBI," http://newcriterion.com:81/archive/16/feb98/app.htm.

15.   *CBS Views the Press*, broadcast transcripts, October 2, 1948, 4; August 20, 1949, 1–3.

16.   Ibid., July 10, 1948, 9–12; September 25, 1948, 1–3; October 2, 1948, 3, 8; August 20, 1949, 1–4.

17.   Ibid., October 2, 1948, 6.

18.   "The Communist Fifth Column in the United States," editorial, *New York Journal-American*, March 21, 1947, 20; Sidney Fields, "Red Portrait Is Black," *New York Mirror*, February 16, 1949, 24.

19.   Daniel Lang, "The Days of Suspicion," *New Yorker*, May 21, 1949, 37–57; *CBS Views the Press*, broadcast transcript, June 4, 1949, 9.

20.   Lang, "Days of Suspicion"; Gary May, *Un-American Activities: The Trials of William Remington* (New York: Oxford University Press, 1994), 135.

21.   Ibid., 212, 214–15, 307, 321. See also Kathryn S. Olmsted, *Red Spy Queen: A Biography of Elizabeth Bentley* (Chapel Hill: University of North Carolina Press, 2002),

53–54; and John Earl Haynes and Harvey Klehr, *Venona: Decoding Soviet Espionage in America* (New Haven, Conn.: Yale University Press, 1999), 161–62.

22. Caute, *Great Fear*, 470. For Hollenbeck's treatment of Condon's case, *CBS Views the Press*, broadcast transcripts, March 7, 1948, 1–11, and February 12, 1949, 1–7.

23. Edward A. Shils, *The Torment of Secrecy: The Background and Consequences of American Security Policies* (Glencoe, Ill.: Free Press, 1956), 188; Caute, *Great Fear*, 462.

24. Caute, *Great Fear*, 457; Thomas is quoted in Kenneth O'Reilly, *Hoover and the Un-Americans: The FBI, HUAC, and the Red Menace* (Philadelphia: Temple University Press, 1983), 123. The Thomas quotation as reported by Hollenbeck was slightly different. Hollenbeck quoted a dispatch from Washington written by the *Herald Tribune*'s Carl Levin that said HUAC had accused Condon of being "one of the weakest links in the security screen protecting this nation's atomic secrets" (*CBS Views the Press*, broadcast transcript, March 7, 1948, 1).

25. J. A. C. Grant, review of *The House Committee on Un-American Activities: 1945–1950*, by Robert Carr (Ithaca, N.Y.: Cornell University Press, 1952), in *Western Political Quarterly* 6, no. 4 (December 1953): 831; *CBS Views the Press*, broadcast transcript, March 7, 1948, 2.

26. *CBS Views the Press*, broadcast transcript, March 7, 1948, 11.

27. Ibid.

28. Typescript of February 20, 1948, *Counterattack* article, 1, in Don Hollenbeck, Broadcast Papers (MS 319), Archives and Special Collections, University of Nebraska–Lincoln Libraries.

29. Ibid.

30. Ibid.; Allen Weinstein, *Perjury: The Hiss-Chambers Case* (New York: Knopf, 1978), 166, 167.

31. Alger Hiss, interview by author, June 16, 1975. Hiss cited Hollenbeck's coverage of his first trial in Alger Hiss, *In the Court of Public Opinion* (New York: Knopf, 1957), 297–98.

32. Joseph Wershba, interview by author, November 10, 1974.

33. Charles Gussman, letter to author, May 15, 1977.

34. *CBS Views the Press*, broadcast transcript, July 9, 1949, 2, 7.

35. Ibid., 7–8.

36. Ibid., 10.

37. *CBS Views the Press*, broadcast transcript, September 11, 1947, 6.

38. Three earlier Robeson concerts in the Peekskill area had been successful.

39. Paul Robeson, "Forge Negro-Labor Unity for Peace and Jobs," speech to the National Labor Conference for Negro Rights, Chicago, June 10, 1950, as reprinted in *Paul Robeson Speaks: Writings, Speeches, Interviews, 1918–1974*, edited by Philip S. Foner (New York: Brunner/Mazel, 1978), 244.

40. The wording attributed to Robeson is quoted in Dorothy Butler Gilliam, *Paul Robeson, All-American* (Washington, D.C.: New Republic, 1976), 137. See

Robeson, *Paul Robeson Speaks*, 198, and Martin Bauml Duberman, *Paul Robeson* (New York: Knopf, 1988), 342, for their version of what Robeson said.

41.   *CBS Views the Press*, broadcast transcript, September 3, 1949, 1.

42.   Duberman, *Paul Robeson*, 364.

43.   Ibid., 365.

44.   *CBS Views the Press*, broadcast transcript, September 3, 1949, 7; "Interrupted Concert," *New York Times*, August 29, 1949, 16.

45.   Ibid., 6, 8.

46.   Ibid., 10.

47.   For the version of the speech McCarthy inserted in the *Congressional Record*, see Lately Thomas, *When Even Angels Wept: The Senator Joseph McCarthy Affair—A Story without a Hero* (New York: Morrow, 1973), 92–98.

48.   Frank Stanton, interview by author, August 4, 1975; Jack Walters, interview by author, August 5, 1975.

49.   Tim Weiner, "A 1950 Plan: Arrest 12,000 and Suspend Due Process," *New York Times*, December 23, 2007, 30. "Don Hollenbeck Security Matter," May 21, 1950, memorandum, SAC, New York, to Director, FBI, in Hollenbeck's FBI file, which I obtained under the Freedom of Information Act.

50.   Ibid. Also see New York FBI's memo of September 28, 1950, in Hollenbeck's FBI file.

51.   Clapper is quoted in Donald A. Ritchie, *Reporting from Washington: The History of the Washington Press Corps* (New York: Oxford University Press, 2005), 72.

52.   Don Hollenbeck, "How It's Done," *PM*, February 27, 1942, 13.

53.   Ralph Leviton, "Myopia at CBS," editorial, *News Workshop*, undated clipping in Hollenbeck scrapbook, Hollenbeck Broadcast Papers, 137; *CBS Views the Press*, broadcast transcript, June 4, 1949, 10.

54.   Reel tape labeled "Here You Are, Dec. 31, 1948," Robert Lewis Shayon Papers, box 92, Howard Gotlieb Archival Research Center, Boston University Library.

55.   Undated *Variety* clipping in Hollenbeck scrapbook, 135.

56.   Ibid.

57.   Harriet Van Horne, "CBS Weighs Words for Words' Sake," undated *New York World-Telegram* clipping in Hollenbeck scrapbook, 135; "Hollenbeck in Slow Burn at CBS' Overture for McCaffrey as 'Word' M.C.," *Variety*, February 9, 1950, in Hollenbeck scrapbook, 135.

58.   Sig Mickelson, interview by author, June 17, 1975.

59.   Paul W. White, *News on the Air* (New York: Harcourt, Brace, 1947), 159.

60.   John Dunning, *On the Air: The Encyclopedia of Old-Time Radio* (New York: Oxford University Press, 1998), 715.

61.   Mike Wallace, interview by author, August 15, 2005.

62.   James Burke, interview by author, August 15, 1975.

63.   Edmund Scott, interview by author, November 10, 1974.

64.   William S. Paley, *As It Happened: A Memoir* (New York, Doubleday, 1979), 142.

65. Wershba interview, November 10, 1974; Sig Mickelson interview, June 17, 1975.

66. Dallas Townsend, interview by author, July 9, 1975; J. A. Sierra, review of *A Sergeant Named Batista*, by Edmund A. Chester (New York: Holt, 1954), www.historyofcuba.com/main/ref.htm; Chester, *A Sergeant Named Batista*, 202, 262, 265.

67. Walters, Wershba (November 10, 1974), and Burke interviews.

68. *CBS Views the Press*, broadcast transcript, February 11, 1950, 2.

69. Burke interview.

70. *CBS Views the Press*, broadcast transcript, May 20, 1950, 5.

71. Ned Calmer, interview by author, August 4, 1975; "California Publishers Want Ad Bribery Charge Aired," *Editor and Publisher*, May 21, 1949, 5.

72. George Herman, letter to author, September 29, 1974.

73. *CBS Views the Press*, broadcast transcript, July 12, 1947, 2–6.

74. Ibid., 7; Wershba interview, November 10, 1974.

75. Anne Hollenbeck, interview by author, October 27, 1974.

76. Wershba interview, November 10, 1974.

77. *CBS Views the Press*, broadcast transcript, July 19, 1947, 8.

78. Ibid.

79. Ibid., 12.

80. Wershba interview, November 10, 1974.

81. Jack Gould, "TV: An Eye for News," *New York Times*, April 24, 1961, 59.

82. "CBS Views the Press," *Variety*, February 15, 1950, 32; Saul Carson, "On the Air: The Reformed Gadfly," *New Republic*, March 13, 1950, 22; Leviton, "Myopia at CBS."

83. "Radio and Television: Schlitz Co. May Sponsor 'The Pulitzer Prize Playhouse' Dramatizations in Fall," *New York Times*, July 1, 1950, 17; "Irony Rides at CBS," *Variety*, June 29, 1950, clipping in Hollenbeck scrapbook, 136.

84. Douglas Edwards, interview by author, July 8, 1975; Leviton, "Myopia at CBS."

12. Jack O'Brian: Traveling with the Conservative, Anti-Commie Crowd

1. "O'Brian, Jack," in Frances C. Locher, ed., *Contemporary Authors* (Detroit: Gale, Research, 1982), 103:370; "Spellman Chosen to Get First Sokolsky Award," *New York Times*, May 13, 1963, 22; Spellman is quoted in Lately Thomas, *When Even Angels Wept: The Senator Joseph McCarthy Affair—A Story without a Hero* (New York: Morrow, 1973), 346.

2. "The Man with the Popular Mind," *Time*, November 20, 1964, 50; "Writer Speaks up for Cohn," undated, unidentified newspaper clipping, stamped July 1, 1964, in the author's files.

3. Nicholas von Hoffman, *Citizen Cohn* (New York: Doubleday, 1988), 12.

4. Gladys K. Drewelow, "Jack O'Brian Reminisces about Buffalo," December 10, 1991, 2A. The original is in the library of the *Buffalo (N.Y.) News.*

5. O'Brian is quoted in M. A. Jones, FBI memorandum to Mr. DeLoach, February 16, 1960, contained in FBI's March 23, 2007, response to my request for O'Brian's FBI files under the Freedom of Information Act; Jack O'Brian, letter to J. Edgar Hoover, February 18, 1960, in O'Brian's FBI file.

6. Hoover to O'Brian, July 27, 1965, in O'Brian's FBI file.

7. Director of FBI, memo to legal attaché, London, June 5, 1963; "Legat, Rome No. 21," FBI memo to director, September 3, 1965, both in O'Brian's FBI file.

8. Drewelow, "Jack O'Brian Reminisces about Buffalo," 6, 11.

9. Jack O'Brian, "Billy's 'Black Magic' Can't Conjure Sponsor," *New York Journal-American*, December 13, 1952, 24; Jack O'Brian, "A Good Ford Show Is in Our TV Future," *New York Journal-American*, October 3, 1952, 33.

10. Jack O'Brian, "Arthur Wants to Get His Moon Over Miami," *New York Journal-American*, November 29, 1952, 24; O'Brian, "A Good Ford Show."

11. See Ted Morgan, *Reds: McCarthyism in Twentieth-Century America* (New York: Random House, 2003), 411–13.

12. Kahn is quoted in Neal Gabler, *Walter Winchell: Gossip, Power, and the Culture of Celebrity* (London: Picador, 1994), 436.

13. Steve Allen, "Jack O'Brian and the Art of Criticism," *Village Voice*, March 19, 1958, 1, 13.

14. Jack O'Brian, "Da Silva Hosts Show on NBC," *New York Journal-American*, July 6, 1960, 28; Jack O'Brian, "A Happy 1961 to Blydens," *New York Journal-American*, July 8, 1960, 20.

15. Les Brown, "Program Blacklisted in '60 Revived by WCBS," *New York Times*, October 7, 1976, 73.

13. The Hearsts Versus Hollenbeck

1. *CBS Views the Press*, broadcast transcript, November 12, 1949, 2; William Randolph Hearst Jr. with Jack Casserly, *The Hearsts: Father and Son* (Lanham, Md.: Roberts Rinehart, 2001), 296, 285.

2. *CBS Views the Press*, broadcast transcript, December 13, 1947, 5, 6.

3. Ibid., March 13, 1948, 5.

4. Arthur Perles, memo to Davidson Taylor, March 15, 1948.

5. *CBS Views the Press*, broadcast transcript, June 12, 1948, 10.

6. Ibid., April 2, 1949, 1, 2.

7. Ibid., January 24, 1948, 3.

8. Ibid., December 10, 1949, 10.

9. Ibid., July 2, 1949, 5.

10. Ibid., 10.

11. Ibid., July 17, 1948, 12.

12. Ibid., 13.

13. "The Soviet Spider," *New York Journal-American*, July 19, 1948, 12; "The Crime of Communism," *New York Journal-American*, October 17, 1949, 16.

14. Lindsay Chaney and Michael Cieply, *The Hearsts: Family and Empire—the Later Years* (New York: Simon and Schuster, 1981), 61, 62, 58.

15. Ibid., 240, 122.

16. Ibid., 128, 129.

17. T. C. Kirkpatrick, letter to William Randolph Hearst Jr., March 21, 1950; Hearst, memo to Matthews, March 29, 1950; Matthews to Hearst, March 31, 1950, all Research Correspondence Series, box 665, W. R. Hearst Jr. file, in J. B. Matthews Papers, Rare Book, Manuscript, and Special Collections Library, Duke University, hereafter Matthews Papers.

18. Matthews, memo to R. E. Berlin, April 24, 1950, box 652, Richard E. Berlin file, Matthews Papers.

19. See, for example, requests from Westbrook Pegler, Victor Lasky, and Victor Riesel, in Matthews Papers (box 675, Westbrook Pegler file; box 670, Victor Lasky file; and box 678, Victor Riesel file). Also, Matthews, memo to Berlin, August 2, 1951, regarding McCarthy's request "about the speech of Sir John Pratt as reported in the July issue of *Intelligence Digest*" (box 652, Richard E. Berlin file, Matthews Papers). For visits to Matthews by federal agents, see "FBI, 1942–1961," box 211, folder 8, vertical files, Matthews Papers. For *Time* magazine's use of Matthews's dossiers, see "Time, Inc.," box 682, Matthews Papers.

20. Berlin to Matthews, March 28, 1949, and Jean Bordeaux, letter to Matthews forwarded by Berlin, November 10, 1952, both in box 652, Berlin file, Matthews Papers.

21. For his file on Hollenbeck see Card File HOL-HUM (card file case 38), box 751, Donald I. Sweany file, Matthews Papers.

22. Ibid.

23. *CBS Views the Press*, broadcast transcript, October 18, 1947, 7.

24. Card File HOL-HUM.

25. Ibid.; *CBS Views the Press*, broadcast transcript, January 31, 1948, 1, 2; May 14, 1949, 4; June 28, 1947, 3. See, for example, "Conspiracy of Silence," *In Fact*, July 14, 1947, 1, in which Seldes praises Hollenbeck for speaking against the "silent treatment" by the press about the debate about section 304 of the Taft-Hartley labor bill.

26. Card File HOL-HUM .

27. *CBS Views the Press*, broadcast transcript, November 22, 1947, 3.

28. Card File HOL-HUM.

29. *Counterattack* was especially annoyed by ABC's response to anti-Communists' attacks on Gypsy Rose Lee, the stripper-turned-actress-writer, who was scheduled to host ABC's *What Makes You Tick?*. Lee was listed in *Red Channels, Counterattack's* 1950 book about 151 people who, the publication claimed, may have

been subversives. ABC put *Counterattack/Red Channels* in the position of having to take responsibility for its demagoguery, which it refused to do. The network also kept Lee on the air and won a special Peabody award for refusing to buckle to "organized pressure." See David Everitt, *A Shadow of Red: Communism and the Blacklist in Radio and Television* (Chicago: Dee, 2007), 74–76.

30. Raymond Swing, *"Good Evening!" A Professional Memoir by Raymond Swing* (New York: Harcourt, Brace and World, 1964), 261.

31. *CBS Views the Press*, broadcast transcript, January 3, 1948, 8 (also on the *Daily Worker*, see *CBS Views the Press*, September 6, 1947, 4); August 15, 1948, 11; Chaney and Cieply, *Hearsts*, 150.

32. David Nasaw, *The Chief: The Life of William Randolph Hearst* (Boston: Houghton Mifflin, 2000), 597.

33. Ibid.

34. Frank Stanton, interview by author, August 4, 1975. Fred Friendly, who began working for CBS in 1948 and became president of CBS News in 1964, said, "I believe there was a conscious effort by William Randolph Hearst Jr. to get CBS" (Fred Friendly, interview by author, July 8, 1975).

35. Stanton interview.

36. Ibid.

37. William Randolph Hearst Jr., letter to author dictated to Jack O'Connell of Hearst's staff and mailed by O'Connell, October 5, 1977.

38. Sally Bedell Smith, *In All His Glory: The Life of William S. Paley—The Legendary Tycoon and His Brilliant Circle* (New York: Simon and Schuster, 1990), 168.

39. Hearst to author; T. S. Holman, letter to author, March 5, 1978.

40. Donald A. Ritchie, *Reporting from Washington: The History of the Washington Press Corps* (New York: Oxford University Press, 2005), 75. See also Roger Burlingame, *Don't Let Them Scare You: The Life and Times of Elmer Davis* (Philadelphia: Lippincott, 1961), 259–61.

41. Harvey Matusow, *False Witness* (New York: Cameron and Kahn, 1955), 29, 33.

42. Ibid., 68, 71.

43. Ibid., 155.

44. "Daily Worker Critic Forced out of Job on Refusal to Attack 'Gone with the Wind,'" *New York Times*, December 22, 1939, 1; Leeds Moberley, "Rushmore Broke with Reds over Movie Review," *New York Daily News*, January 4, 1958, 12.

45. Theo Wilson, "Confidentially Rushmore: Jobless, He Wouldn't Borrow; On Top, He Was Cold and Cruel," *New York Daily News*, January 6, 1958, 28.

46. Ibid. See, for example, Howard Rushmore, "The Subversive Front: Bell for Red Teachers," *New York Journal-American*, September 12, 1953, 10.

47. *CBS Views the Press*, broadcast transcript, August 2, 1947, 7–8.

48. Ibid., 10, 11.

49. Howard Rushmore, "The Subversive Front: McCarthy Held Back Hot Ammo," *New York Journal-American*, June 19, 1954, 6.

50. Frederick Woltman, "The McCarthy Balance Sheet," *New York World-Telegram and Sun*, July 12, 1954; Matthews, letter to Howard Rushmore, December 13, 1954, in box 704, "General Papers of J. B. Matthews, 1954, June–Dec.," Personal Series, 1895–1970, Matthews Papers.

51. Wilson, "Confidentially Rushmore," 2.

52. David M. Oshinsky, *A Conspiracy So Immense: The World of Joe McCarthy* (New York: Oxford University Press, 2005), 168–69; Haynes Johnson, *The Age of Anxiety: McCarthyism to Terrorism* (Orlando, Fla.: Harcourt, 2005), 184. For "serious misstatements" by the Tydings report, see Ted Morgan, *Reds: McCarthyism in Twentieth-Century America* (New York: Random House, 2003), 403–4.

53. "A Shameful Performance," *New York Journal-American*, July 19, 1950, 1.

54. Igor Cassini, with Jeanne Molli, *I'd Do It All over Again* (New York: Putnam, 1977), 113; Dorothy Kilgallen, "Jelke Girls Linked to Capital Intrigue," *New York Journal-American*, February 1, 1953, 1, 16L; Fulton Lewis Jr., "Fulton Lewis Jr · Bares 'Leftist' Plot to Use Radio for Red Propaganda," *New York Journal-American*, February 3, 1950, 11.

55. For the description of Kenny see John McCarten, "The Swan in the 'Mirror,'" *New Yorker*, March 7, 1953, 35–54; Nick Kenny, "Nick Kenny Speaking," *New York Mirror*, January 15, 1949, 12. See also Farnsworth Fowle, "Nick Kenny, Columnist for the *Mirror*, Writer of Verses and Lyrics, Is Dead," *New York Times*, December 2, 1975, 85.

14. Jack O'Brian: Attacking the Communist Broadcasting System

1. Jack O'Brian, "Martha Shines Her Raye of Fun in Tidy Style," *New York Journal-American*, October 22, 1951, 28.

2. Jack O'Brian, "Commie Phone Plot Exposed in Two Minutes," *New York Journal-American*, June 28, 1954, 26.

3. Jack O'Brian, "Only at Midnight Could This Show Be Dreamed Up!" *New York Journal-American*, September 6, 1951, 38.

4. Jack O'Brian, "Video Viewers Talk Back about This and That," *New York Journal-American*, November 11, 1950, 18.

5. Frank Stanton, interview by author, August 4, 1975.

6. Jack O'Brian, "Like Father, Like Daughter; Like Heck!" *New York Journal-American*, April 27, 1951, 36.

7. Jack O'Brian, "Rep. Hill Labels CBS a Supporter of Leftist Trends," *New York Journal-American*, July 26, 1951, 26; Jack O'Brian, "O'Brian Holds Caucus on TV Commentators," *New York Journal-American*, July 28, 1952, 23.

8. Jack O'Brian, "O'Brian Holds Caucus"; Jack O'Brian, "Gleason's Man Saturday Turns down NBC Offer," *New York Journal-American*, November 24, 1953, 34. For

references to "Egbert" and "Egghead" Murrow, see, for example, Jack O'Brian, "Brinkley Wins—By a Smile," *New York Journal-American*, July 15, 1960, 18.

9. Jack O'Brian, "Radio Wastes the Face of Lovely Mary Healy; TV?" *New York Journal-American*, February 15, 1954, 24; Jack O'Brian, "Here's a Road Company of the Great Gleason," *New York Journal-American*, February 16, 1954, 34.

10. Jack O'Brian, "Some Quiz Guests Act Like Pros—Because They Are!" *New York Journal-American*, May 24, 1954, 24; Jack O'Brian, "Jack Webb Discards Last of His 'Dragnet' Partners," *New York Journal-American*, June 18, 1954, 30.

15. Loyalty Oaths, Blacklists, and Joseph McCarthy

1. Edward R. Murrow and Fred W. Friendly, eds., *See It Now* (New York: Simon and Schuster, 1955), xi. On *Washington, U.S.A.*, see "Ray Bolger Plans More TV Programs," *New York Times*, January 13, 1953, 32. On *The Gamblers* see Sidney Lohman, "News and Notes Gathered from the Studios," *New York Times*, January 31, 1954, X13. A copy of *The Gamblers*, January 31, 1954, is available in Don Hollenbeck, Broadcast Papers (MS 319; hereafter Hollenbeck Broadcast Papers), Archives and Special Collections, University of Nebraska–Lincoln Libraries. On *The Candid Microphone* see "On the Radio," *New York Times*, June 6, 1950, 40, and on its early design see R. W. Stewart, "Can't You Take a Practical Joke?" *New York Times*, November 23, 1947, 85.

2. *Hear It Now*, December 15, 1950 (unless otherwise noted, all recordings of *Hear It Now* come from the Audio Classics Archive); Alexander Kendrick, *Prime Time: The Life of Edward R. Murrow* (Boston: Little, Brown, 1969), 330.

3. *Hear It Now*, December 15, 22, 29, 1950.

4. Jack Gould, "'Hear It Now' and 'Voices and Events,'" *New York Times*, December 24, 1950, 51.

5. Ben Gross, "Televiewing and Listening In," *New York Daily News*, May 16, 1952, 58.

6. See Jeff Merron, "Murrow on TV: *See It Now*, *Person to Person*, and the Making of a 'Masscult Personality,'" *Journalism Monographs*, no. 106 (July 1988). A recording of *Westinghouse Studio One: Cardinal Mindszenty*, May 3, 1954, with Hollenbeck as narrator, is available for viewing at the Paley Center for Media (formerly the Museum of Television and Radio) in New York City. See also Jack Gould, "'Studio One' Presents Compelling Drama of Rackets on Waterfront Couched in Human Terms," *New York Times*, January 18, 1952, 33, in which Gould writes that Hollenbeck does "an exceptionally restrained yet authoritative job as narrator," and "Don Hollenbeck Television Newscast for Norwich," *Variety*, December 20, 1950, clipping in Hollenbeck scrapbook, 139, Hollenbeck Broadcast Papers.

7. See *Television Interviews, 1951–1955: A Catalog of Longines Chronoscope Interviews in the National Archives*, compiled by Sarah L. Shamley (Washington, D.C.: National Archives and Records Administration, 1991). For a listing of coronation

coverage by Hollenbeck and Murrow, see "U.S. TV-Radio Coverage," *New York Times*, June 2, 1953, 10.

8. Sidney Lohman, "Convention Coverage: Proceedings in Chicago Will Receive Most Extensive Distribution Ever," *New York Times*, July 6, 1952, X9; Walter Cronkite, *A Reporter's Life* (New York: Knopf, 1996), 177–78. WCBS ads for CBS's television election night coverage listed Don Hollenbeck as one of Murrow's reporting team covering "elections for the Senate."

9. Bill Leonard, *In the Storm of the Eye: A Lifetime at CBS* (New York: Putnam, 1987), 68–69.

10. American Business Consultants, *Red Channels: The Report of Communist Influence in Radio and Television* (New York: American Business Consultants, 1950), 6.

11. Robert Lewis Shayon, interview by author, June 3, 2006. Shayon's statement disagrees slightly with what he wrote in *Odyssey in Prime Time* (Philadelphia: Waymark, 2001): "It took me four years to outlive the blacklist" (134). Shayon also wrote that "Don Hollenbeck, a CBS newsman who had often worked on 'You Are There' and who did a remarkable radio series of his own, 'CBS Views the Press,' an eye-opening analysis of New York papers, and whose name appeared in *Red Channels*, put his head in a gas oven and killed himself" (134). In fact, Hollenbeck was not listed in *Red Channels*, though he was smeared at length in the February 20, 1948, edition of *Counterattack*. On Martin see Karen Sue Cailteux, "The Political Blacklist in the Broadcast Industry: The Decade of the 1950's" (Ph.D. diss., Ohio Sate University, 1972), 289, and David Everitt, *A Shadow of Red: Communism and the Blacklist in Radio and Television* (Chicago: Dee, 2007), 187.

12. Sally Bedell Smith, *In All His Glory: The Life of William S. Paley—The Legendary Tycoon and His Brilliant Circle* (New York: Simon and Schuster, 1990), 306; Stanley Cloud and Lynne Olson, *The Murrow Boys: Pioneers on the Front Lines of Broadcast Journalism* (Boston: Houghton Mifflin, 1996), 301. See also David Sentner, "Newsman on Eisler Ship Cited Fourteen Times for Subversive Links," *New York Journal-American*, May 20, 1949, 4. The article ends with this teaser: "Another article on the employment of Communist fronters by CBS will be published Sunday."

13. Cloud and Olson, *Murrow Boys*, 301; American Business Consultants, "Howard K. Smith" and "Alexander Kendrick," in *Red Channels*, 136–37, 92–93.

14. On the monitoring of CBS press releases, see American Business Consultants, Inc., *Counterattack* files, box 25, file 14-0-1960, Tamiment Library and Robert F. Wagner Labor Archives, Elmer Holmes Bobst Library, New York University, hereafter, *Counterattack* files; T. C. Kilpatrick, memo on Columbia Broadcasting System to Research Office, September 24, 1947, box 12, file 11–33, *Counterattack* files.

15. "Philip Loeb," in American Business Consultants, *Red Channels*, 101–2.

16. David Everitt, *A Shadow of Red: Communism and the Blacklist in Radio and Television* (Chicago: Dee, 2007), 79–80.

17. The *Journal-American* columnist Jack O'Brian happily announced that Loeb's career was over "after a long and luxurious hiatus in [CBS's] pink-tinged boudoir" (O'Brian, "NBC Picks Up 'Goldbergs' after Exit from CBS," *New York Journal-American*, August 25, 1951, 18). See also Jack O'Brian, "A Prize for 'The Doodles Weaver Show?' Read On!" *New York Journal-American*, August 29, 1951, 38; Jack O'Brian, "Goldbergs Back on TV without Philip Loeb," *New York Journal-American*, February 4, 1952, 23.

18. William S. Paley, interview by author, February 16, 1977; Joseph Persico, *Edward R. Murrow: An American Original* (New York: McGraw-Hill, 1988), 341.

19. "McConnell Comments on Communism," *Radio Daily*, July 10, 1959, 1. ABC was honored with a special Peabody award for "resisting organized pressure and its reaffirmation of basic American principles" ("Peabody Awards Given in Radio, TV," *New York Times*, April 27, 1951, 33).

20. Joseph Ream, memo to "The Organization," December 19, 1950, in the Edward R. Murrow files of the Edward R. Murrow Memorial Library, Tufts University, Medford, Massachusetts; Daniel T. O'Shea, interview by author, July 8, 1975.

21. O'Shea interview; John Cogley, *Radio Television*, vol. 2 of *Report on Blacklisting* (New York: Fund for the Republic, 1956), 126.

22. Alfred B. Berry, interview by author, July 11, 1975.

23. Persico, *Edward R. Murrow: An American Original*, 338.

24. Robert Lewis Shayon, *Odyssey in Prime Time* (Philadelphia: Waymark, 2001), 130; Everitt, *A Shadow of Red*, 125, 128.

25. Paley interview.

26. Berry interview.

27. U.S. Congress, Senate, Subcommittee to Investigate the Administration of the Internal Security Act and Other Internal Security Laws, *Strategy and Tactics of World Communism: Recruiting for Espionage*, 84th Cong., 1st sess., June 28–29, 1955, pt. 14 (Washington, D.C.: U.S. Government Printing Office, 1955), 1342, 1346.

28. Ibid., 1356–57, 1343; Edward Alwood, *Dark Days in the Newsroom: McCarthyism Aimed at the Press* (Philadelphia: Temple University Press, 2007), 97, 99.

29. Ralph H. Johnson and Michael Altman, "Communists in the Press: A Senate Witch-Hunt of the 1950s Revisited," *Journalism Quarterly* 55, no. 3 (Fall 1978): 488–90; Cloud and Olson, *Murrow Boys*, 329.

30. Sig Mickelson, interview by author, June 17, 1975.

31. Ibid.

32. William S. Paley, *As It Happened: A Memoir* (New York: Doubleday, 1979), 282; Paley interview; A. M. Sperber, *Murrow: His Life and Times* (New York: Freundlich, 1986), 364.

33. Betty Koenig Van Bergen, interview by author, August 5, 1975; Persico, *Edward R. Murrow: An American Original*, 342.

34. William L. Shirer, *A Native's Return, 1945–1988*, vol. 3 of *Twentieth-Century Journey: A Memoir of a Life and the Times* (Boston: Little, Brown, 1990), 55, 93–94.

35. Cloud and Olson, *Murrow Boys*, 273, 274–75.

36. Jack Gould, "New 'Cure' for Radio," *New York Times*, March 30, 1947, sec. 2, X9.

37. Shirer, *A Native's Return*, 111, 102.

38. William L. Shirer, interview by author, December 10, 1976.

39. *A Conversation with Eric Sevareid*, CBS News Special, transcript, December 13, 1977. In the author's possession.

40. Ibid., broadcast transcript, 8.

41. Cloud and Olson, *Murrow Boys*, 303; Eric Sevareid, letter to author, February 23, 1978.

42. Joseph Wershba, interview by author, November 10, 1974; Nat Brandt, "Don Hollenbeck Remembered," *Silurian News*, May 2006, 3.

43. John Horn, interview by author, March 27, 1978.

44. Ibid.

45. Arthur Bonner, interview by author, September 27, 1975; Bernard Birnbaum, interview by author, October 8, 2005; Jack Walters, interview by author, August 5, 1975.

46. Fred Friendly, interview by author, July 8, 1975; Walter Cronkite, interview by author, October 11, 2005.

47. "Loyalty Letter Accepted by CBS," *New York Journal-American*, February 7, 1951, 10. See also "CBS Dismissing Objectors to Oath," *New York Journal-American*, January 26, 1951, 36.

48. Richard Rovere, *Senator Joe McCarthy* (New York: Bobbs Merrill, 1970), 166.

49. Ibid.; Edwin R. Bayley, *Joe McCarthy and the Press* (Madison: University of Wisconsin Press, 1981), vii.

50. Bayley, *Joe McCarthy and the Press*, 195, 194. Also see Elmer Davis, *By Elmer Davis*, ed. Robert Lloyd Davis (Indianapolis: Bobbs-Merrill, 1964), 69, and Roger Burlingame, *Don't Let Them Scare You: The Life and Times of Elmer Davis* (Philadelphia: Lippincott, 1961), 300–305.

51. Fred Friendly, *Due to Circumstances Beyond Our Control . . .* (New York: Vintage, 1967), 11.

52. Sig Mickelson, *The Decade That Shaped Television News: CBS in the 1950s* (Westport, Conn.: Praeger, 1998), 145.

53. Ibid.

54. Friendly, *Due to Circumstances Beyond Our Control*, 34.

55. Ibid., 35; Paley interview.

56. *See It Now*, March 9, 1954.

57. Ibid.

58. Friendly, *Due to Circumstances Beyond Our Control*, 41.

59. Friendly interview; Charles Collingwood, interview by author, August 5, 1975.

60. Friendly interview. See, for example, Benjamin R. Shute of Cravath, Swaine and Moore, letter to Murrow, May 4, 1954, reel 41, 527, and numerous "Matter of M" memoranda on reel 42, *Edward R. Murrow Papers, 1927–1973* (microform) (Sanford, N.C.: Microfilming Corp. of America, 1982).
61. Friendly interview.
62. Ibid.

16. The Walking Wounded

1. Jack O'Brian, "An Analysis of Murrow's Portsided Political Pitching," *New York Journal-American*, March 10, 1954, 36.
2. Ibid.
3. George Herman, letter to author, September 29, 1974; Jack O'Brian, interview by author, February 3, 1975.
4. Dr. Willis A. Murphy, interview by author, July 3, 1975.
5. Ibid.; Doctors Hospital Discharge Summary, Don Hollenbeck, No. 88814, Discharge date, March 19, 1954.
6. Shirley Wershba, interview by author, November 10, 1974.
7. Doctors Hospital General History, Don Hollenbeck, Admission Number 54-3079; Murphy interview.
8. Anne Hollenbeck, interview by author, October 27, 1974.
9. Sig Mickelson, interview by author, June 17, 1975; Milton Stern, interview by author, May 12, 1975.
10. Margaret Halsey, interview by author, August 20, 1974.
11. Anne Hollenbeck, undated letter to Don Hollenbeck.
12. Hollenbeck interview, October 27, 1974.
13. Marynia Farnham and Ferdinand Lundberg, *Modern Woman: The Lost Sex* (New York: Harper, 1947), quoted in Betty Friedan, *The Feminine Mystique* (New York: Norton, 1963), 42–43.
14. Farnham and Lundberg, *Modern Woman*, 337.
15. Ibid., 377.
16. Ned Calmer, interview by author, August 4, 1975; Marie Coleman Nelson, interview by author, April 24, 1974.
17. Hollenbeck interview, October 27, 1974.
18. Ibid.
19. Ibid.
20. Ibid.; Betty Koenig Van Bergen, interview by author, August 5, 1975.
21. Jack Walters, letter to author, July 21, 1977.
22. Ibid.
23. Hollenbeck interview, October 27, 1974.
24. Zoë H. Barr, interview by author, July 17, 2005.
25. Barr interview; Hollenbeck interview, October 27, 1974.

26. "Tribute to Zoë," 1950 set of records in Don Hollenbeck, Broadcast Papers (MS 319; hereafter Hollenbeck Broadcast Papers), Archives and Special Collections, University of Nebraska–Lincoln Libraries.

27. Ibid.; John Gude, interview by author, June 16, 1975.

28. Anne Hollenbeck, letter to author, August 14, 1974; Stern interview.

29. Manfred Kirchheimer, letter to author, April 12, 1978.

30. Calmer interview.

31. Jack Walters, interview by author, August 5, 1975.

32. Ibid.

33. Robert Rogow, interview by author, August 4, 1974.

34. Walters interview.

35. Ibid.; Jack Walters, "Just Now," in *Saigon and Other Poems* (New York: Spuyten Duyvil, 2005), 59.

36. Walters interview.

37. Ibid.; James Crayhon, interview by author, July 11, 1975; Calmer interview.

38. Hollenbeck interview, October 27, 1974.

39. Van Bergen interview; Shirley Wershba interview.

40. Rogow interview.

41. Calmer interview.

42. Stern interview.

43. Hollenbeck interview, October 27, 1974.

44. "Coast Editor a Suicide," *New York Times*, June 28, 1940, 21; "Suicide? Editor's Car Found on Span" clipping, with "S. F. News" and "Jun 28 1940" stamped on it, inside the back cover of Hollenbeck scrapbook, along with other San Francisco newspaper clippings about Wilbur N. Burhardt's death, Hollenbeck Broadcast Papers; Don Hollenbeck, letter to Anne Murphy, June 14, 1940.

45. "Mrs. Dall Wed Here to John Boettiger," *New York Times*, January 19, 1935, 15; "Mrs. Anna Boettiger Received a Divorce," *New York Times*, August 12, 1949, 40. On other biographical details about the Boettigers, see "Boettigers Buy Phoenix Paper," *New York Times*, February 24, 1946, 5; "Phoenix Paper Suspends; Former Boettiger Enterprise Established in May, 1947," *New York Times*, October 6, 1949, 29; "Boettiger Paper Is Sold; Phoenix Group, Headed by Giragi, Buys Arizona Times," *New York Times*, July 27, 1948, 23; "Boettiger Goes Abroad; Son-in-Law of Roosevelt Plans to Look behind 'Iron Curtain,'" *New York Times*, February 21, 1948, 28; and "Boettiger Arrives in Warsaw," *New York Times*, March 8, 1948, 8.

46. "Boettiger a Suicide in Seven-Floor Plunge; Roosevelt's Ex-Son-in-Law Overpowers Male Nurse to Leap from Hotel Here," *New York Times*, November 1, 1950, 38; Van Bergen interview.

47. Patrick J. Maney, *"Young Bob" La Follette: A Biography of Robert M. La Follette, Jr., 1895–1953* (Columbia: University of Missouri Press, 1978), 313.

48. Wayne Phillips, "Harassing Feared by 'Voice' Suicide," *New York Times*, May 7, 1953, 10.

49.   Kaplan's note is quoted in David M. Oshinsky, *A Conspiracy So Immense: The World of Joe McCarthy* (New York: Oxford University Press, 2005), 271. See also Ted Morgan, *Reds: McCarthyism in Twentieth-Century America* (New York: Random House, 2003), 439–40; David Caute, *The Great Fear: The Anti-Communist Purge Under Truman and Eisenhower* (New York: Simon and Schuster, 1978), 321.

50.   James Aronson, *The Press and the Cold War* (New York: Monthly Review Press, 1970), 51.

51.   C. P. Trussell, "Clark Says Duggan Was Loyal to U.S.," *New York Times*, December 25, 1948, 1. See also "Fall Kills Duggan, Named with Hiss in Spy Ring Inquiry," *New York Times*, December 21, 1948, 1, 3; John Earl Haynes and Harvey Klehr, *Venona: Decoding Soviet Espionage in America* (New Haven, Conn.: Yale University Press, 1999), 203; "Communist Romantics, I: The Reluctant Laurence Duggan," in Allen Weinstein and Alexander Vassiliev, *The Haunted Wood: Soviet Espionage in America—the Stalin Era* (New York: Modern Library, 2000), 3–4, 12–13, 19; Joseph E. Persico, "The Kremlin Connection," *New York Times Book Review*, January 3, 1999, 6.

52.   Arnold A. Rogow, *James Forrestal: A Study of Personality, Politics, and Policy* (New York: Macmillan, 1963), 17–18. See also Townsend Hoopes and Douglas Brinkley, *Driven Patriot: The Life and Times of James Forrestal* (New York: Knopf, 1992), 465–68.

53.   Pegler is quoted in Hoopes and Brinkley, *Driven Patriot*, 36.

54.   Peter D. Bunzel, "He's Man behind the Microphone, Who Views the Press and Finds Not All to His Taste," *Vineyard (Mass.) Gazette*, June 24, 1949, 88.

55.   Jack O'Brian, "Gonna Wash That Color Right out of Our Set," *New York Journal-American*, May 26, 1954, 38.

56.   Jack O'Brian, "Letters from Readers on Slanted Newscasts," *New York Journal-American*, June 14, 1954, 24.

57.   Ibid.

58.   Ibid.

59.   Van Bergen interview; see also Jay Nelson Tuck, "Don Hollenbeck," *New York Post*, June 23, 1954, 72.

60.   Jerry Walker, "Don Hollenbeck Views Much-Honored Show," *Editor and Publisher*, May 15, 1948, 44; Tuck, "Don Hollenbeck," 72.

61.   Fred Friendly, interview by author, July 8, 1975.

62.   Hollenbeck interview, October 26, 1974; Friendly interview.

63.   *CBS Views the Press*, broadcast transcript, January 17, 1948, 2.

64.   Ibid., 6.

65.   Ibid.; George Polk, letter to Don Hollenbeck, February 5, 1948, in Hollenbeck scrapbook, 39, Hollenbeck Broadcast Papers.

66.   Calmer interview.

67.   Herman to author; Alexander Kendrick, *Prime Time: The Life of Edward R. Murrow* (Boston: Little, Brown, 1969), 421; Van Bergen interview.

68. Calmer interview.
69. Ibid.
70. Dr. Isaih Lew, interview by author, December 9, 1974.

17. The Sermon in the Suicide

1. Ted Marvel, interview by author, August 9, 1975.
2. George George, letter to author, March 10, 1978.
3. Nat Brandt, interview by author, April 24, 1978.
4. Anne Hollenbeck, interview by author, October 26, 1974. Anne's clear recollection—and her memory usually was excellent—was that he was on the wagon in 1953–54. However, Betty Koenig Van Bergen, who was Hollenbeck's girlfriend in the last year of his life, said that she thought the year he spent sober was 1950–51. Of course, they both could have been right (Betty Koenig Van Bergen, interview by author, August 5, 1975).
5. Brandt interview; Zoë H. Barr, interview by author, July 17, 2005.
6. Brandt interview.
7. Marvel interview.
8. Brandt interview.
9. James Burke, interview by author, August 15, 1975.
10. Sig Mickelson, interview by author, June 17, 1975.
11. Brandt interview.
12. Hollenbeck interview, October 26, 1974; Sherry Walters, interview by author, August 7, 1975.
13. Walters interview.
14. Walter Cronkite, interview by author, October 11, 2005.
15. Milton Stern, interview by author, May 12, 1975.
16. Hollenbeck interview, October 27, 1974.
17. Ibid.
18. Ibid.
19. Van Bergen interview by author.
20. Ibid.
21. Charles Gussman, interview by author, September 29, 1973.
22. Van Bergen interview.
23. Stern interview.
24. Van Bergen interview.
25. Stern interview.
26. Ibid.
27. Ibid. Jessie Seacrest is the wife Hollenbeck discussed with Stern. Some Lincoln residents also believed that a despondent Seacrest, who died at age thirty-five in Honolulu on September 19, 1940, killed herself. Margery L. Hammond, a Lincoln High School graduate in Hollenbeck's class, wrote that Seacrest "committed sui-

cide" (Margery L. Hammond, letter to author, June 30, 1975). But Seacrest family members are certain Jessie Seacrest died of natural causes. My efforts to determine her cause of death from Hawaiian records were unsuccessful.

28. Stern interview.

29. Ibid.

30. Ibid.

31. Margaret Halsey, interview by author, August 20, 1974.

32. Stern interview.

33. Certificate of death for Don Hollenbeck, Division of Records, Department of Health, Borough of Manhattan, Certificate No. 152-54-113295, dated June 22, 1954; Joe Martin and Henry Lee, "TV's Don Hollenbeck, Ailing, Afraid, Suicide," *New York Daily News*, June 23, 1954, 3, 6.

34. James O'Connor, "Don Hollenbeck of TV Suicide by Gas," *New York Mirror*, June 23, 1954, 3; "Don Hollenbeck Is Suicide by Gas," *New York Times*, June 23, 1954, 16. See Martin and Lee, "TV's Don Hollenbeck"; and Norton Mockridge, "Hollenbeck, TV Newscaster, Takes Own Life," *New York World-Telegram and Sun*, June 22, 1954, 1–2. The most accurate article appeared in the *Herald Tribune*: "Don Hollenbeck, 49, Kills Himself," *New York Herald Tribune*, June 24, 1954, 1, 29.

35. "Don Hollenbeck a Suicide," *New York Journal-American*, June 22, 1954, 1.

36. Jay Nelson Tuck, "Don Hollenbeck," *New York Post*, June 23, 1954, 72.

37. Ibid., 4, 72.

38. Ibid., 4.

39. Cronkite interview; Mike Wallace, interview by author, August 15, 2005.

40. "Myron's Story," interview of Mike Wallace by Morley Safer, *Sixty Minutes*, May 21, 2006. In 1982 General William Westmoreland sued Wallace and CBS for reporting that Westmoreland had deliberately falsified estimates of enemy troop strength in Vietnam. Though the suit eventually was settled without payment, Wallace experienced deep depression during the trial and even attempted to kill himself. He told Safer: "I wrote a note. And Mary [Wallace's wife] found it. And she found the pills that I was taking on the floor. I was asleep." Safer then said on *Sixty Minutes*: "But that was over twenty years ago. . . . Mary got him through it."

41. Wallace interview by author; Joseph Wershba, interview by author, August 10, 2006.

42. See, for example, Jack O'Brian, "An Analysis of Murrow's Portsided Political Pitching," *New York Journal-American*, March 10, 1954, 36.

43. Hollenbeck interview, October 26, 1974.

44. Jack O'Brian, interview by author, February 3, 1975.

45. FBI internal report no. 77-23027-5, New York file no. 77-4336, report by G. W. Chappelear, New York office, May 21, 1942, and FBI internal report no. 77-23027-8, memo dated July 13, 1945, from SAC, New York, to FBI Director John Edgar Hoover re "SODAC, New York City, Internal Security-R." Also see FBI report

on Don Hollenbeck, made at the New York office by Raymond J. Kopp, September 28, 1950, "Security Matter-C," file no. 100–98638 FJS, and FBI report on Don Hollenbeck, made at the New York office on June 22, 1954, file no. 100-369550-5, which I obtained under the Freedom of Information Act.

46. "Hoover Describes Dossiers by F.B.I.," *New York Times*, May 12, 1954, clipping in Benjamin Mandel Series, box 687, FBI General Papers 1952–55, J. B. Matthews Papers, Rare Book, Manuscript, and Special Collections Library, Duke University. See also Kenneth O'Reilly, "Friendly Witnesses," in *Hoover and the Un-Americans: The FBI, HUAC, and the Red Menace*, 230–54 (Philadelphia: Temple University Press, 1983).

47. FBI internal report no. 77-23027-5.

48. FBI internal report no. 77-23027-8.

49. Jack O'Brian, "Continuing Study of the Continuing CBS News 'Slant,'" *New York Journal-American*, June 23, 1954, 37.

50. Ibid.

51. FBI internal report no. 100-369550-0, memo from "SAC, New York (100-98638)," dated July 7, 1954.

52. William S. Paley, interview by author, February 16, 1977; Joseph E. Persico, *Edward R. Murrow: An American Original* (New York: McGraw-Hill, 1988), 392–93; Fred Friendly, *Due to Circumstances Beyond Our Control . . .* (New York: Vintage, 1967), 66.

53. *See It Now*, June 22, 1954, broadcast tape available in the CBS News archives. Murrow's remarks about Hollenbeck from that broadcast are also quoted in Friendly, *Due to Circumstances Beyond Our Control*, 64.

54. Phonograph record of Murrow's June 22, 1954, radio tribute following Hollenbeck's suicide, in Don Hollenbeck, Broadcast Papers, Archives and Special Collections, University of Nebraska–Lincoln Libraries.

Epilogue

1. This—and all other broadcast tributes to Hollenbeck from June 22, 1954—are available in Don Hollenbeck, Broadcast Papers (MS 319), Archives and Special Collections, University of Nebraska–Lincoln Libraries.

2. Ibid.

3. William S. Paley, interview by author, February 16, 1977; Charles Collingwood, interview by author, August 5, 1975.

4. Mike Wallace, interview by author, August 15, 2005; Paley interview.

5. Paley interview.

6. William S. Paley, *1974/1954: Free Broadcast Journalism* (N.p.: CBS, 1974), 26. See also Sally Bedell Smith, *In All His Glory: The Life of William S. Paley—the Legendary Tycoon and His Brilliant Circle* (New York: Simon and Schuster, 1990), 364–65.

7. John Crosby, "A British Opinion of Us," *New York Herald Tribune*, undated 1947 clipping in Hollenbeck scrapbook, 57, Hollenbeck Broadcast Papers.

8. Robert Lewis Shayon, "Scraps of Sound and History," *Saturday Review of Literature*, February 10, 1951, 30.

9. Broadcast tribute to Hollenbeck, June 22, 1954.

10. Alan Jackson, interview by author, January 25, 1975.

11. George George, letter to author, March 10, 1978.

12. George Seldes, *Witness to a Century: Encounters with the Noted, the Notorious, and the Three SOBs* (New York: Ballantine, 1987), 382.

13. Broadcast tribute to Hollenbeck, June 22, 1954.

14. Anne Hollenbeck, letter to Ted Marvel, July 6, 1954.

15. Anne Hollenbeck, interview by author, October 27, 1974; Edward R. Murrow, *In Search of Light: The Broadcasts of Edward R. Murrow, 1938–1961*, ed. Edward Bliss Jr. (New York: Avon, 1967), 369.

16. Murrow, *In Search of Light*, 371.

17. Ibid., 371, 372.

18. Ibid., 373.

19. Tom Wicker, *Shooting Star: The Brief Arc of Joe McCarthy* (Orlando, Fla.: Harcourt, 2006), 177–78; Eisenhower is quoted in Ted Morgan, *Reds: McCarthyism in Twentieth-Century America* (New York: Random House: 2003), 505.

20. Squires is quoted in Jim Lehrer, "Blurring the Lines Hurts Journalism," *Nieman Reports*, Summer 1999, 65.

21. Murrow, *In Search of Light*, 376.

Bibliography

A Conversation with Eric Sevareid. CBS News Special, transcript, December 13, 1977. In the author's possession.

"A Plain Talk with the Readers of This Paper by the Editor." *Omaha Bee-News,* October 28, 1928, 2.

"A Shameful Performance." *New York Journal-American,* July 19, 1950, 1.

Alexander, Jack. "Do Gooder." *Saturday Evening Post,* December 6, 1941, 14–15.

Allen, Frederick Lewis. *The Big Change.* New York: Bantam, 1961.

Allen, Steve. "Jack O'Brian and the Art of Criticism." *Village Voice,* March 19, 1958, 1, 13.

Alterman, Eric. *What Liberal Media? The Truth About Bias and the News.* New York: Basic Books, 2003.

Alwood, Edward. "CBS Correspondent Winston Burdett and His Decision to Become a Government Witness in the Age of McCarthyism." *American Communist History* 5, no. 2 (2006): 153–67.

——. *Dark Days in the Newsroom: McCarthyism Aimed at the Press.* Philadelphia: Temple University Press, 2007.

American Business Consultants. *Red Channels: The Report of Communist Influence in Radio and Television.* New York: American Business Consultants, 1950.

Ames, William E. and Roger A. Simpson. *Unionism or Hearst: The Seattle Post-Intelligencer Strike of 1936.* Seattle: Pacific Northwest Labor History Association, 1978.

Aronson, James. *The Press and the Cold War.* New York: Monthly Review Press, 1970.

Atkinson, Rick. *The Day of Battle: The War in Sicily and Italy, 1943–1944.* New York: Holt, 2007.

Atwood, L. Erwin and Kenneth Starck. "Effects of Community Press Councils: Real and Imagined." *Journalism Quarterly* 49 (Summer 1972): 230–38.

Bagdikian, Ben. "Bagdikian's Post-Mortem: Keep Up Criticism." *Bulletin of the American Society of Newspaper Editors,* October 1972, 1, 12–13.

——. *The Information Machines: Their Impact on Men and the Media.* New York: Harper and Row, 1971.

Balk, Alfred. "Background Paper." In Twentieth Century Fund, *A Free and Responsive Press: The Twentieth Century Fund Task Force Report for a National News Council,* 11–66. New York: Twentieth Century Fund, 1973.

——. *The Rise of Radio: From Marconi Through the Golden Age.* Jefferson, N.C.: McFarland, 2006.

Barnouw, Erik. *A Tower in Babel.* Vol. 1, *to 1933,* of *A History of Broadcasting in the United States.* New York: Oxford University Press, 1966.

——. *The Golden Web.* Vol. 2, *1933 to 1953,* of *A History of Broadcasting in the United States.* New York: Oxford University Press, 1968.

——. *The Sponsor.* New York: Oxford University Press, 1978.

Barron, Jerome. *Freedom of the Press for Whom?* Bloomington: Indiana University Press, 1973.

Baughman, James L. *Same Time, Same Station: Creating American Television, 1948–1961.* Baltimore: John Hopkins University Press, 2007.

Bayley, Edwin R. *Joe McCarthy and the Press.* Madison: University of Wisconsin Press, 1981.

Becker, Stephen. *Marshall Field III: A Biography.* New York: Simon and Schuster, 1964.

Beichman, Arnold. "The Resurrection of *PM*: Liberalism vs. Newspaper Know-How." *New Leader,* May 8, 1948, 8–9.

Bennett, David H. *The Party of Fear: from Nativist Movements to the New Right in American History.* Chapel Hill: University of North Carolina, 1988.

Bent, Silas. *Ballyhoo: The Voice of the Press.* New York: Liveright, 1927.

——. *Newspaper Crusaders: A Neglected Story.* New York: McGraw-Hill, 1939.

——. *Strange Bedfellows: A Review of Politics, Personalities, and the Press.* New York: Liveright, 1928.

Bentley, Eric, ed. *Thirty Years of Treason: Excerpts from Hearings before the House Committee on Un-American Activities, 1938–1968.* New York: Viking, 1971.

Berger, Meyer. *The Story of the* New York Times: *The First 100 Years, 1851–1951.* 1951. Reprint, New York: Arno, 1970.

Berman, Jeffrey. *Surviving Literary Suicide.* Amherst: University of Massachusetts Press, 1999.

Bernstein, Carl. *Loyalties: A Son's Memoir.* New York: Simon and Schuster, 1989.

Bernstein, Mark and Alex Lubertozzi. *World War II on the Air: Edward R. Murrow and the Broadcasts That Riveted a Nation.* Naperville, Ill.: Sourcebooks, 2003.

Bliss, Edward Jr. *Now the News: The Story of Broadcast Journalism.* New York: Columbia University Press, 1991.

Blum, David. *Tick ... Tick ... Tick: The Long Life and Turbulent Times of* 60 Minutes. New York: HarperCollins, 2004.

Blumenson, Martin. *United States Army in World II: The Mediterranean Theater of Op-*

erations, Salerno to Cassino. Washington, D.C.: Office of the Chief of Military History, U.S. Army, 1969.

"Blurt v. Blurb." *Time*, September 16, 1948, 8.

"Boettiger Arrives in Warsaw." *New York Times*, March 8, 1948, 8.

"Boettiger a Suicide in Seven-Floor Plunge; Roosevelt's Ex-Son-in-Law Overpowers Male Nurse to Leap from Hotel Here." *New York Times*, November 1, 1950, 38.

"Boettiger Goes Abroad; Son-in-Law of Roosevelt Plans to Look behind 'Iron Curtain.'" *New York Times*, February 21, 1948, 28.

"Boettiger Paper Is Sold; Phoenix Group, Headed by Giragi, Buys Arizona Times." *New York Times*, July 27, 1948, 23.

"Boettigers Buy Phoenix Paper." *New York Times*, February 24, 1946, 5.

"Boldness Prevented Being Identified, Says Wupper." *Omaha Bee-News*, April 6, 1931, 2.

Boyer, Peter J. *The Undoing of America's Number One News Network*. New York: Random House, 1988.

Bozell, L. Brent III. *Weapons of Mass Distortion: The Coming Meltdown of the Liberal Media*. New York: Crown Forum, 2004.

Brady, Erik. "Bdwy.'s Favorite Scribe Is Buflo.'s Favorite Son." *Buffalo Courier-Express*, May 18, 1979, 3.

Brandt, Nat. "Don Hollenbeck Remembered." *Silurian News* [New York], May 2006, 3, 6.

Brasch, Walter M. *With Just Cause: Unionization of the American Journalist*. Lanham, Md.: University Press of America, 1991.

"'Brass Rail' Walkout Begins Its 518th Day." *PM*, June 18, 1940, 14.

Brown, Lee. *The Reluctant Reformation: On Criticizing the Press in America*. New York: McKay, 1974.

Brown, Les. "Program Blacklisted in '60 Revived by WCBS." *New York Times*, October 7, 1976, 73.

Brucker, Herbert. *Communication Is Power: Unchanging Values in a Changing Journalism*. New York: Oxford University Press, 1973.

——. *Freedom of Information*. New York: Macmillan, 1949.

Bryce, James. *The American Commonwealth*. 2 vols. London: Macmillan, 1899.

Bryce, Oliver. "Thought Control American Style." *New Republic*, January 13, 1947, 11–12.

Buckley, William F. Jr. and L. Brent Bozell. *McCarthy and His Enemies: The Record and Its Meaning*. Chicago: Regnery, 1954.

Buhle, Paul and Wagner, Dave. *Hide in Plain Sight: The Hollywood Blacklistees in Film and Television, 1950–2002*. New York: Palgrave Macmillan, 2003.

Bunzel, Peter D. "He's Man behind the Microphone Who Views the Press and Finds Not All to His Taste." *Vineyard (Mass.) Gazette*, June 24, 1949, 88.

Burlingame, Roger. *Don't Let Them Scare You: The Life and Times of Elmer Davis*. Philadelphia: Lippincott, 1961.

Burton, Michael C. *John Henry Faulk: A Biography*. Austin, Tex.: Eakin, 1993.

Buxton, Frank and Bill Owen. *The Big Broadcast: 1920–1950*. New York: Viking, 1972.

Cailteux, Karen Sue. "The Political Blacklist in the Broadcast Industry: The Decade of the 1950's." Ph.D. diss., Ohio State University, 1972.

"California Publishers Want Ad Bribery Charge Aired." *Editor and Publisher*, May 21, 1949, 5, 60.

Calmer, Ned. *The Anchorman*. New York: Doubleday, 1970.

Campbell, Joseph. *The Hero with a Thousand Faces*. Princeton, N.J.: Princeton University Press, 1972.

"Can Russia Deliver the Bomb?" *Life*, October 10, 1949, 44–45.

Carlisle, Rodney P. "William Randolph Hearst: A Fascist Reputation Reconsidered." *Journalism Quarterly* 50, no. 1 (Spring 1973): 125–33.

Carr, Robert K. *The House Committee on Un-American Activities, 1945–1950*. Ithaca, N.Y.: Cornell University Press, 1952.

Carson, Saul. "On the Air: The Reformed Gadfly." *New Republic*, March 13, 1950, 22.

Carter, Hodding. *Where Main Street Meets the River*. New York: Rinehart, 1953.

Carter, Paul A. *Another Part of the Twenties*. New York: Columbia University Press, 1977.

Cassini, Igor, with Jeanne Molli. *I'd Do It All Over Again*. New York: Putnam, 1977.

Caute, David. *The Great Fear: The Anti-Communist Purge Under Truman and Eisenhower*. New York: Simon and Schuster, 1978.

"CBS Dismissing Objectors to Oath." *New York Journal-American*, January 26, 1951, 36.

CBS News. *Television News Reporting*. New York: McGraw-Hill, 1958.

"CBS Rides Herd on New York Papers." *Nieman Reports*, October 1947, 25–29.

"CBS Station in New York Starts Criticism of Press." *Editor and Publisher*, June 7, 1947, 11, 95.

"CBS Views the Press." *Variety*, February 15, 1950, 32.

Chaney, Lindsay and Michael Cieply. *The Hearsts: Family and Empire—the Later Years*. New York: Simon and Schuster, 1981.

Chapman, John. *Tell It to Sweeney: The Informal History of the New York Daily News*. New York: Doubleday, 1961.

Chester, Edmund A. *A Sergeant Named Batista*. New York: Holt, 1954.

Chester, Giraud and Garnet R. Garrison. *Radio and Television: An Introduction*. New York: Appleton-Century-Crofts, 1950.

Christian, Dick. "Jack O'Brian Hailed for Successful Career." *Buffalo News*, October 30, 1991, B-12.

Clark, David G. "H. V. Kaltenborn and His Sponsors: Controversial Broadcasting and the Sponsor's Role." *Journal of Broadcasting* 12, no. 4 (Fall 1968): 309–21.

Clooney, George and Grant Heslov. "Commentary." *Good Night, and Good Luck*. Widescreen edition. DVD. Directed by George Clooney. Hollywood, Calif.: Warner Independent Pictures, 2005.

——. *Good Night, and Good Luck: The Screenplay and History Behind the Landmark Movie*. New York: Newmarket, 2006. The script is also available at www.script-o-rama.com/movie_scripts/g/good-night-and-good-luck-script.html.

Cloud, Stanley and Lynne Olson. *The Murrow Boys: Pioneers on the Front Lines of Broadcast Journalism*. Boston: Houghton Mifflin, 1996.

"Coast Editor a Suicide." *New York Times*, June 28, 1940, 21.

Cogley, John. *Radio-Television*. Vol. 2 of *Report on Blacklisting*. New York: Fund for the Republic, 1956.

Cohn, Roy. *McCarthy*. New York: New American Library, 1968.

Cole, Hugh M. *The Ardennes: Battle of the Bulge*. Washington, D.C.: U.S. Department of the Army, Office of the Chief of Military History, 1965.

Cole, Wayne S. *Charles A. Lindbergh and the Battle Against American Intervention in World War II*. New York: Harcourt Brace Jovanovich, 1974.

Collins, Karl [Kenneth Crawford]. "The Rise and Decline of a Crusader." *New Leader*, March 1946, 8.

Commager, Henry Steele. *The American Mind: An Interpretation of American Thought and Character since the 1880's*. New Haven, Conn.: Yale University Press, 1959.

Commission on Freedom of the Press. *A Free and Responsible Press: A General Report on Mass Communication: Newspapers, Radio, Motion Pictures, Magazines, and Books*. Chicago: University of Chicago Press, 1947.

"The Communist Fifth Column in the United States." *New York Journal-American*, March 21, 1947, 20.

"Conspiracy of Silence." *In Fact*, July 14, 1947, 1.

Cook, Bruce. *Dalton Trumbo*. New York: Scribner's, 1977.

Cooney, John. *The American Pope: The Life and Times of Frances Cardinal Spellman*. New York: Times Books, 1984.

Coote, Colin R. *The Other Club*. London: Sidgwick and Jackson, 1971.

"Cop Is Hooch Sniffer—'Suspicious' Suitcase Yields Three and a Half Pints of Alleged Booze." *Lincoln (Neb.) Evening State Journal*, December 11, 1926, 6.

Copple, Neale. *Tower on the Plains: Lincoln's Centennial History, 1859–1959*. Lincoln, Neb.: Lincoln Centennial Commission, 1959.

Coulter, Ann. *Treason: Liberal Treachery from the Cold War to the War on Terrorism*. New York: Three Rivers, 2003.

"The Crime of Communism." *New York Journal-American*, October 17, 1949, 16.

"Critics: The Man with the Popular Mind." *Time*, November 20, 1964, 50.

Cronkite, Walter. *A Reporter's Life*. New York: Knopf, 1996.

Crosby, Donald F. *God, Church, and Flag: Senator Joseph R. McCarthy and the Catholic Church 1950–1957*. Chapel Hill: University of North Carolina Press, 1978.

Crosby, John. "A British Opinion of Us." Undated *New York Herald Tribune* article, Hollenbeck scrapbook, 57, Don Hollenbeck, Broadcast Papers (MS 319), Archives and Special Collections, University of Nebraska–Lincoln Libraries.

——. "The Press in Review." *New York Herald Tribune*, June 9, 1947, 15.

——. "Some Irritability Around." *New York Herald Tribune*, April 25, 1958, sec. 2, 1.

Cuppy, Will. *The Decline and Fall of Practically Everybody*. Edited by Fred Feldkamp. New York: Holt, 1950.

"Daily Worker Critic Forced out of Job on Refusal to Attack 'Gone with the Wind.'" *New York Times*, December 22, 1939, 1.

Davey, Harold L. "James E. Davey Descendancy Narrative." Unpublished family genealogy database, June 20, 2006. Contact Davey at hdavey@comcast.net.

Davis, David Brion. *The Fear of Conspiracy: Images of Un-American Subversion from the Revolution to the Present*. Ithaca: Cornell University Press, 1971.

Davis, Elmer. *By Elmer Davis*. Edited by Robert Lloyd Davis. Indianapolis: Bobbs-Merrill, 1964.

Dell, Floyd. *Upton Sinclair: A Study in Social Protest*. New York: Doran, 1927.

Denker, David D. "The Newspaper *PM*, 1937–1942: An Internal Study." Ph.D. diss., Yale University, 1951, box 4, *PM* Collection, Bill Kovach Collection of Contemporary Journalism, Nieman Foundation, Harvard University.

"Dinner Given Here by Mrs. Matthews." *New York Times*, January 12, 1940, 12.

Doherty, Thomas. *Cold War, Cool Medium: Television, McCarthyism, and American Culture*. New York: Columbia University Press, 2003.

"Don Hollenbeck a Suicide." *New York Journal-American*, June 22, 1954, 1.

"Don Hollenbeck, 49, Kills Himself." *New York Herald Tribune*, June 24, 1954, 1, 29.

"Don Hollenbeck Is Suicide by Gas." *New York Times*, June 23, 1954, 16.

Dorinson, Joseph and William Pencak, eds. *Paul Robeson: Essays on His Life and Legacy*. Jefferson, N.C.: McFarland, 2002.

Dreier, Thomas. *The Power of Print—and Men*. New York: Mergenthaler Linotype, 1936.

Drewelow, Gladys K. "Jack O'Brian Reminisces About Buffalo." Summary of her various telephone interviews of Jack O'Brian, and his postinterview addenda, accompanied by her December 10, 1991, letter to Elliott Shapiro, librarian, *Buffalo News* library, where the material is archived. For six weeks in 1991 Drewelow, chair of the Room Dedication Committee of the Buffalo Convention Center, interviewed O'Brian by telephone. She shared her eleven-page summary of those interviews with him. He added corrections and personal notes. The interviews with O'Brian anticipated his October 1991 visit to Buffalo for the unveiling of a public room bearing his name at the Buffalo Convention Center.

D'Souza, Dinesh. *The Enemy at Home: The Cultural Left and Its Responsibility for 9/11*. New York: Doubleday, 2007.

Duberman, Martin Baum. *Paul Robeson*. New York: Knopf, 1988.

Dunning, John. *On the Air: The Encyclopedia of Old-Time Radio*. New York: Oxford University Press, 1998.

Dyson, Lowell K. *Red Harvest: The Communist Party and American Farmers*. Lincoln: University of Nebraska Press, 1982.

Editors of *Freedomways*. *Paul Robeson: The Great Forerunner*. New York: Dodd, Mead, 1978.

Edward R. Murrow Papers, 1927–1973 (microform). Sanford, N.C.: Microfilming Corp. of America, 1982.

Edwards, Bob. *Edward R. Murrow and the Birth of Broadcast Journalism*. Hoboken, N.J.: Wiley, 2004.

Einstein, Daniel. *Special Edition: A Guide to Network Television Documentary Series and Special News Reports, 1955–1979*. Metuchen, N.J.: Scarecrow, 1987.

"Embarrassed Mr. Orr." *Lincoln (Neb.) Evening Journal*, December 8, 1926, 1.

Enright, D. J., ed. *The Oxford Book of Death*. New York: Oxford University Press, 1983.

Ernst, Morris L. and David Loth. *Report on the American Communist*. New York: Holt, 1952.

Erwin, Edward, ed. *The Freud Encyclopedia: Theory, Therapy, and Culture*. New York: Routledge, 2002.

Everitt, David. *A Shadow of Red: Communism and the Blacklist in Radio and Television*. Chicago: Dee, 2007.

Ewald, William Bragg Jr. *Who Killed Joe McCarthy?* New York: Simon and Schuster, 1984.

"Experiment in Progress." *Time*, July 29, 1940, 58.

"Fall Kills Duggan, Named with Hiss in Spy Ring Inquiry." *New York Times*, December 21, 1948, 1, 3.

Fang, Irving E. *Those Radio Commentators!* Ames: Iowa State University Press, 1977.

"Farley Makes (Hello There) Flying Visits; La Platte, Fort Creek Have Big Moments with Party Chief." *Omaha World-Herald*, October 3, 1937, 1.

Farnham, Marynia and Ferdinand Lundberg. *Modern Woman: The Lost Sex*. New York: Harper, 1947.

Fast, Howard. *Peekskill, USA: A Personal Experience*. New York: Civil Rights Congress, 1951.

Faulk, John Henry. *Fear on Trial*. New York: Simon and Schuster, 1964.

Faulkner, Virginia, ed. *Roundup: A Nebraska Reader*. Lincoln: University of Nebraska Press, 1957.

Fenton, Tom. *Bad News: The Decline of Reporting, the Business of News, and the Danger to Us All*. New York: Regan, 2005.

Field, Marshall. *Freedom Is More Than a Word*. Chicago: University of Chicago Press, 1945.

Fields, Sidney. "Red Portrait Is Black." *New York Mirror*, February 16, 1949, 24.

"Finds Moral Turpitude in Bartos' Act." *Lincoln (Neb.) Star*, June 2, 1926, 2.

"First Junior Assembly of Season Held in Colorful Winter Setting; 125 Debutantes, Several Introduced at Party, and Escorts Attend." *New York Times*, December 5, 1936, 15.

Fish, Hamilton. *The Challenge of World Communism*. Milwaukee: Bruce, 1946.

Fleischman, Stephen. *A Red in the House: The Unauthorized Memoir of S. E. Fleischman, My Thirty Years in Network News*. New York: iUniverse, 2004.

Foner, Philip S., ed. *Paul Robeson Speaks: Writings, Speeches, Interviews, 1918–1974*. New York: Brunner/Mazel, 1978.

"$4,000 Prizes for Best Ideas to Advance Omaha, State." *Omaha World-Herald*, May 3, 1939, 1.

Fowle, Farnsworth. "Nick Kenny, Columnist for the *Mirror*, Writer of Verses and Lyrics, Is Dead." *New York Times*, December 2, 1975, 85.

Frank, Thomas. "Taking Names: Anti-liberalism in Theory and Practice." *Harper's Magazine*, February 2006, 85–88.

Franken, Jerry. "CBS Views the Press." *Billboard*, June 14, 1947, 15.

Freud, Sigmund. *Collected Papers*. New York: Basic Books, 1959.

——. *The Standard Edition of the Complete Psychological Works of Sigmund Freud*, translated and edited by James Strachey. London: Hogarth, 1957.

Fried, Richard M. *Men Against McCarthy*. New York: Columbia University Press, 1976.

——. *Nightmare in Red: The McCarthy Era in Perspective*. New York: Oxford University Press, 1990.

Friedan, Betty. *The Feminine Mystique*. New York: Norton, 1963.

Friendly, Fred. *Due to Circumstances Beyond Our Control ...* New York: Vintage, 1967.

Frost, Robert. *Complete Poems of Robert Frost*. New York: Holt, 1949.

Furman, Bess. *Washington By-Line: The Personal History of a Newspaperwoman*. New York: Knopf, 1949.

Gabler, Neal. *Walter Winchell: Gossip, Power, and the Culture of Celebrity*. New York: Knopf, 1994.

Gannett, Lewis. "Books and Things." *New York Herald Tribune*, December 10, 1947, 31.

Gates, Gary Paul. *The Inside Story of CBS News*. New York: Harper and Row, 1978.

Gentry, Curt. *J. Edgar Hoover: The Man and the Secrets*. New York: Norton, 1991.

"Gere Won Race to Start a Newspaper in New Capital." Centennial edition supplement, *Lincoln (Neb.) Evening Journal*, November 2, 1967, 6.

Gibbs, Wolcott. "Ralph Ingersoll—a Very Active Type Man." *New Yorker*, May 2, 1942, 21–30, and May 9, 1942, 21–30.

Gilliam, Dorothy Butler. *Paul Robeson: All-American*. Washington, D.C.: New Republic, 1976.

"Gimbels Big College Fashion Show, Saturday, August 18, at 1 p.m." *New York Times*, August 12, 1945, 42.

"Girls Will Present 'Pageant of Dolls.'" *New York Times*, November 15, 1936, D1.

"Goes to Spier's." *Lincoln (Neb.) State Journal*, October 7, 1926, 14.

Goldberg, Bernard. *Bias: A CBS Insider Exposes How the Media Distort the News*. Washington, D.C.: Regnery, 2002.

Goldman, Eric. *The Crucial Decade—and After: America, 1945–1960*. New York: Vintage, 1960.

Goldman, Mark. *City on the Lake: The Challenge of Change in Buffalo, New York*. Buffalo, N.Y.: Prometheus, 1990.

——. *High Hopes: The Rise and Decline of Buffalo, New York*. Albany: State University of New York Press, 1983.

Goodman, Walter. "Murrow, Advocacy and the Medium's Power." *New York Times*, July 29, 1990, H25.

Goodwin, Frederick K. and Kay Redfield Jamison. *Manic-Depressive Illness*. New York: Oxford University Press, 1990.

Gould, Jack. "CBS and the Press: New Program Appraises Performance of New York Newspapers." *New York Times*, June 8, 1947, sec. 2, 9.

——. "'Hear It Now' and 'Voices and Events.'" *New York Times*, December 24, 1950, 51.

——. "New 'Cure' for Radio." *New York Times*, March 30, 1947, sec. 2, X9.

——. "'Studio One' Presents Compelling Drama of Rackets on Waterfront Couched in Human Terms." *New York Times*, January 18, 1952, 33.

——. "TV: An Eye for News." *New York Times*, April 24, 1961, 59.

Goulden, Joseph G. *The Best Years: 1945–1950*. New York: Atheneum, 1976.

"Gov. Landon Is Only 19 Votes Short of Victory, Poll Shows." *Omaha Bee-News*, October 11, 1936, 1.

Grant, J. A. C. Review of *The House Committee on Un-American Activities: 1945–1950*, by Robert Carr. *Western Political Quarterly* 6, no. 4 (December 1953): 831–32.

Graud, Chester and Garnet R. Garrison. *Radio and Television: An Introduction*. New York: Appleton-Century-Crofts, 1950.

Gray, Barry. "What Can I Do for You?" Partial transcript of WOR, New York, radio broadcast, June 5, 1947. Don Hollenbeck, Broadcast Papers (MS 319), Archives and Special Collections, University of Nebraska–Lincoln Libraries.

"Greet Their Governor; Ray Ronald, Head of 19th District, Rotary, Speaks at Noon Luncheon." *Lincoln (Neb.) State Journal*, December 7, 1926, 14.

Grenier, Judson. "Upton Sinclair and the Press: *The Brass Check* Reconsidered." *Journalism Quarterly* 49, no. 3 (Autumn 1972): 427–36.

Gross, Ben. "Televiewing and Listening In." *New York Daily News*, May 16, 1952, 58.

Hagedorn, Hermann. *The Bomb That Fell on America*. Santa Barbara, Calif.: Pacific Coast Publishing, 1946.

Halberstam, David. "CBS: The Power and the Profits." *Atlantic Monthly*, January 1976, 33–71, and February 1976, 52–91.

——. *The Powers That Be*. New York: Dell, 1980.

Halsey, Margaret. *Color Blind: A White Woman Looks at the Negro*. New York: Simon and Schuster, 1946.

——. *No Laughing Matter: The Autobiography of a WASP*. Philadelphia: Lippincott, 1977.

——. *With Malice toward Some*. New York: Simon and Schuster, 1938.

Hamilton, Virginia. *Paul Robeson: The Life and Times of a Free Black Man*. New York: Harper and Row, 1974.

Harris, Leon. *Upton Sinclair: American Rebel*. New York: Crowell, 1975.

Harwood, Richard L. "Press Criticism: Who Needs It?" *Bulletin of the American Society of Newspaper Editors*, February 1972, 1, 10–11.

"The Hate Season Blossoms in the 'Journal-American.'" *PM*, May 4, 1942, 3.

Hauke, Kathleen A. *Ted Poston: Pioneer American Journalist*. Athens: University of Georgia Press, 1998.

Hausman, Linda Weiner. "Criticism of the Press in U.S. Periodicals, 1900–1939: An Annotated Bibliography." *Journalism Monographs* no. 4 (August 1967).

Haynes, John Earl. *Communism and Anti-Communism in the United States: An Annotated Guide to Historical Writings*. New York: Garland, 1987.

Haynes, John Earl and Harvey Klehr. *Venona: Decoding Soviet Espionage in America*. New Haven, Conn.: Yale University Press, 1999.

"Hearst Hits a New Low." *PM*, May 1, 1942, 2.

"Hearst Keeps Up Barrage of Lies." *PM*, May 5, 1942, 15.

"The Hearst Newspapers Advocate." *Omaha Bee-News*, November 7, 1928, 22.

"Hearst Predicts Defeat of Smith on Rum Issue." *Omaha Bee-News*, September 2, 1928, 1.

"Hearst, Sailing, Shifts to NRA." *New York Times*, May 27, 1934, 3.

Hearst, William Randolph. *Selections from the Writings and Speeches of William Randolph Hearst*. San Francisco: N.p., 1948.

Hearst, William Randolph Jr. with Jack Casserly. *The Hearsts: Father and Son*. Lanham, Md.: Roberts Rinehart, 1991.

Hentoff, Nat. "N.Y. TV Criticism: The Stumbling Eye." *Village Voice*, March 5, 1958, 5.

Herman, Arthur. *Joseph McCarthy: Reexamining the Life and Legacy of America's Most Hated Senator*. New York: Free Press, 2000.

Herzberg, Joseph G. *Late City Edition*. New York: Holt, 1947.

Hewitt, Don. *Tell Me a Story: Fifty Years and 60 Minutes in Television*. New York: Public Affairs, 2002.

Hicks, John D. *My Life with History: An Autobiography*. Lincoln: University of Nebraska Press, 1968.

——. "My Nine Years at the University of Nebraska." *Nebraska History* 46, no. 1 (March 1965): 1–27.

Hilmes, Michele, ed. *NBC: America's Network*. Berkeley: University of California Press, 2007.

Hiss, Alger. *In the Court of Public Opinion*. New York: Knopf, 1957.

Hoffmann, Frederick J. *The Twenties: American Writing in the Postwar Decade*. New York: Viking, 1955.

Hofstadter, Richard. *The Age of Reform: From Bryan to F.D.R.* New York: Knopf, 1956.

Hollenbeck, Don. "America First Committeemen Take Stand on Lindbergh." *PM*, October 1, 1941, 12.

——. "America First Ducks Lindbergh Washington Speech." *PM*, September 23, 1941, 10.

——. "America First Resignations." *PM*, October 29, 1941, 10.

——. "America First's Silence Means It Supports Lindbergh." *PM*, September 16, 1941, 10.

——. "Ashland, Which Lost Capital Because of Mosquitoes." *Omaha Bee-News*, January 17, 1937, sec. B, 6.

——. "A Tribute to Zoë." Three-record set of reminiscences and radio broadcasts created in 1950 by Hollenbeck for his six-year-old daughter, Zoë, Don Hollenbeck, Broadcast Papers (MS 319), Archives and Special Collections, University of Nebraska–Lincoln Libraries.

——. "Badoglio Coalition Plan Doesn't Satisfy." *PM*, November 1, 1943, 8.

——. "CBS Views the Press." *Atlantic Monthly*, September 1948, 49–51.

——. "'Dear Mr. Hollenbeck—.'" Undated article from *Page One* in Hollenbeck scrapbook, 93, Don Hollenbeck, Broadcast Papers (MS 319), Archives and Special Collections, University of Nebraska–Lincoln Libraries.

——. "Existentialism: Fashionable Despondency." *Talks: A Quarterly Digest of Addresses in the Public Interest by the Columbia Network*, January 1947, 41–42.

——. "Fifty-eight Americans Demand Spiked Guns Against Hitler." *PM*, September 15, 1941, 10.

——. "Give Us Time." Unpublished novel in Don Hollenbeck, Broadcast Papers (MS 319), Archives and Special Collections, University of Nebraska–Lincoln Libraries.

——. "Good News, But—." *PM*, February 13, 1942, 12.

——. "How It's Done." *PM*, February 27, 1942, 13.

——. "Hugh Johnson Rolls His Own Rap at Lindbergh." *PM*, September 17, 1941, 11.

——. "Kangaroo Court in the Philippines." *New Republic*, December 5, 1949, 18–19.

——. "Lindbergh's Dirtiest Speech: Attack on Jews." *PM*, September 12, 1941, 14.

——. "Louisville—a Friendly, Bustling Town of Contrasts." *Omaha Bee-News*, November 29, 1936, sec. A, 11.

——. "Nebraska City—a Paradox—an Old City Yet Young." *Omaha Bee-News*, December 6, 1936, sec. A, 12.

——. "New Book Marks a Signal Advance." *Omaha Bee-News*, August 15, 1937, A-8.

——. "On Negroes in the War Effort." *PM*, March 8, 1942, 9.

——. "Plattsmouth—a City That Glories in Its Past and Future." *Omaha Bee-News*, November 15, 1936, sec. A, 10.

——. "Swinging at a Feather Bed." *Saturday Review of Literature*, November 8, 1947, 34–36.

——. "They Ask for Guns, They Get Pemmican." *PM*, January 23, 1942, 3.

——. Transcripts: *American Music, Bridgebuilders, CBS Is There, CBS Views the Press, Men and Books, News of America, Victory Hour, War Journal,* and other Hollenbeck programs and series. Don Hollenbeck, Broadcast Papers (MS 319), Archives and Special Collections, University of Nebraska–Lincoln Libraries.

——. "Two More Replies to *PM* Query." *PM*, September 18, 1941, 11.

——. "Weeping Water—Famous for Its Foursquare Bank System." *Omaha Bee-News*, November 22, 1936, sec. A, 10, as reprinted in brochure, included with letter from John S. Savage to author, May 7, 1975.

——. "Young Man—God to Wahoo—It Lacks Eligibles." *Omaha Bee-News*, January 10, 1937, sec. B, 6.

"Hollenbeck, Don." *Current Biography* 12, no. 2 (February 1951): 28–30.

Hollenbeck, Don and James Reston. "Is the American Press Doing Its Job Today?" Transcript of ABC Radio broadcast of *Town Meeting of the Air*, May 9, 1950. Don Hollenbeck, Broadcast Papers (MS 319), Archives and Special Collections, University of Nebraska–Lincoln Libraries.

Hoopes, Townsend and Douglas Brinkley. *Driven Patriot: The Life and Times of James Forrestal*. New York: Knopf, 1992.

"How Hearst Kept Step with Axis for Eight Years." *PM*, May 21, 1942, 1.

Howe, Quincy. *Ashes of Victory: World War II and Its Aftermath*. New York: Simon and Schuster, 1972.

——. *The News and How to Understand It: In Spite of the Newspapers, in Spite of the Magazines, in Spite of the Radio*. New York: Simon and Schuster, 1940.

Hoyt, Edwin P. *Paul Robeson: The American Othello*. Cleveland: World Publishing, 1967.

Hughes, Frank. *Prejudice and the Press: A Restatement of the Principle of Freedom of the Press with Specific Reference to the Hutchins-Luce Commission*. New York: Devin-Adair, 1950.

Hutchens, John K. "Quiet, Please: The Columbia Network Tells Its Analysts to Keep Their Opinions to Themselves." *New York Times*, September 26, 1943, X9.

"The Hutchins Commission Revisited." Transcript of panel discussion at the University of Colorado, Boulder, Colorado, August 30, 1967, sponsored by the Division of Mass Communications and Society, Association for Education in Journalism and Mass Communication.

"The Hutchins Report: A Twenty-Year Review." *Columbia Journalism Review*, Summer 1967, 5–20.

Hutchison, E. R. and David G. Clark. "Self-censorship in Broadcasting—the Cowardly Lions." *New York Law Forum* 18, no. 1 (Summer 1972): 1–31.

"If N.Y. Press Felt Needle in CBS Jabs, Only *Sun* Winced; Sees Red." *Variety*, June 11, 1947, 39.

Ingersoll, Ralph, "History of this Property." *PM* supplement, June 18, 1946.

——. "Volunteer Gestapo." *PM*, July 12, 1940, 21.

Innis, Harold. *The Bias of Communication*. Toronto: University of Toronto Press, 1951.

"Jack O'Brian Takes Bride." *New York Times*, January 16, 1947, 31.

Jackaway, Gwenyth L. *Media at War: Radio's Challenge to the Newspapers, 1924–1939*. Westport, Conn.: Praeger, 1995.

Jamison, Kay Redfield. *Night Falls Fast: Understanding Suicide*. New York: Knopf, 1999.

——. *Touched with Fire: Manic Depressive Illness and the Artistic Temperament*. New York: Free Press, 1994.

"J. J. Johnston Dies; Ring Promoter, 70." *New York Times*, May 8, 1946, 25.

Johnson, Haynes. *The Age of Anxiety: McCarthyism to Terrorism*. Orlando, Fla.: Harcourt, 2005.

Johnson, Ralph H. and Michael Altman. "Communists in the Press: A Senate Witch-Hunt of the 1950s Revisited." *Journalism Quarterly* 55, no. 3 (Fall 1978): 487–93.

Joiner, Thomas. *Why People Die by Suicide*. Cambridge, Mass.: Harvard University Press, 2005.

Jones, Ira O. "A Study of the Editorial Policy of the *Omaha Bee-News* and the *Omaha World-Herald* with Regard to Social Problems." Master's thesis, University of Omaha, 1937.

Jones, Will Owens. "A Rough Sketch of the Publisher." *Lincoln (Neb.) State Journal*, July 24, 1927, C-2.

Kaplan, Fred. *The Wizards of Armageddon*. New York: Simon and Schuster, 1983.

Kendrick, Alexander. *Prime Time: The Life of Edward R. Murrow*. Boston: Little, Brown, 1969.

Kenny, Nick. "Nick Kenny Speaking." *New York Mirror*, January 15, 1949, 12.

Kessler, Ronald. *The Bureau: The Secret History of the FBI*. New York: St. Martin's, 2002.

Kilgallen, Dorothy. "Jelke Girls Linked to Capital Intrigue." *New York Journal-American*, February 1, 1953, 1, 16L.

"Kills His Bride for Smoking." *Omaha Bee-News*, November 3, 1928, 1.

Kimball, Penn. *The File*. San Diego: Harcourt Brace Jovanovich, 1983.

Klehr, Harvey, John Earl Haynes, and Kyrill M. Anderson. *The Soviet World of American Communism*. New Haven, Conn.: Yale University Press, 1998.

Klurfeld, Herman. *Winchell: His Life and Times*. New York: Praeger, 1976.

Knightley, Phillip. *The First Casualty, from the Crimea to Vietnam: The War Correspondent as Hero, Propagandist, and Myth Maker*. New York: Harcourt Brace Jovanovich, 1975.

Komarovsky, Mirra. *Women in the Modern World: Their Education and Their Dilemmas*. Boston: Little, Brown, 1953.

Kovel, Joel. *Red Hunting in the Promised Land: Anticommunism and the Making of America*. New York: Basic Books, 1994.

Kurtz, Howard et al. "The Erosion of Values: A Debate among Journalists Over How to Cope." *Columbia Journalism Review*, March–April 1998, 44–47.

Landry, Robert J. "Edward R. Murrow." *Scribner's*, December 1938, 7–11, 50, 52.

Lang, Daniel. "The Days of Suspicion." *New Yorker*, May 21, 1949, 37–57.

Larsen, Lawrence H. and Barbara J. Cottrell. *The Gate City: A History of Omaha*. Lincoln: University of Nebraska Press, 1997.

Larsen, Lawrence H., Harl A. Dalstrom, and Kay Calamé Dalstrom. *Upstream Metropolis: An Urban Biography of Omaha and Council Bluffs*. Lincoln: University of Nebraska Press, 2007.

Lasch, Robert. "*PM*'s Post-Mortem." *Atlantic Monthly*, July 1948, 44–49.

Latham, Earl. *The Communist Controversy in Washington: From the New Deal to McCarthy*. Cambridge, Mass.: Harvard University Press, 1966.

Lauerman, Kerry. "Salon Interview: George Clooney." September 16, 2005, www.salon.com/ent/feature/2005/09/16/george_clooney/print.html.

Lazarsfeld, Paul. *Radio and the Printed Page: An Introduction to the Study of Radio and Its Role in the Communication of Ideas*. New York: Duell, Sloan and Pearce, 1940.

Leab, Daniel. *A Union of Individuals: The Formation of the American Newspaper Guild, 1933–1936*. New York: Columbia University Press, 1970.

Leggett, John. *Ross and Tom: Two American Tragedies*. New York: Simon and Schuster, 1974.

Lehrer, Jim. "Blurring the Lines Hurts Journalism." *Nieman Reports*, Summer 1999, 65–66.

Leighton, G. R. "Omaha, Nebraska." *Nebraska History* 19, no. 4 (October–December 1938): 293–329.

Lelyveld, Joseph. *Omaha Blues: A Memory Loop*. New York: Farrar, Straus and Giroux, 2005.

Leonard, Bill. *In the Storm of the Eye: A Lifetime at CBS*. New York: Putnam, 1987.

Leone, Richard and Greg Anrig Jr., eds. *The War on Our Freedoms: Civil Liberties in an Age of Terrorism*. New York: Public Affairs, 2003.

Lerner, Max. "The Six Deadly Press Sins." *PM*, December 4, 1947, 12.

Leuchtenburg, William E. *The Perils of Prosperity: 1914–1932*. Chicago: University of Chicago Press, 1958.

Leviton, Ralph. "Myopia at CBS." Undated editorial from *News Workshop* in Hollenbeck scrapbook, 137, Don Hollenbeck, Broadcast Papers (MS 319), Archives and Special Collections, University of Nebraska–Lincoln Libraries.

Lewis, Fulton Jr. "Fulton Lewis Jr.: Bares 'Leftist' Plot to Use Radio for Red Propaganda." *New York Journal-American*, February 3, 1950, 11.

Lewis, John P. "The Press Gets a Policeman." *PM*, June 3, 1947, 25.

Lewy, Guenter. *The Cause That Failed: Communism in American Political Life*. New York: Oxford University Press, 1990.

Lichtman, Robert M. and Ronald D. Cohen. *Deadly Farce: Harvey Matusow and the Informer System in the McCarthy Era*. Urbana: University of Illinois Press, 2004.

Lichty, Lawrence W. and Malachi C. Topping. *American Broadcasting: A Source Book on the History of Radio and Television*. New York: Hastings House, 1975.

Liebling, A. J. "And the Sun Stood Still." *New Yorker*, August 3, 1946, 46–51.

——. *Mink and Red Herring: The Wayward Pressman's Casebook*. New York: Doubleday, 1949.

——. *The Press*. 2d rev. ed. New York: Ballantine, 1975.

——. "The Rubber-Type Army." In *Problems of Journalism—1951: Proceedings of the 1951 Convention of the American Society of Newspaper Editors*. Washington, D.C.: American Society of Newspaper Editors, 1951.

——. "Some Reflections on the American Press." *Nation*, April 12, 1947, 427.

——. *The Wayward Pressman*. New York: Doubleday, 1948.

Light, Murray B. *From Butler to Buffett: The Story Behind the Buffalo News*. Amherst, N.Y.: Prometheus, 2004.

Lincoln: Nebraska's Capital City 1867–1923. Lincoln, Neb.: Woodruff, 1923.

"Lincoln Woman Is Found Dead." *Lincoln (Neb.) State Journal*, August 1, 1927, p. 1, 12.

Lippmann, Walter and Charles Merz. "A Test of the News. An Examination of the News Reports in the *New York Times* on Aspects of the Russian Revolution of Special Importance to Americans, March 1917–March 1920." Supplement to the *New Republic*, August 4, 1920.

Lo, Alexander C. "Suicide." In *The Freud Encyclopedia: Theory, Therapy, and Culture*, 548–50. Edited by Edward Erwin. New York: Routledge, 2002.

Lohman, Sidney. "Convention Coverage: Proceedings in Chicago Will Receive Most Extensive Distribution Ever." *New York Times*, July 6, 1952, X9.

——. "News and Notes Gathered from the Studios." *New York Times*, January 31, 1954, X13.

"Look Who's Talking." *Time*, June 16, 1947, 54.

"Loyalty Letter Accepted by CBS." *New York Journal-American*, February 7, 1951, 10.

Lukas, J. Anthony. "Where Are You Now, PM Spinney?" *New Republic*, September 9, 1972, 26–30.

Lundberg, Ferdinand. *Imperial Hearst: A Social Biography*. New York: Equinox Cooperative Press, 1936.

——. "PM: The Wall Street-Popular-Front Tabloid." *Harper's*, October 1940, 486–92.

Lyon, Eugene. "The Strange Case of PM." *American Mercury*, August 1940, 484–88.

Lyons, Louis, ed. *Reporting the News: Selections from Nieman Reports*. Cambridge, Mass.: Belknap, 1965.

MacDonald, J. Fred. *Don't Touch That Dial! Radio Programming in American Life, 1920–1960*. Chicago: Nelson-Hall, 1979.

——. *One Nation Under Television: The Rise and Decline of Network TV*. New York: Pantheon, 1990.

——. *Television and the Red Menace: The Video Road to Vietnam*. New York: Praeger, 1985.

MacPherson, Myra. *"All Governments Lie!" The Life and Times of Rebel Journalist I. F. Stone*. New York: Scribner's, 2006.

"Man About the World." *Time*, May 31, 1943, 44.

"Man with a View." *Cue*, December 18, 1948, 17.

"The Man with the Popular Mind." *Time*, November 20, 1964, 50.

Maney, Patrick J. *"Young Bob" La Follette: A Biography of Robert M. La Follette, Jr., 1895–1953*. Columbia: University of Missouri Press, 1978.

Mann, J. John. "A Current Perspective of Suicide and Attempted Suicide." *Annals of Internal Medicine* 136, no. 4 (February 19 2002): 302–11.

——. "Neurobiological Aspects of Suicide." In New York State Office of Mental Health, *Approaches and Special Populations*. Vol. 2 of *Saving Lives in New York: Suicide Prevention and Public Health*. Albany: New York State Office of Mental Health, 2005.

"Marion Davies and Clark Gable Score in Witwer's 'Cain and Mabel.' " *Omaha Bee-News*, November 13, 1936, 19.

Martin, Joe and Henry Lee. "TV's Don Hollenbeck Ailing, Afraid, Suicide." *New York Daily News*, June 23, 1954, 3, 6.

Marton, Kati. *The Polk Conspiracy: Murder and Cover-up in the Case of CBS News Correspondent George Polk*. New York: Farrar, Straus and Giroux, 1990.

Marzolf, Marion T. *Civilizing Voices: American Press Criticism, 1880–1950*. New York: Longman, 1991.

Matthews, Anne McIlhenney. "Jack O'Brian: A Real Puncher." *Buffalo Courier-Express*, May 4, 1973, 27.

Matthews, J. B. *Odyssey of a Fellow Traveler*. New York: Mount Vernon, 1938.

Matusow, Harvey. *False Witness*. New York: Cameron and Kahn, 1955.

May, Gary. *Un-American Activities: The Trials of William Remington*. New York: Oxford University Press, 1994.

Mayer, Milton. *Robert Maynard Hutchins: A Memoir*. Berkeley: University of California Press, 1993.

——. *They Thought They Were Free: The Germans, 1933–45*. Chicago: University of Chicago Press, 1955.

McAuliffe, Mary Sperling. *Crisis on the Left: Cold War Politics and American Liberals, 1947–1954*. Amherst: University of Massachusetts Press, 1978.

McCabe, Peter. *Bad News at Black Rock*. New York: Arbor House, 1987.

McCarten, John. "The Swan in the 'Mirror.'" *New Yorker*, March 7, 1953, 35–54.

McCarthy, Joseph R. *McCarthyism: The Fight for America*. New York: Devin Adair, 1952.

"McConnell Comments on Communism." *Radio Daily*, July 10, 1959, 1.

McConnell, Raymond A. Jr. "The Prairie Capital." In Virginia Faulkner, ed., *Roundup: A Nebraska Reader*, 253–58. Lincoln: University of Nebraska Press, 1957.

McCullough, David. *Truman*. New York: Simon and Schuster, 1992.

McKee, James L. *Remember When … : Memories of Lincoln*. Lincoln, Neb.: Lee, 1998.

McLeod, Elizabeth and Harlan Zinck. "D-Day Documented: A Broadcast Time Capsule." Introductory liner notes to Radio Archives' *D-Day: History as It Happened*, a 2004 collection of seventy-two CDs of NBC and CBS radio coverage.

McLuhan, Marshall. *Understanding Media: The Extensions of Man*. New York: McGraw-Hill, 1965.

McLuhan, Marshall and Quentin Fiore. *The Medium Is the Massage*. New York: Bantam, 1967.

McManus, John T. "Listeners Cry for More CBS Views on the News." *PM*, June 3, 1947, 23.

——. "New CBS Program Will Criticize New York Press." *PM*, May 26, 1947, 19.

"Men and Things." *Lincoln (Neb.) State Journal*, December 8, 1926, 14.

Menard, Orville D. *Political Bossism in Mid-America: Tom Dennison's Omaha, 1900–1933*. Lanham, Md.: University Press of America, 1989.

Mencken, H. L. *A Gang of Pecksniffs*. Edited by Theo Lippman Jr. New York: Arlington House, 1975.

Menen, Aubrey. *Four Days of Naples*. New York: Seaview, 1979.

Merron, Jeff. "Murrow on TV: *See It Now, Person to Person*, and the Making of a 'Masscult Personality.'" *Journalism Monographs*, no. 106 (July 1988).

Metz, Robert. *CBS: Reflections in a Bloodshot Eye*. Chicago: Playboy, 1975.

Mickelson, Sig. *The Decade That Shaped Television News: CBS in the 1950s*. Westport, Conn.: Praeger, 1998.

Midura, Edmund. "An Evaluation of A. J. Liebling's Performance as a Critic of the Press." Ph.D. diss., University of Iowa, 1969.

Milkman, Paul. *PM: A New Deal in Journalism, 1940–1948*. New Brunswick, N.J.: Rutgers University Press, 1997.

Minear, Richard H. *Dr. Seuss Goes to War: The World War II Editorial Cartoons of Theodor Seuss Geisel*. New York: New Press, 1999.

"Miss Betty Francis Is Honored at Party." *New York Times*, December 14, 1936, 30.

"Miss Raleigh Holiday Bride of Hollenbeck." *Omaha Bee-News*, December 21, 1934, 17.

"Mrs. Anna Boettiger Received a Divorce." *New York Times*, August 12, 1949, 40.

"Mrs. Dall Wed Here to John Boettiger." *New York Times*, January 19, 1935, 15.

Moberley, Leeds. "Rushmore Broke with Reds Over Movie Review." *New York Daily News*, January 4, 1958, 12.

Mockridge, Norton. "Hollenbeck, TV Newscaster, Takes Own Life." *New York World-Telegram and Sun*, June 22, 1954, 1–2.

Morgan, Ted. *Reds: McCarthyism in Twentieth-Century America*. New York: Random House, 2003.

Morris, Eric. *Salerno: A Military Fiasco*. New York: Stein and Day, 1983.

Mott, Frank Luther. *American Journalism: A History, 1690–1960*. New York: Macmillan, 1962.

"Move Disbar Frank Bartos." *Lincoln (Neb.) Star*, March 17, 1926, 2.

Mudd, Roger. *The Place to Be: Wshington, CBS, and the Glory Days of Television News*. New York: Public Affairs, 2008.

Mumford, Lewis. *The Golden Day: A Study in American Literature and Culture*. Boston: Beacon, 1957.

Murrow, Edward R. Foreword to *This I Believe: The Living Philosophies of One Hundred Thoughtful Men and Women in All Walks of Life*. Edited by Edward P. Morgan. New York: Simon and Schuster, 1952.

——. *In Search of Light: The Broadcasts of Edward R. Murrow, 1938–1961*. Edited by Edward Bliss Jr. New York: Avon, 1967.

Murrow, Edward R. and Fred W. Friendly, eds. *See It Now*. New York: Simon and Schuster, 1955.

"Myron's Story." Interview of Mike Wallace by Morley Safer, *Sixty Minutes*, May 21, 2006.

Nasaw, David. *The Chief: The Life of William Randolph Hearst*. Boston: Houghton Mifflin, 2000.

Navasky, Victor S. *Naming Names*. New York: Hill and Wang, 2003.

Nevins, Allan. "American Journalism and Its Historical Treatment." *Journalism Quarterly* 36, no. 4 (Fall 1959): 411–422, 519.

"New Firm Plans Negro-Life Plays." *New York Times*, August 28, 1943, 15.

Newlove, Donald. *Those Drinking Days: Myself and Other Writers*. New York: Horizon, 1981.

O'Brian, Jack. "A Good Ford Show Is in Our TV Future." *New York Journal-American*, October 3, 1952, 33.

——. "A Happy 1961 to Blydens." *New York Journal-American*, July 8, 1960, 20.

——. "An Analysis of Murrow's Portsided Political Pitching." *New York Journal-American*, March 10, 1954, 36.

——. "A Prize for 'The Doodles Weaver Show?' Read On!" *New York Journal-American*, August 29, 1951, 38.

——. "Are Networks Keeping Air Clean?" *New York Journal-American*, July 8, 1951, TV section, 1.

——. "Arthur Wants to Get His Moon Over Miami." *New York Journal-American*, November 29, 1952, 24.

——. "Berle, Silvers, Bergen, First in Anti-Red Line." *New York Journal-American*, April 30, 1954, 35.

——. "The Best: Bing, Benny, Cole, Eve, Jo M. M. McB., Groucho." *New York Journal-American*, April 16, 1953, 34.

——. "Billy's 'Black Magic' Can't Conjure Sponsor." *New York Journal-American*, December 13, 1952, 24.

——. "Bob Montgomery Not Too Busy to Belt at Reds." *New York Journal-American*, November 4, 1950, 18.

——. "Brinkley Wins—by a Smile." *New York Journal-American*, July 15, 1960, 18.

——. "Check Grabber Has Ripping Time for $10,000." *New York Journal-American*, February 23, 1952, 23.

——. "'Cholly' Starts New WJZ Radio Show on Monday." *New York Journal-American*, March 31, 1951, 18.

——. "Commie Phone Plot Exposed in Two Minutes." *New York Journal-American*, June 28, 1954, 26.

——. "'The Continental' Has Fanciest Sets on Video." *New York Journal-American*, April 3, 1952, 35.

——. "Continuing Study of the Continuing CBS News 'Slant.'" *New York Journal-American*, June 23, 1954, 37.

——. "Critic's Aunt Sends Letter by Aerial Mail." *New York Journal-American*, June 3, 1952, 31.

——. "Da Silva Hosts Show on NBC." *New York Journal-American*, July 6, 1960, 28.

——. "Don't Tell Us You Missed This One!" *New York Journal-American*, June 16, 1953, 36.

——. "Eve Arden, Jack Benny Are JO'B's Radio Bests." *New York Journal-American*, March 18, 1954, 36.

——. "Gleason's Man Saturday Turns down NBC Offer." *New York Journal-American*, November 24, 1953, 34.

——. "Goldbergs Back on TV Without Philip Loeb." *New York Journal-American*, February 4, 1952, 23.

——. "Gonna Wash That Color Right out of Our Set." *New York Journal-American*, May 26, 1954, 38.

——. "Hearst Vision Traced Through Radio and TV." *New York Journal-American*, August 15, 1951, 34.

——. "Here's a Road Company of the Great Gleason." *New York Journal-American*, February 16, 1954, 34.

——. "It's Wonderful They're Always So Wonderful." *New York Journal-American*, March 12, 1951, 26.

——. "Jack Webb Discards Last of His 'Dragnet' Partners." *New York Journal-American*, June 18, 1954, 30.

——. "Letters from Readers on Slanted Newscast." *New York Journal-American*, June 14, 1954, 24.

——. "Liberace Lives in a Grand Piano; Well, Darned Near!" *New York Journal-American*, February 19, 1954, 26.

——. "Like Father, Like Daughter; Like Heck!" *New York Journal-American*, April 27, 1951, 36.

——. "Martha Shines Her Raye of Fun in Tidy Style." *New York Journal-American*, October 22, 1951, 28.

——. "NBC Picks up 'Goldbergs' after Exit from CBS." *New York Journal-American*, August 29, 1951, 18.

——. "O'Brian Holds Caucus on TV Commentators." *New York Journal-American*, July 28, 1952, 23.

——. "Only at Midnight Could This Show Be Dreamed Up!" *New York Journal-American*, September 6, 1951, 38.

——. "Perry Has Handsome Lead in 'Handsomest Male' Call." *New York Journal-American*, January 5, 1954, 32.

——. "Portsided Political Pitching." *New York Journal American*, March 10, 1954, 36.

——. "Radio Wastes the Face of Lovely Mary Healy; TV?" *New York Journal-American*, February 15, 1954, 24.

——. "Rep. Hill Labels CBS a Supporter of Leftist Trends." *New York Journal-American*, July 26, 1951, 26.

——. "Some Quiz Guests Act Like Pros—Because They Are!" *New York Journal-American*, May 24, 1954, 24.

——. "Story of Radio Free Europe on Video Tonight." *New York Journal-American*, October 23, 1951, 32.

——. "Video Viewers Talk Back About This and That." *New York Journal-American*, November 11, 1950, 18.

——. "What Medium Needs Is to Be Not So Medium." *New York Journal-American*, September 29, 1952, 23.

"O'Brian, Jack." In Frances C. Locher, ed. *Contemporary Authors*, 103:370–71. Detroit: Gale Research, 1982.

O'Connell, Frank. *Farewell to the Farm*. Caldwell, Idaho: Caxton, 1962.

O'Connor, James. "Don Hollenbeck of TV Suicide by Gas." *New York Mirror*, June 23, 1954, 3.

O'Connor, Richard. *Heywood Broun*. New York: Putnam, 1975.

"Off Pitch." *Time*, August 26, 1946, 56.

Oliver, Bryce. "Thought Control—American Style." *New Republic*, January 13, 1947, 11–12.

Ollry, Francis and Elias Smith. "An Index of 'Radio-Mindedness' and Some Applications." *Journal of Applied Psychology* 23, no. 1 (February 1939): 8–18.

Olmsted, Kathryn S. *Red Spy Queen: A Biography of Elizabeth Bentley*. Chapel Hill: University of North Carolina Press, 2002.

"*Omaha Bee-News* Ceases Publication." *Omaha World-Herald*, September 28, 1937, 1.

"On the Radio." *New York Times*, June 6, 1950, 40.

O'Neill, Marty. "Columnist Jack O'Brian Enthralls Advertising Women with Star Tales." *Buffalo Courier-Express*, April 26, 1978, 19.

O'Reilly, Kenneth. *Hoover and the Un-Americans: The FBI, HUAC, and the Red Menace*. Philadelphia: Temple University Press, 1983.

Oshinsky, David M. *A Conspiracy So Immense: The World of Joe McCarthy*. New York: Oxford University Press, 2005.

Overseas Writers. "The George Polk Case: Report of the Overseas Writers of the Special Committee to Inquire into the Murder at Salonika, Greece, May 16, 1948, of Columbia Broadcasting System Correspondent George Polk." ca. 1949. Copy in Northwestern University Library.

Packer, Herbert L. *Ex-Communist Witnesses: Four Studies in Fact Finding*. Stanford, Calif.: Stanford University Press, 1962.

Pages from History. Lincoln, Neb.: *Journal-Star*, 1993.

Paley, William S. *As It Happened: A Memoir*. New York: Doubleday, 1979.

——. "Keeping the Editorial Page out of Radio." *Broadcasting*, December 15, 1937, 20, 34.

——. *1974/1954: Free Broadcast Journalism*. N.p: Columbia Broadcasting System, 1974.

Palmer, Nancy, ed. *Terrorism, War, and the Press*. Hollis, N.H.: Hollis, 2003.

Paper, Lewis J. *Empire: William S. Paley and the Making of CBS*. New York: St. Martin's, 1987.

Parker, Dorothy. *The Viking Portable Library Dorothy Parker*. New York: Viking, 1944.

"Peabody Awards Given in Radio, TV." *New York Times*, April 27, 1951, 33.

Peck, Seymour. "The Press Can Take Its Own Medicine Gracefully." *PM*, June 19, 1947.

"People Are Talking About …" *Vogue*, September 1947, 181.

Perkins, Dexter. *The New Age of Franklin Roosevelt, 1932–45*. Chicago: University of Chicago Press, 1957.

Persico, Joseph E. *Edward R. Murrow: An American Original*. New York: McGraw-Hill, 1988.

——. "The Kremlin Connection." *New York Times Book Review*, January 3, 1999, 6.

Pfaelzer, Jean. *Driven Out: The Forgotten War Against Chinese Americans*. New York: Random House, 2007.

"Philip Loeb Dead: Prominent Actor." *New York Times*, September 1, 1955, 38.

Phillips, Wayne. "Harassing Feared by 'Voice' Suicide." *New York Times*, May 7, 1953, 10.

"Phoenix Paper Suspends; Former Boettiger Enterprise Established in May, 1947." *New York Times*, October 6, 1949, 29.

Pilat, Oliver. *Pegler: Angry Man of the Press*. Boston: Beacon, 1963.

Pitts, Alice Fox. *Read All About It! Fifty Years of ASNE*. Easton, Pa.: American Society of Newspaper Editors, 1974.

Plath, Sylvia. *The Collected Poems*. Edited by Ted Hughes. New York: Harper and Row, 1981.

Polks's Omaha (Neb.) City Directory. Omaha: Polk, 1929.

Portrait and Biographical Album of Lancaster County, Nebraska. Chicago: Chapman, 1888.

Poston, Ted. *A First Draft of History*. Edited by Kathleen A. Hauke. Athens: University of Georgia Press, 2000.

Potter, David M. *People of Plenty: Economic Abundance and the American Character*. Chicago: University of Chicago Press, 1954.

Powers, Richard Gid. *Not Without Honor: The History of American Anticommunism*. New York: Free Press, 1995.

——. *Secrecy and Power: The Life of J. Edgar Hoover*. New York: Free Press, 1987.

"Promises Quiz of 'Pink Profs.'" *New York Journal-American*, January 12, 1947, L6.

Puckette, Charles McD. "Nine Newspapermen Consider Their Profession." *New York Times Book Review*, December 21, 1947, 7.

"Python Injures Dancer." *Lincoln (Neb.) State Journal*, October 19, 1926, 1.

"Radio Takes a Look at the Press—It's Mostly a Mess." *Frontpage*, June 1947, 5.

Radosh, Ronald and Allis Radosh. *Red Star Over Hollywood: The Film Colony's Long Romance with the Left*. San Francisco: Encounter Books, 2005.

"Ray Bolger Plans More TV Programs." *New York Times*, January 13, 1953, 32.

Redish, Martin H. *The Logic of Persecution: Free Expression and the McCarthy Era*. Stanford, Calif.: Stanford University Press, 2005.

Reese, Kay and Mimi Leipzig. "An Interview with Arthur Leipzig." asmp.org, 1996. www.asmp.org/6oth/interview_arthur_leipzig.php.

Reeves, Thomas C. *The Life and Times of Joe McCarthy: A Biography*. New York: Stein and Day, 1982.

"Reporter and News Staff Director for Thirty Years." *Lincoln (Neb.) State Journal*, July 24, 1927, 12F.

Rice, John Andrew. *I Came Out of the Eighteenth Century*. New York: Harper, 1942.

Riley, Sam G. *The American Newspaper Columnist*. Westport, Conn.: Praeger, 1998.

Rips, Michael. *The Face of a Naked Lady: An Omaha Family Mystery*. Boston: Houghton Mifflin, 2005.

Ritchie, Donald A. *Reporting from Washington: The History of the Washington Press Corps*. New York: Oxford University Press, 2005.

Rivers, William L., William B. Blankenburg, Kenneth Starck, and Earl Reeves. *Backtalk: Press Councils in America*. San Francisco: Canfield, 1972.

Robeson, Paul. "Forge Negro-Labor Unity for Peace and Jobs." Speech to the National Labor Conference for Negro Rights, Chicago, June 10, 1950. Reprinted in *Paul Robeson Speaks: Writings, Speeches, Interviews, 1918–1974*. Edited by Philip S. Foner. New York: Brunner/Mazel, 1978.

——. *Here I Stand*. Boston: Beacon, 1988.

Rogow, Arnold A. *James Forrestal: A Study of Personality, Politics, and Policy*. New York: Macmillan, 1963.

Rollyson, Carl. *Rebecca West: A Life*. New York: Scribner's, 1996.

——. "Rebecca West and the FBI." *New Criterion* 16, no. 6 (February 1998): 12–22. An appendix is available at http://newcriterion.com:81/archive/16/feb98/app.htm.

Rorty, James and Moshe Decter. *McCarthy and the Communists*. Boston: Beacon, 1954.

Rorty, James and Winifred Raushenbush. "The Lessons of the Peekskill Riots." *Commentary*, October 1950, 309–23.

Rose, Billy. *Wine, Women, and Words*. New York: Simon and Schuster, n.d.

Ross, Lillian E., George Whitman, Joe Wershba, Helen Ross, and Mel Fiske. *The "Argonauts."* New York: Modern Age Books, 1940.

Rosten, Leo C. "President Roosevelt and the Washington Correspondents." *Public Opinion Quarterly* 1, no. 1 (January 1937): 36–52.

Roth, Philip. *The Plot Against America*. London: Vintage, 2005.

Rovere, Richard H. *Senator Joe McCarthy*. 1959. New York: Bobbs Merrill, 1970.

Rowland, Helen. "Radio and Television." *Writer's Digest*, October 1947, 75.

Rubin, David. "Liebling and Friends: American Press Critics from 1859 to the Present." In possession of the author.

Rushmore, Howard. "The Subversive Front: Bell for Red Teachers." *New York Journal-American*, September 12, 1953, 10.

——. "The Subversive Front: McCarthy Held Back Hot Ammo." *New York Journal-American*, June 19, 1954, 6.

Sandoz, Mari. *Capital City*. Boston: Little, Brown, 1939.

Savage, James W. and John T. Bell. *History of the City of Omaha, Nebraska*. New York: Munsell, 1894.

Savery, Gilbert M. *As I Used to Say*. Lincoln, Neb.: Aluminum Pica Pole Press, 2002.

Sawyer, R. McLaren. *The Modern University*. Vol. 2 of *Centennial History of the University of Nebraska*. Lincoln: Centennial, 1973.

Saylor, Harry T. "A Newspaperman's Newspaper." *Saturday Review of Literature*, December 6, 1947, 74.

Schechter, A. A., with Edward Anthony. *I Live on Air*. New York: Stokes, 1941.

Schieffer, Bob. *Face the Nation: My Favorite Stories from the First Fifty Years of the Award-Winning News Broadcast*. New York: Simon and Schuster, 2004.

Schlesinger, Arthur M. Jr. *The Age of Roosevelt: The Politics of Upheaval*. Boston: Houghton Mifflin, 1960.

Schoenfeld, Herman. "Man-Bites-Dog Act Slays N.Y. Press; Dailies' Reaction Big $64 Question." *Variety*, June 4, 1947, 29.

Schoenstein, Ralph. *Citizen Paul: A Story of Father and Son*. New York: Farrar, Straus and Giroux, 1978.

Schrecker, Ellen. *The Age of McCarthyism: A Brief History with Documents*. Boston: Bedford/St. Martin's, 2002.

———. *Many Are the Crimes: McCarthyism in America*. Boston: Little, Brown, 1998.

Schroth, Raymond A. *The American Journey of Eric Sevareid*. South Royalton, Vt.: Steerforth, 1995.

Schumach, Murray. "A Modern Miracle." *New York Times*, October 13, 1946, sec. 2, 9.

———. *The Face on the Cutting Room Floor: The Story of Movie and Television Censorship*. New York: Morrow, 1964.

Seacrest, Ann Raschke. "Genealogy and Heritage of the J. C. Seacrest Family." Prepared for a family gathering, Colorado Springs, Colorado, August 7, 1980. Ann Raschke Seacrest is married to Kent Seacrest, grandson of J. C. Seacrest. Don Hollenbeck, Broadcast Papers (MS 319), Archives and Special Collections, University of Nebraska–Lincoln Libraries.

Seacrest, Ted C. "J. C. Seacrest Family Orientation Manual, Section 2: History of the J. C. and Jessie E. Seacrest Family," June 2000, Don Hollenbeck, Broadcast Papers (MS 319), Archives and Special Collections, University of Nebraska–Lincoln Libraries.

"The Search." Transcript of television program narrated by Don Hollenbeck, November 20, 1953. Copyright Office, Motion Picture, Broadcasting and Recorded Sound Division, Library of Congress, Washington, D.C.

Seldes, George. *The Great Thoughts*. New York: Ballantine, 1985.

———. *Lords of the Press*. New York: Messner, 1938.

———. *Never Tire of Protesting*. New York: Stuart, 1968.

———. *Tell the Truth and Run*. New York: Greenberg, 1953.

———. *Witness to a Century: Encounters with the Noted, the Notorious, and the Three SOBs*. New York: Ballantine, 1987.

Sentner, David. "Newsman on Eisler Ship Cited Fourteen Times for Subversive Links." *New York Journal-American*, May 20, 1949, 4.

Sevareid, Eric. *The Big Truth*. Minneapolis: Twin Cities Local, American Newspaper Guild, CIO, and School of Journalism, University of Minnesota, 1953.

———. *Not So Wild a Dream*. New York: Knopf, 1946.

Sexton, Anne. *Complete Poems*. Boston: Houghton Mifflin, 1981.

Shafer, Jack. "The Church of Liebling." *Slate*, August 25, 2004. www.slate.com/id/2105627/.

Shamley, Sarah L., comp. *Television Interviews, 1951–1955: A Catalog of Longines Chronoscope Interviews in the National Archives*. Washington, D.C.: National Archives and Records Administration, 1991.

Shayon, Robert Lewis. *Odyssey in Prime Time*. Philadelphia: Waymark, 2001.

———. *Open to Criticism*. Boston: Beacon, 1971.

———. "Scraps of Sound and History." *Saturday Review of Literature*, February 10, 1951, 30.

Shils, Edward A. *The Torment of Secrecy: The Background and Consequences of American Security Policies*. Glencoe, Ill.: Free Press, 1956.

Shirer, William L. *Stranger Come Home*. Boston: Little, Brown, 1954.

———. *The Traitor*. New York: Farrar, Straus, 1950.

——. *Twentieth Century Journey: A Memoir of a Life and the Times.* Vol. 1, *The Start, 1904–1930.* New York: Simon and Schuster, 1976.

——. *Twentieth Century Journey: A Memoir of a Life and the Times.* Vol. 2, *The Nightmare Years, 1930–1940.* Boston: Little, Brown, 1984.

——. *Twentieth Century Journey: A Memoir of a Life and the Times.* Vol. 3, *A Native's Return, 1945–1988.* Boston: Little, Brown, 1990.

Siepmann, Charles A. *Radio, Television, and Society.* New York: Oxford University Press, 1950.

Sierra, J. A. Review of *A Sergeant Named Batista*, by Edmund A. Chester, n.d. www.historyofcuba.com/main/ref.htm.

Sinclair, Upton. *The Autobiography of Upton Sinclair.* New York: Harcourt, Brace and World, 1962.

——. *The Brass Check: A Study of American Journalism.* 1919. Reprint, New York: Arno, 1970.

Sirgiovanni, George. *An Undercurrent of Suspicion: Anti-Communism in America during World War II.* New Brunswick, N.J.: Transaction, 1990.

Slater, Robert. *This … Is CBS: A Chronicle of Sixty Years.* Englewood Cliffs, N.J.: Prentice Hall, 1988.

Smith, Howard K. *Events Leading up to My Death: The Life of a Twentieth-Century Reporter.* New York: St. Martin's, 1996.

Smith, Sally Bedell. *In All His Glory: The Life of William S. Paley—the Legendary Tycoon and His Brilliant Circle.* New York: Simon and Schuster, 1990.

Sokolov, Raymond. *Wayward Reporter: The Life of A. J. Liebling.* New York: Harper and Row, 1980.

Sorenson, Alfred. *The Story of Omaha from the Pioneer Days to the Present Time.* Omaha: N.p., 1923.

"The Soviet Spider." *New York Journal-American*, July 19, 1948, 12.

"Spellman Chosen to Get First Sokolsky Award." *New York Times*, May 13, 1963, 22.

Sperber, A. M. *Murrow: His Life and Times.* New York: Freundlich, 1986.

Steinberg, Julien. "Ferment in the New York Newspaper Guild." *New Leader*, May 10, 1947, 5.

Steinberg, Peter L. *The Great "Red Menace": United States Prosecution of American Communists, 1947–1952.* Westport, Conn.: Greenwood, 1984.

Steiner, Ralph. "Pictures Can Report Labor Strife Better Than Words." In *Picture Stories of the Year.* New York: PM, 1941.

Stettner, Louis, ed. *Weegee.* New York: Knopf, 1977.

Stevens, Betty. *Thirty: A History of the* Lincoln Journal. Henderson, Neb.: Service Press, 1999.

Stewart, Kenneth. *News Is What We Make It: A Running Story of the Working Press.* Westport, Conn.: Greenwood, 1970.

——. "Notes on interview with William McCleery." Undated manuscript, Kenneth Stewart Collection, American Heritage Center, University of Wyoming Library, Laramie.

——. "The People Who Made *PM* and the *Star*." Undated manuscript, Kenneth Stewart Collection, American Heritage Center, University of Wyoming Library, Laramie.

——. "Press Rx: Faith Healing?" *Saturday Review of Literature*, April 5, 1947, 13–14, 27–28.

Stewart, R. W. "Can't You Take a Practical Joke?" *New York Times*, November 23, 1947, 85.

Stolberg, Benjamin. "Muddled Millions." *Saturday Evening Post*, February 15, 1941, 9–10, 88–90, 92.

Strachey, James, ed. *The Standard Edition of the Complete Psychological Works of Sigmund Freud*. London: Hogarth and Institute of Psycho-Analysis, 1957.

Strout, Lawrence N. *Covering McCarthyism: How the* Christian Science Monitor *Handled Joseph R. McCarthy, 1950–1954*. Westport, Conn.: Greenwood, 1999.

Svirsky, Leon, ed. *Your Newspaper: Blueprint for a Better Press*. New York: Macmillan, 1947.

Swanberg, W. A. *Citizen Hearst*. New York: Scribner's, 1961.

Swing, Raymond. *"Good Evening!" A Professional Memoir by Raymond Swing*. New York: Harcourt, Brace and World, 1964.

"The Talk of the Town." *New Yorker*, June 24, 1944, 17–22.

Tebbel, John. *The Marshall Fields: A Study in Wealth*. New York: Dutton, 1947.

Tebbel, John and Kenneth Stewart. *Makers of Modern Journalism*. New York: Prentice-Hall, 1952.

Thomas, Lately. *When Even Angels Wept: The Senator Joseph McCarthy Affair—a Story Without a Hero*. New York: Morrow, 1973.

"To Readers of the *Omaha World-Herald* and Former Readers of the *Omaha Bee-News*." *Omaha Morning World-Herald*, September 29, 1937, 1.

Torrey, Volta. "Hearst Pushes around Newsboys Who Sell *PM*." *PM*, May 22, 1942, 13.

"Total of 110 Years for $1,000,000 Embezzler; Former Nebraska Banker Lost All Speculating." *New York Times*, April 9, 1931, 4.

"To the Readers of *PM*." *PM*, June 18, 1940, 18.

Tripp, Frank. "No More'n a Rabbit." *Binghamton (N.Y.) Press*, June 16, 1947, 6.

Trussell, C. P. "Clark Says Duggan Was Loyal to U.S." *New York Times*, December 25, 1948, 1.

Tuck, Jay Nelson. "Don Hollenbeck." *New York Post*, June 23, 1954, 4, 72.

Tuck, Jim. *McCarthyism and New York's Hearst Press: A Study of Roles in the Witch Hunt*. Lanham, Md.: University Press of America, 1995.

"$2,807 Needed Before July 5." *Omaha World-Herald*, June 15, 1939, 1.

U.S. Congress. House. Committee on Un-American Activities. *Hearings before Committee on Un-American Activities on Communist Infiltration of Hollywood Motion Picture Industry*. 80th Cong., 1st sess., 1947. Washington, D.C.: U.S. Government Printing Office, 1947.

U.S. Congress. House. Committee on Un-American Activities. *H.R. 1884 and H.R. 2122, Bills to Curb or Outlaw the Communist Party of the United States: Hearings before the Committee on Un-American Activities*. 80th Cong., 1st sess., pt. 2, March 26,

1947. Testimony of J. Edgar Hoover. Washington, D.C.: U.S. Government Printing Office, 1947.

U.S. Congress. House. Subcommittee on Legislation of the Committee on Un-American Activities. *Proposed Legislation to Curb or Control the Communist Party of the United States: Hearings before the Subcommittee on Legislation of the Committee on Un-American Activities on H.R. 4422 and H.R. 4581.* 80th Cong., 2d sess., Washington, D.C.: U.S. Government Printing Office, 1948.

U.S. Congress. Senate. Subcommittee to Investigate the Administration of the Internal Security Act and Other Internal Security Laws. *Strategy and Tactics of World Communism: Recruiting for Espionage,* 84th Cong., 1st sess., June 28–29, 1955, pt. 14. Washington, D.C.: U.S. Government Printing Office, 1955.

"U.S. TV-Radio Coverage." *New York Times,* June 2, 1953, 10.

Van Horne, Harriet. "CBS Views the Press, Critic Poses Query." *New York World-Telegram,* June 16, 1947, 10.

——. "The 'Moral Majority' and Us." *Television Quarterly* 18, no. 1 (Spring 1981): 65–75.

"Viewing the Press." *Washington Post,* May 29, 1947, 14.

Villard, Oswald Garrison. *The Disappearing Daily: Chapters in American Newspaper Evolution.* New York: Knopf, 1944.

——. *How Stands Our Press?* Chicago: Human Events Associates, 1947.

——. *Some Newspapers and Newspaper-men.* New York: Knopf, 1923.

Vlanton, Elias, with Zak Mettger. *Who Killed George Polk? The Press Covers up a Death in the Family.* Philadelphia: Temple University Press, 1996.

Von Hoffman, Nicholas. *Citizen Cohn.* New York: Doubleday, 1988.

Walker, Jerry. "Don Hollenbeck Views Much-Honored Show." *Editor and Publisher,* May 15, 1948, 44.

Wallace, Mike. *Between You and Me: A Memoir.* New York: Hyperion, 2005.

——. Remarks titled "Confronting the Crisis" delivered at a December 1997 forum sponsored by the *Columbia Journalism Review* and quoted in "The Erosion of Values: A Debate among Journalists Over How to Cope." *Columbia Journalism Review,* March–April 1998, 44–47.

Wallace, Mike and Gary Paul Gates. *Close Encounters.* New York: Morrow, 1984.

Walters, Jack. *Saigon and Other Poems.* New York: Spuyten Duyvil, 2005.

Wang, Jessica. *American Science in an Age of Anxiety: Scientists, Anticommunism, and the Cold War.* Chapel Hill: University of North Carolina Press, 1998.

"War Correspondents in Person: The McGaffins and the Press; Hollenbeck, Parr, Rundle, Arnot," and "Nebraska's War Correspondents: Charles Arnot, Grant Parr, Walter G. Rundle, William McGaffin, Don Hollenbeck." *Nebraska History* 25, no. 1 (January–March 1944): 56–72.

Watts, Richard Jr. "Which Paper D'Ya Read?" *New Republic,* December 15, 1947, 27–28.

Wechsler, James A. *The Age of Suspicion.* New York: Random House, 1953.

——. "The Life and Death of *PM.*" *Progressive,* March 1949, 9–12, and April 1949, 15–17.

——. *Reflections of an Angry Middle-Aged Editor.* New York: Random House, 1960.

——. "Time, Space, and News." *Nation*, January 17, 1948, 75–77.

"New Paper Out; 'Weekly Block' Has All the News." *New York Herald Tribune*, January 29, 1949, 13.

Weiner, Tim. "A 1950 Plan: Arrest 12,000 and Suspend Due Process." *New York Times*, December 23, 2007, 30.

Weinstein, Allen. "F.B.I.'s Hiss Files Show Bumbling, Not Malice." *New York Times*, February 1, 1976, E-9.

——. *Perjury: The Hiss-Chambers Case.* New York: Knopf, 1978.

Weinstein, Allen and Alexander Vassiliev. *The Haunted House: Soviet Espionage in America—the Stalin Era.* New York: Modern Library, 2000.

Weisberg, Jacob. "Cold War Without End." *New York Times Sunday Magazine*, November 29, 1999, 116–23, 155–58.

Wershba, Joseph. "Murrow vs. McCarthy: See It Now." *New York Times Sunday Magazine*, March 4, 1979, 31–38.

West, Rebecca. "A Briton Looks at 'McCarthyism.'" *U.S. News and World Report*, May 22, 1953, 60–81.

——. "British Observer Is Impressed Most by Stassen's Following." *New York Herald Tribune*, June 23, 1948, 3.

——. "Rebecca West Says Communists Controlled Wallace Convention." *New York Herald Tribune*, July 26, 1948, 2.

——. "The Republicans' Convention as Seen Through British Eyes." *New York Herald Tribune*, July 26, 1948, 4.

Westinghouse Studio One: Cardinal Mindszenty, May 3, 1954, Paley Center for Media (formerly the Museum of Television and Radio), New York.

White, Paul W. *News on the Air.* New York: Harcourt, Brace, 1947.

Wicker, Tom. *Shooting Star: The Brief Arc of Joe McCarthy.* Orlando, Fla.: Harcourt, 2006.

Wiggins, J. Russell. "Nine Nieman Fellows Speak Their Piece About Newspapers." *Washington Post*, November 30, 1947, 7B.

Williams, Helen Jean. "An Evaluation of Criticism of the Daily Press in George Seldes' *In Fact*." Master's thesis, University of Minnesota, 1947.

Williamson, Eunice M. Willman. *Malcolm as It Was: The Story of My Hometown of Malcolm, Nebraska, a Most Wonderful Place to Live and Grow, from Its Very Beginning up to 1948.* Lincoln, Neb.: Dageforde, 1995.

Wilson, Theo. "Confidentially Rushmore: Jobless, He Wouldn't Borrow; On Top, He Was Cold and Cruel." *New York Daily News*, January 6, 1958, 28.

Winfield, Betty Houchin. *FDR and the News Media.* Urbana: University of Illinois Press, 1990.

Winfield, Betty Houchin and Lois B. DeFleur. *The Edward R. Murrow Heritage: Challenge for the Future.* Ames: Iowa State University Press, 1986.

Winkler, John K. *William Randolph Hearst: A New Appraisal* New York: Hastings House, 1955.

"With Spier's." *Lincoln (Neb.) State Journal*, October 7, 1926, 14.

Woltman, Frederick. "The McCarthy Balance Sheet." *New York World-Telegram and Sun*, July 12, 1954, 1.

"Woman Found Dead in Home." *Lincoln (Neb.) Star*, August 1, 1927, 1.

"*World-Herald* Wins Pulitzer Prize Medal; Scrap Drive Example Rated Outstanding Service to Public." *Omaha World-Herald*, May 4, 1943, 1.

"W. R. Hearst Tells Why People Will Elect Roosevelt." *Omaha Bee-News*, October 24, 1932, 1.

Wright, Charles H. *Robeson: Labor's Forgotten Champion*. Detroit: Balamp, 1975.

Wyatt, Wendy N. *Critical Conversations: A Theory of Press Criticism*. Cresskill, N.J.: Hampton, 2007.

Ybarra, Michael J. *Washington Gone Crazy: Senator Pat McCarran and the Great American Communist Hunt*. Hanover, N.H.: Steerforth, 2004.

Yeats, William Butler. *The Collected Poems of W. B. Yeats*. New York: Macmillan, 1956.

Zion, Sidney. *The Autobiography of Roy Cohn*. Secaucus, N.J.: Stuart, 1988.

Index